Bayesian Network Technologies:

Applications and Graphical Models

Ankush Mittal
Indian Institute of Technology, India

Ashraf Kassim
National University of Singapore, Singapore

T0321984

IGI PUBLISHING
Hershey • New York

Acquisition Editor:	Kristin Klinger
Senior Managing Editor:	Jennifer Neidig
Managing Editor:	Sara Reed
Assistant Managing Editor:	Sharon Berger
Development Editor:	Kristin Roth
Copy Editor:	Lanette Ehrhardt
Typesetter:	Michael Brehm
Cover Design:	Lisa Tosheff
Printed at:	Yurchak Printing Inc.

Published in the United States of America by
IGI Publishing (an imprint of IGI Global)
701 E. Chocolate Avenue
Hershey PA 17033
Tel: 717-533-8845
Fax: 717-533-8661
E-mail: cust@idea-group.com
Web site: http://www.idea-group.com

and in the United Kingdom by
IGI Publishing (an imprint of IGI Global)
3 Henrietta Street
Covent Garden
London WC2E 8LU
Tel: 44 20 7240 0856
Fax: 44 20 7379 0609
Web site: http://www.eurospanonline.com

Library of Congress Cataloging-in-Publication Data

Bayesian network technologies : applications and graphical models / Ankush Mittal and Ashraf Kassim, edi-
tors.
      p. cm.
  Summary: "This book provides an excellent, well-balanced collection of areas where Bayesian networks
have been successfully applied; it describes the underlying concepts of Bayesian Networks with the help of
diverse applications, and theories that prove Bayesian networks valid"--Provided by publisher.
  Includes bibliographical references and index.
  ISBN 978-1-59904-141-4 (hardcover) -- ISBN 978-1-59904-143-8 (ebook)
  1. Bayesian statistical decision theory--Data processing. 2. Bayesian statistical decision theory--Computer
programs. 3. Bayesian statistical decision theory--Graphic methods. 4. Decision making--Statistical methods. I. Mittal, Ankush. II. Kassim, Ashraf.
  QA279.5.B3886 2007
  519.5'42--dc22
                              2007007222

British Cataloguing in Publication Data
A Cataloguing in Publication record for this book is available from the British Library.

Bayesian Network Technologies:
Applications and Graphical Models

Table of Contents

Section I:
Modeling and Classification Using Bayesian Networks

Chapter I

Kaizhu Huang, Fujitsu Research and Development Centre Co. Ltd., China
Zenglin Xu, Chinese University of Hong Kong Shatin, Hong Kong
Irwin King, Chinese University of Hong Kong Shatin, Hong Kong
Michael R. Lyu, Chinese University of Hong Kong Shatin, Hong Kong
Zhangbing Zhou, Bell-Labs, Lucent Technologies, China

Chapter II

Ben K. Daniel, University of Saskatchewan, Canada
Juan-Diego Zapata-Rivera, Educational Testing Service, USA
Gordon I. McCalla, University of Saskatchewan, Canada

Section III:
Bayesian networks for Bioinformatics Applications

Foreword

It gives me great pleasure to write the foreword for this book, which gives a simple and lucid understanding of Bayesian networks. Bayesian networks play a central role in the machine learning research and have been successfully applied to different fields due to their flexible nature. A Bayesian network is a high-level representation of a probability distribution over a set of variables that are used for building models of specific problem domains. It is represented by a graphical model where nodes represent the variables and arcs represent the statistical dependence among the variables. The flexibility of choosing the variables and of relationship among the variables based on domain specific nature and strong statistical support lead to high and reliable performance of Bayesian networks.

The book is divided into three major parts. The first part addresses the intricacies involved in modeling a Bayesian network. Modeling complex domains is an active area of research which can be applied to database queries, reliability analysis and classification. Researchers in machine learning will definitely find this part helpful for modeling and applying Bayesian networks to complex domains. The second and third parts of the book present the application of Bayesian networks to the highly mature but complex field of image processing and the newer data intensive field of Bioinformatics.

This book will be very useful for researchers from diverse fields, such as computer science, engineering, mathematics, physics, chemistry, and biology. The structure and applications of the book are quite appealing and I hope the readers will find the book an interesting work of knowledge enhancement tool.

Professor K. R. Rao, University of Texas at Arlington, USA

Preface

Machine learning is an attempt to teach computers to use reasoning methods similar to those employed by humans. In the study of machine learning, it becomes obvious that most of these methods are founded in mathematical fields. The purpose of this book is to describe the underlying concepts of Bayesian network in an interesting manner with the help of diverse applications. A Bayesian network can be represented by a graph with probabilities attached. Thus, a Bayesian network represents a set of variables together with a joint probability distribution with explicit independency assumptions.

A Bayesian network is a high-level representation of a probability distribution over a set of variables that are used for building a model of the problem domain. Bayesian networks are now being used in a variety of artificial intelligence (AI) applications. Bayesian networks offer the AI researcher a convenient way to attack a multitude of problems in which one wants to come to conclusions probabilistically. Because a large number of people are now using Bayesian networks, there is a great deal of research on efficient exact solution methods as well as a variety of approximation schemes. One advantage of Bayesian networks is that it is intuitively easier for a human to understand direct dependencies and local distributions than complete joint distribution. The benefit of the Bayesian network representation lies in the way such a structure can be used as a compact representation for many naturally occurring and complex problem domains. It is believed that Bayesian networks offer the potential solutions to the existing problems in various domains.

Bayesian networks have shown superior performance as compared to neural networks, support vector machines, decision trees, and so forth, for several high-level classification tasks such as data mining, fault monitoring, bioinformatics, and so forth. The time related dependencies can also be encoded in Bayesian network to form a dynamic Bayesian network, which can be applied to speech recognition, visual tracking, and several other problems. Bayesian network shows the dependence-independence relations in a comprehensible form that eases the tasks of decomposition, feature selection, or transformation, besides providing a sound inference mechanism.

The book makes an attempt to make Bayesian networks more accessible to a wider community. Our intention through editing the book is that the ideas and techniques should spread much beyond the research community responsible for developing them. This book fills the lacuna in providing an excellent and well balanced collection of areas where Bayesian network has been successfully applied. The chapters present the theory that make Bayesian networks valid, describe some of the strengths and weaknesses of Bayesian networks, and give specific examples of a Bayesian network in action. The key idea is to help the readers appreciate the importance of Bayesian network as powerful machine learning tools and also to come with grasp of utilizing it oneself for solving typical real-life problems. Several IT applications are crucially dependent on performance of machine learning tools and can be solved using Bayesian networks.

As the book demonstrates, the Bayesian networks can be used for modeling knowledge in gene regulatory networks, medicine, engineering, text analysis, image processing, data fusion, and decision support systems. The book is very relevant for the research community, including graduate student and professors interested in applying Bayesian networks to real-world problems. The book could serve as a reference textbook in several Bayesian network courses that are being taught in numerous universities around the world. There are practically hundreds of universities all over the world which offer courses in Bayesian networks, AI, and so forth, where book finds great relevance. In addition, because the special emphasis in the book is on emerging areas such as bioinformatics, video tracking, and so forth, it can be used by the students in these areas as a starting material to get into the field. Our book takes a practical approach to applications of Bayesian networks. This would help even the naïve user in accomplishing the task of applying Bayesian networks in his or her area. The stress is on how theoretical aspects of Bayesian network can be utilized to yield practical solutions.

Organisation of This Book

The book contains 15 chapters organized under three sections. Each section addresses a major area of applications of Bayesian networks. Within a section, each chapter addresses a unique research or technology issue and how it could be handled by Bayesian networks or its variants.

Section I: Modeling and Classification Using Bayesian Networks

Chapter I, *A Novel Discriminative Naive Bayesian Network for Classification* (Huang, Xu, King, Lyu, & Zhou) explains discriminative naïve Bayesian classifier, which has merits of both discriminative (SVM classifier) and generative (naïve Bayesian) methods. This classifier has good performance and works well in the case of missing information. Improvement is achieved by preserving discriminative information by directly constructing decision rules among data. This chapter explains algorithm, along with experiments which demonstrate the advantages of this classifier. Comparison is given with both SVM and naïve Bayesian classifiers.

Chapter II, *A Bayesian Belief Network Approach for Modeling Complex Domains* (Daniel, Zapata-Rivera, & McCalla) describes use of Bayesian networks for modeling complex environments like social sciences, humanities, and so forth. Bayesian brief networks are used for modeling because brief Bayesian networks offer a mathematically rigorous way to model a complex environment that is flexible and are able to mature as knowledge about the system grows, and are computationally efficient. An example of social capital construct is taken to illustrate BBN techniques for complex domains.

Chapter III, *Data Mining of Bayesian Network Structure Using a Semantic Genetic Algorithm-Based Approach* (Shetty, Song, & Alam) presents semantic genetic algorithm (SGA) for Bayesian network structure generation from database. SGA is a modification of classical GA with modified mutation and crossover operator that incorporates semantics of Bayesian networks to improve accuracy. This chapter explains classical GA followed by SGA with simulation, and shows how SGA is better than classical GA for Bayesian network learning by proper analysis of results.

Chapter IV, *NetCube: Fast, Approximate Database Queries Using Bayesian Networks* (Margaritis, Faloutsos, & Thrun) describes NetCube, a method for fast and approximate queries on large databases. NetCube uses Bayesian network as a model of the database, which can answer aggregate queries approximately without accessing the database. In this chapter we will study methods for producing Bayesian networks for large databases and use of Bayesian networks to answer queries.

Chapter V, *Applications of Bayesian Networks in Reliability Analysis* (Langseth & Portinale) provides insight into Bayesian networks and their application in reliability analysis. The chapter starts with an explanation of Bayesian network and then explains how to model reliability systems using Bayesian networks by using a step by step approach. The chapter explains how to model reliability of both discrete and continuous real life systems under environmental conditions that are given as input to model.

Chapter VI, *Application of Bayesian Modeling to Management Information Systems: A Latent Scores Approach* (Gupta & Kim) discusses the application of Bayesian modeling and structural equation modeling (SEM) as a decision support tool for management information systems (MIS) managers. It shows that SEM is good for empirical validation and Bayesian networks are highly suitable for diagnosis and prediction of customer behavior.

Section II: Bayesian Network for Image Processing and Related Applications

This section deals with the application of Bayesian networks to solve various image processing and computer vision problems like tracking.

Chapter VII, *Bayesian Networks for Image Understanding* (Savakis, Luo, & Kane) describes the use of Bayesian networks for scene classification and object detection. Scene classification means to classify scenes in known categories, such as outdoor or indoor, city or landscape, and so forth, while object detection is to identify known objects. If information is generated for whole image, then it is used for scene classification, and if it is generated for different parts (or regions) then it is used for object detection. Both of these applications are based on generation of semantic information from image. In this chapter, a case of indoor and outdoor scenes is taken for scene classification while a case of face detection is taken for object detection.

Chapter VIII, *Long Term Tracking of Pedestrians with Groups and Occlusions* (Jorge, Abrantes, Lemos, & Marques) explains a two step tracking algorithm for interacting pedestrians, which can cope with occlusions and group tracking. This chapter explains the Bayesian network model used to correctly identify pedestrians (i.e., the labeling problem) in the presence of occlusions and groups. It suggests two strategies, periodic inference and network simplification, to deal with difficulties due to off-line analysis of video sequence.

Chapter IX, *DBN Models for Visual Tracking and Prediction* (Diao, Lu, Hu, Zhang, & Bradski) describes some dynamic Bayesian network (DBN) models for tracking in nonlinear, nonGaussian and multimodal situations, which are difficult to model with traditional methods, such as Kalman filter models. It also presents a prediction method to assist feature extraction part by making a hypothesis for the new observations and demonstrates some experimental results on sampling data and real data. It shows the potential of DBNs to provide a general and flexible tracking tool kit for visual tracking in complex environments.

Chapter X, *Multimodal Human Localization Using Bayesian Network Sensor Fusion* (Lo) presents a flexible, simple, and modular multimodal localization architecture using a Bayesian network as the fusion engine. The issues related to the complexity of analyzing the high amount of data coming out of multiple sensors are discussed. Later on, a case study of deployment of this architecture in the area of video conferencing applications is also presented.

Chapter XI, *Retrieval of Bio-Geophysical Parameters from Remotely Sensing Data by Using Bayesian Methodology* (Notarnicola) discusses the application of Bayesian techniques for the estimation of surface features, soil, and vegetation water content. It describes an algorithm development based on an experimental/modeling scheme aimed at extracting biogeophysical parameters, soil, and vegetation water content from remotely sensed data. This algorithm uses the multisources information, such as different polarizations, frequencies, and sensors for inversion system. This chapter also discusses inversion methodologies for both active and passive systems.

Section III: Bayesian Networks for Bioinformatics Applications

This section explores the application of Bayesian networks in the emerging research area of bioinformatics addressing problems related to gene expression, drug discovery, and protein binding.

Chapter XII, *Application of Bayesian Network in Drug Discovery and Development Process* (Chinnasamy, Patwardhan, & Sung) discusses the application of Bayesian networks in drug discovery and development process. It shows how Bayesian networks revolutionize the speed, quality, and effectiveness of the steps in the drug discovery process, that is, target identification, gene network analysis, protein structure analysis, fold class prediction, protein side chain prediction, protein-protein interaction, and clinical trials.

Chapter XIII, *Bayesian Network Approach to Estimate Gene Networks* (Imoto & Miyano) shows that the Bayesian networks with nonparametric regression provides robust base for the estimation of gene networks. In recent years, a large amount of gene expression data has been collected, and estimating a gene network has become one of the central topics in the field of bioinformatics. Several methodologies have been proposed for constructing a gene network based on gene expression data, such as Boolean networks, and differential equation models. The chapter shows the effectiveness of applying Bayesian networks to this problem.

Chapter XIV, *Bayesian Network Modeling of Transcription Factor Binding Sites: A Tutorial* (Narang, Chowdhary, Mittal, & Sung) discusses some recent improved techniques like "time-delayed Bayesian network" and "semi-fixed Bayesian network" to incorporate the important biological information into Bayesian network to learn gene network.

Chapter XV, *Application of Bayesian Network in Learning Gene Network* (Liu, Sung, & Mittal) introduces how temporal Bayesian network can be applied to learn gene networks and how we can integrate important biological factors into the framework of Bayesian network to improve the learning performance. The special emphasis of the chapter is to discover time dependency in several features using Bayesian networks.

Section I

Modeling and Classification Using Bayesian Networks

Chapter I

A Novel Discriminative Naive Bayesian Network for Classification

Kaizhu Huang, Fujitsu Research and Development Centre Co. Ltd., China

Zenglin Xu, Chinese University of Hong Kong Shatin, Hong Kong

Irwin King, Chinese University of Hong Kong Shatin, Hong Kong

Michael R. Lyu, Chinese University of Hong Kong Shatin, Hong Kong

Zhangbing Zhou, Bell-Labs, Lucent Technologies, China

Abstract

Naive Bayesian network (NB) is a simple yet powerful Bayesian network. Even with a strong independency assumption among the features, it demonstrates competitive performance against other state-of-the-art classifiers, such as support vector machines (SVM). In this chapter, we propose a novel discriminative training approach originated from SVM for deriving the parameters of NB. This new model, called discriminative naive Bayesian network (DNB), combines both merits of discriminative methods (e.g., SVM) and Bayesian networks. We provide theoretic justifications, outline the algorithm, and perform a series of experiments on benchmark real-world datasets to demonstrate our model's advantages. Its performance outperforms NB in classification tasks and outperforms SVM in handling missing information tasks.

Introduction

Bayesian network classifiers, a school of generative classifiers, have shown their advantages in many classification tasks, even though their overall performance is not as good as discriminative classifiers, such as support vector machines (Huang, Yang, King, & Lyu, 2004; Vapnik, 1999). The naive Bayesian network (NB) classifier is a simple yet effective Bayesian network classifier (Duda & Hart, 1973; Langley, Iba, & Thompson, 1992).

NB assumes a conditional independency among the variables or attributes. When used for classification, NB predicts a new data point as the class with the highest posterior probability. This is shown in equation (1), where $A_j (1 \leq j \leq n)$ represents the attribute or variable, and $C_i (1 \leq i \leq k)$ denotes the class variable. In equation (2), this posterior classification rule can be transformed into a joint probability classification rule, because $P(A_1, A_2, \ldots, A_n)$ for a given data point is a constant with respect to C. Finally, by incorporating the independency assumption, that is, $P(A_i, A_j \mid C) = P(A_i \mid C) P(A_j \mid C)$, for $1 \leq i \neq j \leq n$, the classification rule is changed in a decomposable form as equation (3).

$$c = \arg\max_{c_i} P(C_i \mid A_1, A_2, \ldots, A_n)$$

$$= \arg\max_{c_i} \frac{P(C_i) P(A_1, A_2, \ldots, A_n \mid C_i)}{P(A_1, A_2, \ldots, A_n)} \tag{1}$$

$$= \arg\max_{c_i} P(C_i) P(A_1, A_2, \ldots, A_n \mid C_i) \tag{2}$$

$$= \arg\max_{c_i} P(C_i) \prod_{j=1}^{n} P(A_j \mid C_i) \tag{3}$$

When used in real applications, NB first partitions the dataset into several subdatasets by the class label. Then, in each subdataset labelled by C_i, the maximum likelihood (ML) estimator $P(A_j = a_{jk} \mid C_i)$ can be given by the frequency n_{ijk} / n_i, n_{ijk} is the number of the occurrences of the event $\{A_j = a_{jk}\}$ in subdataset C_i; n_i is the number of the samples in subdataset C_i.

The above simple scheme achieves surprising success in many classification tasks (Duda & Hart, 1973; Friedman, Geiger, & Goldszmidt, 1997; Langley et al., 1992). Importantly, a great advantage of NB is its immediate ability to deal with the missing information problem. Assume the attributes set $\{A_1, A_2, \ldots, A_n\}$ be A. When the values of a subset of A, for example T, are unknown or missing, the marginalization inference can be obtained immediately as follows:

$$c = \arg\max_{c_i} P(C_i) P(A - T \mid C_i)$$

$$= \arg\max_{c_i} P(C_i) P(A - T \mid C_i)$$

$$= \arg\max_{c_i} P(C_i) \prod_{j \in A-T} P(A_j \mid C_i) \tag{4}$$

No further computation is needed in handling this missing information problem, because each term $P(A_j \mid C_i)$ has been calculated in training NB. In comparison, other discriminative classifiers are difficult to deal with the missing information problem. Generally speaking, lack of probability formulation makes this school of methods impossible to do marginalization.

However, there are still shortcomings in NB. More specifically, this approach models the joint probability in each subset separately and then applies the Bayes rule to construct the posterior classification rule. This framework appears to be incomplete, because this construction procedure actually discards important discriminative information for classification. Without considering the other classes of data, this method only tries to approximate the information in each subdataset. On the other hand, the discriminative classifiers preserve this information well by directly constructing decision rules among all the data. Therefore, for the Naive Bayesian classifier, it is not enough to approximate the data in each subdataset separately. It should provide a global scheme to preserve the discriminative information among all the data.

One of the solutions is to directly learn a posterior probability model rather than a joint probability model. However, within the framework of Bayesian network classifier, this kind of approach is often computationally hard to perform the optimization. Even for the simple naive Bayesian classifier, the corresponding posterior learning, known as the logistic regression (LR) (Jordan, 1995), will encounter problems in order to deal with missing information tasks. In a two-category classification problem, LR defines the posterior probability as:

$$P(c = C_0 \mid A_1, A_2, ..., A_n) = 1/(1 + \exp(-\sum_{j=1}^{n} \beta_j A_j - \theta)) \tag{5}$$

$$P(c = C_1 \mid A_1, A_2, ..., A_n) = 1 - P(c = C_0 \mid A_1, A_2, ..., A_n) \tag{6}$$

In the above, β and θ are two unknown parameters which can be estimated by the ML criterion. When the values of a subset of attribute set T are unknown, the marginalization on T is obtained in equation (7):

$$P(c = C_0 \mid A - T) = \frac{\sum_T P(c = C_0 \mid A) P(A - T, T)}{\sum_T P(c = C_0 \mid A) P(A - T, T) + \sum_T P(c = C_1 \mid A) P(A - T, T)} \tag{7}$$

The right hand side is hard to calculate. First, $P(A - T, T)$ varies from T, and thus it cannot be omitted. Second, in $P(c = C_0 \mid A)$, the logistic form will be at least calculated $r^{|T|}$ times, where r is the minimum number of values of attributes, and $|T|$ represents the cardinality of set T. This calculation is computationally intractable when the number of missing attributes is large.

In this chapter, we develop a novel discriminative method to train the naive Bayesian classifier. We call this model the discriminative naive Bayesian (DNB) classifier. Beginning with modeling the joint probabilities for the data, we plug into the optimization function a penalty term which describes the divergence between two classes. On one hand, the optimization of the new function tries to approximate the dataset as accurately as possible. On the other hand, it also tries to enlarge the divergence among classes as large as possible. Importantly, when improving the accuracy, this model inherits the NB's ability in handling the missing information problem.

Combining generative classifiers and discriminative classifiers has been one of the active topics in machine learning. A lot of work has been done in this area (Bahl, Brown, de Souza, & Mercer, 1993; Beaufays, Wintraub, & Konig, 1999; Hastie & Tibshirani, 1996; Valtchev, Odell, Woodland, & Young, 1996). However, nearly all of these methods are designed for the Gaussian mixture model (McLachlan & Basford, 1988) or the hidden Markov model (Rabiner & Juang, 1986). By contrast, our discriminative approach is developed for one of the Bayesian network classifiers, the naive Bayesian classifier. On the other hand, Jaakkola & Haussler (1998) develop a method to explore generative models from discriminative classifiers. Different from this approach, our method performs a reverse way to use discriminative information in generative classifiers. In Huang, King, and Lyu (2003), a discriminative training is performed on a kind of tree belief network, a Chow-Liu tree; however, it appears hard to prove the convergence of the algorithm.

This chapter is organized as follows. First, we describe the discriminative naive Bayesian classifier in detail. We then evaluate our algorithm on four benchmark datasets. The relationship between our algorithm and other approaches, such as SVM, and Fisher discriminant analysis, is discussed. Finally, we set out the conclusion.

Discriminative Naive Bayesian Network for Classification

In this section, we first develop the discriminative naive Bayesian classifier in a two-category classification task. Then, in the next section, we exploit a voting scheme to extend our method into multicategory classification tasks.

Two-Category Discriminative Naive Bayesian Classifier

The NB firstly partitions the dataset into several subdatasets by the class variable. Typically, in a two-category classification problem, two subdatasets, S_1 and S_2, represent the data with the class label C_1 and C_2, respectively. Then, in each subdataset, the ML or the cross entropy criterion can be used to find the optimal values for the parameters, namely, $P(A_j \mid C_1)$ and $P(A_j \mid C_2)$, $1 \leq j \leq n$. The cross entropy between a distribution p and a reference distribution q is defined as the Kullback-Leibler function, shown in the following:

$$KL(q, p) = \sum q \log \frac{q}{p} \qquad (8)$$

Within the framework of Bayesian learning, the reference distribution is generally the empirical distribution. Therefore for NB, the optimization function in a two-category classification problem can be written as follows:

$$\{P_1, P_2\} = \underset{\{p_1, p_2\}}{\arg\min}(KL(p_1, \tilde{p}_1) + KL(p_2 = \tilde{p}_2)) \tag{9}$$

$\tilde{p}_1$ and $\tilde{p}_2$ represent the empirical distribution for the subdataset 1 and subdataset 2, respectively. The first term and second term on the right hand side of equation 9 describe how accurately the joint distributions p_1 and p_2 approximate the subdataset 1 and subdataset 2. It is observed again that this function is incomplete, because only the innerclass information is preserved. The important interclass information, namely the divergence information between class 1 and class 2, is actually discarded. To fix this problem, we add into the optimization function an interactive term, which represents the divergence between classes:

$$\{P_1, P_2\} = \underset{\{p_1, p_2\}}{\arg\min} \, f(P_1, P_2)$$
$$= \underset{\{p_1, p_2\}}{\arg\min}(KL(p_1, \tilde{p}_1) + KL(p_2 + \tilde{p}_2) = W \times \mathrm{Div}(p_1, p_2)) \tag{10}$$

$Div(p_1, p_2)$ is a function of the divergence between p_1 and p_2. This function value needs to go up as the divergence goes down. W is a penalty parameter. In this chapter, we use the reciprocal of the Kullback-Leibler measure to represent the function:

$$\mathrm{Div}(p_1, p_2) = \frac{1}{\sum_x p_1 \log \dfrac{p_1}{p_2}} \tag{11}$$

Optimization on this function will make the innerdivergence described in the first two terms on the right hand side as small as possible, while the interclass divergence among classes will be as big as possible, which will benefit the classification greatly. Different from the discriminative classifiers such as the LR, the discriminative information is finally incorporated into the joint probability p_1 and p_2. Thus, the advantages of using joint probabilities will be naturally inherited into the discriminative Naive Bayesian classifier.

However, the disadvantage of plugging this interactive item is that we cannot optimize p_1 and p_2, as in NB, separately in the subdataset 1 and subdataset 2. To clarify this problem, we combine the NB assumption to expand the optimization function in a complete form:

$$\underset{\{P_1, P_2\}}{\min} \sum_{c=1}^{2} \sum_{j=1}^{n} \sum_{A_j} [\tilde{p}_c(a_{jk}) \log \frac{\tilde{p}_c(a_{jk})}{p_c(a_{jk})}] + W \frac{1}{\sum_{j=1}^{n} \sum_{A_j} p_1(a_{jk}) \log(p_1(a_{jk})/p_2(a_{jk}))} \tag{12}$$

$$\text{s.t.}\ 0 \le p_c(a_{jk}) \le 1, \tag{13}$$

$$\sum_{A_j} p_c(a_{jk}) = 1, c = 1, 2; j = 1, 2, ..., n.$$

$p_c(a_{jk})$ is the short form of $p_c(A_j = a_{jk})$. This is the same for $\tilde{p}_c(a_{jk})$. p_1 and p_2 are a set of parameters, namely, $p_1 = \{p_1(A_j), 1 \le j \le n\}$, $p_2 = \{p_2(A_j), 1 \le j \le n\}$. This is a nonlinear optimization problem under linear constraints. p_1 and p_2 are interactive variables. It is clear that they cannot be separately optimized as in equation 9.

To solve this problem, we use a modified Rosen's gradient projection method (Rosen, 1960). We firstly calculate the gradients of the optimization function with respect to p_1 and p_2. We then project this gradient on the constraint plane. In our problem, the projection matrix can be written as in equation 17. The optimal step length α is searched in the projected gradient direction by using the quadratic interpolation method (Lasdon, 1970). The process is repeated until a local minimal is obtained. We write down the detailed steps as follows:

1.   Calculate the gradient according to equation 14-16.

$$\frac{\partial f}{\partial p_1(a_{jk})} = -\tilde{p}_1(a_{jk})/p_1(a_{jk}) - \frac{W}{Z}[1 + \log(p_1(a_{jk})/p_2(a_{jk}))] \tag{14}$$

$$\frac{\partial f}{\partial p_2(a_{jk})} = -\tilde{p}_2(a_{jk})/p_2(a_{jk}) - \frac{W}{Z}p_1(a_{jk})/p_2(a_{jk}) \tag{15}$$

$$Z = \sum_{i=1}^{n}\sum_{A_j} \log(p_1(a_{jk})/p_2(a_{jk})) \tag{16}$$

2.   Project the gradient into the constraint plane: $\nabla f^M = \nabla f \cdot M$

$$M = I - A(A'A)^{-1}A' \tag{17}$$

where A is the coefficient matrix for the constraint, and I is the identity matrix.

3.   Search the optimal step length α by quadratic interpolation method.

4.   Update p_1 and p_2 by the following equations.

$$p_1(a_{jk})^{\text{new}} = p_1(a_{jk})^{\text{old}} - \alpha \nabla f_{1jk}^M \tag{18}$$

$$p_2(a_{jk})^{\text{new}} = p_2(a_{jk})^{\text{old}} - \alpha \nabla f_{2jk}^M \tag{19}$$

5.   Go to step 1 until p_1 and p_2 converge.

Figure 1. Discriminative naive Bayesian classifier committee machine for a four-category problem S_i, $1 \leq i \leq 4$ represent the subdataset for category i, respectively. $C_l m$, $1 \leq l \leq 3$, $l < m$ means the two-category discriminative naive Beyesian classifier for category l and category m.

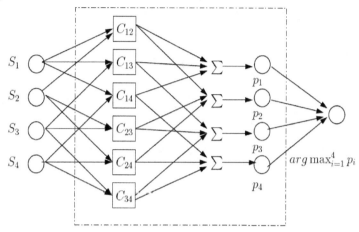

Multicategory Discriminative Naive Classifier

We use a partly connected committee machine scheme to extend the two-category classification problem into the multicategory one. We construct a two-category classifier for each pair of classes. For an *m*-category problem, in total, $m(m - 1)/2$ classifiers will be constructed. Each classifier will output a probability on how confident its vote is. We then sum up the voting probabilities for each class, and return the class with the highest probabilities as the final decision.

In Figure 1, we illustrate a four-category committee machine. In Figure 1, totally $4 \times 3/2 = 6$ DNB two-category classifiers are constructed. Then, these classifiers output the confidence on the class they are voting for. These confidences or probabilities are summed up for each class. Finally, the class with the maximum confidence is output as the classification result.

Table 1. Description of data sets used in the experiments

Dataset	Variables	Class	Train	Test
Iris	4	3	150	CV-5
Segment	19	7	2310	30%
Satimage	36	6	4435	2000
DNA	60	3	2000	1186

Table 2. Parameters used in the experiments

Method	Penalty parameter	Kernel function
DNB	1000	N/A
SVM	1000	3-order polynomial

Evaluations

In this section, we implement the DNB algorithm to evaluate its performance on four bench-mark datasets from Machine Learning Repository in UCI (Blake & Merz, 1998). The detailed information for these datasets is listed in Table 3. These datasets vary in the variable number and the sample size. As observed in Table 3, the variable number ranges from 4 to 60 and the sample size varies from 150 to 6,435. The diversity in choosing the datasets will make the evaluations on the algorithms more reliable. For the Iris dataset, which has a small number of samples, we use a five-fold cross-validation method (CV5) to test the performance. We compare our model's performance with NB and a 3-order polynomial kernel SVM in two cases, namely the case without information missing and the case with information missing. The parameters for DNB and SVM used in the experiments are listed in Table 3.

Table 3. Prediction accuracy without information missing (%)

Dataset	NB	DNB	SVM
Iris	93.33	**97.33**	95.33
Segment	88.44	90.88	**95.96**
Satimage	80.65	82.65	**87.90**
DNA	94.44	**94.52**	94.35

Figure 2. Error rates without information missing (%)

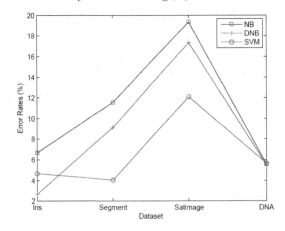

Without Information Missing

We first implement our model in the case without information missing. The experimental results are demonstrated in Table 3. To clearly see the comparison, we also plot the error rates in Figure 2. It can be observed that DNB outperforms NB in all of the four datasets. This implies that incorporating discriminative information in training the generative models benefits the classification greatly. When compared with SVM, DNB wins in two of the datasets, while it loses in the other two. We note that in these two datasets, that is, Segment and Setimage, SVM performs significantly better than DNB. This demerit of DNB roots in the inner scheme of generative classifiers. Later in the chapter, we will present a detailed discussion on this issue.

With Information Missing

It is important to discuss the ability of the DNB in handling the missing information problem, because one of the main advantages for generative classifiers lies in this point. Gradually, we increase the percentages of the number of unknown or missing attributes randomly. We then test the recognition rate on these datasets with different percentages. As mentioned previously for DNB and NB, a principled way to handle the missing information problem

Figure 3. Error rates with information missing for four datasets. The figures on the upper-left, upper-right, bottom-left, bottom-right are the curves for Iris, Segment, Satimage, and DNA, respectively.

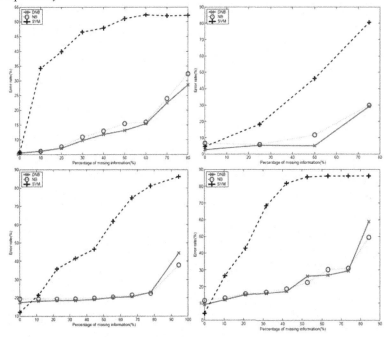

is to use inference under uncertainty: $c = \arg\max_{C_i} P(C_i) \prod_{A_j \in A-T} P(A_j|C_i)$. For SVM, a normal way to force its application in missing information tasks is simply setting zero values for the missing attributes. Because in implementing SVM the values of attributes are prenormalized to the range $[-1,1]$, the zero value can be considered as the average value of the attributes. Thus in a sense, this method can be regarded as replacing the missing values with the corresponding average value. The experiment results for the four datasets are shown in Figure 3. It is shown that NB demonstrates a robust ability to handle the missing information problem. In four datasets, the error rate curves of NB maintain a flat trend when the information does not decay too much. Furthermore, DNB shows a similar resistance ability, while its accuracy is higher than NB. In comparison, SVM's performance gradually runs down as the number of the missing variables goes up. The superiority of DNB over NB and SVM is especially prominent in the Iris dataset. In the Iris dataset the number of samples is relatively small. Thus, the distribution from insufficient training data may not represent the real distribution. Therefore, the discriminative item will contribute more in constructing the classifiers.

Discussion

In this section, we discuss the connections of our model with SVM and Fisher discriminant analysis (FDA) (Fukunaga, 1990) in the concept level. In SVM, a linear classifier $y = w \cdot x + b$ with the maximum margin between two classes is searched by minimizing the following function in equation 20.

$$\Gamma(w,\xi) = \frac{C}{N}\sum_{i=1}^{N}\xi_i + \frac{1}{2}\|w\|^2$$

$$\text{s.t.}\, y_i \cdot ((w \cdot x_i) + b) \geq 1 - \xi_i, \xi_i \geq 0$$

(20)

where, $x_i \in \mathbb{R}^n$, n is the data dimension, $y_i \in \mathbb{R}$ is the class label corresponding to x_i, and $w \in \mathbb{R}^n$ and $b \in \mathbb{R}$ are the variables to be optimized. To handle the nonlinear problem, usually the so-called kernel trick will be used to map the input into a high-dimension feature space, where a linear classifier can be found. This function consists of two parts. Because $\dfrac{2}{\|w\|^2}$ represents the margin between two classes, the second part on the right hand of equation 20, namely $\dfrac{1}{2}\|w\|^2$, describes the extent on how far away two classes are from each other. The first term can be considered as the loss function in the training dataset, that is, how accurate the sample in the training dataset can be classified into the corresponding class. Interestingly, we note this optimization function of SVM is similar to the one of DNB. In the DNB model, two terms form.

The optimization function as equation 10. The second term represents a similar meaning to the one in SVM. The first term in DNB also tries to approximate the training dataset as accurately as possible. The difference is that in SVM, the first part directly minimizes the recognition error rate, while in DNB, this part minimizes an intermediate term representing the difference between the estimated joint distribution and the empirical distribution. As Box once said, "all models are wrong (but some are useful)" (Box & Draper, 1987, p. 424). The estimated distribution under the strong independency assumption may not always coincide with the real data, and therefore may fail to work in practice.

It is also interesting that the Fisher discriminant analysis (FDA) also uses an idea similar to ours to separate two classes. FDA minimizes the innerclass divergence described by the average covariance of all classes and maximizes the interclass divergence represented by the difference of the means between two classes. However, using the difference between the mean values as the divergence between two classes may not be as informative a way as the Kullback-Leibler divergence, a distribution-based approach.

Conclusion

In this chapter, we have improved a typical Bayesian network classifier, that is, the naive Bayesian classifier. We exploit a discriminative way to train the naive Bayesian classifier. This novel training enables the improved method called discriminative naive Bayesian classifier both in merits of discriminative methods and generative methods. When handling the tasks without information missing, the DNB demonstrates superior performance over the Naive Bayesian classifier. When handling tasks with missing information, the DNB outperforms the Support Vector Machine. A series of experiments has been conducted to evaluate our model. The results have demonstrated the effectiveness of our model in comparison with the Naive Bayesian classifier and the Support Vector Machine.

References

Bahl, L.R., Brown, P.F., de Souza, P.V., & Mercer, R.L. (1993). Estimating hidden markov model parameters so as to maximize speech recognition accuracy. *IEEE Transactions on Speech and Audio Processing, 1,*77-82.

Beaufays, F., Wintraub, M. , & Konig, Y. (1999). Discriminative mixture weight estimation for large gaussian mixture models. In *Proceedings of the International Conference on Acoustics, Speech and Signal Processing* (pp. 337-340).

Blake, C.L., & Merz, C.J. (1998). UCI repository of machine learning databases.University of California, Irvine: Department of Information and Computer Sciences. Retrieved December 14, 2006, from http://www.ics.uci.edu/»mlearn/MLRepository.html

Box, G. E. P., & Draper, N. R. (1987). *Empirical model-building and response surfaces.* New York: John Wiley & Sons.

Duda, R., & Hart, P. (1973). *Pattern classification and scene analysis*. New York : John Wiley & Sons.

Friedman, N., Geiger, D., & Goldszmidt, M. (1997). Bayesian network classifiers. *Machine Learning, 29*, 131-161.

Fukunaga, K. (1990). *Introduction to statistical pattern recognition* (2nd ed.). San Diego: Academic Press.

Hastie, T., & Tibshirani, R. (1996). Discriminant analysis by gaussian mixtures. *Journal of the Royal Statistical Society (B), 58*, 155-176.

Huang, K., King, I., & Lyu, M.R. (2003). Discriminative training of bayesian chow-liu tree multinet classifiers. In *Proceedings of the International Joint Conference on Neural Network (IJCNN-2003)* (vol.1, pp. 484-488). Portland, OR.

Huang, K., Yang, H., King, I., & Lyu, M.R. (2004). Learning large margin classifiers locally and globally. In R. Greiner & D. Schuurmans (Eds.), *Proceedings of the Twenty-first International Conference on Machine Learning (ICML-2004)* (pp. 401-408).

Jaakkola, T.S., & Haussler, D. (1999). Exploiting generative models in discriminative classifiers. In *Proceedings of the 1998 conference on Advances in neural information processing systems II* (pp. 487-493). Cambridge, MA: MIT Press.

Jordan, M.I. (1995). Why the logistic function? A tutorial discussion on probabilities and neural networks (Tech. Rep. No. 9503). MIT Computational Cognitive Science Report.

Langley, P., Iba, W., & Thompson, K. (1992). An analysis of bayesian classifiers. In *Proceedings of National Conference on Artificial Intelligence (AAAI-1992)* (pp. 223-228).

Lasdon, L.S. (1970). *Optimization theory for large systems*. The Macmillan Company.

McLachlan, G.J., & Basford, K.E. (1988). *Mixture models: Inference and applications to clustering*. New York: Marcel Dekker.

Rabiner, L.R. & Juang, B.H. (1986, January). An introduction to hidden Markov models. *IEEE ASSP Magazine*, 4-15.

Rosen, J.B. (1960). The gradient projection method for nonlinear programming: Part I-linear constraints. *SIAM Journal of the Society for Industrial and Applied Mathematics, 3*(1), 181-217.

Valtchev, V., Odell, J.J., Woodland, P.C., & Young, S.J. (1996). Lattice-based discriminative training for large vocabulary speech recognition. In *Proceedings of the International Conference on Acoustics, Speech and Signal Processing* (pp. 605-608).

Vapnik, V.N. (1999). *The nature of statistical learning theory* (2nd ed.). New York: Springer-Verlag.

Chapter II

A Bayesian Belief Network Approach for Modeling Complex Domains

Ben K. Daniel, University of Saskatchewan, Canada

Juan-Diego Zapata-Rivera, Educational Testing Service, USA

Gordon I. McCalla, University of Saskatchewan, Canada

Abstract

Bayesian belief networks (BBNs) are increasingly used for understanding and simulating computational models in many domains. Though BBN techniques are elegant ways of capturing uncertainties, knowledge engineering effort required to create and initialize the network has prevented many researchers from using them. Even though the structure of the network and its conditional & initial probabilities could be learned from data, data is not always available or it is too costly to obtain. In addition, current algorithms that can be used to learn relationships among variables, initial and conditional probabilities from data are often complex and cumbersome to employ. Qualitative-based approaches applied to the creation of graphical models can be used to create initial computational models that can help researchers analyze complex problems and provide guidance and support for decision-making. Initial BBN models can be refined once appropriate data is obtained. This chapter extends the use of BBNs to help experts make sense of complex social systems (e.g., social capital in virtual learning communities) using a Bayesian model as an interactive simulation tool. Scenarios are used to find out whether the model is consistent with the expert's beliefs. The sensitivity analysis was conducted to help explain how the model reacted to different sets of evidence. Currently, we are in the process of refining the initial probability values presented in the model using empirical data and developing more authentic scenarios to further validate the model.

Introduction

Bayesian networks, Bayesian models, or Bayesian belief networks (BBNs) can be classified as part of the probabilistic graphical model family. Graphical models provide an elegant and mathematically sound approach to represent uncertainty. It combines advances in graph theory and probability. BBNs are graphs composed of nodes and directional arrows (Pearl, 1988). Nodes in BBNs represent variables, and directed edges (arrows) between pairs of nodes indicate relationships between variables. The nodes in a BBN are usually drawn as circles or ovals. Further, BBNs offer a mathematically rigorous way to model a complex environment that is flexible, able to mature as knowledge about the system grows, and computationally efficient (Druzdzel & Gaag, 2000; Rusell & Norvig, 1995).

Research shows that BBN techniques have significant power to support the use of probabilistic inference to update and revise belief values (Pearl, 1988). In addition, they can readily permit qualitative inferences without the computational inefficiencies of traditional joint probability determinations (Niedermayer, 1998). Furthermore, the causal information encoded in BBNs facilitates the analysis of actions, sequences of events, observations, consequences, and expected utility (Pearl, 1988).

Despite the relevance of BBNs, the ideas and techniques have not spread into the social sciences and humanities research communities. The goal of this chapter is to make Bayesian networks more accessible to a wider community in the social sciences and humanities, especially researchers involved in many aspects of social computing. The common problems, which can prevent the wider use of BBN in other domains, include:

- Building BBNs requires considerable knowledge engineering effort, in which the most difficult part of it is to obtain numerical parameters for the model and apply them in complex, which are the kinds of problems social scientists are attempting to address.

- Constructing a realistic and consistent graph (i.e., the structure of the model) often requires collaboration between knowledge engineers and subject matter experts, which in most cases is hard to establish.

- Combining knowledge from various sources such as textbooks, reports, and statistical data to build models can be susceptible to gross statistical errors and by definition are subjective.

- The graphical representation of a BBN is the outcome of domain specifications. However, in situations where domain knowledge is insufficient or inaccurate, the model's outcomes are prone to error.

- Acquiring knowledge from subject matter experts can be subjective.

Despite the problems outlined above, BBNs still remain a viable modeling approach in many domains, especially domains which are quite imprecise and volatile, such as weather forecasting, stock market, and so forth. This chapter extends the use of BBN approaches to complex and imprecise constructs. We use social capital as an example of showing the modeling procedures involved. The approach presented in the chapter helps experts and researchers build and explore initial computational models and revise and validate them as more data become available. We think that by providing appropriate tools and techniques, the process of building Bayesian models can be extended to address social issues in other domains in the social sciences and the humanities.

The rest of the chapter is described as follows. In section 2, basic Bayesian concepts are presented. The goal is to provide the reader with some of the fundamental principles underlying Bayesian probabilities and the modeling process. Section 3 briefly describes the role of computational models in the area of artificial intelligence in education. In section 4, we provide procedures for building Bayesian models and illustrate them with a model of social capital in virtual communities, which is described in section 5. In section 6, various stages of model construction, updating, and validation are described. Section 7 disuses and summarizes the chapter. It also describes future research directions.

Background

Graphical models draw upon probability theory and graph theory. Graphical models provide a natural way of dealing with two major problems, uncertainty and complexity. In addition, they provide intuitive ways in which both humans and machines can model a highly interactive set of random variables, as well as complex data structures, to enable them to make logical, useful, and valid inferences from data. In mathematical notation, a graph G is simply a collection of vertices V and edges E, that is, $G = (V, E)$ and a typical graph G is associated with a set of variables (nodes) $N = \{X_1 X_2, X_3...X_n\}$ and by establishing one-to-one relationships among the variables in N. Each edge in a graph can be either directed or undirected.

Directed graphs in particular consist only of directed edges. Acyclic directed graphs (ADGs) are special kinds of directed graphs that do not include cycles. One of the advantages of directed graphs over undirected graphs is that ADGs can be used to represent causal relationships among two or more variables, for example an arc from A to B indicates that A causes B. Such property can be used to construct a complex graph with many variables (a causal graph). In addition, directed graphs can encode deterministic as well as probabilistic relationships among variables. BBNs are examples of acyclic directed graphs, where nodes represent random variables and the arcs represent direct probabilistic dependences among the variables (Pearl, 1988).

Building on graph theory and conditional probability, Bayesian modeling is the process of using initial knowledge and updating such belief using Bayes' theorem in relation to probability theory, resulting in Bayesian belief networks (a.k.a., belief networks, Bayesian belief networks, causal probabilistic networks, or causal networks). The Bayesian interpretation of probability is based on the principles of conditional probability theory. In Bayesian statistics, conditional probabilities are used with partial knowledge about an outcome of an experiment. For example, such knowledge is conditional on relationships between two related events A and B, such that the occurrence of one will affect the occurrence of the other. Suppose event B is true, that is, it has occurred, then the probability that A is true given the knowledge about B is expressed by: $P(A|B)$. This notation suggests the following two assumptions:

1.   Two events A and B are independent of each other if $P(A) = P(A|B)$ (1)

2.   Two events A and B are conditionally independent of each other given C if $P(A|C) = P(A|B, C)$ (2)

Drawing from these two assumptions, Bayes' theorem swaps the order of dependence between events. For instance:

3. $$P(A|B) = \frac{P(A, B)}{P(B)}$$ (3)

4.   And Bayes' theorem states that:

$$P(A|B) = \frac{P(B|A)P(A)}{P(B)}$$ (4)

$$P(A|B) = \frac{P(B|A)P(A)}{P(B)} = \frac{P(B|A)P(A)}{\sum_j P(B|A_j)P(A_j)}$$ (5)

where j indicates all possible states of A.

From the above equations, the following can be stated about BBN models relationships to conditional probability:

- $P(A|B)$ is posterior probability given evidence B
- $P(A)$ is the initial probability of A
- $P(B|A)$ is the likelihood probability of the evidence given A
- $P(B)$ is the initial probability of the evidence B

Modeling Process

Models in general are useful tools for representing abstractions and concrete realities. Models provide various ways of organizing, analyzing, and understanding logical relationships among data, objects, and classes. There are several kinds of models used in a variety of contexts and domains. Computational models are useful tools that can help researchers understand social and technical aspect of systems, and provide systems designers and analysts with rich insights to build processes, procedures, and tools to support systems' operations.

Figure 1. Modeling process

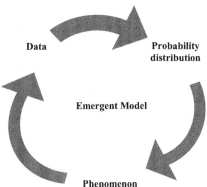

In artificial intelligence in education (AIED), models are used to capture characteristics of learners that can themselves be used by tools to support learning (McCalla, 2000). Models can also be used for representing various educational systems. Baker (2000) summarized three major uses of models within AIED: models as scientific tools for understanding learning problems, models as components of educational systems, and models as educational artifacts. Baker (2000) further observed that the future of artificial intelligence in education (AIED) would involve building models to support learners in learning communities and to help educators manage learning under distributed circumstances.

The process of building models is an iterative one, involving organization of data, establishing logical relationships among the data, and coming up with a knowledge representation scheme. The process involves interaction of data, observation of a phenomenon, a knowledge representation scheme, and an emergent model (see Figure 1).

A fundamental assumption underlying most of the model building process is that data is available in which a researcher can be able to infer logical relationships and draw logical and concrete conclusions from the model. There are modeling approaches that do not allow the introduction of prior knowledge during the modeling process. These approaches normally prevent the introduction of extraneous data to avoid skewing the experimental results. However, there are times when the use of prior knowledge would be a useful contribution to the modeling and evaluation processes and the overall observation of the behaviour of a model.

Related Research and Building Bayesian Models

BBN techniques are increasingly used in a variety of domains, including medical diagnostic systems (Niedermayer, 1998; Pradhan, Provan, Middleton, & Henrion, 1994), student modeling (Conati, Gertner, & VanLehn, 2002; Reye, 2004; VanLehn, Niu, Siler, & Gertner, 1998; Vomlel, 2004; Zapata-Rivera, 2002, 2003; Zapata-Rivera & Greer, 2004), troubleshooting of malfunctioning systems (Finn & Liang, 1994), and intelligent help assistant in Microsoft

Figure 2. Fundamental phases and procedures in building BBN models

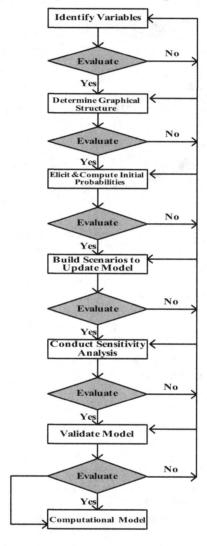

Office (Heckerman & Horwitz, 1998). Recently, Daniel, Zapata-Rivera, and McCalla (2003) extended the use of BBNs to model social interactions in virtual learning communities.

The construction of BBNs consists of several phases (see Figure 2). The first step involves identifying and defining the problem domain, followed by the identification of the relevant variables constituting the problem being modeled. Further, once the variables are established, variable states and their relevant initial probabilities are assigned (Druzdzel & Gaag, 2000). Probability values are normally estimated or appropriated based on certain sources of evidence (empirical data, expert's belief, literature review, or intuition). The second step is to determine the relationships among the variables and establish the graphical structure of the model. The third step, then, is to apply Bayesian rules to compute conditional probability values for each of variables in the model. The fourth stage of model building requires development of scenarios to update and train the model. Once a model is updated, the fifth phase is to run sensitivity analysis to assess the performance of the model against its parameters.

Model validation takes place during the sixth and the last phase of the model development. Validation ensures that the model is useful and valid and that it reflects real world phenomenon. The modeling phases are normally conducted to reach a stable computational model. In some circumstances these are only shown in three steps, but we extended this to 7 phases, as shown in Figure 2. The different phases are elaborated and shown with an example of modeling social capital discussed later in the chapter.

The joint probabilities in Bayesian models can grow exponentially given two or more states of set of variables. For instance, assuming a binary set of variables with no graphical structure specified, the number of probability values needed to determine the joint probability distribution in a BBN model is 2^n, where n = number of variables. In other words, if there are 10 variables in a model, then their joint probability distribution is $2^{10} = 2048$ probability values. But sometimes it is seldom necessary that all these numbers be elicited and stored in the model.

This can be reduced through factorization and exploring independencies among variables through techniques of "explaining away." The notion of "explaining away" suggests that there are two competing causes, A and B, which are conditionally dependent given that their common child, C, is observed, even though they are marginally independent. For example, suppose the grass is wet, but that we also know that it is raining. Then the posterior probability that the sprinkler is on goes down.

The inherent structure of a Bayesian model can be defined in terms of dependency and independency assumptions between variables, and it greatly simplifies the representation of the joint probability distribution capturing any dependencies, independences, conditional independences, and marginal independences between variables.

A Bayesian model is usually composed of n variables and each variable is deliberately associated with those variables that lie under its influence. This is known as conditional independence (see equation 2), and it can be represented in different ways, for example, causal chain, common cause, and common effect. Figure 3 shows a scenario in which A acts as a common cause for B and C. If there is no evidence about A, knowing about B could change the probability of C (by propagating new evidence through A). However, if A is observed (i.e., evidence of A is available), knowing about B will not change the probability

Figure 3. Example of a conditional independence

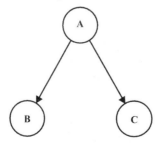

of C (i.e., the path between B and C is blocked given $A - B$ and C are d-separated by A). D-separation is a Bayesian rule describing relationships between two nodes X and Y with respect to another node Z. X and Y are d-separated by Z if no information can flow between them when Z is observed. More information about conditional independence and d-separation can be found in Neapolitan (2004), Korb and Nicholson (2004), and Finn (1996). Additional information regarding learning Bayesian networks can be found in Heckerman (1996) and Neapolitan (2004).

Though initial probabilities can be obtained from many sources, these sources seldom offer the requirements for the quantitative aspect of the model. As a result, several algorithms are required to compute the values needed, most of which are time consuming and difficult to apply in some domains, as noted previously in this chapter. Nonetheless, there are generally two approaches for learning BBNs from data. The first is based on constraint-search (Pearl & Verma, 1991) and the second uses a Bayesian search for graphs with the highest posterior probability (Cooper & Herskovits, 1992).

In building Bayesian graphs, knowledge obtained from human experts is normally determined by drawing causal links among nodes, and probabilities are based on subject estimates. As described previously, the most daunting task of building models is to translate experts' knowledge into numerical values. Subsequently, combinations of quantitative and qualitative approaches are sometimes required. Eliciting probabilities from experts has some drawbacks. For instance, it has been found that experts can exhibit problems such as overconfidence, in initial estimation, disagreement among experts, assigning high probability values events that are easy to remember (availability problem) (Morgan & Henrion, 1990). All these issues are likely to affect the quality of the initial probabilities.

Wellman (1990) introduced a qualitative abstraction of BBNs known as qualitative Bayesian networks (QBN), which uses the concept of positive and negative influences between variables to determine causal relationships between variables in a graph. It assumes an ordered relationship between variables. Qualitative propagation is based on the premise that each variable in a network is provided a sign either positive (+) or negative (−), and that the effect of an observation **e** on **n** variables in a network propagates the sign of change throughout the network. In addition, Renooij and Witteman (1999) proposed a probability scale that contains words as well as numbers to help researchers and domain experts during the elicitation phase of building a belief network.

Drawing from QBN approaches, Daniel, Zapata-Rivera, and McCalla (2003) used a qualitative and quantitative approach of eliciting knowledge from experts (i.e., structure and initial and conditional probabilities) based on the descriptions of the strength of the relationship among variables in a network. This approach takes into account the number of states of a variable, number of parents, degree of strength (e.g., strong, medium, weak), and the kind of relationship or influence (e.g., positive or negative influence) to produce initial and conditional probabilities.

Once an initial model is elicited, particular scenarios are used to refine and document the network. In contrast to QBN, which makes use of its own qualitative propagation algorithms, this approach uses standard Bayesian propagation algorithms. Initial probabilities can also be refined when data becomes available. This approach is illustrated with the help of an example of model social capital in the virtual communities discussed in the proceeding section. In choosing a probabilistic approach to modeling, BBNs offer a number of advantages over other methods for the following reasons:

- BBN models are powerful tools both for graphically representing the relationships among a set of variables and for dealing with uncertainties in expert systems.

- The graphical structure of BBNs provides a visual method of relating relationships among variables in a simple way.

- Graphs in probabilistic modeling are convenient means of expressing substantial assumptions and they facilitate economical representation of a joint probability function to enhance making efficient inferences from observations.

- BBN's approach to modeling permits qualitative inferences without the computational inefficiencies of traditional joint probability determinations (Niedermayer, 1998).

- In BBNs, a network can be easily refined, that is, additional variables can be easily added and mapping from the mathematics to common understanding or reference points could be quickly done.

- The BBN approach allows for evidence to be entered into the network, and updating the network to propagate the probabilities to each node. The resulting probabilities tend to reflect common sense notions, including effects such as "explaining away" and "pooling of evidence."

- BBNs offer an interactive graphical modeling mechanism that researchers can use to understand the behaviour of a system or situation, (e.g., it is possible to add evidence/observe variables and propagate it throughout the whole graphical model to see/inspect the effects on particular variables of interest).

- The fact that BBN has a qualitative and quantitative part gives it more advantages over other methods.

Modeling Social Capital in Virtual Learning Communities

Current research on social capital (SC) suggests that there is no single construct constituting social capital, but rather, social capital is a composite of different variables, each of which can be interpreted independently (Daniel, McCalla, & Schwier, 2005). Daniel, Schwier, and Mc-Calla (2003) define social capital in virtual learning communities as common social resource that facilitates information exchange, knowledge sharing, and knowledge construction through continuous interaction, built on trust and maintained through shared understanding.

There are fundamentally many variables constituting social capital in terrestrial communities. Results of the synthesis of current research on SC revealed that building social capital requires continuous and positive interaction (Cohen & Prusak, 2001; Putnam, 2000; World

Bank, 2000). More specifically, positive interaction provides value to its participants, especially when it is built upon positive attitudes among individuals in a community (Daniel, Schwier, & McCalla, 2003). Interaction enables people to identify common goals, achieve shared understanding and social protocols, build trust, and commit themselves to each other (World Bank, 1999). The value derived from social interactions can include sharing experience, endorsing behavior, surfacing tacit knowledge, sharing information, recommending options, and providing companionship and hospitality (Lee, Danis, Miller, & Jung, 2001).

In virtual learning communities, the quality of interactions can be used to understand the presence or absence of a set of relationships among learners in virtual communities (Daniel, Schwier, & McCalla, 2003). Resnick (2002) noted SC can be understood through the kinds of relationships among individuals, and that the lack of SC in a community reveals the absences of productive relationships. A productive relationship in virtual communities is formed out of positive interactions and positive attitudes among members. Further, productive relationships occur when participants have a common set of expectations, mediated by a set of shared social protocols.

Another important aspect of building SC in virtual communities is when members establish a certain level of shared understanding. The process of establishing shared understanding often draws upon a set of shared beliefs, shared goals and values, experiences, and knowledge (Daniel, O'Brien, & Sarkar, 2003; Schwier & Daniel, in press). Further, research shows that awareness is critical to effective interactions and productive relationships in virtual settings (Gutwin & Greenberg, 1998). Maintaining different forms of awareness in a virtual community can lubricate the value of interaction. For instance, in order to effectively collaborate and function as a community, people need to be *aware* of others, where they are located (*demographic awareness*), what they do (*professional awareness*), what others know (*knowledge awareness*), and what they are able to do (*capability awareness*).

Another influential variable of social capital in communities is trust. Several research studies used trust as proxy for measuring SC in communities (World Bank, 1999; Putnam, 2000). Trust is a critical ingredient and a lubricant to almost any forms of social interactions (Daniel, McCalla, & Schwier, 2002). Trust enables people to work together, collaborate, and smoothly exchange information and share knowledge without time wasted on negotiation and conflict (Cohan & Prusak, 2000). Trust can also be treated as an outcome of positive attitudes among individuals in a community. Further, in virtual settings, trust can only be created and sustained when individuals are provided with an environment that can support different forms of awareness. Based on the literature on social capital, and validating the literature with an expert's knowledge drawn from our research into social capital in virtual learning communities for the last six years, we have identified and summarized the fundamental variables constituting social capital presented in Table 1.

The second step in building a model of SC is to map the variables (see Table 1) into a graphical structure based on logical and coherent qualitative reasoning. Similarly, the knowledge of the structure of the model was grounded in current research into social capital and our work on social capital in virtual communities. The knowledge for specifying the structure of the model was elicited from the literature and our research was based on qualitative reasoning. During the qualitative reasoning, causal relationships among the variables are conjured, resulting into an acyclical graph. For instance, in virtual learning communities, people's attitudes can strongly influence the level of their awareness on various issues, which in turn can influence trust.

Table 1. Social capital variables and their definitions (Daniel, McCalla, & Schwier, 2005)

Variable Name	Variable Definition	Variable States
Interaction	A mutual or reciprocal action between two or more agents determined by the number of messages sent and received	Positive/Negative
Attitudes	Individuals' general perception about each other and others' actions	Positive/Negative
Community Type	The type of environment, tools, goals, and tasks that define the group	Virtual learning community (VLC) and Distributed community of practice (DCoP)
Shared Understanding	A mutual agreement/consensus between two or more agents about the meaning of an object or idea	High/Low
Awareness	Knowledge of people, tasks, or environment, or all of the above	Present/Absent
Demographic Awareness	Knowledge of an individual: country of origin, language, and location	Present/Absent
Professional Awareness	Knowledge of people's background training, affiliation, and so forth	Present/Absent
Competence Awareness	Knowledge about an individual's capabilities, competencies, and skills	Present/Absent
Capability Awareness	Knowledge of people's competences and skills in regard to performing a particular task	Present/Absent
Social protocols	The mutually agreed upon, acceptable and unacceptable ways of behaviour in a community	Present/Absent
Trust	A particular level of certainty or confidence with which an agent uses to assess the action of another agent.	High/Low

Figure 4. Bayesian model of social capital in virtual communities (Daniel, Zapata-Rivera, & McCalla, 2003)

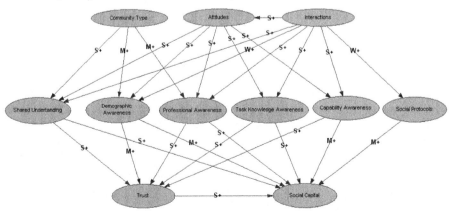

This is indicated in the direction of the arrow, that is, attitudes influencing different forms of awareness and the strength of the influence suggesting strongly positive relationships among the variables. Further, because awareness can contribute to both trust and distrust, the strength of the relationships can be medium positive, medium weak, and so forth, depending on the kind of the awareness. For instance, demographic awareness has a positive and medium effect on trust (see Figure 4), meaning that it is more likely that people will trust others regardless of their demographic backgrounds.

Extending this type of qualitative reasoning resulted in the BBN structure shown in Figure 4. In the model, those nodes that contribute to higher nodes align themselves in "child" to "parent" relationships, where parent nodes are super-ordinate to child nodes. For example in Figure 4, trust is the child of the following variables: shared understanding; different forms of awareness (demographic awareness, competence awareness, professional awareness and capability awareness) and social protocols. The parents of trust are in turn children of two variables: interaction and attitudes.

Figure 4 relates to all forms of virtual communities (VLCs and DCoP), and the graph topology enables different forms of experiments to be conducted, which can apply to both types of communities. Once a BBN graph is developed, the third stage is to obtain initial probability values to populate the network. Initial probabilities can be obtained from different sources, and sometimes obtaining accurate initial numbers that can yield valid and meaningful posteriors can be difficult. This chapter offers an approach for building an initial model that relies on minimal knowledge of sophisticated knowledge engineering techniques for eliciting initial probabilities.

Eliciting and Computing Conditional Probabilities

In Bayesian network, every stage of situation assessment requires assigning initial probabilities to the hypotheses. These initial probabilities are normally obtained from knowledge of the prevailing situation. However, converting a state of knowledge to probability assignment is a problem that lies at the heart of Bayesian probability theory.

In our approach, the initial conditional probabilities were obtained by examining qualitative descriptions of the influence between two or more variables. Each probability value describes strength of relationships, and the letters S (strong), M (medium), and W (weak) represent the different degrees of influence among the variables in the model (Daniel, Zapata-Rivera & McCalla, 2003). The signs + and - represent positive and negative relationships among the variables.

Conditional probability values were obtained by adding weights to the values of the variables, depending on the number of parents and the strength of the relationship between particular parents and children. For example, say *Attitudes* and *Interactions* have positive and strong (S+) relationships with *Knowledge Awareness*. The evidence of *positive interactions* and *positive attitudes* will produce a conditional probability value for *Knowledge Awareness* 0.98 (*threshold value for strong = 0.98*). The weights were obtained by subtracting a base value (1 / number of states, 0.5 in this case) from the threshold value associated to the degree of influence, and dividing the result by the number of parents (i.e., (0.98 - 0.5) / 2 = 0.48

Table 2. Threshold values and weights with two parents

Degree of influence	Thresholds	Weights
Strong	$1-\alpha = 1 - 0.02 = 0.98$	$(0.98-0.5) / 2 = 0.48 / 2 = 0.24$
Medium	0.8	$(0.8-0.5) / 2 = 0.3 / 2 = 0.15$
Weak	0.6	$(0.6-0.5) / 2 = 0.1 / 2 = 0.05$

$/ 2 = 0.24$). This follows the fact that in the graph *knowledge awareness* is a child of both *interactions* and *attitudes*.

Table 2 shows the threshold values and weights used in this example. Because it is more likely that a certain degree of uncertainty can exist, value $\alpha = 0.02$ leaves some room for uncertainty when considering evidence coming from positive and strong relationships. These threshold values can be adjusted based on expert opinion.

Using this approach, it is possible to generate conditional probability tables (CPTs) for each node (variable) regardless of the number of parents, depending on how the initial knowledge is elicited and what decisions are made to process the knowledge into initial probabilities. For instance, assuming some subject matter experts are consulted to obtain initial probabilities, this knowledge is translated into the threshold weighted values, as described in Table 2, depending on the degree of influence among the variables (i.e., evidence coming from one of the parent's states), a decision which can also be obtained from the subject mater expert in a particular domain. However, when experts define degrees of influence for more than one of the parents' states, adding weights could result in ties, which could generate inconsistent CPT. In such cases, one could ask the expert which parent should be used, or which has the most probable high degree of influence depending on the case under investigation.

Computation of Conditional Probability Values

As discussed earlier in the chapter, different forms of awareness are critical to interaction that stimulates positive SC in VLCs. Following the structure of the BBN (see Figure 4), *task knowledge awareness* is influenced by two parents: *interactions* and *attitudes*. Table 3 shows conditional probability values for *task knowledge awareness*s.

Table 3. Conditional probability table for task knowledge awareness given two parents

	Attitudes	positive		negative	
	Interactions	positive	negative	positive	negative
TaskKnowledge Awareness	High	0.98	0.74	0.74	0.5
	Low	0.02	0.26	0.26	0.5

Combining the Bayesian laws of computation already described, and the approach presented in Table 3 in this chapter, the initial probabilities for task knowledge awareness, given different states of interactions and attitudes, are calculated as follows:

- P (TaskKnowledgeAwareness = high | Attitudes = positive & Interactions = positive) = 0.5 + 0.24 + 0.24 = 0.98

- P(TaskKnowledgeAwareness = low | Attitudes = positive & Interactions = positive) = 1 - 0.98 = 0.02

- P (TaskKnowledgeAwareness = high | Attitudes = positive & Interactions = negative) = 0.5 + 0.24 = 0.74

- P (TaskKnowledgeAwareness = low | Attitudes = positive & Interactions = negative) = 1 - 0.74 = 0.26

- P (TaskKnowledgeAwareness = high | Attitudes = negative & Interactions = positive) = 0.5 + 0.24 = 0.74

- P (TaskKnowledgeAwareness = low | Attitudes = negative & Interactions = positive) = 1 - 0.74 = 0.26

- P (TaskKnowledgeAwareness = high | Attitudes = negative & Interactions = negative) = 0.5 **

- P (TaskKnowledgeAwareness = low |Attitudes = negative & Interactions = negative) = 1-0.5 = 0.5

We could ask experts for a threshold value or could offer experts several possibilities and let them decide. Because the expert has not provided any information about what to do when there is evidence of *attitudes* = negative and *interactions* = negative, no value has been added to the base value (0.5 **), Which in most cases can be hypothetical, especially in virtual communities, in that interaction is prerequisite for a community. However, one expects to get a high conditional probability value of *task knowledge awareness* = negative when *attitudes* = negative and *interactions* = negative, a possible alternative would be to use p (*task knowledge awareness* = positive | *attitudes* = negative & *interactions* = negative) = 0.02 And p (*task knowledge awareness* = negative | *attitudes* = negative & *interactions* = negative) = 0.98 Assuming that a positive strong relationship also occurs when *attitudes* = negative and *interactions* = negative. Table 4 shows this conditional probability table.

Table 4. Alternative CPT for two parents with positive strong relationships

| | Attitudes | positive | | negative | |
	Interactions	positive	negative	positive	negative
TaskKnowledge Awareness	High	0.98	0.74	0.74	0.02
	Low	0.02	0.26	0.26	0.98

Querying the Model

The mechanism for drawing conclusions in BBNs is based on probability propagation of evidence. Propagation also refers to model updating based upon a known set of evidence. It is sometimes the case that a BBN contains many variables, each of which can be relevant for some kind of reasoning, but rarely are all variables relevant for all kinds of reasoning at once. Therefore, researchers need to identify the subset of the model, that is, relevant to their needs. Such a decision can be made based on some qualitative inferences from real world data or experts' intuitive experience using scenarios to query relevant part of the network (Daniel, Zapata-Rivera, & McCalla, 2005; Zapata-Rivera, 2002).

Querying a BBN refers to the process of updating the conditional probability table and making inferences based on new evidence. One way of updating a BBN is to develop a detailed number of scenarios that can be used to query the model. A scenario refers to a written synopsis of inferences drawn from observed phenomenon or empirical data. Druzdzel and Henrion (1993) described a scenario as an assignment of values to those variables in Bayesian network which are relevant for a certain conclusion, ordered in such a way that they form a coherent story, a causal story which is compatible with the evidence of the story.

The use of scenarios in Bayesian network is drawn from psychological research (Pennington & Hastie, 1988). This research shows that humans tend to interpret and explain any social situation by weighing up the most credible stories that include hypotheses to test and understand social phenomena. Furthermore, updating a BBN using scenarios is an attempt to understand various relationships among variables in a network. Druzdzel and Suemondt (1994) suggested that one way of querying a network is to instantiate variables to their observed values. They noted that observed evidence could be causally sufficient to imply the values of other yet unobserved variables (for instance, if a patient is male, it implies he is not pregnant).

Case Scenarios and Model Updating

In this section, a number of scenarios are described based on an expert's opinion and knowledge of the operations of virtual communities. The case scenarios described in the previous sections were taken from real communities, in which one of the authors was a participant observer for a period of 2 years. However, the description of the communities is not based on formal experimental study, but rather the scenarios are shown to illustrate the process of updating an initial Bayesian model using any kinds of evidence. It is likely that the results of the model predictions could change in the face of empirical evidence. Though the scenarios presented are not empirically documented, we believe that the scenarios themselves demonstrate real social phenomena in virtual communities.

Case 1

Community A was a formal virtual learning community of graduate students learning fundamental concepts and philosophies of e-learning. The members of this community were drawn from diverse cultural backgrounds and different professional training. In particular, participants were practising teachers teaching in different domains at secondary and primary schools levels. Some individuals in the community had extensive experiences with educational technologies, while others were novices but had extensive experience in classroom pedagogy. These individuals were not exposed to each other beforehand, and thus were not aware of each other's talents and experiences.

Because the community was a formal one, there was a formalised discourse structure and the social protocols for interactions were explained to participants in advance. The special protocols required different forms of interactions, including posting messages, critiquing others, providing feedback to others postings, asking for clarifications, and so forth. As the interactions progressed in this community, intense disagreements were observed. Individuals began to disagree more on the issues under discussion and there was little shared understanding among the participants in most of the discourse.

Case 2

Community B was a distributed community of practice for software engineers who gathered to discuss issues of software development. The main goals of the community were to facilitate exchange of information, and knowledge and peer-support to the members of the community. Members of this community shared common concerns and were drawn from all over the world. In terms of skills, participants composed of highly experienced software developers and novices. Participants were drawn from all over the world and were affiliated to different organisations, including researchers at universities and software support groups.

After a considerable period of interaction, individuals were exposed to each other long enough to start exchanging personal information among each other. It was also observed that individuals offered a lot of help to each other throughout their interactions. Though no formal social protocols were explained to the participants, members interacted as if there were social protocols guiding their interactions. Further, there were no visible roles of community leaders.

Case 3

Community C consisted of a group of individuals learning fundamentals of programming in Java. It was an open community whose members were geographically distributed and had diverse demographic backgrounds and professional cultures. They did not personally know each other, and they used different aliases from time to time while interacting in the community. Diverse programming experiences, skills, and knowledge were also observed among the participants. It was interesting to observe that though these individuals did not know each other in advance, they were willing to offer help and support to each other learning Java. Though there were no formal social protocols of interaction, individuals interacted as if there were clear set social protocols to be followed in the community.

Procedures for Updating the Model

In order to test and update the initial Bayesian model of SC, each case scenario was analysed looking for various evidences regarding the impact of individual variables in the model. Once a piece of evidence was added to the model, typically through tweaking a state of a variable (i.e., observing a particular state of a variable) or through a process commonly known as variable initialisation, the model is updated and results are propagated to the rest of variables in the Bayesian model. This process generates a set of new marginal probabilities for the variables in the model. In the three case scenarios, the goal was to observe changes in probability values for trust and social capital.

The model prediction outcomes were based on the nature of the cases described in the chapter. It is important to note that the cases themselves represent general characteristics of virtual communities, and is not directly based on empirical evidence. However, this is a step to come up with more cases to train the model and run some empirical experiments to validate the model. This phase of a model development further helps experts to examine the model and refine it based on their knowledge of the domain. The Bayesian model therefore serves as an interactive tool that enables experts to create a probabilistic model, simulate scenarios, and reflect on the results of the predictions.

Community A

Community A is a virtual learning community (Community Type = *VLC.*) Based on the case description, shared understanding is set to *low* and professional knowledge awareness is set to *doesnotexist*. Individuals in this community are familiar with their geographical diversity, and so demographic cultural awareness is set to *exists*. There is a well-established formal set of social protocols set previously by the instructor (social protocols = *known.*). Figure 5 shows the Bayesian model after the evidence from community A has been added (shaded nodes) and the results of the posterior probabilities.

*Figure 5. A Bayesian model of SC when evidence from **community A** has been added and propagated through the model*

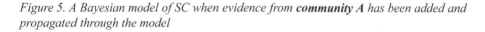

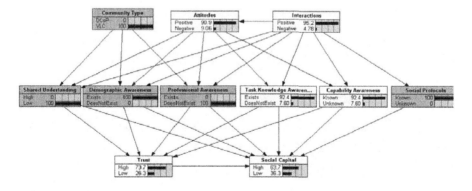

The results of the predictions show the highest level of trust (P (Trust=*high*) =0.565) and a corresponding probability level of SC (P (SC=*high*)=0.491). These values are relatively low. Several explanations can be provided for the drop in the levels of SC and trust. There was a negative interaction in the community and lack of shared understanding in the community. The lack of shared understanding had possibly affected the level of trust and subsequently social capital. It is also possible that negative interactions and attitudes have further affected the levels of task knowledge awareness and individual capability awareness. It could also be inferred that experiences of more knowledgeable individuals in the community were more likely to have been ignored, making individuals less cooperative.

Community B

Variables observed in this case include community type which has been set to community of practice (DCoP). Professional awareness culture was set to *exists*, because after interaction, it was observed that individuals in that community became aware of their individuals talents and skills. Individual's capability awareness and task awareness were set to *exists* as well. Individuals in this community shared common concerns and frame of reference, and so shared understanding was set to *high*. Figure 6 shows the Bayesian model after the evidence from community B has been added (shaded nodes) and propagated through the model.

Propagating this set of evidence, high levels of trust and SC (P (Trust = *high*) = 0.88 and P (SC = *high*) = 0.542) were observed. Given the evidence, it was also observed that interactions and attitudes in the model were positive, which have positively influenced demographic cultural awareness and social protocols. Further, the presence of shared understanding and the high degrees of different kinds of awareness and knowledge of social protocols in this community have resulted into high levels of trust and SC.

In spite of the evidence, demographic cultural awareness has little influence on the level of trust in this kind of a community and subsequently, it has not significantly affected SC. This can be explained by the fact that professionals in most cases are likely to cherish their professional identity more than their demographic backgrounds. This is in line with a previous

Figure 6. A Bayesian model of SC when evidence from community B has been added and propagated through the model

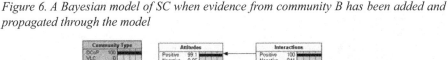
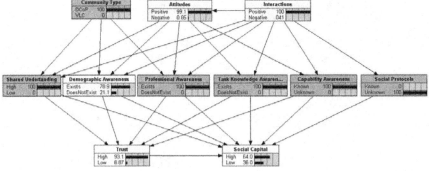

study, which suggested most people in distributed communities of practice mainly build and maintain social relations based on common concerns other than geographical distribution (Daniel, O'Brien, & Sarkar, 2003).

Community C

Variables extracted from this case scenario include community type (*VLC*), shared understanding, and professional cultural awareness, and thus demographic cultural awareness, individual's capability awareness and task awareness were set to *exists*. Figure 7 shows the Bayesian model after the evidence from community C has been added (shaded nodes) and propagated through the model.

In community C, high levels of trust and SC (P (Trust = high) = 0.920 and P (SC = high) = 0.766) were observed after the propagation of the evidence. These high levels of trust and SC can be attributed to the fact that the community was based on an explicit and focused domain and members, though they might have concealed their identities, were willing to positively interact and participate in order to learn the domain. Further increase in the levels of trust and social capital can also be attributed to the presence of shared understanding. In other words, people in that community got along well and understood each other well enough. They used the same frame of reference and had almost common goals of learning a domain (Java programming language).

Model Validation and Sensitivity Analysis (SA)

Further, approximating probabilities elicited from experts and experts' judgments can be prone to errors, and sometimes due to uncertainty of the properties of an event, their accuracy is not guaranteed. For example, if one is asked to toss a coin and estimate the probability that the coin can either land head or tails suggests the probability value to be 0.5, which only assumes that the coin is a fair, but in a situation where one has never seen the coin

Figure 7. A Bayesian model of SC when evidence from community C has been added and propagated through the model

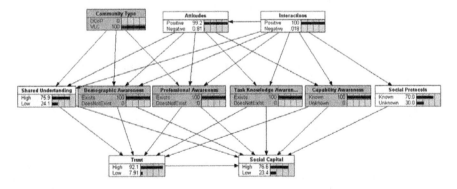

and is uncertain whether it is fair or not, then a degree of belief can be used as an initial knowledge. In other words, initial assumptions are made that the coin is fair, and sometimes such assumptions can be biased.

Sensitivity analysis is primarily used to validate the quantitative part of a Bayesian model. There are two approaches to sensitivity analysis. One approach tests how sensitive the network model is to changes in overall findings, and the other approach aims to find changes in each variable in the model. In the former case, the influence of each of the nodes in the network on a query node can be measured, using a measure such as entropy, and ranked. The results of a sensitivity analysis can be used for initializing the portions of the model for later iterations in the development cycle (Haddaway, 1999). In the latter case, the goal is to determine whether more precision in estimating variables is required and whether it can be useful in later iteration of model development cycle. Sensitivity analysis is a mathematical technique for investigating the effects of inaccuracies in the parameters of a mathematical model. It aims to study how variation in output of a model (numerical or otherwise) can be apportioned, qualitatively or quantitatively, to different sources of data (Morgan & Henrion, 1990). In general, SA is conducted by:

- Defining the model with all its input and output variables
- Assigning probability density functions to each input parameter
- Generating an input matrix through an appropriate random sampling method and evaluating the output
- Assessing the influences or relative importance of each input parameters on the output variable

Sensitivity analysis is relevant to modeling SC model because the states of the input variables are numerous and their individual influence on the model is not precisely known. Sensitive analysis will also help here to further refine the model and conduct further studies to validate the model (Chan & Darwiche, 2004). In order to identify which variables had dominating effects on the query variables, automated analysis (support for this type of analysis was provided in the Netica software package; https://www.norsys.com) on sensitivity of each variable to the target variable in model was conducted.

One-way sensitivity analysis was performed to determine the relative sensitivity of each of the individual variables to social capital and to understand the spread of the distribution of the variables in the model. The results of the sensitivity analysis (see Appendix 1) show that those variables with weak level of influence to social capital show low mutual information values. Trust, capability awareness, and tasks awareness were relatively sensitive to social capital compared to professional awareness, demographic awareness, social protocols, and shared understanding.

In general terms, results indicated that social is not sensitive to only one variable, but rather it is sensitive to a number of variables and even more so to variables that are in strong paths (strong positive paths in the model; see Figure 7). The results of the sensitivity analysis revealed at least three relatively high levels of entropy reduction for three variables, interactions, and attitudes with the same entropy reduction of 0.1533, capability awareness with entropy reduction of 0.1494, shared understanding at 0.1112, and trust at 0.1175. Higher values of entropy reduction correspond to variables in strong paths, and it generally suggests that the qualitative reasoning used for deriving the initial probabilities presented in the social capital model is reasonable. Although results of the sensitivity analysis seem to suggest that different variables can affect social capital at different levels, at this point, further studies are required to determine the effects of individual variables on social capital.

Nonetheless, the results of the sensitivity analysis can be used to improve the model by changing the threshold initial probability values presented earlier in the chapter. Further, drawing from the results, one could speculate that the individual variations in values could be caused by partial knowledge of domain experts used for building the network and early assumptions made during the development of the model, both of which are common problems inherent in the development of any Bayesian model.

Another possible way of rectifying inconsistence in a Bayesian model is to conduct model validation. Model validation in essence is post sensitivity analysis, which is performed by identifying sensitive set of variables given evidence, altering the parameters of a query variable and observing the related changes in the posterior probabilities of the target variable. This is done through help of evidence coming from empirical data (see last phase of figure 2, building Bayesian networks). However, in a situation, where there are N-scenarios, a straightforward analysis can be extremely time consuming and difficult to maintain, especially on larger networks. Coupe and Van der Gaag (1998) addressed this difficulty by identifying a sensitivity set of a variable given evidence.

Discussion and Conclusion

Bayesian network is a tool that helps model a situation involving uncertainty. In the social sciences and indeed in many other fields, uncertainty may arise due to a variety of causes. For instance, it can be the result of gaps in knowledge, complexity, and imprecision of domain knowledge, ignorance, or volatility of a knowledge domain. And so, by representing knowledge in graphical form, researchers can effectively communicate results.

A Bayesian model encodes domain knowledge, showing relationships, interdependencies, and independence among variables. The qualitative part of the model is represented by links showing direction of influence or independence among variables. The information describing the details of the quantitative relationships among the variables is often stored in conditional probability tables (CPT). This enables the model to use probability theory, especially Bayesian statistics to calculate conditional dependencies among the variables in the network, and resolve the uncertainties with probability inferences.

Though BBN techniques are elegant ways of capturing uncertainties, the knowledge engineering effort required to create conditional probability values per each given variable in a network has prevented many researchers from using them in many domains. In addition, current algorithms that can be used to learn initial and conditional probabilities from data are often complex and cumbersome to employ and data is not always available. Even though initial probabilities can be elicited from experts, it sometimes raises the problems of accuracy in values.

In addition, translating experts' qualitative knowledge into numerical probabilistic values is a daunting and often complex task. Because Bayesian network modeling involves establishing cause and effects among variables, it is sometimes difficult to determine causal relationships or to adequately describe all the causes and effects. In such cases, Bayesian networks can be described using probabilities describing what we know or believe is happening in a particular domain.

This chapter has extended the use of BBN techniques to complex domains, and illustrating with an example of social capital construct, it has shown different phases in which a similar model can be built. The approach described in the chapter combined both qualitative and quantitative techniques to elicit knowledge from experts without worrying about computing initial probabilities for training a model. In a later study of one of the virtual communities (**VLC A**) presented earlier in the case scenarios, we have administered a survey to nine members of the community to find out primarily their sense[1] of a community online. Overall results revealed the presences and perceived importance of many instances of social capital in promoting a sense of a community online, and in enhancing information exchange and knowledge sharing. Among the variables reported were different forms of awareness, trust, shared understanding, common goals, and shared values. We intend to use the results of this study to refine the initial conditional probabilities of the variables in the social capital model.

Acknowledgment

We acknowledge support from the Natural Sciences and Engineering Research Council of Canada (NSERC), as well as the Social Sciences and Humanities Research Council of Canada (SSHRC) toward Ben's research. We would also like to thank Educational Testing Service researchers, David Williamson and Russell Almond for reviewing this chapter and providing very constructive feedback.

References

Baker, M. (2000). The roles of models in artificial intelligence and education research: A prospective view. *International Journal of Artificial Intelligence in Education*, (11), 122-143. Retrieved February 21, 2007, from http://icar.univ-lyon2.fr/gric5/home/mbaker/webpublications/BakerIJAIED2000.PDF

Chan, H., & Darwiche, A. (2004). Sensitivity analysis in Bayesian Networks: From single to multiple parameters. In *Proceedings of the 20th Conference on Uncertainty in Artificial Intelligence (UAI)* (pp. 67-75).

Cohen, D., & Prusak, L. (2001). *In good company: How social capital makes organizations work*. MA: Harvard Business School Press.

Cooper, G.F., & Herskovits, E. (1992). A Bayesian method for the induction of probabilistic networks from data. *Machine Learning, 9*(4), 309-347.

Conati, C., Gertner, A., & VanLehn, K. (2002). Using bayesian networks to manage uncertainty in student modeling. *User Modeling and User-Adapted Interaction, 12*(4), 371-417.

Coupé, V.M.H., & Van der Gaag, L.C. (1998). Practicable sensitivity analysis of Bayesian belief networks. In M. Huskova, P. Lachout, & J.A. Visek (Eds.), In *Proceedings of the Joint Session of the 6th Praque Symposium of Asymptotic Statistics and the 13th Praque Conference on Information Theory, Statistical Decision Functions and Random Processes* (pp. 81-86). Praque: Union of Czech Mathematicians and Physicists.

Daniel, B.K., McCalla, G., & Schwier, R. (2003). Social capital in virtual learning communities and distributed communities of practice. *The Canadian Journal of Learning Technology, 29*(3), 113-139.

Daniel, B.K., McCalla, G.I., & Schwier, R.A. (2005, July 18-22). Data mining and modeling social capital in virtual learning communities. In *Proceedings of the 12th International Conference on Artificial Intelligence in Education* (pp. 2000-2008). Amsterdam.

Daniel, B.K., O'Brien, D., & Sarkar, A. (2003). A design approach for Canadian distributed community of practice on governance and international development: A preliminary report. In R.M. Verburg & J.A. De Ridder (Eds.), *Knowledge sharing under distributed circumstances* (pp. 19-24). Enschede: Ipskamps.

Daniel, B.K., Zapata-Rivera, D.J., & McCalla, G.I. (2003). A Bayesian computational model of social capital in virtual communities. In M. Huysman, E. Wenger, & V. Wulf (Eds.), *Communities and technologies* (pp. 287-305). London: Kluwer.

Daniel, B.K., Zapata-Rivera, J.D, & McCalla, G.I. (2005, November 16-18). Computational framework for constructing Bayesian belief network models from incomplete, inconsistent and imprecise data in E-Learning (Poster). In *Proceedings of the Second LORNET International Annual Conference, I2LOR-2005*, Vancouver, Canada.

Druzdzel, M. (1996). Qualitative verbal explanations in Bayesian belief networks. *Artificial Intelligence and Simulation of Behaviour Quarterly, 9*(4), 43-54.

Druzdzel, M.J., & Gaag, L.C. (2000). Building probabilistic networks: Where do the numbers come from?. Guest editor's introduction. *Data Engineering, 12*(4), 481-486.

Druzdzel, M.J., & Henri, J.S. (1994). Relevance in probabilistic models: "Backyards" in a "small world." In *Working Notes of the AAAI-1994 Fall Symposium Series* (pp. 60-63). New Orleans, LA.

Druzdzel, M.J., & Henrion, M. (1993). Efficient reasoning in qualitative probabilistic networks. *AAAI*, 548-553.

Finn, J. (1996). *An introduction to Bayesian networks.* London: University College Press.

Finn, J., & Liang, J. (1994). drHugin: A system for value of information in Bayesian networks. In *Proceedings of the Fifth International Conference on Information Processing and Management of Uncertainty in Knowledge-Based Systems (IPMU)* (pp. 178-183). Paris.

Gutwin, C., & Greenberg, S. (1998). Design for individuals, design for groups: Tradeoffs between power and workspace awareness. In *Proceedings of the ACM Conference on Computer Supported Cooperative Work* (pp. 207-216). ACM Press.

Haddaway, P. (1999, Spring). An overview of some recent developments in Bayesian problem solving techniques. *AI Magazine*. Retrieved February 21, 2007, from http://citeseer. ist.psu.edu/haddaway99overview.html

Heckerman, D. (1996). *A tutorial on learning with Bayesian networks.* Retrieved December 16, 2006, from ftp://ftp.research.microsoft.com/pub/tr/tr-95-06.pdf

Heckerman, D., & Horwitz, E. (1998). Inferring informational goals from free-text queries: A bayesian approach. In *Proceedings of the 14th Conference on Uncertainty in AI* (pp. 230-238).

Korb, K.B., & Nicholson, A.E. (2004). *Bayesian artificial intelligence.* Boca Raton, FL: Chapman & Hall/CRC.

Lacave, C., & Diez, F.J. (2002). Explanation for causal Bayesian networks in Elvira. In *Proceedings of the Workshop on Intelligent Data Analysis in Medicine and Pharmacology (IDAMAP-2002),* Lyon, France.

Lee, A., Danis, C. Miller, T. & Jung, Y. (2001). Fostering social interaction in online spaces. In M. Hirose (Ed.), *Proceedings of the Eighth IFIP TC.13 Conference on Human-Computer Interaction* (INTERACT'01) (pp. 59-66). Amsterdam: IOS Press.

McCalla, G. (2000). The fragmentation of culture, learning, teaching and technology: Implications for artificial intelligence in education research. *International Journal of Artificial Intelligence, 11*(2), 177-196.

McMillan, D.W., & Chavis, D.M. (1986). Sense of community: A definition and theory. *American Journal of Community Psychology, 14*(1), 6-23.

Morgan, M. G., & Henrion, M. (1990). *Uncertainty—a guide to dealing with uncertainty in quantitative risk and policy analysis.* Cambridge: Cambridge University Press.

Neapolitan, R.E. (2004). *Learning Bayesian networks.* London: Prentice Hall.

Niedermayer, D. (1998). *An introduction to Bayesian networks and their contemporary applications.* Retrieved December 16, 2006, from http://www.niedermayer.ca/papers/bayesian/

Pearl, J. (1988). *Probabilistic reasoning in intelligent systems: Networks of plausible inference.* San Mateo, CA: Morgan Kaufmann.

Pearl, J. and T. S. Verma (1991). A theory of inferred causation. In J. A. Allen, R. Fikes, and E. Sandewall (Eds.), *(pp. 441–452). Principles of Knowledge Representation and Reasoning: Proceedings of Second International Conference on Knowledge Representation(KR '91).* San Francisco, CA: Morgan Kaufmann.

Pennington, N., & Hastie, R. (1988). Explanation-based decision-making: Effects of memory structure on judgment. *Journal of Experimental Psychology: Learning, Memory and Cognition, 14*(3), 521-533.

Pradhan, M., Provan, G., Middleton, B., & Henrion, M. (1994). Knowledge engineering for large belief networks. In *Proceedings of the Tenth Conference on Uncertainty in Artificial Intelligence* (pp. 484-490).

Putnam R. (2000). *Bowling alone: The collapse and revival of American community*. New York: Simon Schuster.

Renooij, S., & Witteman, C. (1999). Talking probabilities: Communicating probabilistic information with words and numbers. *International Journal of Approximate Reasoning,* (2), 169-194. Retrieved February 21, 2007, from http://citeseer.ist.psu.edu/renooij99talking.html

Resnick, P. (2002). Beyond bowling together: Sociotechnical capital. In J.M. Carroll (Ed.), *HCI in the new millennium* (pp. 247-272). New York: Addison-Wesley.

Reye, J. (2004). Student modeling based on belief networks. *International Journal of Artificial Intelligence in Education, 14*, 63-96.

Russell, S., & Norvig, P. (1995). *Solution manual for artificial intelligence: A modern approach*. Englewood Cliffs, NJ: Prentice Hall.

Schwier, R.A., & Daniel, B.K. (2007). Did we become a community? Multiple methods for identifying community and its constituent elements in formal online learning environments. In N. Lambropoulos & P. Zaphiris (Eds.), *User-evaluation and online communities*. Hershey, PA: Idea Group.

Van der Gaag, L.C., Renooij, S., Witteman, C., Aleman, B.M.P., & Taal, B.G. (1999). How to elicit many probabilities. In *Proceedings of Uncertainty in Artificial Intelligence, UI99* (pp. 647-654).

VanLehn, K., Niu, Z., Siler, S., & Gertner, A.S. (1998). Student modeling from conversational test data: A bayesian approach without priors. In *ITS'98: Proceedings of the 4th International Conference on Intelligent Tutoring Systems* (pp. 434-443).

Vomlel, J. (2004). Bayesian networks in educational testing. *International Journal of Uncertainty, Fuzziness and Knowledge Based Systems, 12* (Supplementary Issue 1), 83-100.

Wellman, M.P. (1990). Fundamental concepts of qualitative probabilistic networks. *Artificial Intelligence, 44*, 257-303.

World Bank, The (1999). *Social capital research group*. Retrieved December 16, 2006, from http://www.worldbank.org/poverty/scapital/

Zapata-Rivera, J.D. (2002). cbCPT: Knowledge engineering support for CPTs in Bayesian networks. In *Proceedings of the Canadian Conference on AI* (pp. 368-370).

Zapata-Rivera, J.D. (2003). *Learning environments based on inspectable student models*. Doctoral thesis, University of Saskatchewan, Department of Computer Science.

Zapata-Rivera, J.D., & Greer, J. (2004). Interacting with Bayesian student models. *International Journal of Artificial Intelligence in Education, 142*, 127-163.

Endnote

[1]   McMillan and Chavis (1986) defined a sense of a community as a feeling that members have of belonging, a feeling that members matter to one another and to the group, and a shared understanding among the members and that their needs will be met through their commitment to be together.

Appendix: Results of the Sensitivity Analysis

Probability of new finding = 100 %, of all findings = 100 %.

Sensitivity of '*SocialCapital*' to findings at '*SocialCapital*':

Probability ranges: *Change*	Min.	Current	Max.	RMS.
High	0	0.5423	1	0.4982
Low	0	0.4577	1	0.4982

Note: Entropy reduction = 0.9948 (100 %)
    Belief Variance = 0.2482 (100 %)

Sensitivity of 'SocialCapital' to findings at 'Interactions':

Probability ranges: *Change*	Min.	Current	Max.	RMS.
High	0.3168	0.5423	0.7677	0.2255
Low	0.2323	0.4577	0.6832	0.2255

Note: Entropy reduction = 0.1534 (15.4 %)
    Belief Variance = 0.05083 (20.5 %)

Sensitivity of 'SocialCapital' to findings at 'Attitudes':

Probability ranges: *Change*	Min.	Current	Max.	RMS.
High	0.3169	0.5423	0.7676	0.2254
Low	0.2324	0.4577	0.6831	0.2254

Note: Entropy reduction = 0.1533 (15.4 %)
    Belief Variance = 0.05079 (20.5 %)

Sensitivity of 'SocialCapital' to findings at 'TaskKnowledgeAwareness':

Probability ranges: Change	Min.	Current	Max.	RMS.
High	0.3162	0.5423	0.764	0.2239
Low	0.236	0.4577	0.6838	0.2239

Note: Entropy reduction = 0.1511 (15.2 %)
Belief Variance = 0.05012 (20.2 %)

Sensitivity of 'SocialCapital' to findings at 'IndCapabAwareness':

Probability ranges: Change	Min.	Current	Max.	RMS.
High	0.3174	0.5423	0.7628	0.2227
Low	0.2372	0.4577	0.6826	0.2227

Note: Entropy reduction = 0.1494 (15 %)
Belief Variance = 0.04959 (20 %)

Sensitivity of 'SocialCapital' to findings at 'Trust':

Probability ranges: Change	Min.	Current	Max.	RMS.
High	0.3148	0.5423	0.7158	0.1987
Low	0.2842	0.4577	0.6852	0.1987

Note: Entropy reduction = 0.1175 (11.8 %)
Belief Variance = 0.03948 (15.9 %)

Sensitivity of 'SocialCapital' to findings at 'SharedUndertanding':

Probability ranges: Change	Min.	Current	Max.	RMS.
High	0.315	0.5423	0.7069	0.1934
Low	0.2931	0.4577	0.685	0.1934

Note: Entropy reduction = 0.1112 (11.2 %)
Belief Variance   = 0.03742 (15.1 %)

Sensitivity of 'SocialCapital' to findings at 'ProfCultAwareness':

Probability ranges: Change	Min.	Current	Max.	RMS.
High	0.3279	0.5423	0.7076	0.1883
Low	0.2924	0.4577	0.6721	0.1883

Note: Entropy reduction = 0.1052 (10.6 %)
   Belief Variance = 0.03544 (14.3 %)

Sensitivity of 'SocialCapital' to findings at 'DemogCultAwareness':

Probability ranges: Change	Min.	Current	Max.	RMS.
High	0.4328	0.5423	0.6647	0.1157
Low	0.3353	0.4577	0.5672	0.1157

Note: Entropy reduction = 0.03937 (3.96 %)
   Belief Variance = 0.0134 (5.4 %)

Sensitivity of 'SocialCapital' to findings at 'Social Protocols':

Probability ranges: Change	Min.	Current	Max.	RMS.
High	0.4487	0.5423	0.6359	0.0936
Low	0.3641	0.4577	0.5513	0.0936

Note: Entropy reduction = 0.02562 (2.58 %)
   Belief Variance = 0.008761 (3.53 %)

Sensitivity of 'SocialCapital' to findings at 'CommType':

Probability ranges: Change	Min.	Current	Max.	RMS.
High	0.4873	0.5423	0.5972	0.05493
Low	0.4028	0.4577	0.5127	0.05493

Note: Entropy reduction = 0.008786 (0.883 %)
   Belief Variance = 0.003017 (1.22 %)

Chapter III

Data Mining of Bayesian Network Structure Using a Semantic Genetic Algorithm-Based Approach

Sachin Shetty, Old Dominion University, USA

Min Song, Old Dominion University, USA

Mansoor Alam, University of Toledo, USA

Abstract

A Bayesian network model is a popular formalism for data mining due to its intuitive interpretation. This chapter presents a semantic genetic algorithm (SGA) to learn the best Bayesian network structure from a database. SGA builds on recent advances in the field and focuses on the generation of initial population, crossover, and mutation operators. In SGA, we introduce semantic crossover and mutation operators to aid in obtaining accurate solutions. The crossover and mutation operators incorporate the semantic of Bayesian network structures to learn the structure with very minimal errors. SGA has been proven to discover Bayesian networks with greater accuracy than existing classical genetic algorithms. We present empirical results to prove the accuracy of SGA in predicting the Bayesian network structures.

Introduction

One of the most important steps in data mining is building a descriptive model of the database being mined. To do so, probability-based approaches have been considered an effective tool because of the uncertain nature of descriptive models. Unfortunately, high computational requirements and the lack of proper representation have hindered the building of probabilistic models. To alleviate the above twin problems, probabilistic graphical models have been proposed. In the past decade, many variants of probabilistic graphical models have been developed, with the simplest variant being Bayesian networks (BN) (Pearl, 1988). BN is a popular descriptive modeling technique for available data by giving an easily understandable way to see relationships between attributes of a set of records. It has been employed to reason under uncertainty, with wide varying applications in the field of medicine, finance, and military planning (Pearl, 1988; Jensen, 1996). Computationally, BN provides an efficient way to represent relationships between attributes and allow reasonably fast inference of probabilities. Learning BN from raw data can be viewed as an optimization problem where a BN has to be found that best represents the probability distribution that has generated the data in a given database (Heckerman, Geiger, & Chickering, 1995). This has lately been the subject of considerable research because the traditional designer of a BN may not be able to see all of the relationships between the attributes. In this chapter, we focus on the structure learning of a BN from a complete database. The database stores the statistical values of the variables as well as the conditional dependence relationship among the variables. We employ a genetic algorithm technique to learn the structure of BN.

A typical genetic algorithm works with populations of individuals, each of which needs to be coded using a *representative function* and be evaluated using a *fitness function* to measure the adaptiveness of each individual. These two functions are the basic building blocks of a genetic algorithm. To actually perform the algorithm, three genetic operators are used to explore the set of solutions: *reproduction*, *mutation*, and *crossover*. The reproduction operator promotes the best individual structures to the next generation. That is, the individual with the highest fitness in a population will reproduce with a highest probability than the one with the lowest fitness. The mutation operator toggles a position in the symbolic representation of the potential solutions. Mutation avoids local optima by exploring new solutions by introducing a variation in the population. The crossover operator exchanges genetic material to generate new individuals by selecting a point where pieces of parents are swapped. The main parameters, which influence the genetic algorithm search process, are initial population, population size, mutation, and crossover operators.

In this chapter we first introduce the related work in BN structure learning and present the details of our approach for structure learning in a BN structure using a modified genetic algorithm. Then we experiment with two different genetic algorithms. The first one is the genetic algorithm with classical genetic operatiors. In the second algorithm, we extend the standard mutation and crossover operators to incorporate the semantic of the BN structures. Finally, we conclude the chapter and proposes some thoughts for futher resarch.

Related Work

Larranaga, Kuijpers, Murga, and Yurramendi (1996) proposed a genetic algorithm based on the score-based greedy algorithm. In their algorithm, a directed acyclic graph (DAG) is represented by a connectivity matrix that is stored as a string. The recombination is implemented as one-point crossover on these strings, while mutation is implemented as random bit flipping. In a related work, Larranaga, Poza, Yurramendi, Murga, and Kuijpers (1996) employed a wrapper approach by implementing a genetic algorithm that searches for an ordering that is passed on to K2 (Cooper & Herskovits, 1992), a score-based greedy learning algorithm. The results of the wrapper approach were comparable to those of their previous genetic algorithms. Different crossover operators have been implemented in a genetic algorithm to increase the adaptiveness of the learning problem, with good results (Cotta & Muruzabal, 2002). Lam and Bacchus (1994) proposed a hybrid evolutionary programming (HEP) algorithm that combines the use of independence tests with a quality-based search. In the HEP algorithm, the search space of DAG is constrained in the sense that each possible DAG only connects two nodes if they show a strong dependence in the available data. The HEP algorithm evolves a population of DAG to find a solution that minimizes the minimal description length (MDL) score. A common feature of the aforementioned algorithms is that the mutation and crossover operators were classical in nature. These operators do not help the evolution process reach the best solution.

Wong, Lam, and Leung (1999) developed an approach based on MDL score and evolutionary programming. They have integrated a knowledge-guided genetic operator for optimization in the search process. However, the fitness function is not taken into account to guide the search process. Myers and Levitt (1999) have proposed an adaptive mutation operator for learning structure of BN from incomplete data. It is a generalized approach to influence the current recombination process based on previous population. It does not take into account the fitness of a population either. Blanco, Inza, and Larranaga (2003) have adopted the estimation of distribution algorithms method for learning BN without the use of crossover and mutation operators. This is not in accordance with the classical genetic algorithm due to the lack of recombination operators. Recently, Dijk et al. (2003) built another generalized genetic algorithm to improve the search process without taking into account the specific characteristics of the population. As we see, most of the genetic algorithm-based approaches mentioned above adopt a generalized approach to improve the search process. The mutation and crossover operators proposed in this chapter are semantically oriented and thus they aid in a better convergence to the solution. Hence, our BN structure learning algorithm differs from the above algorithms in the design of mutation and crossover operators.

Semantic Genetic Algorithm-Based Approach

Structure Learning of Bayesian Networks

Formally, a BN consists of a set of nodes that represent variables, and a set of directed edges between the nodes. Each node is featured by a finite set of mutually exclusive states. The directed edges between nodes represent the dependence between the linked variables. The strengths of the relationships between the variables are expressed as conditional probability tables (CPT). Thus, a BN efficiently encodes the joint probability distribution of its variables. For n-dimensional random variable $(X_1, \ldots, X_n)$, the joint probability distribution is determined as follows:

$$P(x_i, \ldots, x_n) = \prod_{i=1}^{n} P(x_i \mid pa(x_i)) \tag{1}$$

where x_i represents the value of the random variable X_i and $pa(x_i)$ represents the value of the parents of X_i. Thus, the structure learning problem of a BN is equivalent to the problem of searching the optimum in the space of all DAG. During the search process, a trade-off between the structural network complexity and the network accuracy has to be made. The trade-off is necessary as complex networks suffer from over fitting, making the run time of inference very long. A popular measure to balance complexity and accuracy is based on the principle of MDL from information theory (Lam & Bacchus, 1994). In this chapter, the BN structure learning problem is solved by searching for a DAG that minimizes the MDL score.

Representative Function and Fitness Function

The first task in a genetic algorithm is the representation of initial population. To represent a BN as a genetic algorithm individual, an edge matrix or adjacency matrix is needed. The set of network structures for a specific database characterized by n variables can be represented by an $n \times n$ connectivity matrix C. Each bit represents the edge between two nodes where

$$C_{ij} = \begin{cases} 1, & \text{if } j \text{ is a parent of } i \\ 0, & \text{otherwise} \end{cases}$$. The two-dimensional array of bits can be represented as an

individual of the population by the following string $C_{11} C_{12} \ldots C_{1n} C_{21} C_{22} \ldots C_{2n} \ldots C_{n1} C_{n2} \ldots C_{nn}$, where the first n bits represent the edges to the first node of the network, and so on. It can be easily found that C_{kk} are the irrelevant bits which represent an edge from node k to itself, which can be ignored by the search process.

With the representative function decided, we need to devise the generation of the initial population. There are several approaches to generate initial population. We implemented the Box-Muller random number generator to select how many parents would be chosen for each individual node. The parameters for the Box-Muller algorithm are the desired average and standard deviation. Based on these two input parameters, the algorithm generates a number that fits the distribution. For our implementation, the average corresponds to the average number of parents for each node in the resultant BN. After considerable experimentation with databases whose Bayesian structure is similar to the ASIA network (Lauritzen & Spiegelhalter, 1988), we found that the best average was 1.0 with a standard deviation of 0.5. Although this approach is simple, it creates numerous illegal DAG due to cyclic subnetworks. An algorithm to remove or fix these cyclic structures has to be designed. The basic operation of the algorithm is to remove a random edge of a cycle until cycles are not found in a DAG individual.

Now that the representative function and the population generation have been decided, we need to find a good fitness function. Most of the *state-of-the-art* implementations use the fitness function proposed in the algorithm K2 (Cooper & Herskovits, 1992). The K2 algorithm assumes an ordered list of variables as its input. It maximizes the following function by searching for every node from the ordered list of a set of parent nodes:

$$g(x_i, pa(x_i)) = \prod_{j=1}^{q_i} \frac{(r_i - 1)!}{(N_{ij} + r_i - 1)!} \prod_{k=1}^{r_i} N_{ijk}! \qquad (2)$$

where r_i represents the possible value assignments $(v_{i1}, \ldots, v_{ir_i})$ for the variable with index i, N_{ijk} representing the number of instances in a database in which a variable X_i has value v_{ik}, and q_i represents the number of unique instantiations of $pa(x_i)$.

Mutation and Crossover Operators

We introduce two new operators, semantic mutation (SM) and single point semantic crossover (SPSC), to the existing standard mutation and crossover operators. The SM operator is a heuristic operator that toggles the bit value of a position in the edge matrix to ensure that the fitness function $g(x_i, pa(x_i))$ is maximized. The SPSC operator is specific to our representation function. As the function is a two-dimensional edge matrix consisting of columns and rows, our new crossover operator operates on either columns or rows. Thus, the crossover operator generates two offspring by either manipulating columns or rows.

Box 1. Pseudo code for semantic crossover

Step 1. Initialization

> Read the input individual and populate a parent table for each node

Step 2. Generate new individual

> For each node in the individual do the following n times:

> 2.1   Execute the Box Mueller algorithm to find how many parents need to be altered.

> 2.2   Ensure that the nodes selected as parents do not form cycles. If cycles are formed repeat step 2.1.

> 2.3   Evaluate the network score of the resultant structure.

> 2.4   If current score is higher than previous score, then the chosen parents are the new parents of the selected node.

> Repeat steps 2.1 through 2.4.

Step 3. Return the final modified individual.

The SPSC crosses two parents by manipulating columns or parents and maximizing the function $g(x_i, pa(x_i))$, and b) manipulating rows or children and maximizing the function $\prod_i g(x_i, pa(x_i))$. By combining SM and SPSC, we implement our new genetic algorithm called semantic genetic algorithm (SGA). Following is the pseudo code for the semantic crossover operation. The algorithm expects an individual as input and returns the modified individual after applying semantic crossover operations.

Simulations

SGA Implementation

The SGA algorithm has been implemented and incorporated into the Bayesian network tools in Java (BNJ) (*http://bnj.sourceforge.net*). BNJ is an open-source suite of software tool for research and development using graphical models of probability. Specifically, SGA is implemented as a separate module using the BNJ API. To depict the Bayesian network, BNJ visually provides a visualization tool to create and edit Bayesian networks.

Simulation Methodology

Figure 1 shows the overall simulation setup to evaluate our genetic algorithm. Following are the main steps of the algorithm:

1. Determine a BN and simulate it using a probabilistic logic sampling technique (Henrion, 1988) to obtain a database *D*, which reflects the conditional relations between the variables;

Figure 1. Simulation setup for learning Bayesian network structure

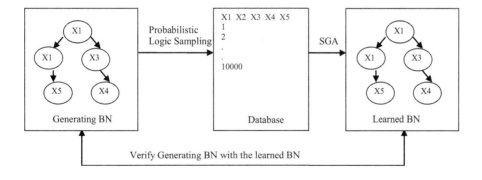

2. Apply our SGA approach to obtain the BN structure B_s, which maximizes the probability $P(D \mid B_s)$; and

3. Evaluate the fitness of the solutions.

Simulations and Analysis

The BN sizes used in our simulations are 8, 12, 18, 24, 30, and 36. The 8-node BN used in the simulations is from the ASIA networks (Lauritzen & Spiegelhalter, 1988) as shown in Figure 2. The ASIA network illustrates their method of propagation of evidence, and considers a small amount of fictitious qualitative medical knowledge. The remaining networks were created by adding extra nodes to the basic ASIA network.

There are several techniques for simulating BN. For our experiments we have adopted the probabilistic logic sampling technique. In this technique, the data generator generates random samples based on the ASIA network's joint probability distribution table. The data generator sorts nodes topologically and picks a value for each root node using the probability distribution, and then generates values for each child node according to its parent's values in the joint probability table. The root mean square error (RMSE) of the data generated compared to the ASIA network is approximately zero. This indicates that the data was generated correctly. We have populated the database with 2000, 3000, 5000, and 10,000 records. This was done to measure the effectiveness of the learning algorithm for a broad range of information sizes. The following input is used in the simulations:

- Population size λ. The experiments have been carried out with $\lambda = 100$.

- Crossover probability p_c we chose $p_c = 0.9$.

- Mutation rate p_m we considered $p_m = 0.1$.

Figure 2. The structure of the ASIA network

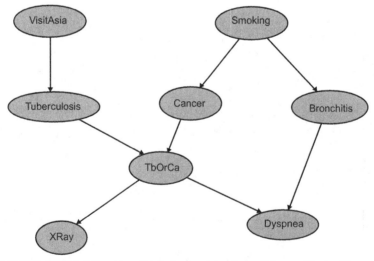

The fitness function used by our algorithm is based on the formula proposed by Cooper and Herskovits (1992). For each of the samples (2000, 3000, 5000, 10000), we executed 10 runs with each of the above parameter combinations. We considered the following four metrics to evaluate the behavior of our algorithm.

- **Average fitness value:** This is an average of fitness function values over 10 runs.

- **Best fitness value:** This value corresponds to the best fitness value throughout the evolution of the genetic algorithm.

- **Average graph errors:** This represents the average of the graph errors between the best BN structure found in each search, and the initial BN structure. Graph errors are defined to be an addition, a deletion, or a reversal of an edge.

- **Average number of generations:** This represents the number of generations taken to find the best fitness function.

For comparison purposes, we also implemented the classical genetic algorithm (CGA) with classical mutation (CM) and single point cyclic crossover (SPCC) operators. Figure 3 plots the average fitness values for the following parameter combination. The average and best fitness values are expressed in terms of $\log P(D \mid B_s)$. The numbers of records are 10,000. The figure also shows the best fitness value for the whole evolution process. One can see that SGA performs better than CGA in the initial 15-20 generations. After 15-20 generations, the genetic algorithm using both operators stabilizes to a common fitness value. The final fitness value is very close to the best fitness value. An important observation is that the average fitness value does not deviate by any significant amount even after 100 generations. The best fitness value is carried over to every generation and is not affected.

The final learned BN was constructed from the final individual generated after 100 gen-

Figure 3. Plot of generations vs. average fitness values (10000 Records)

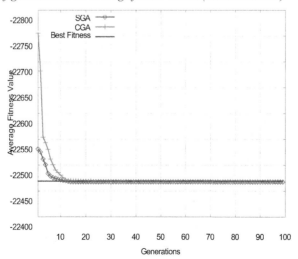

Figure 4. Learned BN after 100 generations for 5,000 records - graph errors = 3

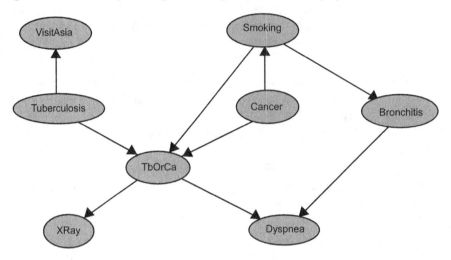

Figure 5. Learned BN after 100 generations for 10,000 records - graph errors = 2

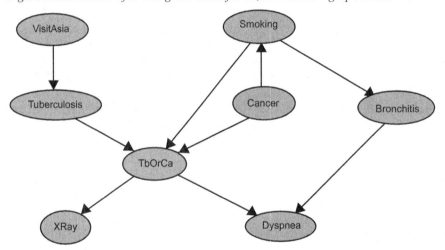

erations. Figures 4 and 5 plot the final learned BN for 5,000 records and 10,000 records, respectively. It can be observed that for both the scenarios, the learned BN differs from the actual generating BN shown in Figure 2 by a small number of graph errors. It is also worth noting that the numbers of graph errors reduce when the total numbers of records increase. This could mean that to reduce the total number of graph errors, a large number of records need to be provided.

Tables 1 and 2 provide the average number of generations and the average graph errors for a different number of records. It is obvious that for 2000 records, the total number of generations taken to achieve the stabilized fitness value is very high. Also, the average number

Table 1. Average number of generations

Records	SGA	CGA
3000	25	30
5000	20	15
10000	20	15

Table 2. Average graph errors for 8-node

Records	SGA	CGA
3000	3	4
5000	2	3
10000	2	3

Table 3. Average graph errors for 12-node

Records	SGA	CGA
3000	21	28
5000	24	29
10000	20	25

Table 4. Average graph errors for 18-node

Records	SGA	CGA
3000	19	24
5000	19.5	25.5
10000	20.7	26

Table 5. Average graph errors for 24-node

Records	SGA	CGA
3000	14.8	22.2
5000	15.3	23.1
10000	10.9	13.3

Table 6. Average graph errors for 30-node

Records	SGA	CGA
3000	15.7	21.5
5000	14.9	20.3
10000	14	18.9

Table 7. Average graph errors for 36-node

Records	SGA	CGA
3000	15.1	19.4
5000	15.6	20.5
10000	13.6	22.5

of graph errors is too high. For the 3,000, 5,000, and 10,000 records, the values for these metrics are reasonable and acceptable.

To compare the performance of SGA with CGA in the presence of larger BN structures, we modified the 8-node ASIA network and generated five additional BN with node sizes 12, 18, 24, 30, and 36. Tables 3-7 show results for simulations carried out on these additional BNs. The tables compare the average graph errors in both approaches. The accuracy of SGA does not deteriorate under increased network sizes.

Conclusion and Future Work

In this chapter, we have presented a new semantic genetic algorithm (SGA) for BN structure learning. This algorithm is another effective contribution to the list of structure learning algorithms. Our results show that SGA discovers BN structures with a greater accuracy than existing classical genetic algorithms. Moreover, for large network sizes, the accuracy of SGA does not degrade and this accuracy improvement does not come with an increase of search space. In all our simulations, 100 to 150 individuals are used in each of the 100 generations. Thus 10,000 to 15,000 networks are completely searched to learn the BN structure. Considering that the exhaustive search space is of 2^{n^2} networks, only a small percentage of the entire search space is needed by our algorithm to learn the BN structure.

One aspect for future work is to change the current random generation of adjacency matrices for the initial population generation. The second is to improve scalability by implementing our genetic algorithm on a distributed platform. We plan to adopt the island model (Tanese, 1989) of computation for implementing the distributed genetic algorithm. The novel aspect of our future work would be to propose a distributed genetic algorithm for a peer-to-peer networking environment. The proposed algorithm would combine the island model of computation with epidemic communications (Birman, Hayden, Ozkasap, Xiao, Budiu, & Minsky, 1999). The epidemic communication paradigm would be adapted to allow the algorithm to be implemented on scalable platforms that would also include fault-tolerance at different levels.

References

Birman, P., Hayden, M., Ozkasap, O., Xiao, Z., Budiu, M., & Minsky, Y. (1999). Bimodal multicast. *ACM Transactions on Computer Systems, 17*(2), 41-88.

Blanco, R., Inza, I., & Larrañaga, P. (2003). Learning Bayesian networks in the space of structures by estimation of distribution algorithms. *International Journal of Intelligent Systems, 18*(2), 205-220.

Cooper, G., & Herskovits, E.A. (1992). A Bayesian method for the induction of probabilistic networks from data. *Machine Learning, 9*(4), 309-347.

Cotta, C., & Muruzabal, J. (2002). Towards more efficient evolutionary induction of Bayesian networks. In *Proceedings of the Parallel Problem Solving from Nature VII* (pp. 730-739). Springer-Verlag.

Dijk, S.V., Thierens, D., & Gaag, L.C. (2003). Building a GA from design principles for learning Bayesian Networks. In *Proceedings of the Genetic and Evolutionary Computation Conference* (pp. 886-897).

Heckerman, D., Geiger, D., & Chickering, D.M. (1995). Learning Bayesian networks: The combination of knowledge and statistical data. *Machine Learning, 20*(3), 197-243.

Henrion, M. (1988). Propagating uncertainty in Bayesian networks by probabilistic logic sampling. *Uncertainty in Artificial Intelligence, 2*, 149-163.

Jensen, F.V. (1996). *Introduction to Bayesian networks.* New York, Inc.; Secaucus, NJ: Springer-Verlag.

Lam, W., & Bacchus, F. (1994). Learning Bayesian Belief Networks: An approach based on the MDL principle. *Computational Intelligence, 10*(4), 269-293.

Larrañaga, P., Kuijpers, C.M.H., Murga, R.H., & Yurramendi, Y. (1996). Learning Bayesian Network structures by searching for best ordering with genetic algorithm. *IEEE Transactions on Systems, Man, and Cybernetics, 26*(4), 487-493.

Larrañaga, P., Poza, M., Yurramendi, Y., Murga, R.H., & Kuijpers, C.M.H. (1996). Structure learning of Bayesian Networks by genetic algorithms: A performance analysis of control parameters. *IEEE Transactions on Pattern Analysis and Machine Intelligence, 18*(9), 912-926.

Lauritzen, S. L., & Spiegelhalter, D.J. (1988). Local computations with probabilities on graphical structures and their application on expert systems. *Journal of the Royal Statistical Society Series, 50*(2), 157-224.

Myers, J., & Levitt, T. (1999). Learning Bayesian Networks from incomplete data with stochastic search algorithms. In *Proceedings of the Fifteenth Conference on Uncertainty in Artificial Intelligence* (pp. 476-485). Morgan Kaufmann.

Pearl, J. (1988). *Probabilistic reasoning in intelligent systems: Networks of plausible inference.* San Mateo: Morgan Kaufman.

Tanese, R. (1989). Distributed genetic algorithms. In *Proceedings of the Third International Conference on Genetic Algorithms* (pp. 434-439).

Wong, M.L., Lam, W., & Leung, K.S. (1999). Using evolutionary programming and minimum description length principle for data mining of Bayesian Networks. *IEEE Transactions on Pattern Analysis and Machine Intelligence, 21*(2), 174-178.

Chapter IV

NetCube:
Fast, Approximate Database Queries Using Bayesian Networks

Dimitris Margaritis, Iowa State University, USA

Christos Faloutsos, Carnegie Mellon University, USA

Sebastian Thrun, Stanford University, USA

Abstract

We present a novel method for answering count queries from a large database approximately and quickly. Our method implements an approximate DataCube of the application domain, which can be used to answer any conjunctive count query that can be formed by the user. The DataCube is a conceptual device that in principle stores the number of matching records for all possible such queries. However, because its size and generation time are inherently exponential, our approach uses one or more Bayesian networks to implement it approximately. Bayesian networks are statistical graphical models that can succinctly represent the underlying joint probability distribution of the domain, and can therefore be used to calculate approximate counts for any conjunctive query combination of attribute values and "don't cares." The structure and parameters of these networks are learned from the database in a preprocessing stage. By means of such a network, the proposed method, called NetCube, exploits correlations and independencies among attributes to answer a count query quickly without accessing the database. Our preprocessing algorithm scales linearly on the size of the database, and is thus scalable; it is also parallelizable with a straightforward parallel implementation. We give an algorithm for estimating the count result of arbitrary queries that is fast (constant) on the database size. Our experimental results show that NetCubes have fast generation and use, achieve excellent compression and have low reconstruction error. Moreover, they naturally allow for visualization and data mining, at no extra cost.

Introduction

In this chapter we will focus on the problem of *estimating* the result of a count query on a very large database, *fast*. The problem of computing counts of records from a database with given desired characteristics is a common one in the area of decision support systems, online analytical processing (OLAP), and data mining. A typical scenario is as follows: a customer analyst has access to a database of customer transaction information (e.g., customer A bought items B, C, and D at the store at location X), and is interested in discovering patterns that exhibit an interesting or unusual behavior that might lead to possibly profitable insights into the company's customer behavior. In other words, the company wants to be able to create a *model* of its customer base (possibly partial), and the better it is able to do that, the more insights it can obtain from the model and more profitable it has the opportunity to be. In this example scenario an analyst would, through an interactive query process, request count information from the database, possibly drilling down in interesting subsets of the database of customer information. It is very important that the results to these queries be returned quickly, because that will greatly facilitate the process of discovery by the analyst. It is also important that the answers to these queries are accurate up to a reasonable degree, although it is not imperative that they are exact. The analyst wants an approximate figure of the result of the query and getting it correct down to the last digit is not necessary.

The methods presented in this chapter are motivated by these observations, that is, the fact that we need great speed coupled with only reasonable accuracy. In the following we present NetCube, a method that can support fast, approximate queries on very large databases. Net-Cube can fit approximately a database of billions of records in the main memory of a single workstation. There is no "trick" to this—it is due to the fact that what is stored in memory is not the actual data themselves, but only *a model of the data*. This model is a **Bayesian network (BN)**, which can be used to answer count queries quickly, albeit only approximately. The speed comes from the fact that only the Bayesian network is used to answer the query, and the database is not accessed at query time. The database is accessed only during the one-time preprocessing phase, when a number of BN models are constructed from it.

There are two important considerations relevant to the problem described above:

- First, the model should be a reasonably accurate description of our database, or at the very least of the quantities derived from them that are of interest. In this problem these quantities are the results of every interesting count query that can be applied to it (e.g., queries with some minimum support such as 10,000 records or 1%).

- Second, the model should be simple enough so that using it instead of the actual data to answer a query should not take an exorbitant amount of time (e.g., more than using the actual database to answer the query) or consume an enormous amount of space (e.g., more space than the actual database uses).

These two issues—accuracy vs. time/space complexity—are conflicting, and the problem of balancing them is a central issue in the AI subfield of machine learning, which concerns itself, among other topics, with the development of models of data. This is because it is always possible to describe the data (or the derived quantities we are interested in) better, or at least as well, with increasingly complex models. However, the cost of such models increases with complexity, in terms of both size (to store the model structure and parameters) and time that it takes to use it (for computing the relevant quantities, that is, the query counts in our case). The reason we use Bayesian networks here is their good performance in estimating probability distributions in practice and their sound mathematical foundations in probability theory, compared to a multitude of other *ad hoc* approaches that exist in the literature.

In this chapter we first describe a conceptual solution to the problem, we then show how this solution, even though it is difficult to implement exactly, can be done so approximately using NetCube, which uses Bayesian networks. Next we describe methods for producing Bayesian networks from a database and using them to answer database queries, followed by implementation details. Finally we conclude with experimental results for two case studies where NetCube is used.

DataCubes: Precomputing All Possible Aggregate Queries

As described above, a typical data mining scenario involving a human requires real-time interaction with the database. In particular, the analyst looking for unusual patterns in the data might hypothesize a relationship and attempt to confirm or refute it by issuing a variety of aggregation queries (e.g., counts or averages for combinations of values for different subsets of attributes) possibly changing the set of attributes; for example, adding or deleting attributes from it. If the current hypothesis is refuted, he or she might move to a completely different subset of attributes to start examining a different hypothesis.

A summary of this interactive data mining procedure, as given by Gray, Bosworth, Layman, and Pirahesh (1996), divides it into four distinct steps:

1.   **Formulate** a query that extracts data from the database.
2.   **Execute** the query, extracting aggregated data from the database into a file or relation.
3.   **Visualize** the results in a graphical way.
4.   **Analyze** the results and formulate a new query (go to step 1).

To facilitate the quick retrieval of the aggregated data, Gray et al. (1996) introduced the idea of the **DataCube**. A DataCube is a conceptual device that contains all possible aggregates over all possible subsets of attributes of a domain of interest. For example, for a hypothetical database containing 1,000 records and 3 attributes A, B, C, each taking values 0 or 1, the count DataCube is shown in Figure 1. There are $2^3 = 8$ possible subsets of these 3 attributes (from the empty set to the entire set $\{A, B, C\}$). For each of these subsets, a table is stored in the DataCube containing the counts for every possible combination of values for the attributes in the subset, for example, for $\{A, B\}$ there are 4 entries in the corresponding table, namely $count(A = 1, B = 1) = 400$, $count(A = 1, B = 0) = 35$, $count(A = 0, B = 1) = 400$, and $count(A = 0, B = 0) = 165$. We will restrict our attention to count DataCubes here, and refer

Figure 1. An example count DataCube for a domain of 3 binary attributes A, B, and C, containing $2^3 = 8$ tables. The notation A corresponds to the assignment $(A = 1)$ and $\bar{A}$ to $(A = 0)$.

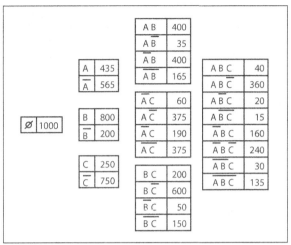

to them simply as "DataCubes" from now on. However, other types of DataCubes exist that correspond to other aggregates, for example, average, max, min, or median DataCubes. Note that some of these can be computed from count DataCubes (e.g., average DataCubes).

We can see that, using the DataCube of a database, computation of any query takes constant time (for a table-lookup implementation). In practice however, computation and storage of the DataCube is exceedingly difficult because of its inherently exponential nature. To solve this problem, several approaches have been proposed. Harinarayan, Rajaraman, and Ullman (1996) suggest materializing only a subset of tables and propose a principled way of selecting which ones to prefer. Their system computes the query from those tables at run time. DataCubes containing only cells of some minimum support are suggested by Beyer and Ramakrishnan (1999), who propose coarse-to-fine traversal that improves speed by condensing cells of less than the minimum support. Histogram-based approaches also exist (Ioannidis & Poosala, 1999), as well as approximations such as histogram compression using the DCT transform (Lee, Kim, & Chung, 1999) or wavelets (Vitter & Wang, 1999). Perhaps closest to the methods described in this chapter is Barbará (1998), which uses linear regression to model DataCubes. Bitmaps are another relatively recent method for efficiently computing counts from highly compressed bitmapped information about the properties of records in the database. Bitmaps are exact techniques that do not maintain counts, but instead store, for every record in the database, one bit for every attribute and value combination. To answer an aggregate query, they perform a pass over several bitmaps at runtime (Chan & Ioannidis, 1999; Johnson, 1999). Even though query optimizers for bitmaps exist (Wu, 1999), the runtime is still linear in the size of the database.

In the next section, we describe the relation that exists between the DataCube of a database and a Bayesian network. Following this, we present methods for constructing BNs from data and using them to implement a DataCube approximately.

Relation Between Bayesian Networks
and DataCubes

In this section, we highlight the aspects of Bayesian networks that relate to our implementation of approximate DataCubes for count queries. We illustrate the relation of DataCubes to BNs using the DataCube of Figure 1, shown again here for convenience in Figure 2(a). This DataCube, possibly taken from the research department of a company that manufactures burglar alarms, is constructed from a database that contains 1,000 records and three Boolean attributes A ("home alarm goes off"), B ("burglar enters the house") and C ("earthquake occurs"). Although we will assume that all attributes are binary, this is not necessary and does not affect the generality of our methods. In Figure 2(b) we can see the corresponding Bayesian network for this domain. The structure of the BN encodes independencies that hold in the domain, for example, the fact that the edge between B and C in the BN is missing indicates that although A may depend on B and A may depend on C, B and C are (unconditionally) independent.

The main idea in this section is that the BN can be used to answer any count query that can be posed on the original database. For example, $count(A = 1, B = 1, C = 0) = 360$, as stored in the DataCube; the same answer can be obtained using the BN as follows:

$$\Pr(A = 1, B = 1, C = 0) = \Pr(A = 1 \mid B = 1, C = 0) \Pr(B = 1, C = 0)$$
$$= \Pr(A = 1 \mid B = 1, C = 0) \Pr(B = 1) \Pr(C = 0)$$

Figure 2. (a) Example DataCube from Figure 1 constructed from a database of 1,000 records containing attributes A, B, and C. (b) Bayesian network generated from the same database. The Bayesian network can describe exactly the same counts as the DataCube but consumes less space in this example because B and C are independent (unconditionally).

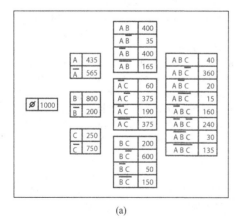
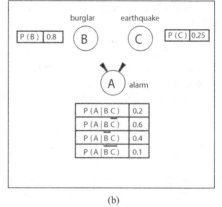

(a)   (b)

$$= 0.6 \cdot 0.8 \cdot 0.75$$
$$= 0.36.$$

The estimated count can be calculated by multiplying with the size of the database, that is, $count(A = 1, B = 1, C = 0) = 0.36 \cdot 1000 = 360$.

In this case, answering the query was relatively easy because it was a *saturated* one. A query is called saturated if it involves all attributes in the database. An unsaturated query may be more difficult to answer using the BN. An example of an unsaturated query is $count(A = 0, B = 1)$. Using the BN we can answer it as follows:

$$\Pr(A = 0, B = 1) = \Pr (A = 0, B = 1, C = 0) + \Pr (A = 0, B = 1, C = 1)$$
$$= \Pr (A = 0 \mid B = 1, C = 0) \Pr (B = 1) \Pr (C = 0) +$$
$$\Pr (A = 0 \mid B = 1, C = 1) \Pr (B = 1) \Pr (C = 1)$$
$$= 0.4 \cdot 0.8 \cdot 0.75 + 0.8 \cdot 0.8 \cdot 0.25$$
$$= 0.4$$

which gives $count(A = 0, B = 1) = 0.4 \cdot 1,000 = 400$, coinciding with the value in the DataCube.

As is well known, a BN represents the joint probability distribution function (**PDF**) of a domain. In general, a probability distribution can be specified with a set of numbers whose size is exponential in the number of attributes in the domain, namely the entries in the joint PDF table. One can represent such a table by a completely connected BN without any great benefit. However, when independencies exist in the domain, using a BN instead of the full joint probability table results in at least two major benefits:

1. **Storage savings:** These may be significant to the point where infeasibly large domains may be representable, provided that they exhibit a sufficient number of independencies among the variables of the domain.

2. **Clear and intuitive representation of independencies:** Given the graphical representation of a BN, it is easy to determine the variables on which a quantity of interest depends on statistically (under assumptions) and which are irrelevant and under what conditions.

Edge omissions indicate the existence of conditional independencies among variables in the domain. As mentioned above, if all variables in the domain are statistically dependent on all others, then there is no storage advantage to using a BN, because the storage required for the specification of the network is exponential in the number of attributes. Fortunately, in practice this is not the norm, and in fact the most interesting domains for data mining are those that exhibit a considerable number of independencies.

The storage space savings in this domain are illustrated in Figure 2(b). The numbers that have to be stored in the DataCube are 20 essential counts. The numbers necessary in the corresponding BN are 6 probability entries. We see that for this particular example this is certainly not a significant improvement, especially considering the overhead of specifying the parents of each node and using floating point numbers for the probability entries. However, for large networks with tens or hundreds of variables, the savings increases exponentially if the corresponding network is sparse. For n attributes, the DataCube has to store 2^n tables of counts, with each table having size equal to the product of the cardinalities of the attributes they include (minus one). No full joint table for hundreds of variables containing either probabilities or counts could ever be stored using today's technology. However, such a domain may be succinctly represented by a Bayesian network instead if a sufficient number of conditional independencies exist.

An interesting application of Bayesian networks that highlights the fact that they can be used to estimate counts is the approach by Getoor, Taskar, and Koller (2001). Getoor et al. (2001) uses a relational extension of Bayesian networks, called probabilistic relational models, to estimate the size of "select" or "select-join" database queries (returning the number of matching records) in cases where data is stored in more than one relations of a database. Their approach is useful for finding the optimal query execution plan before a query is executed, which is an important and difficult problem in database query processing.

Learning Bayesian Networks from Data

Our approach, presented in the next section, uses one or more Bayesian networks to represent the database. In this section we describe the prevalent techniques that are used for learning Bayesian networks. We first describe the easier task of computing the parameters of a BN when its structure is known, followed by one possible method for learning the structure in the next section.

We first describe the notation and symbols we will use. The database is denoted as $\mathcal{D}$ and its size $N = |\mathcal{D}|$. Throughout the chapter, we refer to attributes and variables interchangeably because BN variables correspond to attributes in the database. We assume that set $\mathbf{U} = \{X_1, X_2, \ldots, X_n\}$ contains all n attributes in the domain. A BN is a pair $B = \langle E, T \rangle$, where E is the set of edges among the variables in $\mathbf{U}$ and T is the set of local conditional probability tables (the BN parameters) for the structure defined by E. We denote sets of variables with bold letters. The parents of X_i in the BN are denoted as $\mathbf{Pa}_i$ and their j-th value (attribute value configuration) as $\mathbf{pa}_{ij}$. We assume that variable X_i can take one of r_i values and its parents one of q_i configurations. We assume that all local probability distribution functions of a BN are members of the multinomial family.

Learning the Parameters

A BN is essentially a statistical model. Learning the parameters of a statistical model is a well-known problem in statistics. The parameters of a BN are the probabilities contained in the conditional probability tables representing the local PDF for each variable in the domain. In the BN literature, where Bayesian approaches seem to be dominant, the parameters themselves are assumed to follow a probability distribution.

Before any data are observed, a *prior distribution* Pr(*parameters*) is assumed over the parameters of the local PDFs (for example, this can be uniform). This prior distribution may have parameters of its own—although usually fewer than the number of parameters it covers—which are called *hyperparameters*. Given a data set, a *posterior distribution* Pr(*parameters* | *data*) can be calculated according to Bayes' law:

$$\Pr(parameters \mid data) = \frac{\Pr(data \mid parameters)\Pr(parameters)}{\Pr(data)}$$

The term Pr(*data* | *parameters*) is called the *data likelihood*, or simply *likelihood*. Informally, the term Pr(*data*) can be calculated as a sum (or integral) over all possible parameter values, that is,

$$\Pr(data) = \sum_{parameter\ values} \Pr(data \mid parameters)\Pr(parameters)$$

The parameters of a BN are the probabilities stored in the local PDFs. Let P_{ijk} be the probability that variable X_i takes its k-th value (out of r_i possible ones) when its parents $\mathbf{Pa}_i$ in Bayesian network $B = \langle E, T \rangle$ take their j-th value $\mathbf{pa}_{ij}$ (out of q_i possible ones). The likelihood of a data set $\mathcal{D}$ that contains N_{ijk} records in which $X_i = x_{ik}$ and $\mathbf{Pa}_i = \mathbf{pa}_j$ is given by the *multinomial distribution*

$$\Pr(data \mid parameters) = \Pr(\mathcal{D} \mid \{p_{ijk}\}) = N! \prod_{i=1}^{n} \prod_{j=1}^{q_i} \prod_{k=1}^{r_i} \frac{P_{ijk}^{N_{ijk}}}{N_{ijk}!}$$

For the prior distribution, it is frequently desirable to choose one from a family that is *conjugate prior* to the data distribution. A prior is called conjugate when its posterior belongs to the same family as the prior (albeit possibly with different hyperparameters). The conjugate prior family for multinomial data distribution is the Dirichlet; we present only this case in some detail here. For other cases, such as linear regression with Gaussian noise, see Buntine (1993) and Heckerman and Geiger (1995), or for more complicated ones representable by artificial neural networks, see Monti and Cooper (1998). Also, for more details on conjugate priors, see Casella and Berger (1990).

In a BN, we have a number of Dirichlet priors, one for each variable X_i and value $\mathbf{pa}_{ij}$ of its parents $\mathbf{Pa}_i$ in the network. The Dirichlet distribution over the parameters $p_{ij1}, p_{ij2}, \ldots, p_{ijr_i}$ is expressed by:

$$\Pr(p_{ij1}, p_{ij2}, \ldots, p_{ijr_i} \mid E) = \mathrm{Dir}\,(\alpha_{ij1}, \alpha_{ij2}, \ldots, \alpha_{ijr_i}) = \Gamma(\alpha_{ij}) \prod_{k=1}^{r_i} \frac{p_{ijk}^{\alpha_{ijk}-1}}{\Gamma(\alpha_{ijk})}$$

where α_{ijk} are its hyperparameters, $\alpha_{ij} = \sum_{k=1}^{r_i} \alpha_{ijk}$, and $\Gamma(\cdot)$ is the Gamma function.[1] Assuming *local* and *global parameter independence* (Cooper & Herskovits, 1992; Heckerman,

Geiger, & Chickering, 1995; Spiegelhalter & Lauritzen, 1990), the prior distribution over the entire set of parameters $\mathbf{p} = \{p_{ijk}\}$ of the BN is the product over all priors:

$$\Pr(\mathbf{p} \mid E) = \prod_{i=1}^{n} \prod_{j=1}^{q_i} \Gamma(\alpha_{ij}) \prod_{k=1}^{r_i} \frac{p_{ijk}^{\alpha_{ijk}-1}}{\Gamma(\alpha_{ijk})}.$$

Conditionally, on the data set $\mathcal{D}$, the posterior probability over the parameters is also a member of the Dirichlet family, because it is conjugate prior to the multinomial. It is given by:

$$\Pr(p_{ij1}, p_{ij2}, \ldots, p_{ijr_i} \mid E, \mathcal{D}) = \mathrm{Dir}(N_{ij1} + \alpha_{ij1}, N_{ij2} + \alpha_{ij2}, \ldots, N_{ijr_i} + \alpha_{ijr_i}).$$

The posterior over all parameters is then:

$$\Pr(\mathbf{p} \mid E, \mathrm{D}) = \prod_{i=1}^{n} \prod_{j=1}^{q_i} \Gamma(N_{ij} + \alpha_{ij}) \prod_{k=1}^{r_i} \frac{p_{ijk}^{N_{ijk}+\alpha_{ijk}-1}}{\Gamma(N_{ijk} + \alpha_{ijk})} \qquad (1)$$

where $N_{ij} = \sum_{k=1}^{r_i} N_{ijk}$ is the number of records in $\mathcal{D}$ for which $\mathbf{Pa}_i = \mathbf{pa}_{ij}$. Using this distribution to calculate the (posterior) expected value of an arbitrary quantity $Q(\mathbf{p})$, one averages over all possible values of the (unknown) parameters, weighted by the posterior probability of each value:

$$E[Q(\mathbf{p}) \mid E, \mathcal{D}] = \int Q(X_1, X_2, \ldots, X_n) \Pr(\mathbf{p} \mid E, \mathcal{D}) \, d\mathbf{p}.$$

This general formula can be used to calculate the parameter values stored in the conditional probability tables of the BN, which are $\overline{p}_{ijk} = E[p_{ijk} \mid E, \mathcal{D}]$, that is:

$$\overline{p}_{ijk} = E[p_{ijk} \mid E, \mathcal{D}] = \int p_{ijk} \Pr(\mathbf{p} \mid E, \mathcal{D}) d\mathbf{p} = \frac{\alpha_{ijk} + N_{ijk}}{\alpha_{ij} + N_{ij}}. \qquad (2)$$

Due to the form above, the hyperparameters α_{ijk} can be thought of as a number of "virtual samples" that are added to the real samples N_{ijk} for each variable-parent value combination. Popular choices for the hyperparameters are $\alpha_{ijk} = 1$ (a uniform prior over the parameters of each X_i for each parent value combination), and $\alpha_{ijk} = 1/r_i$.

Frequently, for convenience, especially in cases where data are abundant (i.e., when $\alpha_{ijk} \ll N_{ijk}$) and no N_{ij} is zero, the hyperparameters are ignored and the maximum likelihood estimator $\hat{P}_{ijk} = N_{ijk} / N_{ij}$ is used instead of $\overline{P}_{ijk}$. This happens, for example, in score-based methods, where the BIC score is employed, which is itself a large-sample approximation of the posterior and is already assuming that the effects of a prior are negligible.

Learning the Structure: Score-Based Methods

Broadly speaking, there are two classes of algorithms for learning the structure of BNs. One class "scores" a BN based on how well it fits the data, and attempts to find a structure that maximizes that score, while another class attempts to model the independencies in the data. The former is more appropriate in applications where fitting data well is a priority, while the latter has been used to learn a BN model of the so-called "causal" structure of the domain. Because our method falls into the former category, we only present the scoring approach here.

The score-based approach assigns a score to each candidate BN, typically one that measures how well that BN describes the data set $\mathcal{D}$. The score of structure E given data set $\mathcal{D}$ is

$$Score(E, \mathcal{D}) = \Pr(E \mid \mathcal{D})$$

that is, the posterior probability of E given the data set. A score-based algorithm attempts to maximize this score, that is, to find arg $\max_E Score(E, \mathcal{D})$. Computation of the above can be cast into a more convenient form by using Bayes' law:

$$Score(E, \mathcal{D}) = \Pr(E \mid \mathcal{D}) = \frac{\Pr(\mathcal{D} \mid E)\Pr(E)}{\Pr(\mathcal{D})}.$$

To maximize this we need only maximize the numerator, because the denominator does not depend on E. There are several ways to assess $\Pr(E)$ from prior information; see Heckerman(1995) for a discussion and pointers to the literature. Here we will ignore $\Pr(E)$ (assume it a constant), which is equivalent to assuming a uniform prior over structures.

To calculate $\Pr(\mathcal{D} \mid E)$, the Bayesian approach averages over all possible parameters, weighing each by their probability:

$$\Pr(\mathcal{D} \mid E) = \int \Pr(\mathcal{D} \mid E, \mathbf{p})\, \Pr(\mathbf{p} \mid E) d\mathbf{p}.$$

Cooper and Herskovits (1992) first showed that for multinomial local PDFs, and assuming a Dirichlet prior (see previous section), this can be computed analytically:

$$\Pr(\mathcal{D} \mid E) = \prod_{i=1}^{n} \prod_{j=1}^{q_i} \frac{\Gamma(\alpha_{ij})}{\Gamma(\alpha_{ij} + N_{ij})} \prod_{k=1}^{r_i} \frac{\Gamma(\alpha_{ijk} + N_{ijk})}{\Gamma(\alpha_{ijk})}$$

where, as usual, α_{ijk} and N_{ijk} are respectively the hyperparameters and the counts for k-th value of X_i and the j-th configuration of $\mathbf{Pa}_i$. In the large sample limit the term $\Pr(\mathcal{D} \mid E, \mathbf{p})$ $\Pr(\mathbf{p} \mid E)$ can be reasonably approximated as a multivariate Gaussian (Kass & Raftery, 1995; Kass, Tierney, & Kadane, 1988). Doing that and, in addition approximating the mean of the Gaussian with the maximum likelihood value $\mathbf{p}$ and ignoring terms that do not depend of the data set size N, we end up with the *BIC score* approximation:

$$BICscore(B, \mathcal{D}) = \log \Pr(\mathcal{D} \mid \mathbf{p}, E) - \frac{|T|}{2} \log N, \tag{3}$$

first derived by Schwartz (1978). $|T|$ is the number of free parameters of the multivariate Gaussian, that is, its number of dimensions; this equals the number of free parameters of the multinomial local PDFs, that is, $|T| = \sum_{i=1}^{n} q_i (r_i - 1)$. The usefulness of the BIC score comes from the fact that it does not depend on the prior over the parameters, which makes it useful in practice in cases where prior information is not available or is difficult to obtain. It also has the intuitive interpretation of being equal to the data likelihood minus a "penalty term" $(-\frac{|T|}{2} \log N)$ which has the effect of discouraging overly complicated structures and acting to automatically protect from overfitting. The BIC score has been shown to be equal to minus the minimum description length (MDL) score (described by Rissanen, 1987).

As we mentioned above, score-based algorithms attempt to find the structure whose score is maximum. This poses considerable problems because the space of all possible structures is at least exponential in the number of variables n: there are $n(n-1)/2$ possible undirected edges and $2^{n(n-1)/2}$ possible undirected structures for every subset of these edges. Moreover, there may be more than one orientation of the edges for each such choice, resulting in at least one BN for each undirected structure. Therefore a brute force approach that computes the score of every BN structure is out of the question in all but the most trivial domains, and instead heuristic search algorithms are employed in practice. One popular choice is *hill-climbing*, shown graphically in an example in Figure 3 and in pseudocode in Figure 4. The search is started from either an empty, full, or random network, although if background knowledge exists, it can be used to seed the initial candidate network. The procedure *ProbabilityTables()* estimates the parameters of the local PDFs given a BN structure (see previous section). The algorithm's main loop consists of evaluating the score of the structure resulting from every possible *single-edge* addition, removal, or reversal, making the network that increases the score the most the current candidate, and iterating. The process stops when there is no single-edge change that increases the score. There is no guarantee that this algorithm will settle at a global maximum so, to increase the chances of reaching a global maximum, techniques such as a simple perturbation, multiple restarts from random points (initial networks), or simulated annealing can be used.

It is worthwhile to note that the restricted case of tree-structured BNs has been solved optimally, in the minimum KL-divergence sense, by Chow and Liu (1968). A similar approach has been proposed for the case of polytrees (trees where each node can have more than one parent) by Rebane and Pearl (1989), although its optimality has not been proven.

Hill-climbing is not the only method of heuristic search. Best-first search (e.g., Russell & Norvig, 2002), genetic algorithms (Larranaga, Poza, Yurramendi, Murga, & Kuijpers, 1996), and almost any kind of search procedure can also be used. A more principled approach is to reduce the search space by searching among independence-equivalent classes of networks instead (Chickering, 1996). Recently Chickering (2002) proved a conjecture of Meek (1997) that in the limit of large sample sizes, his greedy equivalence search (GES) algorithm does identify an inclusion-optimal equivalence class of BNs, that is, a class of models such that

Figure 3. Illustration of the hill-climbing BN structure search procedure

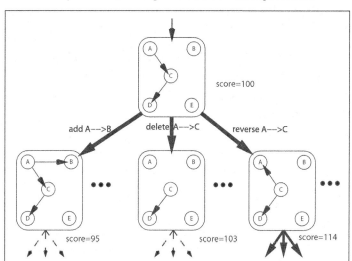

Figure 4. Pseudocode for the algorithm that constructs a BN from a data set $\mathcal{D}$ using hill-climbing search

Procedure B = *BIChillclimb*($\mathcal{D}$)

1. $E \leftarrow \emptyset$
2. $T \leftarrow ProbabilityTables(E, \mathcal{D})$
3. $B \leftarrow \langle E, T \rangle$
4. *score* $\leftarrow -\infty$
5. do:
   (a) *maxscore* $\leftarrow$ *score*
   (b) for each attribute pair (X, Y) do
   (c)   for each $E' \in \{E \cup \{X \to Y\},$
   $$E - \{X \to Y\},$$
   $$(E - \{X \to Y\}) \cup \{Y \to X\}\}$$
   (d) $T' \leftarrow ProbabilityTables(E', \mathcal{D})$
   (e) $B' \leftarrow \langle E', T' \rangle$
   (f)   *newscore* $\leftarrow$ *BICscore*$(B', \mathcal{D})$
   (g)   if *newscore* > *score* then
          $B \leftarrow B'$
          score $\leftarrow$ *newscore*
6. while *score* > *maxscore*
7. Return *B*

Figure 5. Algorithm for preprocessing the database

Procedure $B = BuildFromDisk(\mathcal{D})$:

1. Partition the database $\mathcal{D}$ into K equal partitions $\mathcal{D}_i, i = 1,\ldots,K$ so that each fits in main memory. Let $d = |\mathcal{D}_i|$, for all i.
2. For each $i = 1,\ldots,K$ do the following:
   (a) Read $\mathcal{D}_i$ into memory.
   (b) Build Bayesian network B_i from $\mathcal{D}_i$: $B_i = $ BuildFromMemoryUsingData($\mathcal{D}_i$).
3. For each $i = 1,\ldots,K$ do the following:
   Merge the networks B_i into a single one: $B = RecursivelyMerge(B_1, B_2, \ldots, B_K)$.
4. Return B.

(a) includes the probability distribution from which the dataset was drawn, and (b) no sub-model contains that distribution, if one exists.

NetCube: Implementing the DataCube Using a Bayesian Network

We are now ready to address our main problem, which can be stated as follows:

- **Problem:** We are given a database that may not fit in memory and a procedure *Build-FromMemoryUsingData($\mathcal{D}$)* that is able to generate a BN from a memory-resident database.

- **Desired solution:** A representation that can fit in memory, a procedure *BuildFromDisk()* that generates it from disk, and an *EstimateCount()* procedure that uses it to compute the approximate answer to count queries that may specify an arbitrary number of attribute values.

Our representation is called **NetCube** and uses a single Bayesian network, created from the entire database $\mathcal{D}$, to represent the record counts in the database. Answering a count query works by estimating its probability using the Bayesian network and multiplying by the size of the database to obtain an approximate count of records that satisfy the query. Querying in this way is therefore *constant time* ($O(1)$) in the size of the database, because the database is not accessed. Perhaps the biggest practical problem in our approach is the fact that frequently the database is too large to fit into main memory, something that is required for the algorithms for learning the BN structure and parameters presented previously in this chapter. Below we present a method for solving this problem.

Learning a Single Bayesian Network from a Database that Cannot Fit in Memory

To learn a BN from database $\mathcal{D}$ that fits in main memory, we can use the *BICchillclimb()* procedure, described previously. If $\mathcal{D}$ cannot fit in main memory, we present in Figure 5 the procedure *BuildFromDisk($\mathcal{D}$)* that can be used for that purpose.

The *BuildFromDisk($\mathcal{D}$)* procedure first partitions $\mathcal{D}$ into K subsets (called *chunks* here) $\mathcal{D}_i$ that is, $\bigcup_{i=1}^{k} \mathcal{D}_i = \mathcal{D}$ and $\mathcal{D}_i \neq \mathcal{D}_j$ for $i \neq j$, such that each $\mathcal{D}_i$ fits in memory. It then uses the *BuildFromMemoryUsingData()* procedure to build a BN B_i from each of them. The *BuildFromMemoryUsingData()* contains the implementation of the algorithm for learning the structure of a Bayesian network from data, that is, *BuildFromMemoryUsingData($\mathcal{D}_j$)* = *BICchillclimb($\mathcal{D}_j$)*. (We note that the generation of each B_i can be done in parallel.) Having produced the networks B_i, $i = 1, \ldots, K$, we combine them into a single one B using the *RecursivelyMerge()* procedure, shown in Figure 6.

The *RecursivelyMerge()* procedure uses the *BuildFromMemoryUsingBNs($B_1, \ldots, B_k$)* procedure to combine K BN models from a lower level to one BN at one level higher. It is implemented in exactly the same way as the *BICchillclimb($\mathcal{D}$)* one, with the exception that the score is now computed from the BNs that are passed as its arguments instead of the database, that is, the *BICscore()* procedure is replaced by:

$$BICscoreFromBNs(\tilde{B}, \overbrace{B_1, B_2, \ldots, B_k}^{\text{representing } \mathcal{D}}) =$$

$$\sum_{t \in \tilde{T}} \left\{ \left[\frac{1}{K} \sum_{k=1}^{K} EstimateProbability(t, B_k) \right] \log \left[\frac{1}{K} \sum_{k=1}^{K} EstimateProbability(t, B_k) \right] \right\} - \frac{|\tilde{T}|}{2} \log N$$

In the above formula, the outer sum goes over all table entries t in $\tilde{B} = \langle \tilde{E}, \tilde{T} \rangle$. Each such table entry corresponds to a configuration of variable assignments for the node and the par-

Figure 6. Algorithm for recursively merging K Bayesian networks into a single one

Procedure $B = RecursivelyMerge(B_1, \ldots, B_K)$:

If $B_1, B_2, \ldots, B_K$ simultaneously fit in main memory then:
    $B = BuildFromMemoryUsingBNs(B_1, \ldots, B_K)$
else:
    $\tilde{B}_1 = RecursivelyMerge(B_1, \ldots, B_{\lfloor \frac{K}{2} \rfloor})$.
    $\tilde{B}_2 = RecursivelyMerge(B_{\lfloor \frac{K}{2} \rfloor + 1}, \ldots B_K)$.
    $B = RecursivelyMerge(\tilde{B}_1, \tilde{B}_2)$.

Return B.

ents of the node that it is attached to—the remaining variables are ignored or equivalently assigned "don't care" values—see *Relation Between Bayesian Networks and DataCubes* for an example. The inner equally-weighted sums are simply an average over all networks B_i, $i = 1, \ldots, K$ of the probability of that configuration. (The reason for the equal weighting is the fact that all BNs B_i have been generated from the same number of records from the database.) The *EstimateProbability()* procedure is taken from the literature; possible choices will be discussed in the next section.

The computation of the probability table entries $\Pr(t|\tilde{E})$ in $\tilde{B} = \langle \tilde{E}, \tilde{T} \rangle$ is done from the B_i's without accessing the database; it is also making use of the *EstimateProbability()* procedure:

$$\forall t \in \tilde{T}, \quad \Pr(t \mid \tilde{E}) = \frac{1}{K} \sum_{k=1}^{K} EstimateProbability(t, B_k).$$

Because the database access is $O(N)$ during the *BuildFromDisk($\mathcal{D}$)* procedure, where $N = |\mathcal{D}|$ is the number of records in the database, the number of networks at the base of the recursion is $K = N/d = O(N)$ (where $d = |\mathcal{D}_i|$, for all i) and because accessing a BN does not depend on the database size, it is easy to make the following observation:

- **Observation:** The entire BuildFromDisk() algorithm is $O(N)$ time (linear in the size of the original database) and thus scalable. Moreover, it is parallelizable, with a straightforward parallel implementation.

This observation is supported by the experimental results (Figure 8).

Algorithm for Answering a Count Query from a Bayesian Network

After generating a single BN from database $\mathcal{D}$ (using the *BuildFromDisk()* procedure), the resulting BN B now acts as a representative of the entire database, and we can use it to answer count queries approximately without accessing $\mathcal{D}$. In order to do that, we estimate the probability (expected relative frequency) of the query using the BN, and multiply it with the number of records in the database.

More precisely, to estimate approximate counts for query Q from the Bayesian network B, that is, the output of the *BuildFromDisk()* procedure, we use the *EstimateCount()* procedure, shown below:

$EstimateCount(Q, B) = N \cdot EstimateProbability(Q, B).$

For the procedure *EstimateProbability()* in our implementation we use the join-tree algorithm. *EstimateProbability()* returns the probability of query Q according to the probability distribution represented by B. Because B is a representative of the N records contained in D, $(N \cdot EstimateProbability(Q,B))$ is an estimate of the number of records within D for which Q evaluates to "true," and thus is the (approximate) answer to the original query.

The computation of the probability of an arbitrary query is called *probabilistic inference*.[2] Probabilistic inference may involve an exponential number of calculations and is NP-complete in general. Two kinds of methods for probabilistic inference exist: approximate and exact. Approximate ones (Henrion, 1988; Fung & Chang, 1989; Schachter & Peot, 1989) are sample-based, and generate an artificial database of samples during the process of estimation (the generated samples are discarded immediately and only the count of those than matched the query is kept). Their main disadvantage is that they are slow and may need a great number of samples to estimate the probability of the query to a sufficient degree. For exact inference, the most popular method is the join-tree algorithm. The details of the algorithm are beyond the scope of this chapter; see Pearl (1997) and Huang and Darwiche (1994). Its running time depends on the number of variables and the complexity of the BN, but in practice for typical BNs of a few tens of variables, it runs in under a second. This is the method we use here, contained in the *EstimateProbability()* procedure.

Because the *EstimateCount(Q,B)* algorithm does not access the database, we can make the following observation:

- **Observation:** The *EstimateCount(Q,B)* procedure is $O(1)$ time in the size of the database.

Note that the answers computed using the BN may be approximate. This happens for several reasons:

- There are size and accuracy trade-offs during the learning of the BN using the database, stemming from the use of the BIC score, which may produce a slightly less accurate BN but consuming less space (compared to the fully connected one, for example, which requires exponential space).
- An approximate algorithm for probabilistic inference may be used. In general, exact probabilistic inference may take exponential time, and depends on the complexity of the BN structure.
- The use of floating point numbers for the local PDF parameters may introduce round-off errors.

Case Studies

We experimentally tested the above methods on real and synthetic data. The real data consists of customer transaction data, obtained from a large anonymous retailer.[3] It consists of over 3 million (3,261,809) customer transactions containing information on whether the customer purchased any of the 20 most popular items in the store. The data represents one week of activity and its concise representation occupies around 8 MB. This size coincides with the size of its uncompressed bitmap. Although this database is not large in size, we use it in order to obtain performance results on the compression ratio we can hope to obtain on real-world data.

In order to assess the scalability of our system as the database size grows, we need larger sets that are usually not publicly available. For this reason we used synthetic data for our scalability study. All remaining experiments, except the compression size results, used the synthetic data produced by a program available from IBM's QUEST site.[4] The generation program produces a user-specified number of random association rules involving a number of attributes (their number is also randomly distributed around a user-specified mean), and then generates an arbitrarily large number of market-basket transactions whose statistical behavior conforms to those rules. We produced a database of 100 thousand and 1, 10, and 100 million transaction records from a store inventory of 5,000 items (products) using 10,000 customer patterns having an average length of 4 items. (Each customer pattern corresponds to an "association rule.") The average transaction length was 10 items. Contrary to our real database, we used the 50 most frequently used items. Such a DataCube cannot fit in main memory because it consists of 2^{50} tables totaling much more than 2^{50} DataCube entries.

From both real and synthetic databases we then constructed a number of Bayesian networks from that data in order to model their joint probability distribution. We split the data set in a number of chunks $\mathcal{D}_i$, each containing at most d records, where $d = 815,452$ for the anonymous retailer data set (4 chunks) and $d = 20,000$ for the QUEST data set (5,000 chunks). We then used each chunk $\mathcal{D}_i$ to construct the corresponding Bayesian network B_i. Finally, we recursively combined the networks using a two-level hierarchy for the real data set and a six-level hierarchy, depicted in Figure 7, for the QUEST data set. For the latter, at every level five networks are combined, with the exception of the last level where eight networks were combined.

We compare our results against an uncompressed and compressed bitmap, as well as a compressed bitmap produced after sampling the database for 1% and 10% of its records uniformly. Our experiments evaluate our approach with respect to the following dimensions:

- Build time and scalability
- Space to store models and effective compression of the database
- Time to answer a query
- Query count accuracy
- Visualization of the dependencies in the database

Because the number of possible queries grows exponentially with the number of variables that are involved in it, it was infeasible in practice to perform every possible query of any length. Instead, we generated 10,000 random queries of length up to 5 variables. Each query is more general than one traditionally used in association rule discovery, allowing testing for the presence *or absence* of any particular item in a transaction, from the 20 or 50 most frequently

Figure 7. Illustration of the recursive combination of the QUEST database at 6 levels. At every level, five networks are combined, with the exception of the last level, where the eight networks of level 4 were combined into the final BN of level 5.

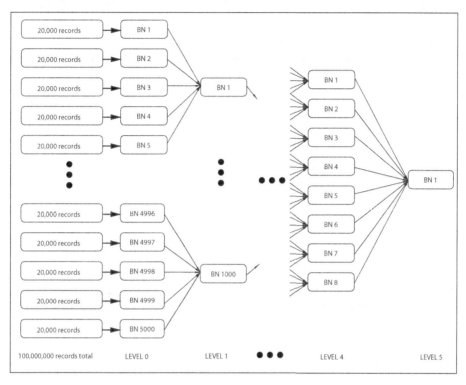

purchased items. For example, one such query may be "what is the number of transactions in the database in which a customer purchased milk and orange juice but not bread?"

Build Time

To measure the effect of database size on build time (scalability) we used the QUEST data set only, as it was the only one with a sufficient number of records. We plot build time vs. number of records in Figure 8. As we can see, NetCube is linear on the database size, and thus scalable. As we can observe from this plot, there exist a number of jumps at certain sizes, which correspond to additional time spent combining BNs from lower levels (i.e., levels closer to the data in Figure 7) to the next higher one, and occur at 100,000, 200,000, and so forth, of the records (level 0 to level 1), 500,000, 1,000,000, and so forth, of the records (level 1 to level 2). However, because the total number of nodes in the recursion tree of Figure 7 is at most twice the number of nodes at level 0, the overall build time is also linear in the database size.

Each database chunk can be processed in parallel, and the merging of the BNs can also be done in parallel across the same recursion depth. Thus, our method is parallelizable in a straightforward manner. Parallelization over a cluster of workstations scales linearly, making the generation of a database of 200 million transactions a matter of hours on a modest cluster of 10 workstations, as shown in Figure 8.

We note here that our attempts to create a single BN by using the straightforward *BuildFrom-MemoryUsingData*() algorithm on the entire QUEST database (for comparison purposes) were unsuccessful for very large problems of size 100 million records or more; the algorithm did not terminate after 4 days and had to be manually aborted. This underscores the usefulness of using our recursive combination procedure (*BuildFromDisk*() procedure) for any kind of practical application that involves very large databases.

Compression

In this set of experiments, we compare the size of our representation to that of compressed bitmaps and sampling by 10%, also compressed. Compressing the bitmaps of each of our databases produced an approximate 7:1 compression ratio for the synthetic QUEST databases and a 3.8:1 ratio for the real-world data. Compressing the sampled database predictably produces linear compression with respect to compressed bitmaps. In contrast, the NetCube approach typically produced compression ratios of 85:1 to 1,211,477:1 for synthetic data, and 1,800:1 or more for real data. The compression ratios and BN sizes are shown in Table 1 and are also plotted in Figure 9. The price for such a high compression performance is the fact that it is lossy. However, if the user can tolerate a certain amount of error (see below),

Figure 8. Build time for the QUEST data set increases approximately linearly with the number of records in the database. Parallelization over a number of workstation scales the build time down linearly.

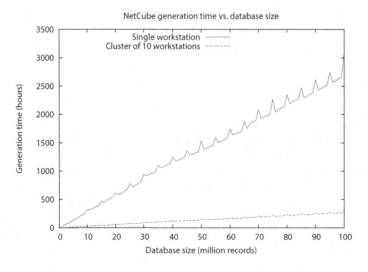

Figure 9. Comparison of the size of the compressed database using bitmaps, sampling by 10%, and NetCubes. The difference between gzip *and* bzip2 *is small (see Table 1), so only the best of the two (*bzip2*) is shown here.*

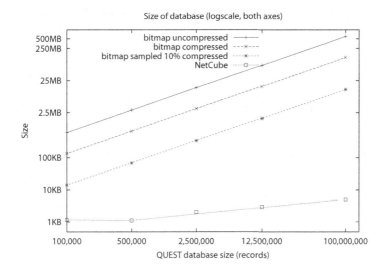

then it may be the method of choice for the data analyst, because its space requirements are modest and has the inherent advantage of visualization.

Note that the network produced from real data, corresponding to one week of transactions, occupies only 4 KB. If we are allowed to make the conservative assumption that the network from any given week is 10 times this one (40 KB), and the assumption that doubling the database size doubles the size of the resulting network (even though our experiments indicate that it might not grow at that rate but a much smaller one), then a NetCube makes it possible to fit 20 billion transactions in the memory of a regular workstation with 256 MB of main memory, corresponding to more than 100 years of transactions at this rate, effectively spanning the lifetime of most businesses.

Query Time

We used a workstation with 128 MB of physical memory for our query time experiments. Running our set of queries on the bitmaps we noticed a slowdown for the larger QUEST databases whose bitmap cannot fit into main memory. This happens because the bitmap system had to use part of the virtual memory system which resides on the disk (thrashing). An important observation we can make here is that although bitmap compression will temporarily alleviate this problem, a database of more than 4.5 times our largest one would again force the bitmap method into the same thrashing behavior (note the compression ratio 4.5:1 for bitmaps in Table 1). A database of such a problematic size would not be unusual in today's real-world problems.

We plot query times in Figure 10. As we can see in general query times are modest except in the case of the NetCube at levels 0 and 1, and compressed bitmaps. Most of the time for queries on bitmaps is used for loading the bitmap into memory, and this can only become worse as the size of the database grows since the bitmap size grows linearly. The NetCube at levels 0 and 1 does poorly due to the large number of BN models it needs to query.

Figure 11 depicts the performance of querying using the NetCube as a function of the level that we use to answer the query. For example, using only a level 1 NetCube for a QUEST query would use 1,000 BNs at that level each being a representative of 100,000 records in the database. As was noted above, using a low level incurs a large performance penalty due to the large number of BNs that we need to use inference on in order to answer the query. This is especially dramatic in the case of level 0, where 5,000 BNs need to be queried. On the other end of the spectrum, a single BN used in level 5 is not ideal either, because it is significantly more complex (densely connected) and thus a query takes more time. As Figure 11 suggests, the ideal level to use in this case is 4, which represents an interesting balance between the number of BN models and their complexity.

Table 1. Comparison of compression ratios for various databases used for the experiments. The first rows correspond to the QUEST-generated databases, while the last one corresponds to real data obtained from an anonymous retailer. The sampling figures refer to 10% sampling and after bzip2 *compression. For the NetCube, the trend of compression ratios that are increasing with database size is due to increasing benefits from using an approximately fixed-sized probabilistic model of a domain in place of data drawn from it.*

Database	Records	Bitmap size (byte)	compression rations (before:after)				
			gzip	bzip2	Sample 10% & bzip2	NetCube	
QUEST	20,000	125,009	4.2:1	4.4:1	40:1	85:1 (1,469 bytes)
	100,000	625,010	4.3:1	4.5:1	42:1	523:1 (1,195bytes)
	500,000	3,125,010	4.4:1	4.5:1	43:1	2,741:1 (1,140 bytes)
	2,500,000	15,625,011	4.4:1	4.5:1	43:1	7,508:1 (2,081bytes)
	12,500,000	78,125,012	4.0:1	4.5:1	44:1	26,050:1 (2,999 bytes)
	100,000,000	625,000,013	4.4:1	4.5:1	45:1	1,211,477:1 (5,145 bytes)
Anonymous retailer	3,261,809	8,154,540	3.8:1	3.8:1	37:1	1889:1 (4,317 bytes)

Figure 10. Average query times for the QUEST data set as a function of the number of variables in a query

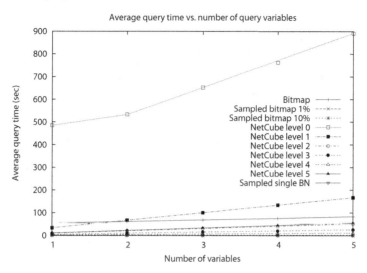

Figure 11. Average query times for the QUEST data set as a function of the recursion level that was used to answer queries

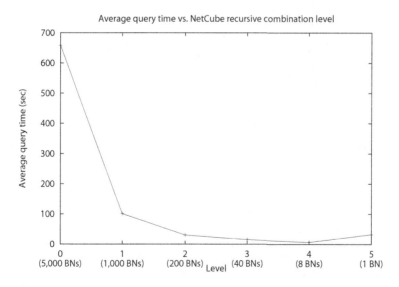

Query Accuracy

We conducted an assessment of the query accuracy using a set of 10,000 random queries containing up to 5 variables (only 300 queries were used for "NetCube level 0" and 1,000 queries for "NetCube level 1" due to large running times). Because relative error becomes artificially large for queries of very little support even when the count difference is not very large, we used queries that had support of 10,000 records or more. Apart from artificially weighing the error rate, queries of very small support are arguably "uninteresting" or can be due to spurious factors. Such treatment is consistent with other approaches in the literature (e.g., Beyer and Ramakrishnan, 1999). Note that our minimum support is not a percent of the entire database; this means that our assessment applies to cases where the user is looking for subtle events even as the database size increases. We used 10,000 as the cutoff for the support of these subtle events, but more research must be done to determine this threshold of significance.

To better understand the effect that the chunk size has on the query accuracy, we compared against another approach, namely sampling 20,000 records from the QUEST database (equal to the number of records used in level 0 of the recursive combination depicted in Figure 7) and producing a single Bayesian network from those. To answer a query using this method we use only the resulting network as our estimate of the joint PDF. This is called "sampled single BN" in the results of Figure 12.

In Table 2 we list the percentage of queries that achieve a 95% accuracy or more, for each method. From the table we see that the NetCube does not achieve a good accuracy when using levels greater than 0. That is to be expected given the levels of compression that are achievable. The actual error distribution is shown in detail in Figure 12. As we can see i this graph, there is significant mass at error levels less than 50%. We also notice that the NetCube at level 0, as well as the sampled single BN, exhibit an increase in errors at around 200%, meaning that they return double the actual count of records of the database. Both of these approaches essentially use 20,000 records per model (answering a query using a NetCube at level 0 corresponds to averaging over all level 0 BN models, each constructed from 20,000 records). Using higher levels of the NetCube alleviates this particular behavior, and is consistent with the fact that they take into account a larger number of records when creating the model, perhaps discounting certain transient effects which might be present when using 20,000 records only. Further investigation and a detailed analysis of phenomena of using different database chunk sizes and datasets that contain transient changes in the distribution or slow "drifting" of the distribution is the subject of future work.

Visualization

As an additional benefit of NetCube, we can visualize the significant associations contained in the database. For example, in Figure 13 we show the BN produced from real data corresponding to a week of activity of the 20 most frequently purchased items at a large anonymous retailer. We also show in Figure 14 the network produced at level 5 (top level) using the 50 most frequently used attributes of the QUEST data set. The advantage of the graphical representation of the BN, that our approach generates, is that it can be used to

Figure 12. Error distribution for different approaches

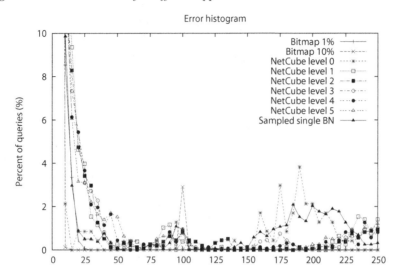

Table 2. Percent of queries for which the accuracy is at least 95%

Method	95-percentile of query accuracy (%)
Bitmap	100
Sampled bitmap 10%	95
Sampled bitmap 01%	88
NetCube level 0	70
NetCube level 1	33
NetCube level 2	33
NetCube level 3	33
NetCube level 4	33
NetCube level 5	32
Sampled single BN	56

clearly depict variables that are the most influential to the ones that the analyst might be examining. Moreover, the conditional probability tables will give our analyst the exact nature and strength of these influences. Therefore our approach fits well with the data mining procedure and can save the analyst time that would be otherwise spent on exploration, drill-down analysis, and so forth, of the customer database.

Summary

In this chapter, we presented NetCube, an approach for answering count queries approximately and fast. To accomplish that, NetCube constructs a Bayesian network model of the database in a preprocessing phase, and uses it to answer count queries approximately without accessing the database. In summary, the benefits of NetCube are:

Figure 13. Bayesian network produced from real data obtained from a large anonymous retailer. For confidentiality reasons, we have anonymized the names of the products that are displayed in the graph.

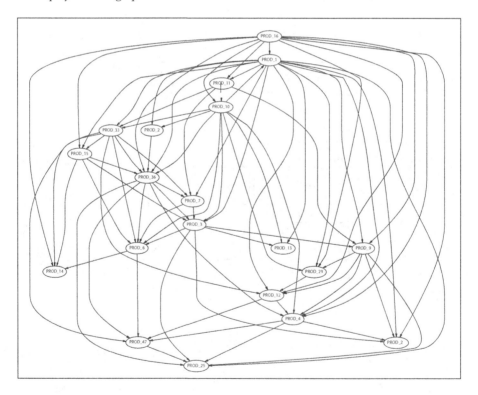

Figure 14. The final Bayesian network produced at level 5 from the QUEST data set

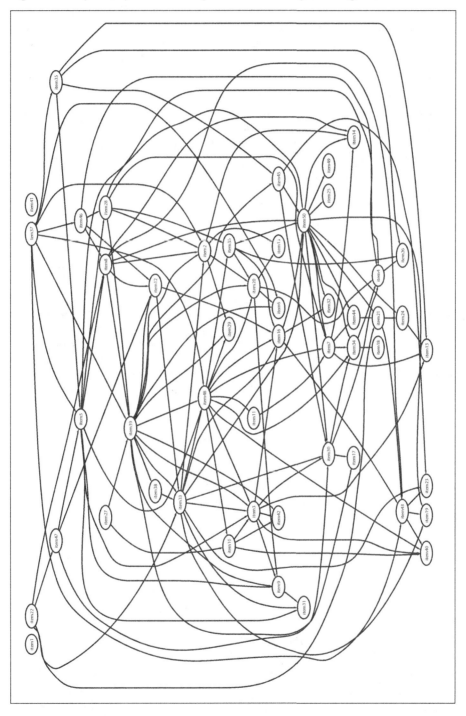

- **Small space:** The resulting BN takes up a very small fraction of the space used for the database. We produced greater than 1800:1 compression ratios on real data.

- **Scalability:** We can handle databases of arbitrarily large number of records; the method's preprocessing time scales linearly with the size of the database. Moreover, it is parallelizable with a straightforward parallel implementation.

- **Query time:** The method can answer arbitrary queries in a short time when used appropriately, that is, a few seconds for a NetCube of level 4.

- **Accuracy:** The method has reasonable accuracy when using low levels (closer to the data) to answer queries. More research is needed for effective error reduction when higher level, recursively combined BN models are used.

- **Suitability to data mining:** The representation that is used by the algorithm, namely Bayesian networks, are an excellent method for visually eliciting the most relevant causes of a quantity of interest and are a natural method to support data mining.

Acknowledgment

Dr. Faloutsos's material is based upon work supported by the National Science Foundation under Grants No. DMS-9873442, IIS-9817496, IIS-9910606, IIS-9988876, LIS 9720374, IIS-0083148, and IIS-0113089, and by the Defense Advanced Research Projects Agency under Contracts No. N66001-97-C-8517 and N66001-00-1-8936. Additional funding was provided by donations from Intel. Any opinions, findings, and conclusions or recommendations expressed in this material are those of the author(s) and do not necessarily reflect the views of the National Science Foundation, DARPA, or other funding parties.

Dr. Thrun's research is sponsored by the National Science Foundation (CAREER grant number IIS-9876136 and regular grant number IIS-9877033), and by DARPA-ATO via TACOM (contract number DAAE07-98-C-L032), which is gratefully acknowledged. The views and conclusions contained in this document are those of the author and should not be interpreted as necessarily representing official policies or endorsements, either expressed or implied, of the United States Government or any of the sponsoring institutions.

References

Barbará, D. (1998). *Quasi-cubes: A space-efficient way to support approximate multidimensional databases* (Tech. Rep.). George Mason University, ISE Department.

Beyer, K., & Ramakrishnan, R. (1999). Bottom-up computation of sparse and Iceberg CUBEs. In *Proceedings of the 25th VLDB Conference* (pp. 359-370).

Buntine, W. (1993). Learning classification trees. In D.J. Hand (Ed.), *Artificial intelligence frontiers in statistics* (pp. 182-201). London: Chapman & Hall.

Casella, G., & Berger, R. (1990). *Statistical inference*. Pacific Grove, CA: Brooks/Cole (Wadsworth).

Chan, C.-Y., & Ioannidis, Y. (1999). Hierarchical cubes for range-sum queries. In *Proceedings of the 25th VLDB Conference* (pp. 675-686). Morgan Kaufmann.

Chickering, D. (1996). Learning equivalence classes of Bayesian-network structures. In *Proceedings of the Twelfth Conference in Artificial Intelligence*. Portland, OR: Morgan Kaufmann.

Chickering, D. (2002, November). Optimal structure identification with greedy search. *Journal of Machine Learning Research*, *3*, 507-554.

Chow, C.K., & Liu, C.N. (1968). Approximating discrete probability distributions with dependence trees. *IEEE Transactions on Information Theory*, *14*, 462-467.

Cooper, G.F., & Herskovits, E.H. (1992). A Bayesian method for the induction of probabilistic networks from data. *Machine Learning*, *9*, 309-347.

Fung, R., & Chang, K.C. (1989). Weighting and integrating evidence for stochastic simulation in Bayesian networks. In L. Kanal, T. Levitt, & J. Lemmer (Eds.), *Uncertainty in artificial intelligence*. North-Holland: Elsevier Science Publishers B.V.

Getoor, L., Taskar, B., & Koller, D. (2001). Selectivity estimation using probabilistic relational models. In *Proceedings of the ACM SIGMOD Conference* (pp. 461-472).

Gray, J., Bosworth, A., Layman, A., & Pirahesh, H. (1996). Data cube: A relational aggregation operator generalizing group-by, cross-tab, and sub-totals. In *Proceedings of the International Conference on Data Engineering* (pp. 152-159).

Harinarayan, V., Rajaraman, A., & Ullman, J.D. (1996). Implementing data cubes efficiently. In *Proceedings of the ACM SIGMOD Conference* (pp. 205-216).

Heckerman, D. (1995, March). *A tutorial on learning with Bayesian networks* (Tech. Rep. No. MSR-TR- 95-06). Microsoft Research, Advanced Technology Division.

Heckerman, D., & Geiger, D. (1995, November). *Likelihoods and parameter priors for Bayesian networks* (Tech. Rep. No. MSR-TR-95-54). Redmond, WA: Microsoft Research.

Heckerman, D., Geiger, D., & Chickering, D.M. (1995). Learning Bayesian networks: The combination of knowledge and statistical data. *Machine Learning*, *20*, 197-243.

Henrion, M. (1988). Propagation of uncertainty by probabilistic logic sampling in Bayesian networks. In J.F. Lemmer & L.N. Kanal (Eds.), *Uncertainty in artificial intelligence 2*. North-Holland: Elsevier Science Publishers B.V.

Huang, C., & Darwiche, A. (1994). Inference in belief networks: A procedural guide. *International Journal of Approximate Reasoning*, *11*, 1-158.

Ioannidis, Y., & Poosala, V. (1999). Histogram-based approximation of set-valued query answers. In *Proceedings of the 25th VLDB Conference* (pp. 174-185).

Johnson, T. (1999). Performance measurements of compressed bitmap indices. In *Proceedings of the 25th VLDB Conference* (pp. 278-289).

Kass, R., & Raftery, A. (1995). Bayes factors. *Journal of the American Statistical Association*, *90*, 773-795.

Kass, R., Tierney, L., & Kadane, J. (1988). Asymptotics in Bayesian computations. In J. Bernardo, M. DeGroot, D. Lindley, & A. Smith (Eds.), *Bayesian statistics 3* (pp. 261-278). Oxford University Press.

Larranaga, P., Poza, M., Yurramendi, Y., Murga, R.H., & Kuijpers, C.M.H. (1996). Structure learning of Bayesian networks by genetic algorithms: A performance analysis of control parameters. *IEEE Journal on Pattern Analysis and Machine Intelligence (PAMI), 18*(9), 912-926.

Lee, J.-H., Kim, D.-H., & Chung, C.-W. (1999). Multi-dimensional selectivity estimation using compressed histogram information. In *Proceedings of the ACM SIGMOD Conference* (pp. 205-214).

Meek, C. (1997). *Graphical models: Selecting causal and statistical models*. Doctoral thesis, Carnegie Mellon University, Department of Philosophy.

Monti, S., & Cooper, G. (1998). Learning hybrid Bayesian networks from data. In M. Jordan (Ed.), *Learning and inference in graphical models*. Cambridge MA: MIT Press.

Pearl, J. (1997). *Probabilistic reasoning in intelligent systems: Networks of plausible inference* (2nd ed.). San Francisco CA: Morgan Kaufmann.

Rebane, G., & Pearl, J. (1989). The recovery of causal poly-trees from statistical data. In L.N. Kanal, T.S. Levitt, & J.F. Lemmer (Eds.), *Uncertainty in artificial intelligence 3* (pp. 222-228). North-Holland: Elsevier Science Publishers B.V.

Rissanen, J. (1987). Stochastic complexity (with discussion). *Journal of the Royal Statistical Society, Series B, 49*, 223-239 and 253-265.

Russell, S., & Norvig, P. (2002). *Artificial intelligence: A modern approach* (2nd ed.). Prentice Hall.

Schachter, R.D., & Peot, M.A. (1989). Simulation approaches to general probabilistic inference on belief networks. In M. Henrion, R.D. Schachter, L.N. Konal & J.F. Lemmer (Eds.), *Proceedings of the Uncertainty in Artificial Intelligence (UAI) Conference* (pp. 221-234). North-Holland: Elsevier Science Publishers B.V.

Schwartz, G. (1978). Estimating the dimension of a model. *Annals of Statistics, 6*, 461-464.

Spiegelhalter, D., & Lauritzen, S. (1990). Sequential updating of conditional probabilities on directed graphical structures. *Networks, 20*, 579-605.

Vitter, J., & Wang, M. (1999). Approximate computation of multidimensional aggregates of sparse data using wavelets. In *Proceedings of the ACM SIGMOD Conference* (pp. 193-204).

Wu, M.-C. (1999). Query optimization for selections using bitmaps. In *Proceedings of the 25th VLDB Conference* (pp. 227-238).

Endnotes

[1]   The Gamma function is defined as $\Gamma(x) = \int_0^{+\infty} e^{-t} t^{x-1} \mathrm{d}t$. For the case where x is a non-negative integer, $\Gamma(x + 1) = x!$.

[2]   Probabilistic inference is a generalization of logical inference—given a BN, it computes the probability of the truth of a compound predicate (query) rather than a true/false value.

[3]   For confidentiality reasons, we cannot reveal the name of the retailer or the products involved.

[4]   http://www.almaden.ibm.com/cs/quest/

Chapter V

Applications of Bayesian Networks in Reliability Analysis

Helge Langseth, Norwegian University of Science and Technology, Norway

Luigi Portinale, University of Eastern Piedmont, Italy

Abstract

Over the last decade, Bayesian networks (BNs) have become a popular tool for modeling many kinds of statistical problems. In this chapter we will discuss the properties of the modeling framework that make BNs particularly well suited for reliability applications. This discussion is closely linked to the analysis of a real-world example.

Introduction

A typical task for the reliability analyst is to give inputs to a decision problem. An example can be to examine the effect that environmental conditions have on a component's time to failure, and give this as input to a maintenance optimization problem. As the quantities in such studies are uncertain or due to random fluctuations, the end result should be a statistical model describing a set of random variables. This model must be mathematically sound, and at the same time easy to understand for the decision maker. Furthermore, the model must be represented such that the quantities we are interested in can be calculated efficiently. In a statistical setting, the numbers we would like to find are either conditional probabilities (e.g., the probability that a component will survive for more than one year in a given environment), or deduced numbers (for instance, the expected life-length of the component).

All these requirements have led to an increased focus among reliability analysts on flexible modeling frameworks like Bayesian network (BN) models. A current research-trend is to compare classical reliability formalisms to BNs, and it has been shown that BNs have significant advantages over the traditional frameworks, partly because BNs are easy to use in interaction with domain experts in the reliability field (Sigurdsson, Walls, & Quigley, 2001). The history of BNs in reliability can (at least) be traced back to Barlow (1988) and Almond (1992).

We see a partiality to discrete variables in the BN community, mainly due to the technicalities of the calculation scheme (see, for example, Jensen, (2001)). We note that the BNs' applicability in reliability analysis would be enormously limited if one would only consider discrete variables, and we will therefore not limit our attention in this way, but rather embrace models containing both continuous as well as discrete variables. (See Moral, Rumi, and Salmeron (2001) and Gilks, Richardson, and Spiegelhalter (1996) for two methods of handling continuous distributions in BNs.)

In this chapter, we will consider applications for BNs in reliability, and discover some of the most prominent reasons for the increasing popularity of BN models in that field of science. The chapter is organized as follows: We start by giving the basics of the BN framework, then we consider BN modeling. Next we analyze the reliability of a real-life system using a BN. Finally, we offer some conclusions.

Bayesian Networks

A Bayesian Network (Cowell, Dawid, Lauritzen, & Spiegelhalter, 1999; Jensen, 2001; Pearl, 1988) is a compact representation of a multivariate statistical distribution function. A BN encodes the probability density function governing a set of n random variables $\mathbf{X} = (X_1, \ldots, X_n)$ by specifying a set of conditional independence statements together with a set of conditional probability functions (CPFs). More specifically, a BN consists of a qualitative part, a *directed acyclic graph* where the nodes mirror the random variables, and a quantitative part, the set of CPFs. An example of a BN over the variables $\mathbf{X} = (X_1, \ldots, X_5)$ is shown in Figure 1. Only the qualitative part is given.

The driving force when making BN models is the set of *conditional independence* statements the model encodes. We will use the notation $\mathbf{X} \perp\!\!\!\perp \mathbf{Y} \mid \mathbf{Z}$ to denote that the random variables in the two sets $\mathbf{X}$ and $\mathbf{Y}$ are conditionally independent given the variables in $\mathbf{Z}$. If $\mathbf{Z}$ is the empty set, we simply write $\mathbf{X} \perp\!\!\!\perp \mathbf{Y}$ to denote that the sets $\mathbf{X}$ and $\mathbf{Y}$ are marginally independent. We use $\mathbf{X} \not\perp\!\!\!\perp \mathbf{Y} \mid \mathbf{Z}$ to make explicit that $\mathbf{X}$ and $\mathbf{Y}$ are conditionally *dependent* given $\mathbf{Z}$.

The qualitative part of the BN is used to encode the conditional independence statements, but before we present the mathematical properties of the BN structure, we need some notation: We call the nodes with outgoing edges pointing into a specific node the *parents* of that node, and say that X_j is a *descendant* of X_i if and only if there exists a directed path from X_i to X_j in the graph. In Figure 1, X_1 and X_2 are the parents of X_3, written pa$(X_3) = \{X_1, X_2\}$ for short. Furthermore, pa $(X_4) = \{X_3\}$ and because there are no directed paths from X_4 to any of the other nodes, the descendants of X_4 are given by the empty set and, accordingly, its nondescendants are $\{X_1, X_2, X_3, X_5\}$. The edges of the graph represent the assertion that a variable is conditionally independent of its nondescendants in the graph given its parents in the same graph. The graph in Figure 1 does, for instance, assert that for all distributions compatible with it, we have that X_4 is conditionally independent of $\{X_1, X_2, X_5\}$ when conditioned on $\{X_3\}$, $X_4 \perp\!\!\!\perp \{X_1, X_2, X_5\} \mid X_3$. Another example is obtained by looking at X_1: pa$(X_1) = \varnothing$, and the descendants of X_1 are $\{X_3, X_4, X_5\}$, so its only nondescendant is X_2. This gives us that $X_1 \perp\!\!\!\perp X_2$ in this model.

All conditional independence statements can be read off a BN structure by using the rules of *d-separation* (Pearl, 1988). The general analysis of d-separation centers around the three categories of network fragments shown in Figure 2: The *serial*, the *converging*, and the *diverging* connection. We will now look at examples where each of these three types of connections are given meaning in the context of reliability analysis.

Let X_1 denote the *planned* preventive maintenance (PM) program for a given component, let X_2 be the *implemented* PM, and X_3 the life-length of the component. To model the interplay between the three quantities, we want to encode conditional independence statements in a model s.t. If we do not know the implemented PM program, then the planned PM can tell us something about the life-length of the component. However, as soon as we learn about the *implemented* PM program, the *plans* are irrelevant for the life-length. This is exactly the implications of the serial connection (Figure 2(a)), which encodes that $X_1 \perp\!\!\!\perp X_3 \mid X_2$, but $X_1 \not\perp\!\!\!\perp X_3$, marginally.

Figure 1. An example BN over the nodes $\{X_1, \ldots, X_5\}$. Only the qualitative part of the BN is shown.

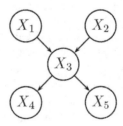

Next, let us look at the quality of the production from an assembly line. The three random variables we will consider are the quality of the first item that was produced at this line (Y_1), the quality of the second item (Y_3), and a measure of how well the assembly line operates overall (Y_2). Now, if Y_2 is unknown to us, information about Y_1 being good (bad) would make us infer that the quality of the line as such (Y_2) was good (bad) as well, and finally that Y_3 therefore would be good (bad) too. Thus, $Y_1 \not\perp\!\!\!\perp Y_3$. On the other hand, if the quality of the production line is known, the quality of each produced item may be seen as independent of each other. Figure 2(b), the diverging connection, dictates these properties: $Y_1 \perp\!\!\!\perp Y_3 \mid Y_2$, but $Y_1 \not\perp\!\!\!\perp Y_3$, marginally. Note that parts (a) and (b) in Figure 2 in principle encode the same conditional independence statements. However, if we look at the network fragments as *causal models* (Pearl, 2000), the two are obviously different.

Finally, we consider again the assembly line, and let Z_1 be the quality of an assembly line, Z_3 the environmental conditions of the production (temperature, humidity, etc.), and Z_2 the quality of a product coming from the assembly line. The quality of the assembly line is a priori independent of the environmental conditions; however, as soon as we observe the quality of the product, we can make inference regarding the quality of the line from what is known about the environmental conditions. If, for instance, the environment is poor when the quality of the product is good, one would assume that the quality of the line is favorable as well. The converging connection in part (c) encodes these properties, as we have $Z_1 \perp\!\!\!\perp Z_3$, but $Z_1 \not\perp\!\!\!\perp Z_3 \mid Z_2$.

When it comes to the quantitative part, we will use $f(\mathbf{x} \mid \mathbf{y})$ to denote the CPF of $\mathbf{x}$ given $\mathbf{y}$. The same notation is used whether $\mathbf{x}$ is a vector of discrete or continuous (or mixed) variables. We will sometimes call $f(\mathbf{x} \mid \mathbf{y})$ a CPF even if $\mathbf{y}$ is empty, but will use $f(\mathbf{x})$ as a shortcut for $f(\mathbf{x} \mid \varnothing)$.

Now, each variable is described by the CPF of that variable *given its parents* in the graph, that is, the collection of CPFs $\{f(x_i \mid \mathrm{pa}\,(x_i))\}_{i=1}^{n}$. The underlying assumptions of conditional independence encoded in the graph allow us to calculate the joint probability function as:

Figure 2. Three small network fragments describing different structural situations: (a) serial, (b) diverging, and (c) converging

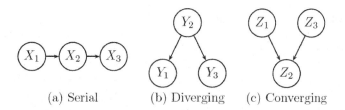

(a) Serial   (b) Diverging   (c) Converging

$$f(x_1, \ldots, x_n) = \prod_{i=1}^{n} f(x_i | \mathrm{pa}(x_i)) \qquad\qquad (1)$$

and this is in fact the main point when working with BNs: assume that a distribution function $f(x_1, \ldots, x_n)$ factorizes according to Eq. 1. This defines the parent set of each X_i, which in turn defines the graph, and from the graph we can read off the conditional independence statements encoded in the model. Hence, the graphical representation is the bridging of the gap between the (high level) conditional independence statements we want to encode in the model and the (low level) constraints this enforces on the CPF. To fully specify the set of CPFs, we must (i) select parametric families for each $f(x_i | \mathrm{pa}(x_i))$, and (ii) determine values for all parameters of each CPF. Alternatively, we can make nonparametric statements regarding $f(x_i | \mathrm{pa}(x_i))$.

Building BN Models

When we want to build a BN, we rely on two sources of information: Input from domain experts and statistical data. In the reliability community, most applications are built in interaction with domain experts. In this section, we will therefore briefly describe the basics when building BN models based on elicitation of domain experts. Building BNs from expert input can be a difficult and time consuming task. This is typically an assignment given to a group of specialists. A BN expert guides the model building, asks relevant questions, and explains the assumptions that are encoded in the model to the rest of the group. The domain experts, on the other hand, supply their knowledge to the BN expert in a structured fashion. In our experience, it will pay off to start the model building by familiarization. The BN expert should study the domain, and the reliability analysts require basic knowledge about BNs. As soon as this is established, model building will proceed through a number of phases:

0. **Decide what to model:** Select the boundary for what to include in the model, and what to leave aside.

1. **Defining variables:** Select the important variables in the model. The *range* of the continuous variables and the *states* of the discrete variables are also determined at this point.

2. **The qualitative part:** Next, we define the graphical structure that connects the variables. In this phase, it can be beneficial to consider the edges in the graph as *causal*, but the trained domain expert may also be confident about conditional dependencies/ independencies to include in the model. Domain experts can often be very eager to incorporate impractically many links in the structure in an attempt to "get it right." The BN expert's task in this setting is to balance the model's complexity with the modeling assumptions the domain experts are willing to accept. Often, a post processing of the structure may reveal void edges (e.g., those creating triangles in the graph (Abramson, Brown, Edwards, Murphy, & Winkler, 1996)).

3. **The quantitative part:** To define the quantitative part, one must select distributional

families for all variables and fix parameters to specify the distributions. If the BN structure has not been carefully elicited (and pruned) this may be a formidable task. Luckily, the consistency problems common when eliciting large probability distribution functions are tackled by a "divide-and-conquer" strategy here. If each CPF $f(x_i \mid$ pa $(x_i))$ is defined consistently, then this implies global consistency as well (Charniak, 1991). To elicit the quantitative part from experts, one must acquire all CPFs $\{f(x_i \mid$ pa $(x_i))\}_{i=1}^{n}$ in Eq. 1, and once again the causal interpretation can come in as a handy tool. Alternatively, the expert can supply a mix of both marginal and conditional distributions, which can then be glued together by the IPFP algorithm (Whittaker, 1990).

4. **Verification:** Verification should be performed both through sensitivity analysis and by testing how the model behaves when analyzing well-known scenarios. Typically, this step gives need for refinement and redefinition of the model, and this is repeated until the work put into improving the model does not lead to substantial benefits. As pointed out by, for example, Druzdzel and van der Gaag (2000), the sensitivity with respect to BN structure is relatively large, and the graph is thus the most vital part. Sensitivity with respect to the parameters is in large dependent on the application.

Lately, some tools that are aimed at guiding the model-building have emerged. These tools attempt to enable a domain expert to build a BN without interacting with a BN expert. For instance, Skaanning (2000) describes a system that can be used to build troubleshooter systems efficiently.

Reliability Analysis with Bayesian Networks

The aim of this section is to give some ideas regarding how BNs can be used to naturally model systems that are considered in reliability analysis calculations. In particular, we will study features like:

*   Calculating the system's reliability
*   Uncertainty regarding local dependencies (i.e., probabilistic gates)
*   Multistate variables (i.e., multiple behavioral modes)
*   Uncertainty on model parameters
*   Dependence between components (e.g., introduced by a common environment)

We will discuss these issues by way of a real-world example: A simple *programmable logic controller* (PLC).

The most common technique for performing the type of calculations we will look into is called fault tree analysis (FTA). However, as we will see in this section, BNs offer more than FTAs when it comes to modeling power. We will not dwell upon FTAs here, just mention that a FTA model can be transformed into an equivalent discrete BN using quite straightforward techniques (Bobbio, Portinale, Minichino, & Ciancamerla, 2001).

System Description

We start by giving a brief description of the PLC controller. The block diagram of the system is shown in Figure 3.

The PLC system is intended to process a digital signal by means of suitable processing units. A redundancy technique is adopted in order to achieve fault tolerance; three different channels are used to process the signal, and a voter hardware device (with 2-out-of-3 majority voting), is collecting channel results to produce the output. For each channel (identified as channels A, B, and C, respectively) a *digital input unit* (DI), a *processing unit* (CPU) and a *digital output unit* (DO) are employed. The digital signal elaborated by a given channel is transmitted among the units through a special dedicated bus called IObus. This design ensures that each channel has dedicated components to avoid *common cause* failures.

Next, the reliability of the system is increased even further by introducing redundancy also at the CPU level. Each processing unit does not only relate to the digital input unit in its own channel, but it also receives a copy of the signal from the other input channels. Three buses called $TriBus_A$, $TriBus_B$ and $TriBus_C$ are used to obtain this. $IOBus_X$ of channel X delivers the signal of DI_X, the digital input of that channel, to the tribuses of other channels (i.e., to $TriBus_Y$ with $Y \neq X$). Thereby, CPU_X can read the signal from other input channels using $TriBus_X$. In case there are conflicts between the tree signals obtained by a processing unit, it uses a majority voting to determine the input signal.

Figure 3. The PLC controller

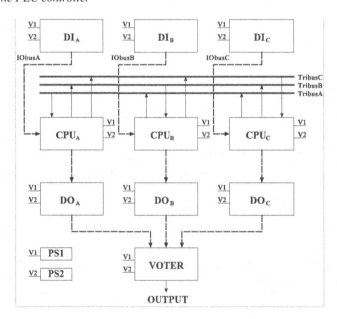

Finally, the system is completed by a redundancy on the power supply system as two independent power supply units (PS_1 and PS_2) are connected to the components. Failure of only one PS unit is (in principle) not critical for the system's operation. In the analysis we consider the event that the controller fails to provide the correct control function. This happens if the power supply, the voter, or at least two of the three channels fail.

The Bayesian Network Model

In this section we follow the outline given in Section 3 to build a BN model of the controller:

Step 0: Decide What to Model

Only the physical system is modeled in this example. A more detailed model may try to capture, for example, the effect that corrective maintenance, functional testing, and operating conditions have on the availability of the system, but this is not considered here.

Step 1: Defining Variables

Each physical component's state is modeled by a dedicated random variable. It also seems reasonable to create a variable PLC, which models the status of the whole controller. Each variable will have two states, and we use "F" for "Failed," and "W" for "Working."

Step 2: The Qualitative Part

As none of the physical components influence any of the others, they should be marginally independent. All components influence the status of the PLC, as any component failure would increase the probability of system failure. Furthermore, knowing the system's state would make the components conditionally dependent. Hence, at this stage of the modeling we assume that a *converging structure* (Figure 2(c)) is the best modeling option. The resulting BN structure is shown in Figure 4.

Step 3: The Quantitative Part

The domain experts assumed that all the components had constant failure rates (as reported in Table 1), and we used that to allocate probabilities to the corresponding nodes. The probability for a component being failed at a given mission time t is calculated as follows: Consider a generic component C with failure rate λ_c. Then, $P(C = F) = 1 - e^{-\lambda_c t}$ at any given time t.

Figure 4. The first attempt to describe the system using a Bayesian network. Note the lack of interpretability, and also the (way too) large parent set of the node **PLC***.*

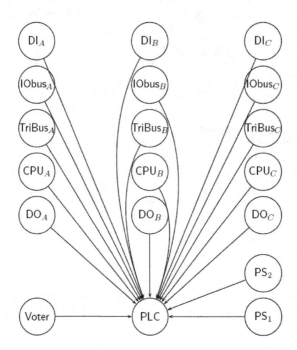

A more difficult task is to determine the CPF of **PLC**. The BN structure has not made the internal structure of the example system explicit, and we have not been able to break the system model down into smaller parts. As usual we have to determine the probability distribution of the variable (**PLC**, in this case) given all possible combinations of the node's parents, but due to the lack of modularity, we have a total of $2^{18}=262\ 144$ different numbers to elicit to define this CPF. Obviously, this is too much to take on, even if all numbers are either 0 or 1. It therefore turns out to be difficult to create a BN using the structure we selected in Step 2 above.

To overcome this problem, the most common method when working with such reliability problems is to use the bottom-up principle, often combined with a top-down approach. The bottom-up principle (closely related to the concept "*divorcing,*" (Jensen, 2001, p. 60)) means that one looks at how components combine to define the subfunctions that make the system work. To this end, we decided to insert a number of extra variables into the model to represent these subfunctions. These nodes are introduced to simplify the modeling, to make the built-in redundancy in the controller system visible in the BN structure, and to make the model more modular. For instance, DI_A and $IObus_A$ together send the signal to CPU_A. We call this subfunction (sending the signal to CPU_A) Inp_{AA}, and introduce the node Inp_{AA} to denote whether the two components achieve that task. Hence, Inp_{AA} takes on the two states "Failed" and "Working;" whether it is working or not is determined by the status of DI_A and $IObus_A$. Inp_{AA} therefore gets these two nodes as its parents in the BN. Similarly, Inp_{AB} is introduced to control if a signal from input B reaches CPU_A (so, Inp_{AB} is monitoring the combined effort by DI_B, $IOBus_B$, and $TriBus_A$), and Inp_{AC} is introduced in the same way. We also make new variables to model the signals arriving at CPU_B and CPU_C.

Next, we introduce the variable In_A, which tells the state of the input signal received by CPU_A after majority voting (recall that each CPU will perform a 2-out-of-3 voting if there is a conflict between the signals). In_A will therefore tell how Inp_{AA}, Inp_{AB}, and Inp_{AC} work when combined. Due to the symmetry of the controller, we introduce the variables In_B and In_C in the same way.

Sig_A is introduced to model the correctness of the signal sent from CPU_A to the output card, and finally Ch_A models the dependability of the signal from channel A to the voter. Again, symmetry makes us introduce similar nodes taking care of the signals from channels B and C. Figure 5 shows the final BN structure. The new nodes all model the availability of the different substructures of the system, and we assume their statuses as given deterministically by the status of their components.

Alternatively, one could use the top-down way of thinking, and would then ask questions like "How does the PLC fail?", and use the answer ("Failure to the power supply, voter, or the signal channels") to motivate the two new nodes PS (power supply, determined by PS_1 and PS_2) and Ch (telling whether at least two of the channels work). Next, one would focus on how Ch could fail, which would give rise to Ch_A, Ch_B, Ch_C, and so forth.

Step 4: Verification

Verification did not relieve any fundamental flaws in the modeling. The model was therefore considered complete. Note that the BN is multiply connected (it has a number of undirected cycles), essentially because of the influence the physical components have on the different channels.

Basic Reliability Results

We can now evaluate the system's unreliability by computing the probability $P(PLC=F)$ in our BN. The calculated unreliability is plotted with a solid line in Figure 7 as a function of the mission time t.

Next, we consider how to analyze the criticality of the system components with respect to system failure. To this end, we should consider system failure as evidence provided to the BN. There are two main computations that can be performed:

Figure 5. A Bayesian network model describing this system. A number of "dummy" vari-ables are introduced to improve readability; only the double-lined nodes were included in the initial model. The PLC node models the status of the whole controller.

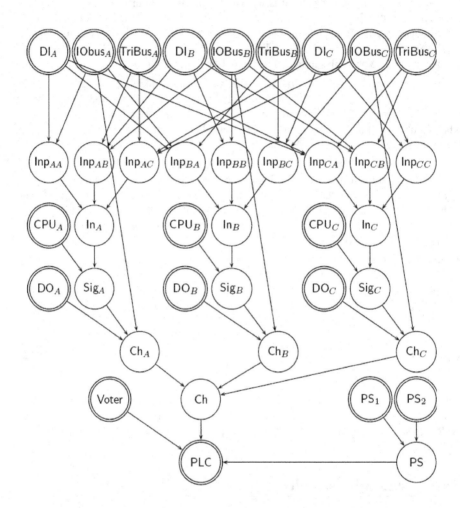

1.   The posterior probability of each single component having failed given that the system has failed

2.   The most probable configuration over the set of components given system failure

The first analysis allows one to obtain information about the criticality of each component. It is calculated by entering evidence that the top event has occurred, and the probability of each component having failed is computed. The right column of Table 1 reports these numbers computed at mission time $t=4\cdot10^5$ hours. The component criticality is obviously a more significant measure than their prior failure probability, for instance, when we want to repair the system. We notice that the processing units are the most critical components with an importance measure of about 38%.

The second kind of analysis is more sophisticated, as it calculates failure probabilities over sets of components. One can think of the calculations taking place as finding the posterior joint probability of all sets of components, given the fact that the system has failed (see Nilsson (1998) for practical algorithms).

Table 2 reports the sets of failed components that have the highest probability of failure given that the system has failed. Table 2 should be read such that the mentioned components are faulty, whereas all the others are working (e.g., out of the 262,144 possible configurations, the most probable given system failure is that two CPUs are faulty, whereas all other components work properly; the probability for this situation is about 4.5%).

Table 1. Failure rates (per hour) and component importance calculated at mission time $t=4 \cdot 10^5$ h

Component	Failure rate	Posterior prob.
IObus	$\lambda_{IO} = 2.0 10^{-9}$	0.002
Tribus	$\lambda_{Tri} = 2.0 10^{-9}$	0.002
Voter	$\lambda_{V} = 6.6 10^{-8}$	0.118
DO	$\lambda_{DO} = 2.45 10^{-7}$	0.204
DI	$\lambda_{DI} = 2.8 10^{-7}$	0.172
PS	$\lambda_{PS} = 3.37 10^{-7}$	0.176
CPU	$\lambda_{CPU} = 4.82 10^{-7}$	0.383

Table 2. Most probable posterior configurations

Components	Posterior probability
$\{CPU_A, CPU_B\}$	0.045
$\{CPU_B, CPU_C\}$	0.045
$\{CPU_A, CPU_C\}$	0.045
$\{Voter\}$	0.027
$\{CPU_A, DO_C\}$	0.022
$\{CPU_A, DO_B\}$	0.022
$\{CPU_B, DO_A\}$	0.022
$\{CPU_B, DO_C\}$	0.022
$\{CPU_C, DO_A\}$	0.022
$\{CPU_C, DO_B\}$	0.022
$\{PS_1, PS_2\}$	0.021

Coverage Factors in BNs

An important modeling improvement in redundant systems considers *coverage* factors. The coverage factor is defined as the probability that a single failure in a redundant system entails a complete system failure. This accounts for the fact that the recovery mechanism can be inaccurate, and that the redundancy therefore becomes inoperative even when only one component has failed. Coverage factors find a natural application in BNs, where we resort to defining probabilistic gates.

Figure 6 reports an excerpt of Figure 5 related to the gate labeled PS (modeling the power supply subsystem composed of the two single units PS_1 and PS_2). It shows a probabilistic AND-gate and the CPF, which models the situation. Recall that the events are binary, with values denoted by W (working) or F (failed). When using the deterministic AND-gate, PS has failed (with probability 1) when both inputs are down, and working (with probability 1) otherwise. In the probabilistic case, the power supply may be down with some probability $1-c$ even when only one input is down. Here, c is called the coverage factor, and in our case we interpret it by noting that $1-c$ gives the probability that a failure of one power supply unit destroys the whole power supply system (e.g., by short circuiting).

To show the effect of the coverage factor on the availability of the system, we introduced a coverage factor c to the gate PS. We calculated the unavailability of the system for $c=0.9$, $c=0.95$, and $c=0.99$, and give the results in Figure 7 (for a time horizon of $t=10^5$ h). For the sake of comparison, also the deterministic case (coverage factor $c=1$) is reported.

Multistate Nodes

Next, we will look at events whose behavior is best described by multistate variables. This is usually related to another modeling issue that may be quite problematic to deal with when using traditional tools in the reliability community, namely components failing in some dependent way. Consider, for instance, the case in which the power supply may induce a control logic failure when failing, for example, due to over voltage. This can be naturally modeled in a BN by connecting each power supply to the CPU nodes. This simply means that new edges are added from nodes PS_1 and PS_2 to each CPU node in the BN of Figure

Figure 6. An AND gate with coverage and the corresponding CPF

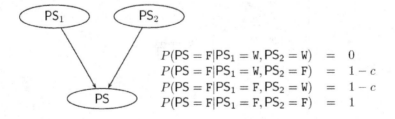

$$P(\mathrm{PS} = \mathrm{F}|\mathrm{PS}_1 = \mathrm{W}, \mathrm{PS}_2 = \mathrm{W}) = 0$$
$$P(\mathrm{PS} = \mathrm{F}|\mathrm{PS}_1 = \mathrm{W}, \mathrm{PS}_2 = \mathrm{F}) = 1 - c$$
$$P(\mathrm{PS} = \mathrm{F}|\mathrm{PS}_1 = \mathrm{F}, \mathrm{PS}_2 = \mathrm{W}) = 1 - c$$
$$P(\mathrm{PS} = \mathrm{F}|\mathrm{PS}_1 = \mathrm{F}, \mathrm{PS}_2 = \mathrm{F}) = 1$$

Figure 7. System unreliability for different coverage factors

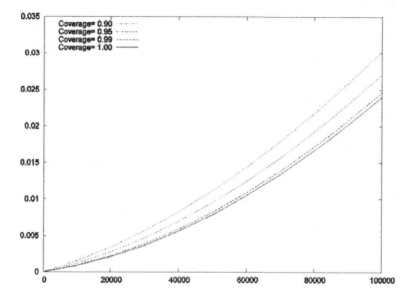

5. One can be even more precise by resorting to multistate variable modeling: Each PS_i unit ($i=1, 2$) can be modeled as having the three states *Working, Over voltage*, and *Failed*, and connected as a parent to each CPU node CPU_A, CPU_B, and CPU_C.

The CPF of each CPU is defined such that it is unaffected by the power-supply as long as it is either working or failed, but as soon as PS goes into "over voltage," we can assign a probability to the event that the CPU immediately fails as well.

This shows how a flexible combination of basic features of a BN can naturally overcome limitations of other modeling frameworks. The abnormal status of a power supply now has both a direct as well as an indirect effect on the system dependability, where the latter originates from the power supplies' (potentially) negative influence on the processing units in the system.

Note that we have introduced this extra aspect to our model without problems; in fact, only a small part of the model is changed, and this is seamlessly integrated into the overall BN.

Parameter Uncertainty

Our next example takes a closer look at parameter uncertainty. In the Bayesian setting, parameters are considered random variables, and are modeled using probability distributions. Accordingly, the system's unreliability is calculated as a weighted average over the possible parameters values, and do not reflect a single deterministic value.

To illustrate this point, we can carry out the following experiment, again focusing on the power supply nodes. The parameter we require is in this case the failure rate of a power supply, λ_{PS}. In the Bayesian setting, we may assume that Λ_{PS} is a random variable, for instance by using a Gamma-distribution: $\Lambda_{PS} \sim G(\alpha, \beta)$. It seems reasonable to assume that the hyper-parameters α and β are chosen such that Λ_{PS} gets expectation corresponding to the value given in Table 1 (i.e., $E[\Lambda_{PS}] = \alpha \cdot \beta = 3.37 \cdot 10^{-7}$). We can then set α to tune the head and tail of the distribution.

In the BN structure, each PS node gets Λ_{PS} as a new parent (see Figure 8). We must also define its CPF, and do that by insisting that $P(\text{PS}_i = F \mid \Lambda_{PS} = \lambda_{PS}) = 1 - \exp(-\lambda_{PS} \cdot t)$ for $i=1, 2$.

We can now take the parameter uncertainty into account by calculating the system's unavailability at a given mission time t from our (extended) BN. Figure 9 provides the system's unreliability under the assumption of different Gamma-distribution for the power supplies' failure rates. We notice that there is a small sensitivity in the assumed distribution. However, as the system's unavailability is essentially linear in Λ_{PS} (in particular we have that $1 - \exp(-\Lambda_{PS} \cdot t) \approx \Lambda_{PS} \cdot t$ for small values of $\Lambda_{PS} \cdot t$), the effect of the parameter uncertainty is limited in our example. A more interesting situation occurs when the parameter uncertainty induces dependence between the different components, and this is examined in Section 4.7.

Figure 8. Λ_{PS} is the failure rate of PS. It is modeled as a random variable.

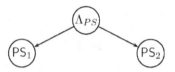

Figure 9. Unreliability for different prior distributions for Λ_{ps}

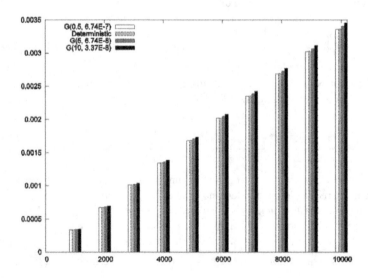

Components Sharing a Common Environment

When modeling complex coherent systems, it is quite common to assume that components can be considered independent, even when they are operating in a common environment. Several researchers have been trying to overcome this defect by explicitly modeling the correlation between components' life-lengths that the shared environment introduces. In this subsection we will elaborate on a solution to this problem described by Lindley and Singpurwalla (1986).

Consider a system of two components, where the system works if at least one of the components works. The components have life-lengths T_1 and T_2 respectively, and the system's life-length is thus given as $R = \max(T_1, T_2)$. Lindley and Singpurwalla (1986) assume that when the components are operating in a controlled laboratory environment, their life-lengths T_i have constant failure rates λ_i ($i = 1, 2$).

Next, the two components are exposed to some common environment, and this introduces a correlation between T_1 and T_2. A rough environment will lead to reduced life-lengths for both components, whereas a gentle environment would imply that the expected life-lengths of both components were increased. We use a random variable E to model the effect of the common environment. It is assumed that the effect of the environment is proportional to the failure rate, that is, $T_i | \{E = \xi\}$ is exponentially distributed with parameter $\xi \cdot \lambda_i$. In this way, a hash environment would correspond to a high value of E, whereas a friendlier environment corresponds to a smaller value of E. A correlation between T_1 and T_2 is introduced if E is not observed, whereas $T_1 \perp\!\!\!\perp T_2 | E$ (compare Figure 10(a) to Figure 2(b)). Lindley and Singpurwalla (1986) continue their modeling by assuming E to follow a Gamma distribution with known parameters, and (amongst other things) derive the marginal distribution of R when E is unobserved.

We can extend this example by assuming that we can characterize the environmental effect E by regression. That is, we presume the existence of a number of covariates $\Upsilon_1, \ldots, \Upsilon_\ell$ such that E follows a distribution with parameters defined as functions of these covariates. The corresponding model with $\ell = 2$ is shown in Figure 10(b). Finally, in Figure 10(c) we have included measurement uncertainty for the covariates. This model applies if we are not able to measure the covariates (Υ_i) themselves; only the noisy measurements (Z_i) are observable.

To exemplify the use of this model, we quantify the CPFs as follows: The covariates Υ_i must be assumed to be realizations of some distribution for this to work. Here we have no a priori information, and they are therefore allocated vague prior distributions (Gaussian distributions with expectation 0 and variance 10^6 were used). Measurements are assumed unbiased with variance 0.1, that is, $Z_i | \{\Upsilon_i = \upsilon_i\} \sim N(\upsilon_i, 0.1)$. We follow Lindley and Singpurwalla (1986) and let the environment be determined by a Gamma distribution, $E \sim \Gamma(r, \mu)$. We define the rate by $\mu = \exp(-\boldsymbol{\beta}^\mathrm{T} \upsilon)$, and assume known shape $r = 2$. $\beta_1 = 0.01$ and $\beta_2 = 0.04$ were chosen rather arbitrarily in this example. Finally, $T_i | \{E = \xi\}$ follows the exponential distribution with parameter $\xi \cdot \lambda_i$; $\lambda_1 = 3 \cdot 10^{-3}$ and $\lambda_2 = 2 \cdot 10^{-3}$ respectively. We used BUGS (Gilks, Thomas, & Spiegelhalter, 1994) to calculate $P(R > 1000 | Z_1 = 1, Z_2 = 2) = 0.29$ and $corr(T_1, T_2 | Z_1 = 1, Z_2 = 2) = 0.90$. If we fail to model the correlation between the two life-lengths, and use the model depicted in Figure 10(d), we would calculate $P(R > 1000 | Z_1 = 1, Z_2 = 2) = 0.41$.

This example highlights the importance of being able to make mathematical models that

Figure 10. (a) Two components in a parallel system have life-lengths T_1 and T_2, respectively, giving the system a life-length of $R = max(T_1, T_2)$. The random variables T_1 and T_2 are traditionally assumed independent, but when exposed to a common environment, E, dependence is introduced. (b) Covariates Υ_1 and Υ_2 are measured to infer properties of the environment. (c) The model is enhanced by introducing measurement error on the covariates. Z_1 and Z_2 denote the measured values of Υ_1 and Υ_2, respectively. (d) The model that is (implicitly) used if the common environment is neglected. See text for further details.

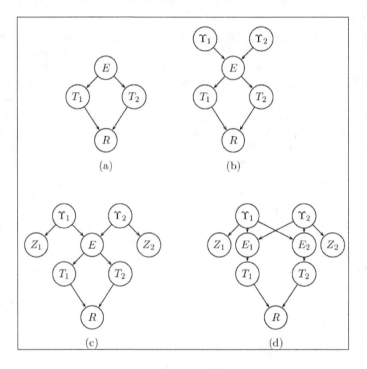

we actually believe in. BNs can be a framework to make such models, also in the context of reliability analysis.

Conclusion

In this chapter. we have considered the applicability of Bayesian networks for reliability analysis. BNs constitute a modeling framework which is particularly easy to use for interaction with domain experts, and this makes it a useful tool in practice. Furthermore, as BNs rest upon probability theory, many of the fundamental discussions obstructing other modeling frameworks are avoided. The sound mathematical formulation has been utilized to generate efficient learning methods. BNs are equipped with an efficient calculation scheme, which often makes them preferable to traditional tools like fault trees.

Many BN tools are available to the practitioners. Examples of commercial tools available online include Hugin (http://www.hugin.com/), BayesiaLab (http://www.bayesia.com/), and Netica (http://www.norsys.com/). BUGS (http://www.mrc-bsu.cam.ac.uk/bugs/) is a general-purpose modeling framework where inference is based on simulation.

Acknowledgment

The example system analyzed in Section 4 was provided by ENEA, the Italian Agency for Energy and Environment. This chapter is partly based on a paper by Langseth and Portinale (2007).

References

Abramson, B., Brown, J., Edwards, W., Murphy, A., & Winkler, R.L. (1996). Hailfinder: A Bayesian system for forecasting severe weather. *International Journal of Forecasting, 12*, 57-71.

Almond, R.G. (1992). *An extended example for testing graphical belief* (Tech. Rep. No. 6). Statistical Sciences Inc.

Barlow, R.E. (1988). Using influence diagrams. In C.A. Clarotti & D.V. Lindley (Eds.), *Accelerated life testing and experts' opinions in reliability, Proceedings of the International School of Physics "Enrico Fermi"* (course CII, pp. 145-157). North-Holland.

Bobbio, A., Portinale, L., Minichino, M., & Ciancamerla, E. (2001). Improving the analysis of dependable systems by mapping fault trees into Bayesian networks. *Reliability Engineering and System Safety, 71*(3), 249-260.

Charniak, E. (1991). Bayesian networks without tears. *AI Magazine, 12*(4), 50-63.

Cowell, R.G., Dawid, A.P., Lauritzen, S.L., & Spiegelhalter, D.J. (1999). *Probabilistic networks and expert systems*. New York: Springer-Verlag.

Druzdzel, M., & van der Gaag, L. (2000). *Building probabilistic networks: Where do the numbers come from?: A guide to the literature* (Tech. Rep. No. UU-CS-2000-20). Institute of Information & Computing Sciences, University of Utrecht, The Netherlands.

Gilks, W., Richardson, S., & Spiegelhalter, D. (1996). *Markov chain Monte Carlo in practice*. London: Chapmann & Hall.

Gilks, W., Thomas, A., & Spiegelhalter, D.J. (1994). A language and program for complex Bayesian modelling. *The Statistician, 43*, 169-178.

Jensen, F.V. (2001). *Bayesian networks and decision graphs*. New York: Springer-Verlag.

Langseth, H., & Portinale, L. (2007). Bayesian networks in reliability. *Reliability Engineering and System Safety, 92*(1), 92-108.

Lindley, D.V., & Singpurwalla, N.D. (1986). Multivariate distributions for the lifelengths ofcomponents of a system sharing a common environment. *Journal of Applied Probability, 23*, 418-431.

Moral, S., Rumi, R., & Salmeron, A. (2001). Mixtures of truncated exponentials in hybrid Bayesian networks. In *Proceedings of the Sixth European Conference on Symbolic and Quantitative Approaches to Reasoning with Uncertainty* (Vol. 2143, pp. 145-167). Berlin, Germany: Springer-Verlag.

Nilsson, D. (1998). Finding the *M* most probable configurations in probabilistic expert systems. *Statistics and Computing, 8*(2), 159-173.

Pearl, J. (1988). *Probabilistic reasoning in intelligent systems: Networks of plausible inference*. San Mateo, CA: Morgan Kaufmann.

Pearl, J. (2000). *Causality – models, reasoning, and inference*. Cambridge, UK: Cambridge University Press.

Sigurdsson, J.H., Walls, L.A., & Quigley, J.L. (2001). Bayesian belief nets for managing expert judgment and modeling reliability. *Quality and Reliability Engineering International, 17*, 181-190.

Skaanning, C. (2000). A knowledge acquisition tool for Bayesian-network troubleshooters. In *Proceedings of the Sixteenth Conference on Uncertainty in Artificial Intelligence* (pp. 549-557).

Whittaker, J. (1990). *Graphical models in applied multivariate statistics*. Chichester, UK: John Wiley & Sons.

Chapter VI

Application of Bayesian Modeling to Management Information Systems:
A Latent Scores Approach

Sumeet Gupta, National University of Singapore, Singapore

Hee-Wong Kim, National University of Singapore, Singapore

Abstract

This chapter deals with the application of Bayesian modeling as a management decision support tool for management information systems (MIS) managers. MIS managers have to deal with problems which require prediction and diagnosis for decision making. Lacking a proper tool for making informed decisions, MIS managers feel hard-pressed for a scenario analysis which can take into account the proper causal relationships existing in the real world. Bayesian modeling could be an appropriate support tool for such decision making. However, its application to decision support in MIS is different from application to other fields, as the variables in field of MIS are hypothetical. This brings in a need for Bayesian modeling at a hypothetical variable level rather than at the observed variable level. In this chapter we will study how Bayesian modeling can be used as a tool for managerial decision support in MIS. The conclusions of this chapter can also be extended to other social science researches where the variables are hypothetical in nature.

Structural equation modeling (SEM) is good for empirical validation but it is not suitable for prediction and diagnosis. Prediction and diagnosis are useful for managerial decision support and can be done using Bayesian networks. Bayesian networks, however, do not differentiate between causal and spurious relationships. The capability of SEM in empirical validation combined with the prediction and diagnosis capabilities of Bayesian modeling offers an excellent tool for managerial decision support. This study proposes the linkage of SEM to Bayesian testing, for prediction and diagnosis from an empirically validated model. We apply the proposed approach to management decision support for customer retention in a virtual community. This research helps SEM researchers in extending their models for managerial prediction and diagnosis. It benefits Bayesian researchers by providing for the application of modeling causal relationships at a latent variable level. Modeling at the latent variable level, before Bayesian testing, would help in simplifying and uncovering the situation under study, and facilitating the identification of causal relationships.

Introduction

Structural equation modeling (SEM) is a causal modeling approach which combines cause-effect information with statistical data to provide a quantitative assessment of relationships among the studied variables. If the relationships are significant, the theoretical construction is considered valid and can be used to provide guidelines for the application of the model in practice. Although SEM is good for empirical validation of theoretically based causal relationships, and to some extent for prediction also, it is not suitable for diagnosis of the situation and thus has limitations in managerial decision making. Moreover, SEM primarily models linear relationships. In case the relationships are nonlinear, the potential effect of independent variables in explaining the variance in dependent variables would not be accurately known, resulting in poor prediction and diagnosis.

These limitations of SEM can be overcome by using Bayesian networks. Bayesian networks are especially suited for prediction and diagnosis and can be trained on the same structure with new data. Moreover, Bayesian networks are suitable for modeling nonlinear relationships. They are, therefore, useful for assessing the impact of changes in the modeled situation. Bayesian networks, however, have certain limitations in causal modeling from the viewpoint of social science research. To establish causality, three criteria, namely temporal order, association, and elimination of plausible alternatives must be fulfilled (Neuman, 2003). In Bayesian modeling, the relationships are based on association (conditional independence), and to some extent temporal order, but the third criterion of elimination of plausible alternatives is not fulfilled. The result is that Bayesian networks do not differentiate between a causal and a spurious relationship. Although, the theoretically valid structural model can be forced as a Bayesian net, the Bayesian networks are not as capable as SEM for theoretical explanation (Anderson, Mackoy, Thompson, & Harrell, 2004). Another limitation of Bayesian networks from MIS research perspective is that they do not differentiate between a latent construct and its measures (observed variables).

These limitations of Bayesian networks can be overcome by using a theoretically based and empirically validated model (which is possible by using SEM) and developing the

Bayesian model at the hypothetical variable level. Therefore, this study aims to propose a causal modeling approach for management decision making by linking SEM to Bayesian modeling. We conduct our study in the context of a virtual community (VC). At the heart of the success of a VC is increased traffic and participation among customers. Customer retention in a VC is therefore critical to its success (Efraim & King, 2003). This study shows how the proposed approach can be used for identifying causal relationships and supporting MIS decision-making.

Linking SEM to Bayesian Modeling

SEM and Bayesian networks are different from each other in numerous ways (Anderson & Vastag, 2004). First, SEM is a causal modeling approach based on reasoning by cause and effect, while Bayesian networks are based on probabilistic causation (occurrence of a cause increasing the probability of an effect). Second, SEM is suitable for empirical validation of a theoretical construction at the latent variable level, while Bayesian networks are especially suited for prediction and diagnosis of any situation at the individual item (observed variable) level. Third, while Bayesian networks can be trained further on the same structure with new data, SEM is not suitable for modeling with new data as the structure may change. Moreover, unlike Bayesian networks, SEM does not support diagnosis. Despite their numerous other differences (Anderson & Vastag, 2004), the two approaches may be combined on the basis that Bayesian networks can represent causality under certain conditions, as explained later in this section.

Causal Modeling and Probabilistic Causation

Probabilistic Causation Theory

Causal modeling is an interdisciplinary field devoted to the study of methods of causal inference. According to Hume (1969), causation can be characterized as regularity of constantly conjoined pairs of events [*effect = f(cause)*] under conditions of temporal priority (a cause must precede the effect) and contiguity (a cause is temporally adjacent to an effect). Hume (1969), however, does not account for imperfect regularities and does not distinguish between a genuine causal relation and a spurious association (Anderson & Vastag, 2004). This gives rise to probabilistic causation, which characterizes the relationship between cause and effect using the tools of probability theory (Hitchcock, 2002), and is a paradigm switch from the absolute determination of an effect due to the occurrence of a cause to the occurrence of a cause increasing the probability of an effect. The underlying assumption is that incomplete knowledge of causes results in uncertain cause-effect relationships. Probabilistic causation implies that the effect is produced by specified causes (direct or known causes) and unspecified causes (indirect causes such as errors and unknown causes) (Anderson & Vastag, 2004). In other words, effect $= f$(*specified causes, unspecified causes*). This is the basis for SEM. This idea can be represented by conditional probability as $p(effect \mid cause) = p(effect \cap cause) / p(cause)$, which forms the basis for Bayesian modeling.

SEM and Bayesian networks are viewed as causal models when they satisfy the conditions of causal sufficiency, causal Markov and faithfulness conditions, and independence of specified and unspecified causes (Anderson & Vastag, 2004). The principle of common cause states that if two variables in a population are associated and neither is a cause of the other, they must share a common cause (Reichenbach, 1956). For example, if variables X and Y are related, but not causally, then they must share some (a set of) common cause(s), say Z. The justification of the causal Markov condition states that every effect variable, conditional on its direct causes, is independent of all variables that are not its causes (Spirtes, Glymour, & Schienes, 1993). This means if X does not cause Y, then $p\{X|Y \& Parents(X)\} = p\{X/\text{Parents}(X)\}$. The faithfulness condition states that probabilistic independencies are a stable result of the causal structure and not due to happenstance or specific parameter values (Anderson & Vastag, 2004). Therefore, the joint population probability distribution over a defined variable set is assumed to be stable or faithful to the underlying causal structure. A model is said to be causally sufficient if the variable set includes all relevant common causes.

A causal model may be expressed as $M = \{S, \Theta_s\}$, where S is the structure of the causal assertion of the variable set V portrayed by a directed acyclic graph (DAG) and Θ_s is a set of parameters compatible with S (Anderson & Vastag, 2004). With the encoded structure characterized as directed (two-headed arrows depicting noncausal association are not allowed) and acyclic (feedback loops such as "$A \rightarrow B \rightarrow A$" are not allowed), a DAG can be translated into a set of recursive structural equations with independent errors, which satisfies the causal Markov condition. A discrete Bayesian network is a specialization of a causal model $M = \{S, \Theta_s\}$, where the structure S implies a set of conditional probability distributions and $\Theta_s = [p\{V_1|\text{Parents}(V_1),\theta_1\}, p\{V_2|\text{Parents}(V_2),\theta_2\}, \ldots\ldots, p\{V_m|\text{Parents}(V_m),\theta_m\}]$.

Each variable has c_i discrete values or states, and each θ_i is assumed to be a collection of multinomial distributions, one for each parent configuration. The associated joint probability distribution of the network is the product of the conditional probabilities in Θ_s, $p(v_1,\ldots,v_m) = \prod_m p\{V_i|\text{Parents}(V_i),\theta_i\}$.

A Brief Overview of Bayesian Networks

A Bayesian network is used to model a domain containing uncertainty in some manner. The network consists of a qualitative part and a quantitative part. The qualitative part is a DAG consisting of nodes and arrows similar to constructs and their connectors in SEM. The nodes represent stochastic variables and arrowheads represent dependencies among the variables. The quantitative part is a set of conditional probability distributions. Thus, each node contains the states of the random variable it represents and a conditional probability table (CPT). The CPT of a node contains probabilities of the node being in a specific state, given the states of its parents.

Figure 1 represents the technology acceptance model (TAM) as a Bayesian network. Consider that the variables—perceived usefulness (PU), perceived ease of use (PEOU), and adoption intention (AI)—can take the states {low, high}, {low, moderate, high}, and {yes, no}, respectively. For example, this means that the variable, PU, of a system is deemed either low or high by the user, and so forth for the other variables. Probabilities are assigned subjectively or according to frequency ratios from a database or a combination of both (Anderson & Vastag, 2004). Assume that the prior probabilities of these states are as

Figure 1. A Bayesian network

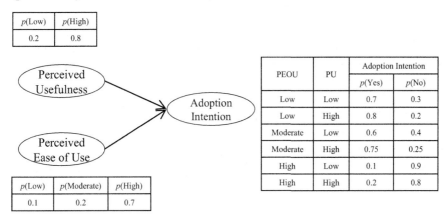

p(Low)	p(High)
0.2	0.8

PEOU	PU	Adoption Intention	
		p(Yes)	p(No)
Low	Low	0.7	0.3
Low	High	0.8	0.2
Moderate	Low	0.6	0.4
Moderate	High	0.75	0.25
High	Low	0.1	0.9
High	High	0.2	0.8

p(Low)	p(Moderate)	p(High)
0.1	0.2	0.7

shown in Figure 1. The values imply, for example, that 80% of the subjects perceive the PU of the system as high and 20% perceive it as low. The CPT of the dependent variable IOU shows the probability of the two states of AI for all combinations of the probabilities of the independent variables, namely PU and PEOU.

Once the Bayesian network is defined, it can be used for making predictions (estimation of forward inference from cause to effect) and diagnosis (backward inference from effect to cause) about real or hypothetical cases. The basis of prediction and diagnosis is probabilistic inference, which is concerned with the revision of probabilities for a variable or a set of variables when an intervention fixes the values of another variable or a set of variables called evidence (Anderson & Vastag, 2004).

Prediction Using a Bayesian Network

Suppose we have evidence that the PU of a customer for an IT product is high and his PEOU is low. We would want to know the probability that his AI for the IT product is "Yes." This can be computed using the chain rule of probability, according to which:

$$p(H|e_1,...,e_n) = \frac{p(H)p(e_1|H)...p(e_n|H)}{\sum_{h \in H} p(e_1|h)...p(e_n|h)p(h)}$$

$$p(AI = Yes|PU = High, PEOU = Low) = \frac{p(AI = Yes)p(PU = High|AI = Yes)p(PEOU = Low|AI = Yes)}{\sum_{i \in AI} p(PU = High|AI = i)p(PEOU = Low|AI = i)p(AI = i)}$$

$$p(AI = Yes | PU = High, PEOU = Low) = \frac{0.348 * 0.296 * 0.078}{0.296 * 0.078 * 0.348 + 0.504 * 0.022 * 0.652} = 0.526$$

Similarly, for AI being "No" given that perceived ease of use is low and perceived usefulness is high, the probability would be:

$$p(AI = No | PU = High, PEOU = Low) = \frac{0.504 * 0.022 * 0.652}{0.296 * 0.078 * 0.348 + 0.504 * 0.022 * 0.652} = 0.473$$

Thus, probability of intention to use being Yes is 0.526 and being No is 0.473. The likelihood ratio is 0.526/0.473 = 1.11.

Diagnosis Using a Bayesian Network

Consider the case in which we have evidence that a person's AI is "No." We would want to know which of PEOU and PU is the more likely reason for AI being "No." We can use Bayes' rule to compute the posterior probability of each explanation:

$$p(PU = Low, AI = No) = \frac{p(PU = Low \cap AI = No)}{p(AI = No)} = \frac{\sum_e p(PU = Low, PEOU = e, AI = No)}{\sum_{u,e} p(PU = u, PEOU = e, AI = No)} = \frac{0.148}{0.652} = 0.226$$

... *Where, u and e denote different states of PU and PEOU, respectively.*
Similarly:

$$p(PU = Low, AI = No) = \frac{p(PU = Low \cap AI = No)}{p(AI = No)} = \frac{\sum_e p(PU = u, PEOU = low, AI = No)}{\sum_{u,e} p(PU = u, PEOU = e, AI = No)} = \frac{0.022}{0.652} = 0.033$$

$p(AI = No)$ is a normalizing constant, equal to the probability (likelihood) of the data. The results imply that a person's perceived usefulness of the system is the more likely cause of a person's AI being "No" (the likelihood ratio is 0.226/0.033 = 6.84). By the chain rule of probability, the joint probability of all the nodes in Figure 1 is $p(PU, PEOU, AI) = p(PU) * p(PEOU) * p(AI|PU, PEOU)$.

Linking SEM to Bayesian Testing

SEM can provide an empirically validated model based on theoretical construction. Also, as SEM is particularly suited for latent variable modeling, it can provide the latent scores of variables to serve as raw data for Bayesian modeling at the hypothetical construct (latent variable) level. The computation of latent variable scores has been briefly described below and is discussed in detail by Joreskog (2000).

The measurement model in SEM can be written as:

$x = \Lambda_x \xi + \delta$, for exogenous or independent variables,

Where, x represents the individual items for independent variables,

$\quad$ ξ is the latent variable corresponding to item x,

$\quad$ Λ_x is the standardized coefficient of relationship between x and ξ, and

$\quad$ δ Is the measurement error for item x.

Once the coefficients of Λx are estimated, they can be treated as fixed and the latent scores. ξ can be computed for each observation in the sample by minimizing:

$$\sum_{i=1}^{N} (x_i - \Lambda_x \xi_i)^T \Theta_\delta^{-1} (x_i - \Lambda_x \xi_i), \text{subject to the consraint: } (1/N)\sum_{i=1}^{N} \xi_i \xi_i^T = \Phi,$$

Where, N is the sample size,

$\quad$ 'i' is the subscript for each observation,

$\quad$ Θ_δ is the covariance matrix of the residual errors,

$\quad$ ϕ is the covariance matrix of latent variables, and

$\quad$ the superscript "T" denotes transpose of the computed matrix.

LISREL 8.54 (SEM software) facilitates computation of latent variable scores for the latent variables of the model being tested. One of the possible uses of latent variable scores is to estimate non-linear relationships among latent variables (Joreskog, 2000). As the functional form of a Bayesian network is nonlinear, latent scores can be used for latent variable modeling in Bayesian networks based on the assumptions under which Bayesian networks represent causality. Based on the validated causal model resulting from SEM testing and the latent variable scores, Bayesian modeling can facilitate management decision support such as diagnosis and prediction of a business/managerial decision. Now we study the theoretical development and empirical validation of a model for customer retention in a VC. This model would be an application ground for Bayesian modeling.

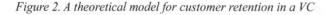

Figure 2. A theoretical model for customer retention in a VC

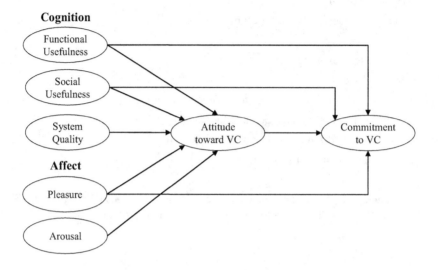

A Model for Customer Retention in a Virtual Community

Virtual communities (VCs) can be defined as groups of people with common interests and practices that communicate regularly and for some duration in an organized way over the Internet through a common location or mechanism. A virtual community (VC) of committed members is of great strategic value to online firms and vendors owing to its ability to attract and retain members. However, online firms and vendors find it difficult to instill commitment among their VC members. Based on the theory of reasoned action (TRA) (Fishbein & Ajzen, 1975), Gupta and Kim (2007) developed a research model (Figure 2) for examining customer commitment formation in a relationship-cum-interest based VC. By understanding the mechanism of customer commitment formation in a VC, online firms and vendors can enhance customer commitment to the VC.

TRA is a widely-studied model from social psychology, which is concerned with the determinants of consciously intended behaviors (Fishbein & Ajzen, 1975). TRA links beliefs, attitudes, intentions, and behaviors. Beliefs influence one's overall attitude about an object. This, in turn, guides the individual's intentions, which influence behaviors regarding the subject. TRA can provide the basic framework for understanding the members' commitment to a VC.

As commitment is not the intended behavior of customer participation, but rather an outcome of customer participation in the VC, Gupta & Kim (2007) proposed the direct link from attitude to behavior (commitment) rather than through commitment intention. This modification is supported by attitude-behavior theory (e.g., Fazio, Powell, & Williams, 1989). According to Fazio et al. (1989), influence of attitude on behavior is strong when the attitude is based on direct experience, or is readily accessible from memory when based on past experience. As the VC members already have direct experience of participation, the likely outcome of their positive attitude toward participation in the VC would be commitment to the VC.

According to TRA, customers' attitude toward the attitude object is influenced by their beliefs about the attitude object. The commonly used beliefs in IS studies are perceived usefulness and perceived ease of use (Davis, 1989). Gupta and Kim (2007) used these beliefs in studying members' attitude toward participation in the VC. Usefulness of a VC refers to the degree to which individuals believe that interaction in a VC is useful for fulfilling their purposes. Usefulness of a VC can be of two types, namely, functional usefulness and social usefulness. Functional usefulness refers to the benefits related to functional, utilitarian, or physical performance of a product or a service. In the case of a VC, such functional benefits would be sharing information, sharing interests, or knowledge. Social usefulness refers to the benefits related to the social standing one obtains in being a part of the VC, such as recognition and social approval from other VC members. Ease of use refers to the degree to which an individual believes that using a particular system would be free of physical and mental effort. Gupta and Kim (2007) used system quality to represent the ease of using a VC (see McKinney, Yoon, & Zahedi, 2002). System quality is the basic component of any information system and represents the effort required on the part of a member to participate in the VC.

Usefulness and ease of use represent the cognitive aspect of human decision making. Studies in consumer behavior (e.g., Batra & Ahtola, 1991) and social psychology (Zajonc, 1980) also consider the affective aspects of human decision-making in studying attitude formation, which represent the feelings side of consciousness (Oliver, 1997). From the affective perspective, Gupta and Kim (2007) considered pleasure and arousal. Pleasure and arousal allow

Table 1. Results of hypothesis testing using LISREL (SEM)

Dependent Variable	Independent Variables	Std. Beta	R^2
Commitment to VC	Attitude	0.28**	0.32
	Functional Usefulness	0.22**	
	Social Usefulness	ns	
	System Quality	--	
	Pleasure	0.21*	
	Arousal	--	
Attitude toward VC	Functional Usefulness	0.27***	0.55
	Social Usefulness	ns	
	System Quality	0.13*	
	Pleasure	0.42***	
	Arousal	ns	

*Note: ns = not significant, * = p < 0.05; ** = p < 0.01; *** = p < 0.001*

for a greater range of positive emotions as compared to only joy, happiness, and interest in other emotion models (Oliver, 1997). As members experience enjoyment in interacting with other members of the VC (Hiltz & Wellman, 1997; Rheingold, 1993), affect can represent the emotional experience of a member from such interaction in the VC.

This model was then subjected to empirical examination using SEM. The data for the empirical examination was collected from the Web site of *Urii.com*—a relationship-cum-interest-based VC—for 2 weeks. The reason for choosing a relationship-cum-interest-based VC is that most of the VCs which are successful in terms of instilling commitment among its members are either relationship-based or interest-based or a mixture of the two. The survey results show that almost all (97.45%) the members in *Urii.com* are women (mostly housewives). The mean age of the members of *Urii.com* is 30.43 years and the mean VC usage experience is 1.27 years. The data was then subjected to analysis using SEM. The outcome of SEM testing is shown in Table 1.

The fit indices (Normed χ^2 = 1.82, GFI=0.89, AGFI=0.86, NFI=0.96, NNFI=0.97, CFI=0.98, RMSEA=0.055, Std. RMR=0.066) suggest an excellent fit (Gefen, Straub, & Boudreau, 2000). The hypothesis testing results indicate that functional usefulness, system quality, and pleasure significantly influence attitude toward VC (R^2=55%) and functional useful-ness, pleasure, and attitude significantly influence customer commitment to VC (R^2=32%). The results support the significant role of affect in predicting attitude toward behavior. The effect of functional usefulness and system quality on attitude is significant and is consis-tent with the TAM model. The effect of pleasure is significant in predicting attitude and is consistent with the previous studies (e.g., Batra & Ahtola, 1990) which study the role of affect in predicting attitude. Now, we will subject this model for further examination us-ing Bayesian modeling. Because social usefulness and arousal had insignificant effect on attitude and commitment, we drop them for further examination. Also, because the effect of system quality on commitment is insignificant, for the sake of simplicity, we also drop system quality in Bayesian testing.

Causal Modeling Using Bayesian Networks

Developing a Bayesian Model

The two steps in developing a Bayesian model are structure learning and prior conditional probability estimation. The empirically validated model using LISREL (Table 1) forms the structure which is applied to the data for estimating conditional probabilities. The latent variable scores obtained from LISREL are used as data for learning the conditional prob-abilities of the latent variables in the structure obtained from LISREL. As depicted earlier, the latent scores are computed by minimizing (Joreskog, 2000):

$$\sum_{i=1}^{N}(x_i - \Lambda_x\xi_i)^T \Theta_\delta^{-1}(x_i - \Lambda_x\xi_i), \text{subject to the constraint:} (1/N)\sum_{i=1}^{N}\xi_i\xi_i^T = \Phi$$

The matrices for the above computation are:

$$X = \begin{pmatrix} \text{FUSE1} \\ \text{FUSE2} \\ \text{FUSE3} \\ \text{PLEA1} \\ \text{PLEA2} \\ \text{PLEA3} \\ \text{PLEA4} \end{pmatrix}; \Lambda_x = \begin{pmatrix} \lambda_{\text{FUSE1}} & 0 \\ \lambda_{\text{FUSE2}} & 0 \\ \lambda_{\text{FUSE3}} & 0 \\ 0 & \lambda_{\text{PLEA1}} \\ 0 & \lambda_{\text{PLEA2}} \\ 0 & \lambda_{\text{PLEA3}} \\ 0 & \lambda_{\text{PLEA4}} \end{pmatrix}; \xi = \begin{pmatrix} \text{FUSE} \\ \text{PLEA} \end{pmatrix}; \delta = \begin{pmatrix} \delta_{\text{FUSE1}} \\ \delta_{\text{FUSE2}} \\ \delta_{\text{FUSE3}} \\ \delta_{\text{PLEA1}} \\ \delta_{\text{PLEA2}} \\ \delta_{\text{PLEA3}} \\ \delta_{\text{PLEA4}} \end{pmatrix}; \Phi = \begin{pmatrix} 1 & \\ \phi_{\text{FUSE-PLEA}} & 1 \end{pmatrix}$$

Similarly, computations may be done for endogenous variables, namely, attitude and commitment in this research.

Bayesian Network Structure Learning

Structure learning refers to the specification of the structure and the parameters of conditional probability distribution of each node. Bayesian networks can either be generated by learning the structure from the data or a structure can be forced. In case of the latter the conditional probability of each node can be estimated either from the observed data or from experience. In learning the structure from the observed data, there are chances of spurious relationships. Hence, we apply a theoretically validated framework on the data for estimating conditional probabilities. The set of model variables for Bayesian network application can be defined as $V = \{$Functional usefulness, Pleasure, Attitude, and Commitment$\}$ and $U = \{u_1, u_2, u_3, u_4\}$. The complete structure of a Bayesian network (Figure 3) implies the following equations:

1.   Functional Usefulness $= f_1(u_1)$

2.   Pleasure $= f_2(u_2)$

3.   Attitude $= f_3($Functional usefulness, Pleasure, $u_3)$

4.   Commitment $= f_4($Functional usefulness, Pleasure, Attitude, $u_4)$

Figure 3. A Bayesian network of customer retention in an online store using a VC

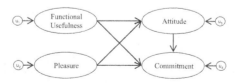

Prior Conditional Probability Estimation

Prior conditional probabilities are estimated from the latent scores obtained from SEM (LISREL). Latent scores cannot be estimated in practice, but they can be computed (Joreskog, 2000). The knowledge discoverer program (Sebastiani & Ramoni, 2000) was used to estimate prior conditional probabilities. Each variable is first discretized into three states (named as low, medium, and high). Any number of states could be chosen, but it is better to use fewer states to identify a variable as this prevents complexities in judging the results. The conditional probability of these states was estimated based on frequency. This means that the data range is divided into three equal parts, and the frequency of each part in the data is calculated. The prior conditional probabilities obtained, using the knowledge discoverer program (Sebastiani & Ramoni, 2000) are shown in Table 2.

Table 2. Prior conditional probabilities

State	Variables			
	Functional Usefulness	Pleasure	Attitude	Commitment
Low	0.02	0.01	0.01	0.01
Medium	0.26	0.55	0.39	0.54
High	0.72	0.44	0.60	0.45

Figure 4. A Bayesian network of customer retention in an online store using a VC

FUSE	PLEA	Attitude		
		p(Low)	p(Med)	p(High)
Low	Low	0.99	0.00	0.00
Low	Med	0.00	0.67	0.33
Low	High	0.00	0.99	0.00
Med	Low	0.33	0.33	0.33
Med	Med	0.00	0.79	0.21
Med	High	0.00	0.40	0.60
High	Low	0.99	0.00	0.00
High	Med	0.00	0.47	0.53
High	High	0.00	0.09	0.91

FUSE	PLEA	ATTI	Commitment		
			p(Low)	p(Med)	p(High)
Low	Low	Low	0.00	1.00	0.00
Low	Low	Med	0.33	0.33	0.33
Low	Low	High	0.33	0.33	0.33
Low	Med	Low	0.33	0.33	0.33
Low	Med	Med	0.00	1.00	0.00
Low	Med	High	1.00	0.00	0.00
Low	High	Low	0.33	0.33	0.33
Low	High	Med	0.00	1.00	0.00
Low	High	High	0.33	0.33	0.33
Med	Low	Low	0.33	0.33	0.33
Med	Low	Med	0.33	0.33	0.33
Med	Low	High	0.33	0.33	0.33
Med	Med	Low	0.33	0.33	0.33
Med	Med	Med	0.00	0.98	0.02
Med	Med	High	0.00	0.83	0.17
Med	High	Low	0.33	0.33	0.33
Med	High	Med	0.00	0.33	0.67
Med	High	High	0.00	0.44	0.56
High	Low	Low	1.00	0.00	0.00
High	Low	Med	0.33	0.33	0.33
High	Low	High	0.33	0.33	0.33
High	Med	Low	0.33	0.33	0.33
High	Med	Med	0.00	0.84	0.16
High	Med	High	0.00	0.71	0.29
High	High	Low	0.33	0.33	0.33
High	High	Med	0.00	0.40	0.60
High	High	High	0.00	0.10	0.90

Functional Usefulness		
p(Low)	p(Med)	p(High)
0.02	0.26	0.72

Pleasure		
p(Low)	p(Med)	p(High)
0.01	0.55	0.44

Based on the prior conditional probabilities, conditional probability distribution (CPD) for the dependent variables is calculated using the knowledge discoverer program (Sebastiani & Ramoni, 2000). The CPD is shown in Figure 4. Once the structure is learned, it can be used to further train the network if more data is available, in which case, the conditional probabilities (Table 2) of the nodes in the network will change. The dynamic modeling does not change the theoretical structure, unlike SEM, where new data may imply change in the model structure.

Table 3. Comparison of marginal log likelihood for various models

INDEPENDENT VARIABLES					DEPENDENT VARIABLES		MARGINAL LOG-LIKELIHOOD
FUSE	SUSE	SYSQ	PLEA	AROU	ATTI	COMM	
✓	✓	✓	✓	✓	✓	✓	**-1507.76**
✓	✗	✓	✓	✓	✓	✓	**-1181.19**
✗	✓	✓	✓	✓	✓	✓	-1284.21
✓	✓	✓	✓	✗	✓	✓	-1292.33
✓	✗	✗	✓	✓	✓	✓	**-929.36**
✗	✗	✓	✓	✓	✓	✓	-966.68
✓	✗	✓	✓	✗	✓	✓	-970.16
✓	✗	✓	✗	✓	✓	✓	-985.46
✗	✓	✗	✓	✓	✓	✓	-1007.74
✓	✓	✗	✓	✗	✓	✓	-1016.95
✓	✓	✗	✗	✓	✓	✓	-1017.67
✗	✓	✓	✓	✗	✓	✓	-1057.89
✗	✓	✓	✗	✓	✓	✓	-1060.05
✓	✓	✓	✗	✗	✓	✓	-1062.39
✓	✓	✗	✓	✓	✓	✓	-1246.88
✓	✓	✓	✗	✓	✓	✓	-1265.71
✓	✗	✗	✓	✗	✓	✓	**-709.65**
✗	✗	✗	✓	✓	✓	✓	-713.53
✓	✗	✗	✗	✓	✓	✓	-729.84
✗	✗	✓	✓	✗	✓	✓	-757.44
✓	✗	✓	✗	✗	✓	✓	-783.11
✗	✗	✓	✗	✓	✓	✓	-790.56
✗	✓	✗	✓	✗	✓	✓	-790.91
✗	✓	✗	✗	✓	✓	✓	-811.06
✓	✓	✗	✗	✗	✓	✓	-812.57
✗	✓	✓	✗	✗	✓	✓	-861.87

FUSE: Functional Usefulness, SUSE: Social Usefulness, SYSQ: System Quality, PLEA: Pleasure, AROU: Arousal, ATTI: Attitude, COMM: Commitment

Model Evaluations

Parsimonious Model Based on Marginal Log-Likelihood

The Bayesian network gives marginal log-likelihood estimates for the network. Marginal log-likelihood is a comparative measure proportional to posterior probability of the model and is used to assess the goodness of fit of the model. It is a good enough measure for identifying the best model but it does not give an idea of how much a model is better than compared to another model. Our interest here is to assess the match between the Bayesian scores of the model and the theoretically validated model obtained from SEM. We compare various models in terms of their marginal log-likelihood value. Because the marginal log-likelihood is minimized, the lesser its magnitude the closer is the predicted model to the original one.

The comparison shows (Table 3) that the full model has a marginal log-likelihood value of -1507.76. In the group of four variables, the best model includes *functional usefulness*, *system quality*, *pleasure,* and *arousal* as independent variables, and the marginal log likelihood for this model is -1181.19. In the group of three variables, the best model has *functional usefulness*, *pleasure,* and *arousal* as independent variables and the marginal log-likelihood for this model is -929.36. In the group of two variables, the best model has *functional usefulness* and *pleasure* as independent variables, and the marginal log-likelihood for this model is -709.65. From SEM, we obtain the best model with *functional usefulness* and *pleasure* as significant indicators. This is also confirmed using Bayesian modeling, which shows that the best model has *functional usefulness* and *pleasure* as independent variables (-709.65).

Network Validation

Network validation tests the predictive accuracy of a model. A cross-validation procedure assesses the internal consistency of the adopted Bayesian model (Anderson et al., 2004; Stone, 1977). The method starts by dividing the database into "n" parts. Then, for each part, the technique predicts the values of a set of variables by estimating the conditional probabilities of the network from the remaining parts. In our current model, we choose five parts, as the

Table 4. Network validation results

RESPONSE VARIABLE	ACCURACY	
	PERCENTAGE	Standard Deviation
Attitude	85.38	2.13
Commitment	92.87	1.55
Functional Usefulness	73.82	2.65
Pleasure	89.53	1.85
Overall	85.40	2.13

data set has only 275 points. The procedure selects 55 cases as the response set and uses the remaining 220 cases to predict the response. This procedure is repeated five times, with each case being included in a response set over the course of the cross-validation. Table 4 shows the results of cross-validation for the four constructs. The prediction accuracy of individual variables and the overall model is quite high and within three standard deviations.

Application of Bayesian Model to Managerial Decision Support in a VC

Prediction (Forward Inference) Using the Current Research Model

When the variable set as evidence node allows inference from cause to effect, the process of inference is called prediction or forward inference. For example, if a person joins a VC having low functional usefulness perception, then this information can be fed to the network as evidence that the probability of functional usefulness being low is 1.0. The revised conditional probability of the consequent nodes (attitude and commitment) is then calculated by the Bayesian network for the three states, namely, low, medium, and high. From Table 5 (state = low), it is clear that the conditional probability of his attitude and commitment being low or medium is increasing, while the conditional probability of his attitude and commitment being high is decreasing. This is known as prediction. Two applications of prediction in VC, namely, modeling customer retention and modeling impact of changes are discussed below.

Table 5. Forward inference due to change in different states of functional usefulness on different states of attitude and commitment

State	Variables					
	Functional Usefulness		Attitude		Commitment	
	PCP	NCP	PCP	NCP	PCP	NCP
Low	**0.02**	**1.00**	0.01	0.01	0.01	0.18
Medium	0.26	0.00	0.39	0.81	0.54	0.81
High	0.72	0.00	0.60	0.18	0.45	0.00

PCP: Prior conditional probability, NCP: New conditional probability

Customer Retention

A customer is considered retained if he/she has high commitment to the VC, a necessary but not sufficient condition for which is a positive attitude toward interaction in the VC. So, we need to model both attitude and commitment for modeling customer retention. The expected changes in attitude due to changes in functional usefulness and pleasure are shown in Figure 5.

From Figure 5 it can be noted that as functional usefulness changes from low to medium to high, the high state of attitude shows an increasing trend, the medium state of attitude shows a decreasing trend, and the low state of attitude shows a constant trend. It can also be noted that as pleasure changes from low to medium to high, the high state of attitude shows an increasing trend, the medium state of attitude shows a mixed trend, and low state of attitude shows a decreasing trend. An increasing trend in high state means an increase in attitude; increasing trend in medium state means a moderate attitude; an increasing trend in low state means decrease in attitude. The results therefore imply a positive relationship between functional usefulness and attitude and between pleasure and attitude. This is the same as the results obtained from SEM. For gaining positive attitude of customers toward interaction in the VC, a VC vendor would like to enhance the high state, and possibly the medium state, and lower the low state of attitude. A VC vendor should therefore make efforts to enhance customers' functional usefulness and pleasure in the VC, so that the overall attitude of the customer towards the VC increases. Figure 5 also depicts that even when functional usefulness is low, the probability of attitude being low is low (which means attitude is high). Meanwhile, when pleasure is low, the probability of attitude being low is high (which means low attitude). This means pleasure has a stronger relationship with attitude; hence, to increase the attitude of customers, it is more important to enhance their pleasure than to enhance functional usefulness.

Figure 5. Separate influence of changes in functional usefulness and pleasure on attitude

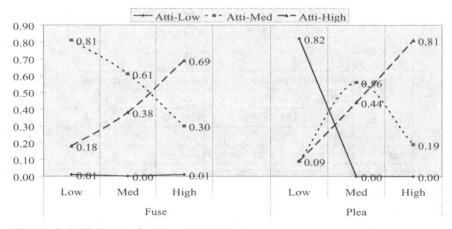

ATTI: Attitude, FUSE: Functional usefulness, PLEA: Pleasure

Figure 6. Separate influence of changes in functional usefulness, pleasure, and attitude on commitment

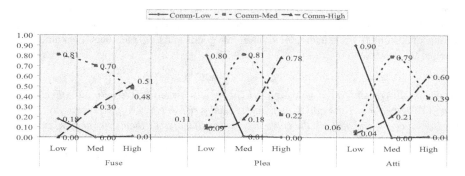

The effect of functional usefulness, pleasure, and attitude on commitment is modeled as shown in Figure 6.

There is an increase in the high state of commitment with the increase in functional usefulness, pleasure, and attitude from low to high. The medium state of commitment shows a mixed trend with increase in pleasure and attitude from low to high, and a decreasing trend with increase in functional usefulness from low to high. The results are the same as obtained from SEM. The medium state of commitment is high even when functional usefulness is low. This implies that there is some commitment among customers, even when the functional usefulness of the site is low. On the other hand, when the pleasure and attitude are low, medium state of commitment is low. This implies that there is a strong direct relationship between pleasure and commitment and attitude and commitment. In other words, pleasure and attitude are more important predictors of the customer's commitment to the VC.

The above prediction can also be accomplished using SEM. However, Bayesian modeling offers some advantages over SEM. First, while, SEM gives the prediction output in terms of mean and standard deviation at a particular data-point, the Bayesian output is in terms of probability distribution of various states of the dependent variable at the given state of independent variable, which is more accurate. The number of states can be increased, and thus the right probability distribution can be obtained. Second, the Bayesian networks can be trained with new data on the same structure very easily, which is not the case with SEM. Third, SEM assumes linear relationships among variables, while Bayesian networks can model a nonlinear relationship among variables as the output is in terms of probability of various states. In such a case, SEM may avoid some crucial variables by rendering them insignificant in case the relationship is nonlinear. The Bayesian network would capture its effect. Fourth, SEM can model only one Y-variable at a time, whereas a Bayesian network can show the impact of any number of Y- and X-variables at a time.

Impact of Incorporating Changes in a VC

A Bayesian network can also be used to measure the likely impact of incorporating changes in a VC. Let us consider a scenario of a real VC, which was facing a problem of decreasing attitude of customers when it attempted to sell the goods to its VC members (the names are changed for privacy).

By way of background, a few years ago ABC.com was owned by the online retailer XYZ. com. XYZ hoped to sell its goods (which included wristwatches) to the community. They had little success, and many in the community were alienated by their cynical approach. In 2001, XYZ sold its VC to the current owner, who is an avid wristwatch collector. For him, ABC is essentially a hobby, and he is very much concerned about the community's happiness, and their attitudes toward the site. To overcome the community's hostility to the prior "commercial" owner, the new owner has gone to great lengths to avoid any perception that ABC seeks to profit directly from the community.

The above scenario requires that the impact of such changes in the VC be ascertained beforehand to avoid such problems in the future which may lead to closure of the VC. To model the above scenario, let us consider a hypothetical case in which a vendor introduces a new forum in the VC for discussion on products sold at the VC Web site. In an attempt to understand the impact on customers' attitude and commitment to the VC, the vendor takes the input of the VC customers on their likely functional usefulness and pleasure after the introduction of such a forum on the scale of low, medium, and high.

Assume that 100 customers took part in the survey, and the frequency (Column a in Table 6) for various combinations of functional usefulness and pleasure is as shown in Table 5. Column b and Column c are the probabilities of various states of attitude and commitment for various combinations of functional usefulness and pleasure as obtained from the conditional probability table in Figure 4. These values are then multiplied by the frequency and their total is calculated for each state of attitude and commitment (Row d). The current state (Row e) is obtained from prior conditional probabilities as shown in Table 2. The total value (Row d) is then compared with the current state (Row e). The result as shown in Row f implies that there is an increase in the low and medium states of attitude and a decrease in the high state of attitude, thus implying an overall decrease of attitude among customers. Similarly, there is an increase in the low state of commitment and a decrease in the medium and high states of commitment, which implies an overall decrease of customer commitment toward the VC. The survey results thus indicate that introduction of the forum in the VC may result in an overall decrease of customers' attitude and commitment to the VC. A vendor therefore needs to take steps to enhance the image of the product forum in the minds of the customers, before introducing the forum. Similarly, the impact of other changes can be measured. Usually, vendors organizing online/offline events and prediction using the Bayesian model can help the vendor in evaluating his decision in terms of customers' overall attitude and commitment toward the VC.

Table 6. Measuring the impact of incorporating changes in the VC

Profiles		Freq. (a)	Attitude (b)			Commitment (c)			Attitude (a*b/100)			Commitment (a*c/100)		
Fuse	Plea		p(low)	p(med)	p(high)	p(low)	p(med)	p(high)	p(low)	p(med)	p(high)	p(low)	p(med)	p(high)
Low	Low	0	0.99	0.00	0.00	0.00	0.99	0.00	0.00	0.00	0.00	0.00	0.00	0.00
Low	Med	10	0.00	0.67	0.33	0.33	0.67	0.00	0.00	0.07	0.03	0.03	0.07	0.00
Low	High	5	0.00	0.99	0.00	0.00	0.99	0.00	0.00	0.05	0.00	0.00	0.05	0.00
Med	Low	15	0.33	0.33	0.33	0.33	0.33	0.33	0.05	0.05	0.05	0.05	0.05	0.05
Med	Med	15	0.00	0.79	0.21	0.00	0.95	0.05	0.00	0.12	0.03	0.00	0.14	0.01
Med	High	10	0.00	0.40	0.60	0.00	0.40	0.60	0.00	0.04	0.06	0.00	0.04	0.06
High	Low	5	0.99	0.00	0.00	0.99	0.00	0.00	0.05	0.00	0.00	0.05	0.00	0.00
High	Med	20	0.00	0.47	0.53	0.00	0.77	0.23	0.00	0.09	0.11	0.00	0.15	0.05
High	High	20	0.00	0.09	0.91	0.00	0.13	0.87	0.00	0.02	0.18	0.00	0.03	0.17
					Total (d)				0.10	0.44	0.46	0.13	0.53	0.34
					Current State (e)				0.01	0.39	0.6	0.01	0.54	0.45
					Change (f)				Inc	Inc	Dec	Inc	Dec	Dec

Fuse: Functional usefulness, Plea: Pleasure

Diagnostic (Backward Inference) Using the Current Research Model

When the variable which serves as an evidence node allows inference from effect to causes, the process of inference is called diagnostic or backward inference. In this, the child nodes (attitude and commitment) are given evidence. Assume the evidence given is that the customers' attitude toward the VC is high. This evidence is fed to the network by setting the probability of the high state of attitude as 1.00 and observing the changes in the parent variables (functional usefulness and pleasure). From Table 7, we can see that the probability of the high state of pleasure and functional usefulness is increasing, while the probability of low and medium state of pleasure and functional usefulness is decreasing. This implies that the members increased attitude toward participation in the VC is due to his/her increased favorable perception of pleasure and functional usefulness in the VC. Two applications of diagnosis to decreasing customer commitment and modeling contradictory behavior of customers are discussed next.

Table 7. Backward inference due to change in attitude on different states of functional usefulness and pleasure

State	Variables					
	Attitude		Functional Usefulness		Pleasure	
	PCP	NCP	PCP	NCP	PCP	NCP
Low	0.01	0.00	0.02	0.01	0.01	0.00
Medium	0.39	0.00	0.26	0.17	0.55	0.40
High	0.60	1.00	0.72	0.83	0.44	0.60

PCP: Prior conditional probability, NCP: New conditional probability

Table 8. Backward inference of low commitment on attitude, functional usefulness, and pleasure

State	Variables							
	Commitment		Attitude		Functional Usefulness		Pleasure	
	PCP	NCP	PCP	NCP	PCP	NCP	PCP	NCP
Low	0.01	1.00	0.01	0.59	0.02	0.36	0.01	0.64
Medium	0.54	0.00	0.39	0.02	0.26	0.07	0.55	0.36
High	0.45	0.00	0.60	0.39	0.72	0.57	0.44	0.00

PCP: Prior conditional probability, NCP: New conditional probability

Decreasing Customers' Commitment to VC

Suppose the online vendor observes decreasing commitment toward participation among its customers, he can then give evidence to the network that the probability of commitment is low and see the effect on parent variables (attitude, functional usefulness, and pleasure). From Table 8, it can be noted that there is an increase in low state of attitude, functional usefulness, and pleasure, and decrease in medium and high state of attitude, functional usefulness, and pleasure. Functional usefulness and attitude are slightly higher than pleasure, as is evident from Table 8 (the probability of high state of pleasure is zero, while there is positive probability in high state of attitude and functional usefulness). A vendor, therefore, needs to take corrective action to enhance customers' pleasure in the VC, to improve customers' commitment toward the VC. Table 8 seems to give a static picture of commitment and attitude toward the VC. As the customers of the VC are changing, the vendor needs to train the Bayesian structure with new data and obtain the conditional probabilities. The modeling then becomes dynamic and gives proper feedback as to the aspect needed to be improved for gaining customers' commitment to the VC.

Modeling Contradictory Behavior of Customers

Apparent contradictory behavior of persons can be modeled using diagnosis with more than one variable. For example, some customers interact in the VC to seek information from the VC but do not participate in VC activities. Such customers can be characterized as persons with high attitude and low commitment. The Bayesian tool can provide an answer to the reasons behind such behavior. The probability of high state of attitude and low state of commitment is set as 1.00. The resulting change in probabilities, as obtained from the knowledge discoverer program (Sebastiani & Ramoni, 2000), of various states of functional usefulness and pleasure is as shown in Table 9. From Table 9 it can be noted that the conditional probability of high and medium states of functional usefulness is decreasing and that of low state is increasing. Moreover, conditional probability of high state of pleasure is decreasing and that of medium and low state of pleasure is increasing. This implies that functional usefulness is low and pleasure is medium. In other words, customers interact primarily because of fun, and they do not perceive the VC to be sufficiently useful for them to commit to it.

Table 9. Diagnostic of functional usefulness and pleasure from attitude and commitment

	Attitude		Commitment		Functional Usefulness		Pleasure	
	PCP	NCP	PCP	NCP	PCP	NCP	PCP	NCP
Low	0.01	0.00	0.01	1.00	0.02	0.94	0.01	0.06
Medium	0.39	0.00	0.54	0.00	0.26	0.06	0.55	0.94
High	0.60	1.00	0.45	0.00	0.72	0.00	0.44	0.00

PCP: Prior conditional probability, NCP: New conditional probability

Discussion and Limitations

The Bayesian model validation results confirm that the model obtained from SEM is parsimonious and better than other models; this is apparent from the lowest marginal log-likelihood (-709.65) of the model. However, it is difficult to conclude from the marginal log-likelihood why other models cannot be chosen. Therefore, the use of SEM for empirical validation of the theoretical model is necessary and complements Bayesian modeling. The prediction accuracy of the Bayesian model is quite high, ranging from 73.82% to 92.87%.

The linking of SEM to Bayesian modeling is in essence a two-step approach. Both SEM and Bayesian modeling complement each other. The latent scores obtained from SEM have been used as data for Bayesian modeling. The marginal log-likelihood results confirm that the results obtained from Bayesian modeling using latent scores give results similar to SEM (as the most parsimonious model predicted by both modeling approaches is the same.)

The prior conditional probabilities shown in Table 2 represent the current state of the model, according to which *attitude* is more on the high side and *commitment* is more on the medium side. The results in Figure 4 show the conditional probability distribution for various combinations of states of *functional usefulness, pleasure,* and *attitude*. The results for many combinations are a little abrupt (e.g., "med, low" for *attitude*; "med, low, low" for *commitment*). This is because the data set used in the research is small. As Bayesian networks work well with large data, it is better to obtain a large data set so that probabilities of all the states and combinations can be observed and set optimally.

The limitation of this study is that it is based on one VC. For generalizability, the Bayesian model needs to be validated in more IS studies. Bayesian networks can also be used with continuous data. However, we have adopted the discretization method to prevent mathematical complexity and to retain the managerial usefulness of the Bayesian model. The dataset used in this research is a little too small to give an overall probability distribution for a Bayesian network; a large dataset would give better results. Bayesian networks can be used with new data to train the current model, which is not possible with SEM. However, due to the limited scope of this chapter, we have not explored this possibility. It can be explored in future research.

Conclusion and Implications

The objective of our study was to develop an approach for managerial decision support in IS studies. We developed a combinatorial SEM-Bayesian approach by combining the strengths of both the SEM and Bayesian approaches. Latent variable modeling, as well as theoretical prediction, are two primary requirements for applying Bayesian modeling in IS research. The combinatorial SEM-Bayesian approach fulfills both these requirements.

From the theoretical perspective, the linking of SEM to Bayesian networks provides an excellent tool for managerial decision support that offers numerous advantages. First, the tool is based on an empirically validated theoretical construction and not on some structure obtained from the data. Structure obtained from data does not account for differences between causal and spurious relationships and therefore any relationship found significant is modeled. Second, the Bayesian modeling of latent variables gives a better understanding of reality. Bayesian modeling of observed variables produces unwieldy networks, which are difficult to interpret. Latent variable modeling helps to simplify the system and uncover the underlying mechanism of the system. Third, in Bayesian networks, relationships are measured in terms of probability of various states of the variables. This adds to the flexibility of managerial prediction and diagnosis by means of the probability distribution of the effect variable. Fourth, linking SEM and Bayesian networks allows for diagnosis based on causal relationships (and not spurious relationships).

SEM researchers can benefit from our proposed approach by extending their empirically validated models to managerial decision support using prediction and diagnosis. As our approach uses a theoretically-based and empirically-validated model for prediction and diagnosis, prediction and diagnosis would strengthen the practical applicability of their research models. Bayesian researchers can benefit by extending the application of latent variable level modeling as used in this research in their domains. This research introduces latent scores approach for latent variable modeling. A latent variable is any quantity which, either in practice or in principle cannot be directly observed (Bartholomew, 1994). Social science studies are based on latent variable modeling. Bayesian modeling approaches in other fields disregards the differences between spurious and causal relationship and therefore the causality of the network generated from the data is in question. Although, it is possible to force relationships which are causally related, theoretical explanation in Bayesian network is poorer than SEM (Anderson et al., 2004). A model based on causal relationships would depict a better picture of reality than a model randomly generated from data. Bayesian researchers can benefit by developing a causal model of the situation they are modeling and then testing using Bayesian networks at latent variable level.

From the practical perspective, our study has shown some examples of how combinatorial approaches of SEM and Bayesian networks can be useful for prediction and diagnosis in IS research. Prediction and diagnosis can be extended to various situations for decision making. In this research we used prediction for modeling customer retention, modeling the impact of changes in the VC, and diagnosis for problem diagnosis and modeling contradictory behavior of the customers. Prediction and diagnosis can similarly be extended to provide quantitative support to various other managerial decisions.

References

Anderson, R.D., & Vastag, G. (2004). Causal modeling alternatives in operations research: Overview and application. *European Journal of Operational Research*, *156*(1), 92-109.

Anderson, R.D., Mackoy, R.D., Thompson, V.B., & Harrell, G. (2004). A bayesian network estimation of the service-profit chain for transport service satisfaction. *Decision Sciences*, *35*(4), 665-688.

Bartholomew, D.J. (1994). Baye's theorem in latent variable modeling. In P.R. Freeman & A.F.M Smith (Eds.), *Aspects of Uncertainty: A Tribute to D.V. Lindley* (pp. 41-50). Chichester, UK: John Wiley.

Batra, R., & Ahtola, O.T. (1991). Measuring the hedonic and utilitarian sources of consumer attitudes. *Marketing Letters*, *2*(2), 159-170.

Davis, F.D. (1989). Perceived usefulness, perceived ease of use, and user acceptance of information technology. *MIS Quarterly*, *13*(3), 319-340.

Efraim T., & King D. (2003). *Introduction to e-commerce*. NJ: Prentice Hall.

Fazio, R.H., Powell, M., & Williams, C. (1989). The role of attitude accessibility in the attitude-to-behavior process. *Journal of Consumer Research*, *16*(3), 280-289.

Fishbein, M., & Ajzen, I. (1975). *Belief, attitude, intention and behavior: An introduction to theory and research*. Reading, MA: Addison-Wesley.

Gefen, D., Straub, D., & Boudreau, M.C. (2000). Structural equation modeling and regression: Guidelines for research practice. *Communications of the Association for Information Systems*, *4*(7), 1-80.

Gupta, S., & Kim, H.W. (2007). Developing the commitment to virtual community: The balanced effects of cognition and affect. *Information Resource Management Journal*, *20*(1), 28-45.

Hiltz, S.R., & Wellman, B. (1997). Asynchronous learning networks as a virtual classroom. *Communications of the ACM*, *40*(9), 44-49.

Hitchcock, C. (2002). Probabilistic causation. In E.N. Zalta (Ed.), *The Stanford encyclopedia of philosophy*. Retrieved December 22, 2006, from http://plato.stanford.edu/entries/causation-probabilistic/

Hume, D. (1969). *A treatise of human nature*. London: Penguin Books.

Joreskog, K.G. (2000). *Latent variable scores and their uses*. Retrieved December 22, 2006, from http://www.ssicentral.com/lisrel/advancedtopics.html

McKinney, V., Yoon, K., & Zahedi, F.M. (2002). The measurement of web-customer satisfaction: An expectation and disconfirmation approach. *Information Systems Research*, *13*(3), 296-315.

Neuman, W. L. (2003). *Social research methods: Qualitative and quantitative approaches, 5th edition*. Boston: Allyn and Bacon.

Oliver, R.L. (1997). *Satisfaction: A behavioral perspective on the consumer*. New York: McGraw-Hill.

Reichenbach, H. (1956). *The direction of time*. Berkeley: University of California Press.

Rheingold H. (1993). *The virtual community: Homesteading on the electronic frontier*. Colorado, MA: Addison–Wesley.

Sebastiani, P., & Ramoni, M. (2000). Bayesian inference with missing data using bound and collapse. *Journal of Computational and Graphical Statistics, 9*(4), 779-800.

Spirtes, P., Glymour, C., & Schienes, R. (1993). *Causation, prediction, and search.* New York: Springer-Verlag.

Stone, M. (1977). Asymptotics for and against cross-validation. *Biometrika, 64*(1), 29-35.

Zajonc, R. B. (1980) Feeling and thinking: Preferences need no inferences. *American Psychologist, 35*(2), 117-123.

Section II:

Bayesian Network for Image Processing and Related Applications

Chapter VII

Bayesian Networks for Image Understanding

Andreas Savakis, Rochester Institute of Technology, USA

Jiebo Luo, Kodak Research Laboratories, USA

Michael Kane, Yale University, USA

Abstract

Image understanding deals with extracting and interpreting scene content for use in various applications. In this chapter, we illustrate that Bayesian networks are particularly well-suited for image understanding problems, and present case studies in indoor-outdoor scene classification and parts-based object detection. First, improved scene classification is accomplished using both low-level features, such as color and texture, and semantic features, such as the presence of sky and grass. Integration of low-level and semantic features is achieved using a Bayesian network framework. The network structure can be determined by expert opinion or by automated structure learning methods. Second, object detection at multiple views relies on a parts-based approach, where specialized detectors locate object parts and a Bayesian network acts as the arbitrator in order to determine the object presence. In general, Bayesian networks are found to be powerful integrators of different features and help improve the performance of image understanding systems.

Introduction

Bayesian networks, also known as belief networks or Bayes nets, have emerged as an effective tool for knowledge representation and inference (Neapolitan, 2003; Pearl, 1988). A Bayesian network is a directed, acyclic graph that can be used to represent the dependency between random variables, represented by nodes. Links between nodes represent conditional probabilities and link directions represent causality between the parent and children nodes. A distinct advantage of Bayesian networks is the ability to incorporate domain-specific knowledge in the network structure, so that the overall joint probability distribution is expressed as a set of conditionally independent relationships that are easier to characterize. According to Bayes' rule, the posterior probability can be expressed in terms of the joint probability, which can be further expressed by conditional probability and prior probability:

$$P(S|E) = \frac{P(S,E)}{P(E)} = \frac{P(E|S)P(S)}{P(E)},$$

where S denotes semantic task and E denotes evidence. Probabilistic reasoning uses the joint probability distribution of a given domain to answer a question about this domain. However, as the number of variables grows, the joint probability can become intractable. With Bayesian networks, the computation of the joint probability distribution over the entire system, given partial evidences about the state of the system, is greatly simplified by using Bayes' rule to exploit the conditional independence relationships among variables.

A Bayes network can be viewed as a knowledge representation and an inference engine that can be useful for many problems. Its advantages include explicit uncertainty characterization, representation of domain-specific knowledge in a human reasoning framework, efficient computation, quick training, easy construction, adaptability, good generalization with limited training data, and easy retraining when pruning or adding new features or new training data. These advantages make them particularly suitable for real-world applications where information can be incomplete or inaccurate. In this chapter, we discuss the application of Bayes nets to two major types of image understanding problems, namely, scene classification and object detection.

Image understanding is the highest processing level in computer vision (Sonka, Hlavac, & Boyle, 1999), where semantic information is extracted from the image, in contrast to image processing, which converts one image representation to another (e.g., by converting an intensity image to an edge map). Early successes in image understanding were limited to applications dealing with constrained environments, for example, military target recognition (Dudgeon & Lacoss, 1993), document processing (Schurmann, Bartneck, Bayer, Franke, Mandler, & Oberlander, 1992), and medical imaging (Robinson & Colchester, 1994). While image understanding in unconstrained environments remains a challenging problem, progress is being made in object detection and scene classification. Object detection deals with identifying known objects within the image, while scene classification characterizes an image into one of the known categories, for example, indoor or outdoor, city or landscape, beach or sunset, and so forth (Serrano, Savakis, & Luo, 2004; Szummer & Picard, 1998; Vailaya, Jain, & Zhang, 1998).

Both scene classification and object recognition can benefit significantly from the use of Bayes nets, and this chapter outlines relevant work in this area. Section 2 provides an overview of the methodology for Bayesian network training and model selection. Section 3 discusses indoor vs. outdoor categorization as part of the larger scene classification problem. Section 4 presents work that incorporates the use of Bayesian networks to accomplish object detection by parts. Section 5 includes conclusions and thoughts for future directions.

Bayesian Network Training and Topology

Bayesian Network Training

A Bayes net consists of four components: priors, the initial beliefs about various nodes in the Bayes net; conditional probability matrices (CPMs), knowledge about the relationship between two connected nodes in the Bayes net; evidences, observations from feature detectors that are input to the Bayes net; and posteriors, the final computed beliefs after the evidences have been propagated through the Bayes net. Various methods have been proposed for learning the parameters (conditional probability matrices, priors, etc.) associated with a Bayesian network (Heckerman, 1995). Given a network structure, a common approach is to use Bayesian statistics to learn the network parameters from data through simple frequency counting where likelihoods of observing a set of variables are generated from the training samples, that is, the observed data.

There are two standard methods, expert knowledge and frequency counting, for obtaining the conditional probability matrices for each parent-child node pair. In expert knowledge-based training, an expert, who has intimate knowledge of the relationships between various entities in the domain, is consulted about the relationship between the label sets of the two nodes joined by each link. Using this knowledge, the CPM for each node pair can be generated. If the desired conditional relationships are well understood or reliable training data is not available, then expert knowledge-based training of the network may be the best option. Frequency counting-based training is a sampling and correlation method that can be used for learning the CPMs directly from training data. A large set of observations and ground truth is first collected. Ground truth, in its normal sense, refers to knowing the label of each training sample with absolute certainty. The conditional probability matrix for a link can be trained using frequency counting only when ground truth for the parent node is available. Multiple observations of each child node are recorded along with ground truth on the parent node. These observations are then compiled together to create frequency tables which, when normalized, can be used as the CPM.

Bayesian Network Model Selection

While Bayesian networks are often constructed by experts, this is not always the best strategy, and automatic structure learning provides a consistent alternative. Many times it is not clear what the optimal structure should be for a given set of variables. In some cases, experts may disagree on an accurate model. In other cases, a model may contain many variables with complex interactions. Automatic structure learning in the former may confirm the validity of a model, while in the latter, structure learning provides a model that is guaranteed to have some degree of fidelity with respect to the training data. Structure learning may also be used for knowledge discovery where, instead of using the model to perform a task such as inference, the relationships between variables are of primary interest.

Bayesian network structure learning approaches generally fall into two categories. The first analyzes dependency relationships between nodes and incorporates this information into an asymptotically correct structure learning algorithm. Methods in this category are deemed asymptotically correct, because the derived structure approaches the optimal asymptotically as the number events in the database increases. One such algorithm (Cheng, Bell, & Liu, 1997), uses mutual information between nodes as a criterion for determining undirected parent-child relationships. Dependency relationships between adjacent nodes are then analyzed to determine arc orientation in the network. Algorithms such as these have the benefit of relatively low computational complexity. In particular, Cheng's algorithm is among the most parsimonious structure finding algorithms with a computational complexity of $O(N^2)$.

Empirically, it has been found that when generating a database from a Bayesian network and trying to relearn the network based on the database, the structure derived from the asymptotically correct algorithm is generally very similar to the original structure. However, there are structure learning algorithms that often come closer to the original structure.

The second category uses a scoring function to induce a search space in the space of possible networks. A local optimum is then found using techniques such as a gradient search, genetic algorithms, or particle swarm optimization (de Campos, Fernandez, Gamez, & Puerta, 2002; Larranaga, Poza, Yurramendi, Murga, & Kuijpers, 1996). In the selection of an appropriate scoring function, one that mitigates expectation maximization of a structure with the probability of the underlying event is desirable.

A variety of scoring functions have been proposed in the space search optimization in structure learning. Akaike's information criterion (AIC) and the Bayesian information criterion (BIC), which were traditionally scoring functions for performing variable selection in linear regression, are widely used. However, both scoring functions tend to overlearn the data and thus yield a network with an overabundance of arcs, resulting in unnecessary structure complexity. As complexity may cause difficulty in performing operations such as inference and structure updating, this is a rather unappealing characteristic. Other techniques, such as using the minimum description length (MDL) (Lam & Bacchus, 1994), have been applied with varying degrees of success. It should be noted that, empirically, it has been found that none of these scoring functions, when applied to a bottom-up search, yields a structure that is as close to the original as the asymptotically correct information theory approach discussed earlier.

The Bayesian Dirichlet equivalent (BDE) (Heckerman, 1995) is a scoring function which, when applied to a bottom-up search, empirically tends to generate structures that are closer to the underlying model than the other techniques mentioned. This scoring function models variables as Dirichelet distributions. The joint probability of a given structure (M_1) and the training data (D) is found and compared to another joint probability corresponding to a different structure (M_2) to form a likelihood ratio, as shown below:

$$\frac{P(M_1|D)}{P(M_2|D)} = \frac{\dfrac{P(M_1,D)}{P(D)}}{\dfrac{P(M_2,D)}{P(D)}} = \frac{P(M_1,D)}{P(M_2,D)}$$

Because the distribution of the data is the same in both cases, there is no need to marginalize over all models to find the probability of the data.

Although they do have the potential to find structures that more accurately represent dependence relationships between nodes, space searching techniques suffer from a high degree of computational complexity. The complexity is generally $O(N^4)$ but may be as high as $O(N^5)$ depending on the scoring function. The majority of this complexity comes from potentially needing to iterate a space searching scheme many times.

Another structure learning approach attempts to alleviate the computational difficulty involved in some fitness functions in the second category. It employs the computationally efficient, although generally less accurate, first approach as an initial "guess" for the node conditional relationships, and then uses the second approach to refine the initial network. This refining step is sometimes called a middle-out search. This technique has been shown to reduce the computational complexity incurred by a bottom-up gradient search, while retaining its potential accuracy (Kane, Sahin, & Savakis, 2003). In the context of image understanding, the work in Kane and Savakis (2004) proposes model selection to determine the structure of a Bayesian network that provides for the knowledge representation and inference of the indoor vs. outdoor scene classification problem, as will be discussed in Section 3.3.

Bayesian Networks for Scene Classification

Framework

The goal of image understanding is to generate a semantic description of a scene, so that it can be used in a particular application. In essence, such a description can be done at the whole scene level or at the parts level (e.g., image regions). The former is referred to as scene classification (i.e., what type of scene this is; is it indoor or outdoor? is it sunset or beach?) and the latter corresponds to object detection and recognition (what is the object and where is it?). In this chapter, we describe the use of Bayesian networks in both scene classification and object detection, respectively. While there are differences in the ways Bayesian networks are applied to these two problems, conceptually it is perhaps easier to incorporate Bayesian networks first at the whole scene level and then progress to the object or parts level.

The primary approach to image understanding is based on collecting training data and identifying decision boundaries between classes in the feature space, that is, training a classifier. After training is completed, these classifiers can be used to characterize novel samples. Both low-level and semantic features have been used for scene classification, and Bayes nets provide a framework for effective integration of such features. Low level features, such as color, texture, and shape, have been widely used (Amit & Geman, 1999; Hjelmas & Low, 2001) and were found to be effective for certain tasks, such as "query by example." However, they are of limited value in important multimedia applications, such as efficient browsing and organization of large collections of digital photos and videos, which require semantic content extraction (Vailaya, Figueiredo, Jain, & Zhang, 1999). Semantic features are important when dealing with photographic images due to the unconstrained nature of photographs and the difficulty in extracting low-level features reliably from them. Bayesian networks provide a unified framework for fusing both low-level and semantic features and allow for diversity in the feature extraction process, and ultimately can improve classification results (Luo, Savakis, & Singhal, 2005).

For tasks such as indoor-outdoor image classification (Luo & Savakis, 2001; Serrano et al., 2004) and scene classification (Valaiya et al., 1998), good performance has been achieved. However, even for the same tasks, higher level features or cues are clearly demanded. For instance, there are natural images where even a human may have difficulty determining the correct orientation, particularly at a low resolution where object recognition is difficult or impossible (Luo, Crandall, Singhal, Boutell, & Gray, 2003). Some may not even have a preferred orientation. Another major concern with low-level feature-driven, exemplar-based approaches is the ability to generalize to real-world, unconstrained images which do not fall into well-defined scene prototypes, and for which a comprehensive collection of prototype exemplars is not readily available.

Model-based approaches are built on expected configuration of a specific type of scene. A scene configuration is the layout of its objects, created from expert or learned knowledge of the scene. Relatively little research has been done on using model-based approaches for unconstrained natural image understanding, because it is usually only possible to build a model for a well-defined scene type, and such a model may not generalize to other scene types (Lipson, Grimson, & Sinha, 1997). For example, while it is possible to build scene models *manually* and *individually* for scene types such as "fields," "snowy mountains," "snowy mountains with lakes," and "waterfalls," it would be far more difficult to do so for other scenes types such as typical indoor scenes. A trainable scene configuration model called composite region template was proposed in Smith and Li (1999) and shown to be promising for a selected set of scene types exhibiting distinctive spatial configuration patterns.

The framework proposed in Luo et al. (2005) may be viewed as a hybrid approach. First, both low-level and semantic features are utilized. In fact, it is a great challenge to find a way to combine such diverse information, measured by different metrics, and represented by different means. For example, color features are represented by histograms, and the presence of a face is Boolean. A probabilistic knowledge integration framework would allow all the information to be integrated in equal terms of probabilities. Bayesian networks allow domain knowledge to be incorporated in the structure as well as parameters of the networks, which is more difficult, if not impossible, for other inference engines such as neural networks or support vector machines (Bishop, 1996; Cristianini & Shawe-Taylor, 2000).

A general framework for semantic understanding of pictorial images, such as the one in Luo et al. (2005), would have an input that is a digital image of a natural scene and is used to extract two sets of descriptors. The first set corresponds to low-level features, for example color, texture, and edge information, and the second set corresponds to semantic objects that can be automatically detected. The low-level features are extracted on a pixel or block basis, using a bank of predetermined filters. The semantic features are obtained using a bank of predesigned object detectors that have been trained for accuracy. The state of the art in object detection, both in terms of accuracy and speed, determines what is included in the object detector bank. The outputs of the low-level and semantic detectors are evidences that are fed into a Bayesian network-based inference engine. The Bayes net is capable of incorporating domain knowledge, as well as dealing with a variable number of input evidences, and producing semantic predicates, which may be in the forms of semantic labels of the entire images or importance maps indicating different scene content. In the next section, we provide an illustrative example of the Bayesian network-based scene classification in indoor vs. outdoor categorization.

Indoor vs. Outdoor Classification

Scene categorization is important in a number of applications that deal with consumer photographs. Knowledge of the scene type is useful for event classification, which constitutes a fundamental component of automatic albuming systems (Loui & Savakis, 2003). Scene categorization is also valuable in image retrieval from databases because it provides high-level semantic understanding of scene content that can be used along with lower-level features such as color, texture, and shape for database browsing (Vogel & Schiele, 2006). Furthermore, when images are processed through a complex imaging path, processing operations may be adjusted depending on the scene type so that the best image rendering can be achieved.

The general problem of automatic scene categorization is difficult to solve and is best approached by a divide-and-conquer strategy. A good first step is to consider only two classes such as indoor vs. outdoor (Serrano et al., 2004; Szummer & Picard, 1998), where outdoor may be further subdivided into city vs. landscape (Vailaya et al., 1998), and so forth. Scene categorization is often approached by computing low-level features, which are processed with a classifier engine for inferring high-level information about the image. In (Szummer & Picard, 1998), color and texture features were computed for the entire image or for image subsections. One of the issues when dealing with a diverse set of features is how to integrate them into a classification engine. The solution proposed was to independently classify image subsections and obtain a final result using a majority classifier. One problem with the methods using low-level features in scene categorization is that it is often difficult to generalize them to diverse image data beyond the training set. More importantly, they lack high-level semantic image interpretation that is extremely valuable in determining the scene type.

Scene content such as the presence of people, sky, grass, and so forth, may be used as additional cues for improving the classification performance obtained by low level features alone. Sky

Figure 1. Bayesian network for indoor vs. outdoor classification

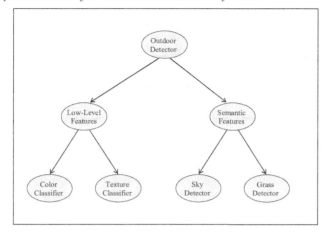

and grass regions can be identified using color and texture features and classifiers that are tuned in a supervised fashion for sky and grass detection (Singhal, Luo, & Zhu, 2003).

A Bayesian network approach can be used to integrate low-level color and texture features and semantic features, including sky and grass, in order to improve the classification performance over using low-level features alone. The Bayesian network structure shown in Figure 1 was proposed for classifying images to indoor vs. outdoor (Luo & Savakis, 2001; Serrano et al., 2004). The network integrates low-level features, that is, color and texture classification, and semantic features, that is, sky and grass detection, using a single inference engine. The conditional probability matrices for each node were derived using the frequency counting method based on a Kodak database of consumer images (Luo & Savakis, 2001). The color features are based on the quantized color histogram (3 x 64 bins) in the Ohta color space with the following components: $I_1 = R + G + B$, $I_2 = R - B$, $I_3 = R - 2G + B$ (Ohta, Kanade, & Sakai, 1980). The texture features were based on the multiresolution simultaneous autoregressive (MRSAR) model (Mao & Jain, 1992). The classification based on color or texture features used a k-nearest neighbor classifier ($k=1$), and yielded 74% and 82%, respectively, for a database of 1300 images (Luo & Savakis, 2001).

The sky and grass features were extracted using two methods. First, the ground truth information about the images was used, that is, the sky and grass detection is always correct. The indoor/outdoor classification results obtained with perfect semantic features reflect an upper bound in performance, because the accuracy of any actual sky and grass classifier would be suboptimal. The second method involved using actual detectors to obtain sky and grass information (Luo & Etz, 2002; Vailaya & Jain, 2000). Sky and grass detectors are based on color/texture features and yield an average accuracy of 95% true detection with 10% false positives.

After all the evidences propagate through the Bayesian network in Figure 1, a threshold is chosen to determine whether the image is indoor or outdoor. When the output belief value at the root node is above the threshold, the image is characterized as outdoor, and vice versa. The threshold value was determined from one-fifth of the available data and applied

Table 1. Indoor vs. outdoor classification results with integration of computed low-level features and semantic sky/grass features obtained from ground truth data

Indoor vs. Outdoor Classification using "Best Case" Semantic Features						
	Color [C]	Texture [T]	C and T	Semantic [S] and C	T and S	S and C and T
Percent Correct	74.2%	82.2%	82.3%	80.9%	86.9%	90.1%

Table 2. Indoor vs. outdoor classification results with integration of computed low-level features and computed semantic sky/grass features

Indoor vs. Outdoor Classification using Computed Semantic Features						
	Color [C]	Texture [T]	C and T	Semantic [S] and C	T and S	S and C and T
Percent Correct	74.2%	82.2%	82.3%	75.2%	84.0%	84.7%

to the remaining testing data. The value of 0.35 yielded the best overall results for both the training and testing data. In fact, the performance is statistically the same on both data sets under 2-fold cross-validation.

The indoor/outdoor classification results with ground truth information for sky and grass are shown in Table 1, where an overall classification of 90.1% is obtained. This level of performance can be viewed as an upper bound when these semantic features are used. The indoor/outdoor classification results that are shown in Table 2 were obtained by computing sky and grass detection and provide a more realistic performance estimate. In all the cases, the use of semantic features improves the system performance, and an overall percent accuracy of 84.7% was obtained when using both low-level and semantic features.

These results provide an improvement over the classification results based on color or texture alone. The major reason for such an improvement is due to the incorporation of semantic features. The Bayesian network provides a good framework for integrating all of the features, as shown in Tables 1 and 2. It should be noted that the low threshold for the combined belief values indicates that even moderate evidence of the presence of prominent outdoor features (sky and grass) is sufficient reason to classify the image as outdoor. If the belief values were to be strictly interpreted as probability, the threshold would have been 0.5.

Examples of correctly and incorrectly classified indoor and outdoor scenes are shown in Figures 2 and 3, respectively. Figure 3 shows that classification errors can be attributed to misleading illumination sources. For instance, the incorrectly classified outdoor scene was taken at dusk and is largely illuminated by camera flash. Conversely, the incorrectly classified indoor scene is highly textured, which is uncharacteristic of most indoor scenes. On one hand, the small patch of sky in Figure 2(d) was correctly detected to help correctly classify the image as outdoor. On the other hand, imperfect semantic feature detector actu-

Figure 2. Examples of correctly classified indoor and outdoor scenes (left and right column, respectively)

Figure 3. Examples of incorrectly classified (a) indoor and (b) outdoor scenes

ally further confounded the misclassification of Figure 3(a), while ironically helped classify Figure 2(f) correctly.

Bayesian Network Structure Learning for Scene Classification

Structure learning can sometimes be used to achieve improved classification performance over applying expert opinion to structure determination. This section presents an overview of the model selection technique employed, an overview of the inference technique used, results using this technique, and a comparison with past results to show improvement in accuracy.

The feature extraction techniques were employed on the same Kodak database of consumer images, which consists of 1308 images. The feature probabilities for 654 of these images were used for training and the remaining 654 were used in the inference experiment. The feature extraction techniques for color, texture, blue sky, and grass, were the same as described in the previous section. After the feature extraction stage, k-nearest neighbor probabilities were extracted and quantized to the nearest 10% for a total of 11 possible states per feature node. The total number of possible feature instantiations is found by taking the number of nodes multiplied by the number of states per node yielding 29,282 possible node instantiations.

The total number of possible directed acyclic graphs given the number of nodes is given in (Cowell, Dawid, Lauritzen, & Spiegelhalter, 1999) as:

$$f(n) = \sum_{i=1}^{n} (-1)^{(i+1)} \frac{n!}{(n-i)!\, i!} 2^{i(n-i)} f(n-i)$$

where n is the number of nodes in the network. In the case of the presented five-node network, there are potentially 29,281 possible graph structures. As this is a relatively small network, it was decided to forgo the model refining technique in favor of a pure gradient search. The fitness function used was the (BDE) score with a uniform prior on the space of network structures. The result is the data given model (DGM) probability calculated using the equation:

$$P(D|M) = \prod_{i=1}^{I} \prod_{j=1}^{qi} \frac{(c_i - 1)! \prod_{k=1}^{c_i} n(x_{ik}|\pi_{ij})!}{(c_i + n(\pi_{ij}) - 1)!}$$

where c_i is the number of states of the ith node, x_{ik} is the ith node with instantiation k and π_{ij} denotes the parent nodes of the ith node with node instantiation j. The model derived using this technique is shown in Figure 4.

Figure 4. Flow graph for indoor vs. outdoor scene classification

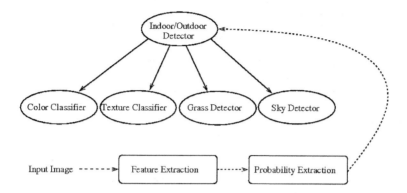

It is worth noting that the model selection structure prefers a naïve Bayes probability model compared to the multilayered structure crafted by experts. In this bottom-up approach, the semantic task is an explanation for the feature probabilities, which serve as states of respective nodes. The inference technique used differs from the one previously used. In the network generated by expert opinion, the goal was to create an outdoor image detector. For a given image, an indoor classification is implied, if the Bayesian Network response is below a chosen threshold; otherwise the image is classified as outdoor. In the network derived from structure learning, full inference was performed. In other words, an indoor classification is implied if it has higher probability of being indoor than outdoor. The technique uses Bayes' rule to compute the posterior probability of the indoor/outdoor states. This is accomplished by first realizing that the joint probability of the network is given by:

$$P(IO, C, T, B, G) = P(IO)\, P(C \mid IO)\, P(T \mid IO)\, P(B \mid IO)\, P(G \mid IO),$$

where *IO, C, T, B, G* represent Indoor/Outdoor, Color, Texture, Blue Sky, and Grass, respectively. Understanding this, we can then compute an indoor vs. outdoor probability with the equation:

$$P(IO = io \mid C = c, T = t, B = b, G = g) = \frac{P(IO = io, C = c, T = t, B = b, G = g)}{\sum_{io} P(IO = io, C = c, T = t, B = b, G = g)}$$

Results of using the described inference technique on the model selection structure on the testing half of the database are shown in Table 3. We see that the proposed procedure for indoor vs. outdoor scene classification performs with approximately 12% greater accuracy than when expert opinion and thresholding are employed.

Table 3. Indoor vs. outdoor scene classification results using model selection

Indoor vs. Outdoor Classification using Computed Semantic Features Model Selection Approach			
	Correct	Incorrect	Percent Correct
Indoor	288	9	97.0%
Outdoor	350	7	98.0%
Overall	638	16	97.3%

Along with inference, the posterior probabilities can also be used on the training set for error estimation. For a given event, we can use the error estimated by expectation maximization along with the frequency of the event to get some idea as to how often our inference will be incorrect. The expected error rate can then be calculated as:

$$\sum_{c,t,s,g} (1 - P(Inf(IO|...)|C = c, T = t, B = b, G = g))n(C = c, T = t, B = b, G = g)$$

where *Inf(IO|...)* is the inferred state of the network give the feature probabilities and *n*(...) is the number of events in the training set where the states are as given by the arguments. This equation gives the expected rate per number of events in the database. By normalizing by the number of events of the databases, the error rate can be expressed as a percentage of the total number of training images. By employing this technique, a resulting error rate of 18.6 per 654 images is found, where the actual error rate is 16 per 654 images. After normalization, an expected error rate of 2.8% is obtained, which matches very well with the actual error of 2.7%

The indoor/outdoor classification results show that, when model selection was used in model determination and posterior probabilities were used in inference, there is a significant improvement in inference accuracy compared with previous results based on expert opinion. In this case, by using model selection, a network structure is found that more accurately encodes the conditional dependencies between network nodes given the training database. In general, model selection is likely to outperform an expert if there is enough representative data available.

Bayesian Networks for Object Detection

Overview

Bayesian networks are particularly well suited to the problem of object detection, and have proven useful in the analysis of the intraclass variations of categories such as faces. Bayesian networks provide a "smoothing" effect upon incomplete data. This feature reinforces the collective power of part detectors without requiring that they detect parts with perfect accuracy. In addition, Bayesian networks offer natural resistance to overfitting and ability to incorporate incomplete data and cause-and-effect relationships (Heckerman, 1995). They have been applied to a wide variety of tasks in machine learning, including high-level applications, such as extracting semantic information from consumer photographs (Luo, Savakis, Etz, & Singhal, 2000), video frames (Vasconcelos & Lippman, 1998), and multimedia (Paek, Sable, Hatzivassiloglou, Jaimes, Schiffman, Chang, & McKeown, 1999). All these works utilize a number of detectors as inputs to Bayesian networks, which then make a decision on multiple sources of information. Individual detectors do not need to be precise, as conflicting information often can be effectively disambiguated by the modeling network.

One such example is using a Bayesian network to integrate the results of multiple individual material detectors (Singhal et al., 2003). Material detection refers to the problem of identifying key semantic material types, such as sky, grass, foliage, water, and snow. The limitation with individual material detectors is the high percentage of misclassifications because of the ambiguities in the color and texture characteristics of various material types. A holistic approach was employed to determine the scene content from a set of individual material detectors using a probabilistic spatial context model, which is encoded and enforced by a Bayesian network. This approach helps reduce misclassification by constraining the material beliefs to conform to the spatial context model, and in turn improve the accuracy of materials detection significantly over the individual material detectors themselves. In the same spirit, to capture the interplay among individually estimated elements of the scene (e.g., cars and pedestrians), a Bayesian network model is used to capture the conditional independence for viewpoint, object identities, and the 3D geometry of surfaces surrounding the objects (Hoiem, Efros, & Hebert, 2006). Viewpoint describes the horizon position in the image and the height of the camera in the 3D scene in relation to the objects of interest. Each image has n object hypotheses, where n varies by image. The object hypothesis involves assigning an identity (e.g., pedestrian or background) and a bounding box. The surface geometry describes the 3D orientations of the object surface and nearby surfaces in the scene.

Bayesian methods have been applied within the context of human face detection as well. Rehg, Murphy, and Fieguth (1999) presented a videoconferencing system that used a Bayes net to determine the speaker. Several features were incorporated, including a neural net-based face detector and a motion-based mouth detector, so that the system could distinguish the speaker if there were multiple faces present.

In particular, face detection using Bayesian networks was employed by Yow and Cipolla (1996, 1997). They detected feature points using spatial filtering and grouped them into face candidates using geometric constraints. Bayesian networks were used to reinforce probabilities and evaluate the likelihood of a candidate as a face. This approach adopts a bottom-up feature-based approach where the face is modeled in terms of six oriented facial features: two eyes, two eyebrows, a nose, and a mouth. Feature detection is simplified as pairs of oriented edges that can be detected at various scales and illuminations. Due to the simplicity of the feature detectors considered, there are many false positives and perceptual grouping is used to eliminate most of them. Feature candidates are grouped into face candidates based on geometrical, intensity, and spatial constraints.

To deal with both frontal and profile faces, a new Bayesian network was constructed with six child nodes, where each node corresponds to one of the facial features. Another stage of processing was performed by a second, more complex multilayer Bayesian network, which assembled the landmarks from primitive edge components based on similarity to spatial relationships gathered from true face data.

A recently developed framework for generalized object detection (Higgs & Savakis, 2005) is presented next, and it is tailored toward the specific application of human face detection under pose variations. Face detection was selected because it is a well-explored area of research, which allows new approaches to be evaluated on a comparative basis to existing, known solutions. For a generalized method, initially applying a new methodology to a known problem can provide valuable feedback during the implementation process by illustrating the limitations with respect to a specialized approach. Furthermore, human faces are expected to be rigid geometric bodies with specific features (parts) that are always present (though potentially occluded), which can be leveraged in the form of assumptions about the problem set. Recent work on parts-based object detection has demonstrated the potential of this approach (Fergus, Perona, & Zisserman, 2003; Schneiderman & Kanade, 2004).

The presence and locations of specific features, for example eyes, nose, and mouth in a face, lend themselves to a bottom-up approach to detection that is intuitive and computationally tractable. If a significant number of these parts are detected, there stands to reason that the object is probably present. The converse is also true: if an image contains none or few of these parts, it is unlikely for the object to be present. If a parts-based detection scheme is flexible enough, the detection of a partially-occluded object can still be successful, whereas a top-down scheme may have more difficulty making an accurate decision.

Another common problem in the field of object detection is caused by the nature of three-dimensional objects being projected onto a two dimensional plane (Schneiderman & Kanade, 2000; Jones & Viola, 2001). Because a true 3D representation is typically unavailable, it is hard to register matching object features between two different views. The task becomes even more complex when applied to flexible objects, as in the case of limbs on an animal. One way to combat this difficulty is to create a detection system explicitly with the capacity to detect multiple views. Within a parts-based framework, the parts for object detection can be selected to correspond to different object pose angles. The easiest way is to separate the object detection into discrete views; for example, a car detector might use headlights for a frontal view and wheel parts for a side view. Alternatively, a more flexible model could use part detectors that activate for multiple views; for example, the same car detection scenario might utilize both curved contour detectors and right-angle detectors for many possible viewing angles.

An object detection system combining these two important concepts, parts-based detection and multiple viewpoints, is presented in this section. To introduce and establish a comparative benchmark with other object detection schemes, it has been applied to the specific task

Figure 5. Parts-based object detection framework

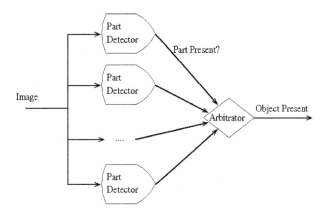

of human face detection. Within the field of face detection, there are roughly two different schools of thought with respect to the overall approach: feature-based and image-based. Surveys of recent work can be found in Hjelmas and Low (2001) and Yang, Kriegman, and Ahuja (2002). The detection framework presented here is feature-based and uses neural network part detectors that are typically used independently for detecting and locating objects or their parts (Rowley, Baluja, & Kanade, 1998; Schimmel, Savakis, & Ray, 2004).

System Architecture

The basic framework for a parts-based object detection system is shown in Figure 5. Specialized part detectors scan an image to find the part for which they have been tuned. The belief value for each part is passed on to an arbitrator, which determines the likelihood that the object is present, given the individual part probabilities. Splitting objects into various component features allows for detection that can account for occlusion over small portions of the object, without requiring that the training set model all possible ways of obscuring parts. This structure is more suited for a single view, in which the appearance is relatively constant.

Expanding on the basic framework to support multiple, discrete views results in a structure where the parts for each view are arbitrated separately, providing a belief value or probability to the final view arbitration stage. If the presence of an object can be established by any of the individual views, the arbitration can be performed by a simple comparison operation. Otherwise, if the views are competitive or mutually exclusive, the arbitrator should leverage any correlation between the view responses to make a more informed decision.

By tying multiple parts to specific views, rather than selecting a number of parts that correspond to multiple views, hierarchical arbitration methods and structures can be used. In this manner, the detection of parts common to one view avoids "competition" with those in a second, which could result in a decreased chance of detecting either view.

Figure 6. Bayesian network for parts-based object detection

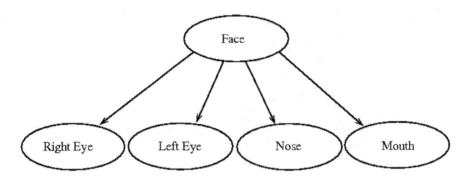

Each part detector is a standard multilayer feed-forward network with an input layer, a fixed-size hidden layer, and a single output neuron. The input layer for each part is implemented as a rectangular window, with dimensions specific to the part size on an object at some reference scale. The neural network is used as a sliding window, such that the network responses for each possible subwindow are recorded in an activation map.

Bayesian networks exhibit excellent "smoothing" capabilities across incomplete datasets, as well as resistance to overfitting. It is safe to assume that no part detector is 100% accurate, and therefore Bayes nets are chosen as view arbitrators due to their ability to implicitly account for these inaccuracies. Figure 6 illustrates a sample Bayesian network and how it would be used to arbitrate over a single view. The node hierarchy and arrow direction indicate that the presence of an object within an image "causes" the detection of the object's constituent parts. The conditional probability table (CPT) for each part shows that they are all treated in a conditionally independent manner, and thus network is a naive Bayes model.

A second design decision made when using Bayesian techniques relates to the variable representation at each node. An object's detection is a binary value: either present or absent; however, the neural network part detectors output a continuous value. Thus, the part activation values must be similarly discretized into presence and absence. Because the continuous distributions underlying neural nets are inherently unknown and very difficult to model, this is a helpful and intuitive step. A view can be detected by making observations of the part states, and selecting the view state that maximizes the network probability, as calculated by inference.

Because detection at different pose angles can never be evidence against the presence of the object, the final decision can be made with a simple logical OR operation. As long as any single view can represent the object and there is no destructive interference, little additional leverage can be gained by applying a more complex decision-making process.

Performance Evaluation

The FERET database (Phillips, Moon, Rizvi, & Rauss, 2000) was chosen to provide images of human faces for training and testing, primarily because it contains multiple viewing angles of human faces. Other desirable characteristics include the large number of different subjects, and good diversity across age, race, and gender. Although various pose angles were available within the FERET image database, only the Frontal A and Quarter Left views were selected to illustrate the capabilities of the system, henceforth referred to as "frontal" and "side." The four parts most commonly associated with the human face detection are the two eyes, the nose, and the mouth. The choices of pose angles allow for all four facial subfeatures to be visible in both views. The size of the window used to detect individual parts was selected so that each part would fully fit into the neural network input at a reference scale, that is, with 400 or less input neurons. All eyes were detected by a 12×20 pixel window, with the exception of the right eye of the side view; it was 12×16 pixels due to foreshortening effects. The nose and mouth detectors were 18×20 and 14×32 pixel windows, respectively. The resulting faces had approximate dimensions of 50 pixels high by 55 wide.

Bootstrapping was used to train the part detectors (Sung & Poggio, 1998), and a corpus of "non-face" images was required to provide false-positives. The Background dataset in Weber (1999) was chosen; it consists of several hundred images showing a variety of cluttered indoor office settings as well as outdoor scenes with both natural flora and man-made architecture.

The detection system was trained and tested under a cross-validation scheme, with each dataset divided into four subsets. The bootstrapping process similar to the work in Sung and Poggio (1998) was used to train individual parts detectors. Artificial neural networks for part detection were trained using standard backpropagation. The component parts were extracted from the training images, preprocessed, and added to the training set as positive examples. The background images were scanned for false-positive examples to add to the training set and the image order was randomized for each bootstrap iteration. Once a sufficient number of false-positives were found, the neural networks were retrained. This step was repeated until the number of false-positives fell below a particular threshold, at which point the bootstrapping process was considered complete.

The goal of training the individual view arbitration networks was to "teach" the arbitration components how to use the detection patterns of a view's parts to make a decision about the presence or absence of the object in the scene. Using these separate training images from both object-present and no-object-present databases, part activation values were gathered using a search similar to that in the bootstrapping process. Activation responses were used to determine event thresholds for determining a part's detection by plotting a receiver operating characteristic (ROC) curve.

Table 4. Part detection thresholds and CPT entries

	Frontal View				Side View			
	Left Eye	Right Eye	Nose	Mouth	Left Eye	Right Eye	Nose	Mouth
Threshold	0.5926	0.6097	0.5190	0.5605	0.3959	0.5290	0.3270	0.5096
P(Part=T | View=F)	0.0798	0.1079	0.0458	0.0790	0.0791	0.0924	0.0658	0.1145
P(Part=T | View=T)	0.8964	0.8624	0.9519	0.8663	0.9111	0.8560	0.9227	0.8449

Table 5. Detection rates on testing images

	Face images detected (%)	Non-face images detected (%)
Frontal Face	96.7%	3.3%
Side Face	97.2%	2.8%
Background	5.7%	94.3%
Overall Face	96.9%	3.1%

The use of Bayes nets allowed for the integration of the individual neural network responses. Conditional probability tables were constructed by counting the frequency of detection with respect to whether the candidate image contained a face or not, as shown in summarized form in Table 4. Note that the entries in Table 4 reflect the performance of the individual part detectors.

Bayes' rule was applied to each view's arbitration network to find an expression relating the presence of an object at a certain view to the conditional part probabilities, as shown in the equation below:

$$P(v \mid d_1, d_2, d_3, d_4) = P(v)P(d_1 \mid v) \, P(d_2 \mid v) \, P(d_3 \mid v) \, P(d_4 \mid v)$$

where v represents view and $d_1 - d_4$ represent detected features. For a given set of part detections, the equation was evaluated twice: once for each state of the view detection, substituting in the corresponding CPTs for each part. The view state with the larger network probability was the view belief for the image. In most cases, two or more of the four parts at any particular view indicated the presence of the object.

The testing results illustrate the face detection capabilities of the system on images outside the training set, and are summarized in Table 5. It is worth noting that the overall detection performance is better than that of any of the individual part detectors, which illustrates the strength of using Bayesian Networks to make decisions in this context.

Conclusion

In this chapter, we illustrate the usefulness of Bayesian networks for image understanding applications including object detection and scene classification, and we outline the principles and methodologies for applying Bayesian networks to such applications. We provide examples that demonstrate that Bayes nets can be built according to specific domain knowledge and available training data to solve inherently uncertain vision problems.

In particular, the latter part of the chapter focuses on an extension of parts-based object detection that utilizes Bayesian networks for decision making and includes support for multiple viewing angles. The domain of human face detection was used to investigate the power of this approach. The detectors were implemented using neural networks trained through bootstrapping and against manually selected facial features from frontal and side images. Four features were chosen from each view: the right and left eyes, the nose, and the mouth. Bayesian networks were used to integrate part detections in a flexible manner, and were trained on a separate dataset so that the experimental performance of each part detector could be incorporated into the final decision. Future work will apply this framework to the detection of other types of objects.

Acknowledgment

This research was funded in part by the Eastman Kodak Company and the Center for Electronic Imaging Systems (CEIS), a NYSTAR-designated Center for Advanced Technology in New York State. The authors would also like to thank Dr. Amit Singhal, Mr. Navid Serrano, and Mr. David Higgs for their help and contributions to various parts of this chapter.

References

Amit, Y., & Geman, D. (1999). A computational model for visual selection. *Neural Computation, 11*(7), 1691-1715.

Bishop, C.M. (1996). *Neural networks for pattern recognition.* Oxford, UK: Oxford University Press.

Cheng, J., Bell, D., & Liu, W. (1997). An algorithm for Bayesian network construction from data. In *Proceedings of the 6th International Workshop on Artificial Intelligence and Statistics.* Fort Lauderdale, Florida: The Society for Artificial Intelligence and Statistics.

Cowell, R.G., Dawid, A.P., Lauritzen, S.L., & Spiegelhalter, D.J. (1999). *Probabilistic networks and expert systems.* New York: Springer-Verlag.

Cristianini, N., & Shawe-Taylor, J. (2000). *An introduction to Support Vector Machines (and other kernel-based learning methods).* Cambridge, UK: Cambridge University Press.

de Campos, L.M., Fernández-Luna, J.M., Gámez, J.A. & Puerta, J.M. (2002). Ant colony optimization for learning Bayesian networks. *International Journal of Approximate Reasoning, 31*(3), 291-311.

Dudgeon, D.E., & Lacoss, R.T. (1993). An overview of automatic target recognition. *Lincoln Laboratory Journal, 6*(1), 3-10.

Fergus, R., Perona, P., & Zisserman, A. (2003). Object class recognition by unsupervised scale-invariant learning. In *Proceedings of the IEEE Conference in Computer Vision and Pattern Recognition* (pp. II-264-II-271). Madison, Wisconsin: IEEE Computer Society.

Heckerman, D. (1995). *A tutorial on learning with Bayesian networks* (Tech. Rep. MSD-TR-95-06). Redmond, WA: Microsoft Research.

Higgs, D., & Savakis, A. (2005). Object detection framework based on parts identification at multiple views. In *Proceedings of the IEEE Western New York Image Processing Workshop.* Rochester, NY: IEEE Signal Processing Society.

Hjelmås, E., & Low, B.K. (2001). Face detection: A survey. *Computer Vision and Image Understanding, 83*(3), 236-274.

Hoiem, D., Efros, A., & Hebert, M. (2006). Putting objects in perspective. In *Proceedings of the IEEE Conference on Computer Vision and Pattern Recognition* (pp. 2137-2144). New York: IEEE Computer Society.

Jones, M.J., & Viola, P. (2001). Rapid object detection using a boosted cascade of simple features. In *Proceedings of the IEEE Conference on Computer Vision and Pattern Recognition* (pp. I-511-I-518). Kauai, Hawaii: IEEE Computer Society.

Kane, M., Sahin, F., & Savakis, A. (2003). A two phase approach to Bayesian network model selection and comparison between the MDL and DGM scoring heuristics. In *Proceedings of the IEEE International Conference on Systems, Man and Cybernetics* (pp. 4601-4606). Washington, DC: IEEE Systems, Man and Cybernetics Society.

Kane, M., & Savakis, A. (2004). Bayesian network structure learning and inference in indoor vs. outdoor image classification. In *Proceedings of the IEEE International Conference On Pattern Recognition* (pp. 479-482). Cambridge, UK: The International Association for Pattern Recognition.

Lam, W., & Bacchus, F. (1994). Learning Bayesian belief networks: An approach based on the MDL principle. *Computational Intelligence, 10*(3), 269-293.

Larranaga, P.P., Poza, M., Yurramendi, Y., Murga, R.H., & Kuijpers, C.M.H. (1996). Structure learning of Bayesian networks by genetic algorithms: A performance analysis of control parameters. *IEEE Transactions on Pattern Analysis and Machine Intelligence, 18*(9), 912-926.

Lipson, P., Grimson, E., & Sinha, P. (1997). Configuration-based scene classification and image indexing. In *Proceedings of the IEEE Conference on Computer Vision and Pattern Recognition* (pp. 1007-1013). San Juan, Puerto Rico: IEEE Computer Society.

Loui, A., & Savakis, A. (2003). Automated event clustering and quality screening of consumer pictures for digital albuming. *IEEE Transactions on Multimedia, 5*(3), 390-402.

Luo, J., Crandall, D., Singhal, A., Boutell, M., & Gray, R.T. (2003). Psychophysical study of image orientation perception. *Spatial Vision, 16*(5), 429-457.

Luo, J., & Etz, S.P. (2002). A physical model-based approach to detecting sky in photographic images. *IEEE Transactions on Image Processing, 11*(3), 201-212.

Luo, J., & Savakis, A. (2001). Indoor vs. outdoor classification of consumer photographs. In *Proceedings of the IEEE International Conference on Image Processing* (pp. 745-748). Thessaloniki, Greece: IEEE Signal Processing Society.

Luo, J., Savakis, A., Etz, S., & Singhal, A. (2000). On the application of Bayes networks to semantic understanding of consumer photographs. In *Proceedings of the IEEE International Conference on Image Processing* (pp. 512-515). Vancouver, Canada: IEEE Signal Processing Society.

Luo, J., Savakis, A., & Singhal, A. (2005). A Bayesian networks-based framework for semantic image understanding. *Pattern Recognition, 38*(6), 919-934.

Mao, J., & Jain, A.K. (1992). Texture classification and segmentation using multiresolution simultaneous autoregressive models. *Pattern Recognition, 25*(2), 173-188.

Neapolitan, R. (2003). *Learning Bayesian networks*. Upper Saddle River, NJ: Prentice Hall.

Ohta, Y.I., Kanade, T., & Sakai, T. (1980). Color information for region segmentation. *Computer Graphics Image Processing, 13*(3), 222-241.

Paek, S., Sable, C.L., Hatzivassiloglou, V., Jaimes, A., Schiffman, B.H., Chang, S.F., & McKeown, K.R. (1999). Integration of visual and text based approaches for the content labeling and classification of photographs. In *Proceedings of the ACM SIGIR '99 Workshop on Multimedia Indexing and Retrieval*. Berkeley, CA: ACM Press.

Pearl, J. (1988). *Probabilistic reasoning in intelligent systems*. San Francisco, CA: Morgan Kaufmann.

Phillips, P.J., Moon, H., Rizvi, S.A., & Rauss, P.J. (2000). The FERET evaluation methodology for face-recognition algorithms. *IEEE Transactions on Pattern Analysis and Machine Intelligence, 22*(10), 1090-1104.

Rehg, J.M., Murphy, K.P., & Fieguth, P.W. (1999). Vision-based speaker detection using Bayesian networks. In *Proceedings of the IEEE Conference on Computer Vision and Pattern Recognition* (pp. 2110-2116). Ft. Collins, CO: IEEE Computer Society.

Robinson, G.P., & Colchester, A.C.F. (1994). Model-based recognition of anatomical objects from medical images. *Image and Vision Computing, 12*(8), 499-507.

Rowley, H.A., Baluja, S., & Kanade, T. (1998). Neural network-based face detection. *IEEE Transactions on Pattern Analysis and Machine Intelligence, 20*(1), 23-38.

Schimmel, J., Savakis, A., & Ray, L. (2004). Geometric head model approach to facial pose estimation. In *Proceedings of the IEEE Western New York Image Processing Workshop*. Rochester, NY: IEEE Signal Processing Society.

Schneiderman, H., & Kanade, T. (2000). A statistical method for 3D object detection applied to faces and cars. In *Proceedings of the IEEE Conference on Computer Vision and Pattern Recognition* (pp. 746-751). Hilton Head Island, SC: IEEE Computer Society.

Schneiderman, H., & Kanade, T. (2004). Object detection using the statistics of parts. *International Journal of Computer Vision, 56*, 151-177.

Schurmann, J., Bartneck, N., Bayer, T., Franke, J., Mandler, E., & Oberlander, M. (1992). Document analysis - from pixels to contents. *Proceedings of the IEEE, 80*(7), 1101-1119.

Serrano, N., Savakis, A., & Luo, J. (2004). Improved scene classification using efficient low-level features and semantic cues. *Pattern Recognition, 37*(9), 1773-1784.

Singhal, A., Luo, J., & Zhu, W. (2003). Probabilistic spatial context models for scene content understanding. In *Proceedings of the IEEE Conference on Computer Vision and Pattern Recognition* (pp. 457-460). Madison, WI: IEEE Computer Society.

Smith, J.R., & Li, C.S. (1999). Image classification and querying using composite region templates. *Journal of Computer Vision and Image Understanding, 75*(1), 165-174.

Sonka, M., Hlavac, V., & Boyle, R. (1999). *Image processing, analysis, and machine vision* (2nd ed.). Pacific Grove, CA: Brooks & Cole.

Sung, K.K., & Poggio, T. (1998). Example-based learning for view-based human face detection. *IEEE Transactions on Pattern Analysis and Machine Intelligence, 20*(1), 39-51.

Szummer, M., & Picard, R.W. (1998). Indoor-outdoor image classification. In *Proceedings of the IEEE International Workshop on Content-Based Access of Image and Video Databases* (pp. 42-51). Bombay, India: IEEE Computer Society.

Vailaya, A., Figueriredo, M., Jain, A., & Zhang, H.J. (1999). Content-based hierarchical classification of vacation images. In *Proceedings of the IEEE International Conference on Multimedia Computing and Systems* (pp. 518-523). Florence, Italy: IEEE Computer Society.

Vailaya, A., & Jain, A. (2000). Detecting sky and vegetation in outdoor images. In *Proceedings of the SPIE-IS&T Electronic Imaging Conference: Storage and Retrieval for Image and Video Databases VIII* (pp. 411-420). San Jose, CA: SPIE Press.

Vailaya, A., Jain, A., & Zhang, H.J. (1998). On image classification: City images vs. landscapes. *Pattern Recognition, 31*(12), 1921-1935.

Vasconcelos, N., & Lippman, A. (1998). A Bayesian framework for semantic content characterization. In *Proceedings of the IEEE Conference on Computer Vision and Pattern Recognition* (pp. 566-571). Santa Barbara, CA: IEEE Computer Society.

Vogel, J., & Schiele, B. (2007). Semantic scene modeling and retrieval for content-based image retrieval. *International Journal of Computer Vision, 72*(2), 133-157 .

Weber, M. (1999). Background image dataset. Retrieved December 22, 2006, from http://vision.caltech.edu/html-files/archive.html

Yang, M.H., Kriegman, D., & Ahuja, N. (2002). Detecting faces in images: A survey. *IEEE Transactions on Pattern Analysis and Machine Intelligence, 24*(1), 34-58.

Yow, K.C., & Cipolla, R. (1996). A probabilistic framework for perceptual grouping of features in human face detection. In *Proceedings of the 2nd International Conference on Automatic Face and Gesture Recognition* (pp. 16-21). Killington, VT: IEEE Computer Society.

Yow, K.C., & Cipolla, R. (1997). Feature-based human face detection. *Image and Vision Computing, 15*(9), 713-735.

Chapter VIII

Long Term Tracking of Pedestrians with Groups and Occlusions

Pedro M. Jorge, Polytechnic Institute of Lisbon, Portugal

Arnaldo J. Abrantes, Polytechnic Institute of Lisbon, Portugal

João M. Lemos, INESC-ID/Instituto Superior Técnico, Portugal

Jorge S. Marques, Instituto de Sistemas e Róbotica &
Instituto Superior Técnico, Lisbon, Portugal

Abstract

This chapter describes an algorithm for tracking groups of pedestrians in video sequences. The main difficulties addressed in this work concern total occlusions of the objects to be tracked, as well as group merging and splitting. Because there is ambiguity, the algorithm should be able to provide the most probable interpretation of the data. A two layer solution is proposed. The first layer produces a set of spatio-temporal trajectories based on low level operations which manage to track the pedestrians most of the time. The second layer performs a consistent labeling of the detected segments using a statistical model based on Bayesian networks. The Bayesian network is recursively computed during the tracking operation and allows the update of the tracker results every time new information is available. Interpreta-

tion/recognition errors can thus be detected after receiving enough information about the group of interacting objects. Experimental tests are included to show the performance of the algorithm in complex situations. This work was supported by FEDER and FCT under project LT (POSI 37844/01).

Introduction

Pedestrian tracking has been extensively studied because it is a key operation in many image analysis systems (Bar-Shalom & Fortmann, 1998; Bredmond & Thonnat, 1998; Cohen & Medioni, 1999; Collins, Lipton, Kanade, Fujiyoshi, Duggins, Tsin et al., 2000; Comaniciu & Meer, 2002; Cox & Hingorani, 1996; Haritaoglu, Harwood, & Davis, 2000; Hue, Le, & Cadre, 2002; Isard & Blake, 1998; Isard & MacCormick, 2001; Okuma, Taleghani, De Freitas, Little, & Lowe, 2004, Oliver, Rosario, & Pentland, 2000; Stauffer & Grimson, 2000; Wren, Azabayejani, Darrel, & Pentland, 1997). This is an easy task when pedestrians appear isolated in the scene. The main difficulties concern occlusions that is, when the pedestrians are occluded by the scene or by another group of pedestrians and cannot be easily detected. In these cases, it is not possible to track each pedestrian with simple image analysis techniques.

The goal of this chapter is to develop a tracking algorithm for interacting pedestrians, which can cope with occlusions and groups. The proposed tracker should be able to recover the track of a pedestrian after its occlusion by the scene or by other objects.

This seems to be possible because a human being is able to solve these situations in many cases. *How do we do that?* To solve ambiguous situations, as the ones mentioned before, we often wait until objects become separate again. Let us consider an example to illustrate the difficulties. Figure 1 shows a group of four persons. Suppose the group splits into two subgroups, each one with two persons. At this point, it is not easy to know who is in each

Figure 1. Tracking a group of pedestrians: Merge and split

subgroup. However, if after a while, one of the subgroups separates, then we can reliably identify each active region.

Most tracking systems are not able to solve this problem because they attempt to provide an instantaneous and independent classification of the active regions, detected in the scene. In order to obtain a reliable interpretation of the moving regions we must be able to consider multiple interpretations and delay the decision, in order to integrate information along time. This provides an uncertainty propagation strategy which is necessary to cope with the occlusion problem.

The tracking algorithm should have the following properties:

- online operation
- detect and track active regions even in the presence of groups and occlusions
- recover from groups and occlusions
- correct wrong decisions when new information is available

The algorithm proposed in this chapter meets these requirements in two steps. First, simple image analysis techniques are used to track moving regions in the video signal. These techniques efficiently track the pedestrians most of the time. However, they can not deal with occlusions or groups. This problem is solved by data interpretation techniques in the second step. The estimation of the pedestrians trajectories in a long time horizon (with groups and occlusions) is obtained by associating elementary trajectories detected by the simple tracking methods. This operation is formulated as a labeling problem, modeled by a Bayesian network and solved by probabilistic inference methods.

Both steps can be incorporated in an online surveillance system. The first step updates the tracks of the moving pedestrians every new frame and the second step periodically (e.g., every 2 seconds) assigns labels (object identifiers) to the detected tracks.

The chapter is organized as follows. Firstly we describe the previous work. Secondly we present the overall ideas of the proposed tracker. Next we consider the Bayesian network model. Then we address online tracking and extensions of the tracker to more complex situations. Lastly we present the experimental results and offer our conclusion.

Previous Work

Many tracking systems are based on two stages. First, active regions are detected in the video signal using motion detection algorithms performed by, for example, optical flow segmentation, background subtraction, frame differences, or a combination of techniques (Collins et al, 2000; Haritaoglu et al., 2000; Wren et al., 1997). These operations can be considered as low level processing because they do not use specific information about the object shape, color, or motion. In a second stage, the detected regions are tracked using region association methods, which can be considered as middle level processing.

Region association methods attempt to match pairs of active regions in consecutive images. This operation should be able to deal with the birth and death of video objects, ambiguous matching, and detection errors. A simple approach consists of using a nearest neighbor tracker which associates each estimated trajectory with the closest moving region (Bar-Shalom & Fortmann, 1998). Because the coordinates of the detected regions are corrupted by measurement noise, Kalman filters have been used to reduce the uncertainty about the target position and velocity. However, the Kalman filter is not able to deal with outliers generated by object detection methods. Robust estimation techniques (e.g., the probabilistic data association filter (PDAF) and its extensions to multiple objects (Bar-Shalom & Fortmann, 1998)) have been used to overcome these difficulties. Another way of propagating the uncertainty under non-Gaussian conditions is based on particle filters which approximate the probability distribution of the unknown parameters (e.g., target location) by a set of samples (particles) drawn from the *a posteriori* distribution, given the observed data (Isard & Blake, 1998; Okuma et al., 2004). These methods were first proposed to deal with outliers and nonGaussian distributions in single target problems, but they were later extended to cope with multiple targets and temporary occlusions (Hue et al., 2002; Okuma et al., 2004).

Another alternative is the multihypothesis tree (MHT), which considers multiple association scenarios and chooses the best at each instant of time (Cox & Hingorani, 1996). This approach is able to cope with outliers. Furthermore, it also allows delayed decisions that is, to delay the labeling of an active region in order to improve the performance.

Some of these techniques were initially proposed in a target tracking paradigm, which has been extensively used in radar surveillance systems since the '80s (Bar-Shalom & Fortmann, 1998). However, object tracking in video sequences is a different problem. Video objects are much larger than point targets. Therefore, there is much more information about the target properties (e.g., color distribution, shape, texture) which is not available in radar systems. As a consequence, the low level operations associated with object detection in video sequences are more reliable. However, the pedestrian motion in video signals is less predictable than a point target (e.g., airplane) in a radar system. Therefore, it is not easy to accurately predict the object position many frames ahead. These differences make pedestrian tracking different from point target tracking, for example, in radar systems.

The tracking operations become harder in the presence of occlusions and groups.

Several attempts have also been recently made to deal with groups of objects. For example, in Haritaoglu et al. (2000) a method is proposed to locate the position of each pedestrian inside the group, using silhouette boundaries. A histogram representation is used in McKenna, Jabri, Duric, Rosenfeld, and Wechsler (2000) to compute the visibility indices of each pedestrian inside the group and to recognize the group members.

This chapter proposes a tracking system for multiple pedestrians in video signals. There is a difference between the previous trackers and the methods proposed in this chapter. While many trackers try to accurately estimate the position of each object, the emphasis of the proposed algorithm lies in the correct identification of pedestrians (labeling problem) in the presence of occlusions and groups.

Figure 2. Two step approach: Stroke detection (left) and labeling (right)

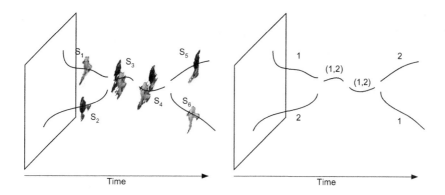

Overall Description

The approach described in this work is based on two steps. First, simple algorithms are used to track moving active regions. Second, the pedestrians' trajectories are labeled in such a way that trajectories associated to the same object receive the same label. Figure 2 shows the two steps for a specific problem in which two persons meet and separate. It is assumed that the first step can be easily solved by standard image analysis techniques (e.g., background subtraction with region matching based on the mutual choice criterion). Short trajectories lasting less than 10 frames are eliminated and considered as false alarms.

Because pedestrian motion is slow compared to the frame rate of 25 fps, no motion model is explicitly used, that is, we assume that the position of each pedestrian in the next frame is close to the position of the pedestrian in the current frame.

The main difficulty in this strategy concerns how to label the detected trajectories, denoted here as strokes, in order to obtain a consistent interpretation of the data, that is, in order to know *where* each object is at each instant of time: this is formulated below as a probabilistic inference problem to be solved by Bayesian networks.

Let $\{(s_i, y_i)\}$ be the set of detected strokes, s_i, and corresponding measurements, y_i, (e.g., color histogram, speed) and let x_i be the label associated to the i-th stroke s_i. It is assumed that $x_i \in L_i$ is a random variable where $L_i = \{l_i\}$ is the set of admissible labels and $y_i \in R^m$; the label l_i identifies a person or a group of persons. For example $l_i = 3$ means that the $i-th$ region is associated with pedestrian 3, while $l_i = (1,3)$ is a group of two pedestrians with labels 1 and 3.

The labeling problem can be formulated as follows: *how can we estimate the unknown labels $x = \{x_i\}$ given the observations $y = \{y_i\}$?* This can be seen as an inference problem to be solved by Bayesian inference techniques. The most probable labeling configuration is obtained by solving

Figure 3. Bayesian network tracker

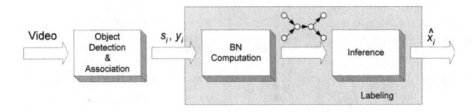

$$\hat{x} = \arg\max_{x} P(x|y) \qquad (1)$$

$$= \arg\max_{x} P(y|x)P(x) \qquad (2)$$

where $p(y|x)$ is the observation model and $P(x)$ is the prior. As mentioned before, $x = \{x_i\}$ is the set of all stroke labels to be estimated and $y = \{y_i\}$ is the set of stroke observations. Furthermore, the observation model can be written as:

$$p(y|x) = \prod_{i} p(y_i|x_i), y_i \in R^m, x_i \in L_i \qquad (3)$$

assuming that observations of different strokes are conditionally independent random variables if the stroke labels are known.

To solve the labeling problem, one has to define the observation model $p(y_i|x_i)$ which accounts for the visual appearance of the pedestrian (or group) x_i and the prior distribution $P(x)$ which model the interaction among pedestrians. For example, $P(x)$ should be zero if x is an inconsistent labeling. This happens, for example, if the same pedestrian appears in two different strokes at the same time instant.

Both model (pior and observation) will be represented using a Bayesian network, which is built in real time during the tracking operation. The estimation of the most probable labeling (1) is preformed by inference techniques for Bayesian network every T seconds (see Figure 3).

Bayesian Network Model

A Bayesian network (BN) is a graph model which represents the joint probability distribution of a set of random variables $x_1, \ldots, x_n$ in terms of simple factors involving few variables (Jensen, 2001).

A Bayesian network is defined by a directed acyclic graph (an oriented graph without loops) where each node is associated to a random variable x_i and the links represent causal dependencies (Pearl, 1997). After defining the graph, the user must also specify the conditional distribution of each node x_i given its parents a_i. This is usually a simple distribution, involving a small number of variables.

The joint probability density function associated to a BN is the product of all the node conditional distributions.

$$P(x) = \prod_{i=1}^{n} P(x_i | a_i)$$

(4)

The Bayesian network is therefore a simple way to model complex distributions of a large number of variables in terms of factors. Furthermore, there are inference algorithms to compute the most probable configuration which efficiently exploit the structure of the probability distribution (equation 4) (e.g., see Jensen, 2001 and Murphy, 2001).

Network Architecture

As mentioned before, the BN used in this chapter is automatically built from the video signal. The main question is: *how is the BN generated?* Figure 4(a) shows an example for the two-person problem shown in Figure 2. This model associates a node x_i to each stroke s_i detected in the video signal; x_i is the label of the stroke s_i that is, a variable which identifies all the pedestrians associated to the stroke trajectory, for example, $x_i = 1$ if s_i is the trajectory of pedestrian 1 and $x_i = (1, 2)$ if s_i is the trajectory of a group of two pedestrains with labels 1 and 2. In this model, the unknown variables are the node labels x_i which can not be directly observed.

The next question is how to define the links which represent causal dependencies. The main idea is simple: two hidden nodes x_i, x_j are linked if s_i, s_j may correspond to sub trajectories of the same object or group. Link creation is performed using simple criteria: (i) causality

Figure 4. Bayesian network: (a) hidden labels; (b) full network

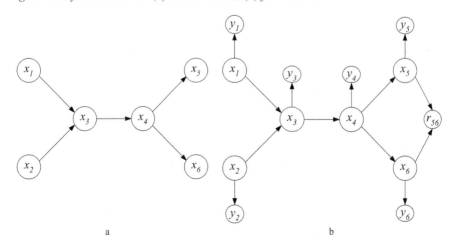

a   b

Figure 5. Basic topologies: Occlusion, merge, split, and three merge-splits

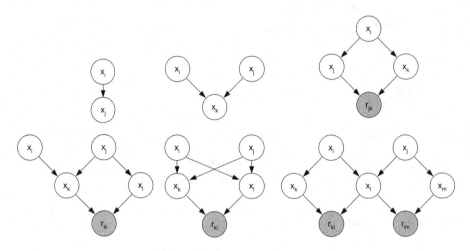

$(s_j$ should start after the end of s_i); (ii) maximum speed (the mean speed of the pedestrian during occlusion should be smaller than a threshold). The speed threshold allows the system to eliminate fast motions during occlusion times, which could not be performed by a pedestrian. The threshold may depend on the image location as well as the average velocity of the pedestrian before the occlusion.

The measurements $\{y_i\}$ can also be included in the BN because they are considered as realizations of a random variable which depends on the stroke labels $\{x_i\} : x_i$ is the parent of y_i. Figure 4(b) shows the complete BN for the two-person problem. (r_{56} is a restriction node associated to the split, which will be explained at the end of this section). The network conveys information about the stroke interaction, namely the propagation of causal dependencies in the presence of occlusions, group merging, and splitting. It also describes the relationship between the stroke labels x_i and the image features y_i. Finally, it also guarantees that physical restrictions hold, for example, the same object cannot belong to two strokes at the same time.

To keep the network simple each node is only allowed to have a maximum number of two parents and two children (this restriction is relaxed in *Online Tracking*). This is done by pruning the network. Pruning can be based on several criteria. For example, if a node has more than two children, the links corresponding to larger occlusion times are eliminated because they are considered as less probable.

Assuming that the number of parents and children is limited to two, there are six basic topologies (see Figure 5). They correspond to the following situations: total occlusion, group merge, group split, and three types of merge-splits. The first topology is used to represent the trajectory of a pedestrian (or group) which is being tracked (stroke s_i), becomes occluded and it is then detected after a while (stroke s_j). The second topology corresponds to a merge of two trajectories (s_i, s_j) into a single trajectory (s_k). This topology corresponds to a merge of two pedestrians (or groups) into a single group. It also accounts for the possibility of x_k being the continuation of x_i (or x_j), and x_j (x_i) disappears. The third topology corresponds to a split of a trajectory into two trajectories. This accounts for group splits and it may also represent other situations for example, x_j (or x_k) is the continuation of x_i and x_k (x_j) is a new stroke. The other topologies correspond to merge-splits.

Every time there is a split, a mutual dependency is created between the children x_i, x_j. This happens because the same person cannot be in two active regions at the same time. To model this dependency, a binary restriction node r_{ij} is created. This node takes the binary value 1 if we have a consistent labeling (no common labels are assigned to the children nodes) and it takes the value 0 otherwise. This variable guarantees that the network does not produce inconsistent configurations in which the same object belongs to two or more trajectories at the same time. To guarantee that the inference algorithm produces a consistent labeling, the restriction nodes are considered as observable nodes with $r_{ij} = 1$.

Admissible Labels

Let us consider the computation of the set of admissible labels L_i for each node x_i. Isolated objects are identified by an integer label l and groups are characterized by a set of labels of the group members, for example, (1,2) is a group with the objects 1 and 2.

The set of admissible labels for each node is obtained by recursively propagating the labels through the network (see below). This operation depends on the graph links in the vicinity of each node x_k which can be classified into one of the six basic topologies: occlusion, merge, split, or tree types of merge-splits (see Figure 5). Therefore only six label propagation rules have to be defined.

The label propagation rules for the first three topologies are:

occlusion:
$$L_k = L_i \cup l_{new} \tag{5}$$

merge:
$$L_k = L_i \cup L_j \cup L_{merge} \cup l_{new} \tag{6}$$

$$L_{merge} = \{a \cup b : a \subset L_i, b \subset L_j, a \cap b = \varnothing\} \tag{7}$$

Table 1. Admissible node labels: creation (1,2), merge (3), occlusion (4), and split (5,6)

k	L_k
1	1
2	2
3	1 2 (1,2) 3
4	1 2 (1,2) 3 4
5	1 2 (1,2) 3 4 5
6	1 2 (1,2) 3 4 5 6

split: $$L_k = \mathcal{P}(L_i) \cup l_{new_k} \quad L_j = \mathcal{P}(L_i) \cup l_{new_j} \tag{8}$$

where $\mathcal{P}(L_i)$ is the partition of the set L_i, excluding the empty set. Label propagation in merge-splits is performed by combining the merge and split rules.

In all these examples, l_{new} stands for a new label, corresponding to a new object entering the scene. Table 1 shows the admissible labels for the example considered in this section. For example, nodes 1,2 correspond to new pedestrians entering the scene, node 3 is a merge of two pedestrians, node 4 is a group occlusion, and nodes 5,6 correspond to a group split.

Node Conditional Distributions

There are three types of nodes in the BN network: *hidden nodes, observation nodes, and restriction nodes.* We have to automatically define the conditional probability tables $p(x_i \mid a_i)$ for each type of node. Let us consider the hidden nodes first because they represent the variables we want to estimate.

Hidden Nodes

Hidden nodes can either have simple labels, representing a single pedestrian, or a compound label. The label of a given node is inherited from the parent nodes using one of three mechanisms: occlusion, group merge, or group split. In addition, we also assume that each node can have a new label corresponding to new objects entering the scene.

To define a probability distribution of the node variable x_i we must specify the probability of each of the four previous mechanisms (new, occlusion, merge, split) which will be denoted by $P_{new}, P_{occl}, P_{merge}, P_{split}$. These probabilities can be set as constant or they may vary according to the stroke geometry and position.

Because there are six basic topologies, we have six types of conditional distributions $p(x_k \mid a_k)$. For example, in the case of occlusion (first topology) the node x_i is either equal to its parent label or it is a new label. Therefore:

$$P(x_k \mid x_i) = \begin{cases} 1 - P_{new} & x_k = x_i \\ P_{new} & x_k = l_{new} \end{cases} \tag{9}$$

In the other cases, the probability distribution is slightly more complex. For example, if x_k has a merge topology with parents x_i, x_j, then we must consider 4 hypotheses: (i) x_k receives the label of x_i, (ii) x_k receives the label of x_j, (iii) x_k is a merge of both labels, or (iv) it is a new label. This leads to:

$$P(x_k|x_i,x_j) = \begin{cases} P_{merge} & x_k = x_i \cup x_j \\ P_{occli} & x_k = x_i \\ P_{occlj} & x_k = x_j \\ P_{new} & x_k = 1_{new} \end{cases} \qquad (10)$$

In the case of splits, similar arguments lead to:

$$P(x_k|x_i) = \begin{cases} P_{split}/(2^{N_i} - 2) & x_k \subset \mathcal{P}(x_i) \setminus x_i \\ P_{occlu} & x_k = x_i \\ P_{new} & x_k = 1_{new} \end{cases} \qquad (11)$$

where $N_i \geq 2$ is the number of objects in the group label x_i. If $x_k \subset \mathcal{P}(x_i) \setminus x_i$, x_k is a subset of the group x_i, we assume that all the $2^{N_i} - 2$ subsets are equiprobable. If $x_k = x_i$ then the node k has all the labels of the parent node. In this case, the group does not separate and has simply suffered a temporary occlusion. If $x_k = 1_{new}$ the stroke k corresponds to a new pedestrian and is not related to the parent node.

The conditional distributions of the other topologies follow similar guidelines and they are defined in the appendix. The above parameters P_{new}, P_{occl}, P_{merge}, P_{split} are heuristically defined or learned from the data. They can be independently specified provided that their sum is equal to 1 for each type of topology. In this chapter, the parameters were heuristically chosen, but they depend on the stroke geometry for example, the occlusion probability is higher if the occlusion time is smaller.

Restriction Nodes

Every time there is a split, a binary node is included to create a dependency between the two children: the same object cannot simultaneously belong to two groups at the same instant of time.

The conditional probability table of the restriction node r_{ij} is created in such a way that $r_{ij} = 1$ if there is no labelling conflict (common labels) and $r_{ij} = 0$ otherwise. Therefore:

$$P(r_{ij} = 1|x_i,x_j) = \begin{cases} 1 & x_i \cap x_j = \varnothing \\ 0 & otherwise \end{cases} \qquad (12)$$

Because we want to avoid common labels in group splits, r_{ij} is considered as an observed node with value 1 and it does not have to be estimated by the inference algorithms.

Figure 6. Dominant colors: (a) image dominant colors and (b) color matching between dominant colors of a stroke and a color model

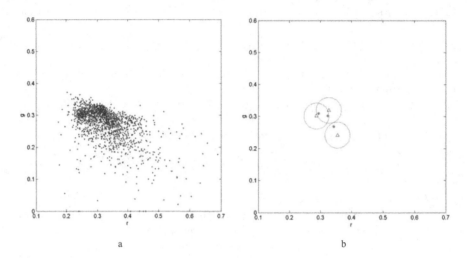

a   b

Observation Nodes

Each stroke detected in the video signal is characterized by a set of features for example, average color histogram, average speed, region shape, key colors obtained by clustering, or by the mean shift (Comaniciu & Meer, 2002) or invariant features such as scale invariant feature transform (SIFT) (Lowe, 1999).

Let y_k be the set of features extracted in stroke s_k. It is assumed that y_k is a random variable which depends on the label x_k. Therefore, we must be able to define the conditional probability $p(y_k \mid x_k)$. This distribution depends on the specific choice we make about the features.

In this chapter, we have used a simple set of features consisting of the M ($M = 5$) dominant colors obtained by clustering the color components of the pixels of all the active regions associated to a given stroke s_k. Each color is represented by two features: the normalized r and g color coefficients. Therefore, y_k is a $2M$ dimensional feature vector. The computation of the dominant colors is performed using the k-means algorithm.

Every time a new pedestrian enters the scene, the set of dominant colors is computed and used to characterize the pedestrian during its evolution in the camera field of view. Therefore, each simple label is defined by M dominant colors $c_k \in R^{2M}$. A group of labels is characterized by the dominant colors of all the objects inside the group. We assume that a stroke s_k is well represented by a tentative label x_k if the dominant colors of s_k match the dominant colors of a tentative label x_k. Figure 6 shows the color scatter diagram of a given stroke and its dominant colors, computed by clustering in the *rg* space. It is also shown the dominant colors of a tentative label. The matched colors are represented by circles.

Let y_{ki} be the $i - th$ dominant color of the video stroke k and let c_{x_kj} be the $j - th$ dominant color of the label x_k. We will assume that:

$$p(y_k|x_k) = \prod_{i=1}^{M} p(y_{ki}|x_k)$$ (13)

where $p(y_{ki} \mid x_k)$ has a high value α in the case of matched colors and a low value β in the case of unmatched ones

$$p(y_{ki} \mid x_k) = \begin{cases} \alpha & \min_j \| y_{ki} - c_{x_kj} \| < \delta \\ \beta & otherwise \end{cases}$$ (14)

where δ is a matching threshold.

Inference

Inference methods are used to compute the most probable configuration of the hidden nodes (labels) given the observed nodes $\{y_i\}$ and restriction nodes $\{r_{ij}\}$. This is equivalent to the solution of (1). Fortunately, there are several well known methods to compute the most probable configuration for example, message passing method for polytrees (Pearl, 1997) or the junction tree algorithm (Jensen, 2001). The complexity of the inference procedure grows if there are multiple paths. In this chapter, inference was performed using the Bayes Net Matlab toolbox, developed by Murphy (2001).

The system described before is able to track moving objects in video sequences, managing to deal with complex situations (occlusions and groups). However, it has two major drawbacks: it is an off-line algorithm (the network complexity and delay grow to infinity as time goes by) and the topological restrictions (two parents and two children) cannot cope with complex situations involving several objects.

These issues are addressed in the following sections and the proposed algorithm is then experimentally evaluated in real video sequences.

Online Tracking

The algorithm previously described in *Bayesian Network Model* is tailored to off-line analysis of video sequences in batch mode. We have to wait until the end of the sequence before doing inference. Furthermore, it cannot be applied to long video sequences because the network complexity and the computational time grow to infinity as time goes by.

A tracking system should provide labeling results in real time, with a small delay. Therefore it is not possible to analise the video sequence in a batch mode, that is, performing inference after detecting the object trajectories in the whole video sequence.

To avoid these difficulties, two strategies are suggested: periodic inference and network simplification. The first strategy consists of incrementally building the network and performing the inference every T seconds. Denoting by $x(0 : kT)$, $y(0 : kT)$ the variables of the Bayesian network associated to strokes detected in the interval $[0,kT]$, then the object labeling can be periodically performed by solving:

$$\hat{x}(0:kT) = \arg \max_{x(0:kT)} \ p(x(0:kT), y(0:kT)) \tag{15}$$

The network grows as before but the labeling delay is reduced to less than T seconds. The solution of (15) can be obtained by standard techniques as before (e.g., junction tree algorithm (Jensen, 2001)).

Figure 7. Evolution of the Bayesian network at three time instants. Gray circles represent frozen past nodes and white circles represent active nodes to be labeled by the inference process.

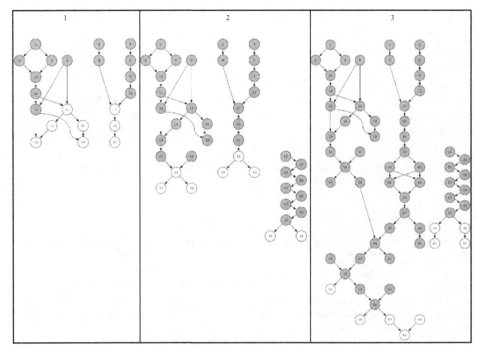

In practice we wish to have an instantaneous labeling of all the objects, that is, we do not wish to wait T seconds for a new global inference. *Can we obtain an instantaneous labeling of the trajectories with a Bayesian network ?* To obtain online labeling, a suboptimal approach can be devised which combines the optimal decision obtained at the instant kT with the new information collected after the instant KT.

Let x_i be a hidden node associated to a trajectory active in the interval $[kT,t]$. Exact inference is performed by computing $P(x_i \mid y(0 : t))$. In order to derive a suboptimal estimate, we shall assume that the information available to estimate x_i is the combination of $y(0 : kT)$ (past) and $y_i(kT : t)$ (recent) that is, we consider the recent observations of stroke s_i and neglect the observations of the other strokes after the last inference instant kT. Applying the Bayes law:

$$P(x_i \mid y(0:t)) = P(x_i \mid y(0 : kT), y_i(kT : t))$$
$$= \alpha \, p(y_i(kT : t) \mid x_i) P(x_i \mid y(0 : kT)) \qquad (16)$$

where $\alpha = 1/P(y_i(kT : t) \mid y(0 : kT))$ is a normalization constant, $P(x_i \mid y(0 : kT))$ is a global prior, computed before in the inference step at time kT using all the information about the interaction among nodes and $p(y_i(kT : t) \mid x_i)$ represents new local information. The choice of the best label $\hat{x}_i$ is performed by selecting the highest a posteriori probability $P(x_i \mid y(0: t))$. When x_i is a new variable that is, when a new stroke is detected after kT, we assume a uniform prior: no label is preferred based on past information.

The above strategies convert the batch algorithm into a online algorithm that is, they solve the first problem. However, the network size increases as before. To overcome this difficulty, a simplification is needed. The main idea used in this work is to bound the memory of the system by freezing a subset of the network nodes with their most probable values.

Old (hidden and observed) nodes influence the labeling assignment of current nodes. However, this influence decreases and tends to zero as time goes by: recent variables are more important than old ones. So, we need to use techniques to forget the past. In this chapter, we allow a

Figure 8. General network: (a) merge-split (b) merge; (c) split)

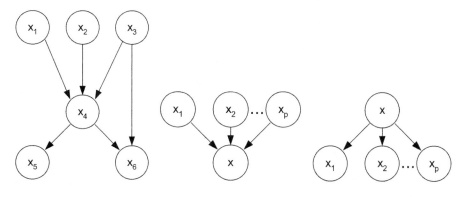

maximum of N active nodes and freeze all the other nodes by assigning them the most probable label obtained in previous inferences. In this way, the complexity of the network remains bounded and can be adapted to the computational resources available for tracking.

Several strategies can be used to select the nodes to be frozen (dead nodes). A simple approach is used for this purpose: oldest nodes are eliminated and the most recent N nodes are kept active.

Figure 7 shows the evolution of the Bayesian network at three instants, for a PETS 2001 sequence. Although the number of nodes grows linearly with time, only the most recent ones are active and updated by the inference algorithm, therefore keeping the computational burden under control.

Extensions

Until now, we have restricted the number of children and parents of each node to a maximum of 2^1. This is too restrictive to cope with many practical situations. The key question is: *how can we deal with more complex situations as shown in Figure 8(a)?*

The extension of merge and split topologies defined in section 3 to deal with arbitrary numbers of parents or children is straightforward. The most difficult problem concerns the merge-splits because there is a combinatorial explosion of different merge-split topologies. In the sequel, we will first define the extensions of merge and split nodes to the general case and then address the merge-split problem.

Figures 8(b) and 8(c) show the merge and split topologies with multiple parents and children. The simplest case is the split because the label propagation rules and conditional probability distribution defined in (8,11) remain valid. The merge has different rules however, because we must consider the association of $2^p - n - 1$ subsets of parent nodes, that is, we should

Figure 9. Modified Bayesian net with mediating nodes x_{mi}

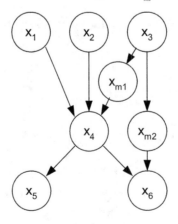

consider the association of any pair of nodes (x_i, x_j), any triplet (x_i, x_j, x_k), and so forth. The set of admissible labels L can be recursively computed as follows:

$$L = L^p \cup l_{new} \tag{17}$$

$$L^i = \text{Merge}(L^{i-1}, L_i) \quad i = 1, \ldots, p \quad L^0 = \phi \tag{18}$$

where L_i is the set of admissible labels of x_i. The Merge(.,.) is defined in (7). The set of admissible labels L can be split into three subsets L_{cont}, L_{merge}, $L_{new} = l_{new}$ associated with stroke continuation, merge, and new. The conditional distribution must consider all these three types of labels as follows:

$$P(x|x_1, \ldots, x_p) - \begin{cases} P_{occl_j} & x = x_j \\ P_{merge} / |L_{merge}| & x \in L_{merge} \\ P_{new} & x = l_{new} \end{cases} \tag{19}$$

where $|L_{merge}|$ denotes the number of elements of set L_{merge}.

Concerning the merge-splits, it is not possible to explicitly consider all the different topologies when the number of children or parents is higher than 2. A different approach is followed. We will detect all such nodes, x_k in the BN and introduce mediating nodes between

Figure 10. Example PETS 2001: (a) detected strokes; (b) most probable labeling obtained with the online algorithm

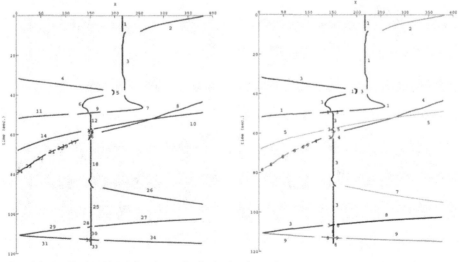

Table 2. Experimental results: Number of strokes (NS); number of objects (NO); number of groups (NG); duration (D sec.); number of labeling errors (NE); computational time (CT sec.)

Seq.	NS	NO	NG	D	NE	CT
PETS 2001	34	8	5	120	2	12.8
Campus	62	11	10	54.8	2	42.8
PETS 2004	67	7	4	36	5	26.6

x_k and its parents with more children (see Figure 9). In this way, splits and merges become separate and can be dealt with the previous rules. Mediating nodes allow solving the split-merge problem in an elegant way.

Tracking Experiments

The proposed algorithm was used to track multiple pedestrians in video sequences. This section shows tracking results obtained in three video sequences: an indoor sequence extracted from PETS 2004 database ("Meet Split 3rd Guy") (*http://www.dai.ed.ac.uk/homes/rbf/ CAVIAR.*) and two outdoor sequences, one from the PETS 2001 database (test set example 1 (*ftp://pets2001.cs.rdg.ac.uk.*)) and one sequence recorded at a university campus. All these

Figure 11. PETS 2001: labeling results at time instants (in sec.) (a) 32.8; (b) 42.4; (c) 49.2; (d) 49.9; (e) 57.6 and (f) 60.8

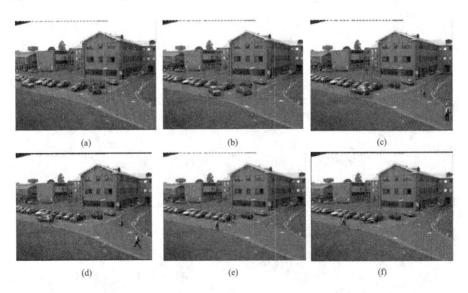

sequences have multiple interacting objects (typically less than 10) with group associations and occlusions. The sampling rate is 25 fps.

Inference was performed every 15 seconds using the online algorithm[2] and a maximum number of ancestor nodes $N = 10$, which prevents the network from growing. The Bayesian network was automatically built during the tracking operation without human intervention and the inference results were obtained using Murphy's Bayes Net toolbox for Matlab (Murphy, 2001).

Example 1: PETS 2001

Figure 10 shows the performance of the tracker in the PETS 2001 sequence sampled at 25 fps, during the first 120 seconds. Figure 10(a) shows the evolution of all active regions detected in the video stream. This figure displays one of the coordinates of the mass center (column) as a function of time. Every time there is an occlusion or when two or more objects overlap it is no longer possible to associate the detected regions with past ones. In such cases the trajectories are interrupted.

Figure 10(b) shows the labeling results obtained with the online algorithm described in the chapter with a maximum of two parents and two children per node. The algorithm manages to disambiguate most of the occlusions well. Only two labeling errors are observed in a total of 34 strokes (3000 frames). The errors are in label 6 and in a switch of labels 3 and 8 at $t = 110sec$. The output of the online algorithm was compared with the results of the batch version of the tracker. The same labeling was obtained in both cases with important computational savings (CPU times[3]: 258 sec (batch) and 12.8 sec (online)). In this example, the computa-

Figure 12. Campus sequence: (a) detected strokes; (b) most probable labeling obtained with the online algorithm

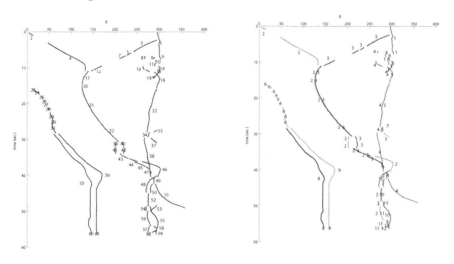

*Figure 13. Campus sequence: Labeling results at time instants (in sec.) (a) 4.4; (b) 10.4;
(c) 22.5; (d) 31.9; (e) 34.8 and (f) 36.2*

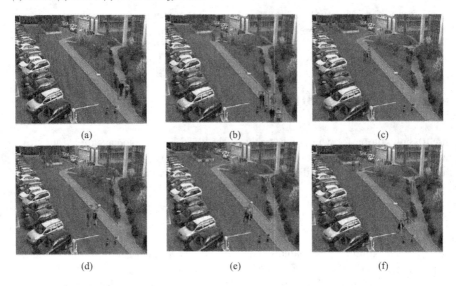

(a)   (b)   (c)

(d)   (e)   (f)

*Figure 14. PETS 2004: (a) detected strokes; (b) most probable labeling obtained with the
online algorithm*

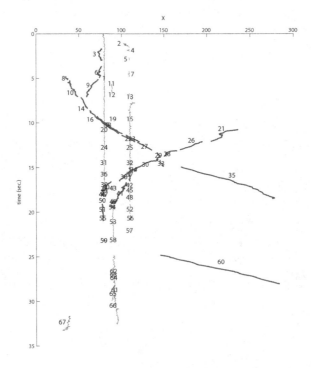

tion time of the labeling algorithm is about 10% of the sequence duration. The statistics of the sequence complexity (number of objects, number of groups, number of tracks, duration) and tracker performance (labeling errors, computational time) are shown in Table 2.

Figure 11 shows an example of the labeling interpretation obtained with the proposed algorithm. This example shows a group merging and splitting involving two vehicles, while the other objects are being tracked by the system. This situation is correctly solved.

Example 2: University Campus

This sequence contains the trajectories of 10 pedestrians walking in an university campus for 54.8 s. The number of groups (10) is much larger than in the previous example. Figure 12 shows the detected stokes as well as the labeling results obtained by the Bayesian network. The BN tracker managed to solve most of the occlusions and group merging and splitting well. Only two labeling errors were obtained (see Table 2).

Figure 13 illustrates the performance of the tracker in a typical situation in which two persons meet, forming a group and then separate (pedestrians with labels 2 and 3).

Figure 7 shows the Bayesian network architecture at three time instants (visible nodes are not represented). Although the number of nodes grows quickly with time, only the most recent ones are updated by the inference algorithm, therefore keeping the computational burden under control. The gray nodes were classified as frozen by the pruning algorithm, and their labels and are not allowed to change.

Figure 15. PETS 2004: Labeling results at time instants (in sec.) (a) 9.6; (b) 12.3; (c) 14.4; (d) 15.0; (e) 15.5, and (f) 17.3

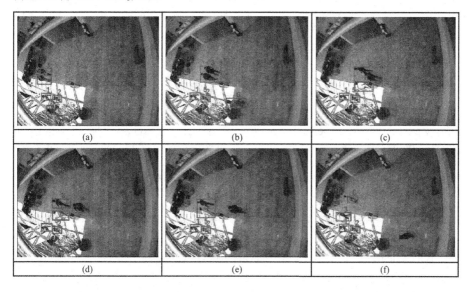

Example 3: PETS 2004

Figure 14 shows the performance of the tracker in the indoor sequence "Meet Split 3rd Guy" (PETS 2004) allowing general topologies, that is, more than two parents and two children per node. This is a difficult example, and useful to illustrate the performance of the tracker in the presence of occlusions, group merging, and splitting. The low level operations needed for object detection produce detection errors (mainly false positives) due to drastic illumination changes and the presence of static objects (persons) which remain undetected during some intervals of time and generate small active regions due to small movements. Even under these conditions the BN tracker manages to produce good results.

Figure 14(a) shows the evolution of all active regions detected in the video stream as in previous examples. Figure 4(b) shows the labeling results obtained with the online algorithm described in the chapter. The BN tracker manages to disambiguate most of the occlusions well (only the yellow stroke is misclassified).

Figure 14(b) shows examples of the tracker performance in group merging and splitting. This sequence has three moving objects (3,4,6) and three static objects. The tracker manages to correctly track the three moving objects most of the time, as shown in Figure 15. Three persons walk in separately (Figure 15(a)), they merge in groups of two (Figures 15(b), 15(c), 15(e)) and they split after a while (Figures 15(d), 15(f)). All these events are correctly interpreted by the tracker. Namely, the correct label is assigned after the two splits of Figures 15(d) and 15(f).

The tracker has some difficulty dealing with the static objects (labels 1, 2, and 5) because they are not correctly detected by the low level algorithms (background subtraction). These objects remain in the same place during the whole sequence. They should be considered as background. However, there are small movements which are detected and appear in Figure 14.

The performance of the BN tracker in this example is summarized in Table 2.

We have tried to repeat the experimental tests without freezing past nodes, but the amount of memory needed increases exponentially and exhausts the computer resources. This is an important issue to be addressed in the future.

Future Work

Future work should consider several issues. Complexity is an important problem to be further addressed in the future. Because the system complexity depends on the video stream, it is important to devise strategies to monitor and control the network complexity. A first step toward this direction is proposed here by network pruning and the use of frozen nodes associated with past information. However, additional work is needed to prevent an exponential increase of the number of labels. Future work should consider label pruning by discarding the less probable labels, keeping, however, the model consistency.

The image features characterizing each stroke should also be studied. The use of dominant colors is a crude representation of the object appearance. More sophisticated features (e.g., local and invariant features (Lowe, 1999; Wren et al., 1997) should be studied in this context as a way to improve the systems performance.

Conclusion

This chapter presents a system for long term tracking of multiple pedestrians in the presence of occlusions and group merging and splitting. The system tries to follow all moving objects present in the scene by performing a low level detection of spatio-temporal trajectories (strokes), followed by a labeling procedure which attempts to assign consistent labels to all the strokes associated to the same pedestrian. The interaction among pedestrians is modeled using a Bayesian network, that is automatically built during the surveillance task. This allows formulation of the labeling problem as an inference task that integrates all the available information extracted from the video stream, allowing to update the interpretation of the detected tracks every time new information is available. For example, sometimes when a group of objects splits, there is not enough information to perform a reliable identification of each object. However the proposed system is able to improve its output, when additional information is extracted from the video signal.

The proposed system is able to deal with occlusions of pedestrians by static objects or by other pedestrians forming groups. The system estimates the identifier (label) of each isolated object (or group) after the end of the occlusion.

The labeling model used in this chapter (Bayesian network) is not time driven. It is event driven: it tries to assign labels to the object trajectories (strokes) detected by simple low level operations. Therefore, only a single variable is used to identify each stroke even if the stroke lasts for tens or hundreds of frames. The Bayesian network does not try to describe the evolution of labels from frame to frame. It describes data conflicts: occlusions, group merging, and splitting.

References

Bar-Shalom, Y., & Fortmann, T. (1998). *Tracking and Data Association*. Academic Press.

Bremond, F., & Thonnat, M. (1998). Tracking multiple nonrigid objects in video sequences. *IEEE Transaction Circuits, Systems and Video Technology, 8*, 585-591.

Cohen, I., & Medioni, G. (1999, June). Detecting and tracking moving objects for video surveillance. In *IEEE Proceedings on Computer Vision and Pattern Recognition* (pp. 1-7). Fort Collins.

Collins, R., Lipton, A., Kanade, T., Fujiyoshi, H., Duggins, D., Tsin, Y. et al. (2000). *A system for video surveillance and monitoring: VSAM final report* (Tech. Rep. No.) CMU.

Comaniciu, D., & Meer, P. (2002). Mean shift: A robust approach toward feature space analysis. *IEEE Transaction on Pattern Analysis and Machine Intelligence, 24*(5) 603-619.

Cox, I., & Hingorani, S. (1996, February). An efficient implementation of Reid's Multiple Hypothesis Traking Algorithm and its evaluation for the purpose of visaul tracking. *IEEE Transactions on Pattern Analysis and Machine Intelligence, 18*(2), 138-150.

Haritaoglu, I., Harwood, D., & Davis, L. (2000, August). W^4: Real-time surveillance of people and their activities. *IEEE Transactions on Pattern Analysis and Machine Intelligence, 22*(8), 809-830.

Hue, C., Le, J.-P., & Cadre, P.P. (2002). Tracking multiple objects with particle filtering. *IEEE Transactions on Aerospace and Electronic Systems, 38*(3), 791-812.

Isard, M., & Blake, A. (1998). Condensation: Conditional density propagation for visual tracking. *IEEE Inter. Journal of Computer Vision, 29*(1), 5-28.

Isard, M., & MacCormick, J. (2001, July). BraMBLe: A Bayesian multiple-blob tracker. In *Proceedings of the IEEE 8th International Conference on Computer Vision* (Vol. 2, pp. 34-41), Vancouver, Canada.

Jensen, F. (2001). *Bayesian networks and decision graphs*. Springer-Verlag.

Lowe, D. (1999, September). Object recognition from local scale-invariant features. In *Proceedings of the IEEE 7th International Conference on Computer Vision* (pp. 1-8).

McKenna, S., Jabri, S., Duric, Z., Rosenfeld, A., & Wechsler, H. (2000). Tracking groups of people. *Journal of Comp. Vision Image Understanding, 80*, 42-56.

Murphy, K. (2001). *The Bayes net toolbox for Matlab*. Computing Science and Statistics, vol 33.

Okuma, K., Taleghani, A., De Freitas, N., Little, J., & Lowe, D. (2004). A boosted particle filter: Multitarget detection and tracking. ECCV.

Oliver, N., Rosario, B., & Pentland, A. (2000). A Bayesian computer vision system for modeling human interactions. *IEEE Transactions on Pattern Analysis and Machine Intelligence, 22*(8), 831-843.

Pearl, J. (1997). *Probabilistic reasoning in intelligent systems: Networks of plausible inference*. Morgan Kaufmann.

Stauffer, C., & Grimson, E. (2000, August). Learning patterns of activity using real-time tracking. *IEEE Transactions on Pattern Analysis and Machine Intelligence, 22*(8), 747-757.

Wren, C., Azabayejani, A., Darrel, T., & Pentland, A. (1997). Pfinder: Real time tracking of the human body. *IEEE Transactions on Pattern Analysis and Machine Intelligence, 19*, 780-785.

Endnotes

[1]   This restriction applies to hidden nodes only.

[2]   The update rate depends on the application; $15sec$ is an acceptable delay in some surveillance tasks.

[3]   These tests were performed on a P4 at 2.8 GHz.

Appendix: Merge-Splits

This appendix defines the expressions for the conditional probability tables of merge-splits.

Merge-Split 1

$$P(x_k | x_i, x_j) = \begin{cases} P_{split} / (2^{N_j} - 2) & x_k \subset \mathcal{P}(x_j) \setminus x_j \\ P_{merge} / (2^{N_j} - 2) & x_k \subset M_{ij} \\ P_{occl_i} & x_k = x_i \\ P_{occl_j} & x_k = x_j \\ P_{new} & x_k = l_{new} \end{cases} \tag{20}$$

where M_{ij} contains group labels including label x_i and a subgroup of x_j without common objects. Specifically,

$$M_{ij} = \{ a \cup b : a = x_i,\ b \subset \mathcal{P}(x_j),\ a \cap b = \varphi \} \tag{21}$$

Merge-Split 2

$$P(x_k | x_i, x_j) = \begin{cases} P_{split_i} / (2^{N_i} - 2) & x_k \subset \mathcal{P}(x_i) \setminus x_i \\ P_{split_j} / (2^{N_j} - 2) & x_k \subset \mathcal{P}(x_j) \setminus x_j \\ P_{merge} / [(2^{N_i} - 1)(2^{N_j} - 1)] & x_k \subset M^*_{ij} \\ P_{occl_i} & x_k = x_i \\ P_{occl_j} & x_k = x_j \\ P_{new} & x_k = l_{new} \end{cases} \tag{22}$$

where M^*_{ij} contains the group labels of all subset of x_i merged with a subgroup of x_j without common objects. Specifically:

$$M^*_{ij} = \{ a \cup b : a \subset \mathcal{P}(x_i),\ b \subset \mathcal{P}(x_j) a \cap b = \varphi \} \tag{23}$$

Merge-Split 3 is a special case of merge-split 2 when two of the parent nodes are the same. The conditional distribution of the merge-split 3 is therefore given by (22).

Chapter IX

DBN Models for Visual Tracking and Prediction

Qian Diao, Intel China Research Center, China

Jianye Lu, Intel China Research Center, China

Wei Hu, Intel China Research Center, China

Yimin Zhang, Intel China Research Center, China

Gary Bradski, Microprocessor Research Lab/ Intel Research, USA

Abstract

In a visual tracking task, the object may exhibit rich dynamic behavior in complex environments that can corrupt target observations via background clutter and occlusion. Such dynamics and background induce nonlinear, nonGaussian and multimodal observation densities. These densities are difficult to model with traditional methods such as Kalman filter models (KFMs) due to their Gaussian assumptions. Dynamic Bayesian networks (DBNs) provide a more general framework in which to solve these problems. DBNs generalize KFMs by allowing arbitrary probability distributions, not just (unimodal) linear-Gaussian. Under the DBN umbrella, a broad class of learning and inference algorithms for time-series models can be used in visual tracking. Furthermore, DBNs provide a natural way to combine multiple vision cues. In this chapter, we describe some DBN models for tracking in nonlinear, nonGaussian and multimodal situations, and present a prediction method to assist feature extraction part by making a hypothesis for the new observations.

Introduction

Reliable visual tracking in complex environments is an important task. Its applications include human computer interaction, teleconferencing, smart surveillance, virtual reality, and motion analysis. It is a very challenging task because the objects' state space representation can be highly nonlinear and the observations are often corrupted by background clutter or occlusion. Traditional tracking methods, such as KFMs, are limited by their Gaussian assumptions. KFMs assume that the dynamics of the target can be modeled, and that noise affecting the target dynamics and sensor data is stationary and zero mean. In cases where the target is actively maneuvering, the disturbance is not zero mean, and the performance of the KFM degrades.

Dynamic Bayesian networks (DBNs) provide a more general framework in which to solve these problems. DBNs are directed graphical models of stochastic processes. They generalize hidden Markov models (HMMs) and linear dynamical systems (LDSs), also called KFMs, by representing the hidden (and observed) state in terms of state variables, which can have complex interdependencies. Bayesian networks (BN) are attractive for vision applications because they combine a natural mechanism for expressing domain knowledge with efficient algorithms for learning and inference (Rehg, Murphy, & Fieguth, 1999). DBNs provide two distinct benefits: Flexible modeling choices and schemes that can be tailored to fit the complexity of the visual tracking task, all of which can be conceptualized in a single framework with an intuitively-appealing graph notation. Second, there exists many effective and efficient inference and learning algorithms for BN that can be applied to visual tracking systems (Pavlovic, Rehg, Cham, & Murphy, 1999).

This chapter makes two contributions. First, we design some DBN models for nonlinear, nonGaussian and multimodal assumptions, and test tracking performance using exact and approximate DBN inference algorithms. The models in Figure 3 combine the advantages of models in references Wu and Huang (2001) and Pavlovic et al. (1999), and handle the case where observations have nonGaussian noise, by approximating it as a mixture of Gaussians. We also consider methods of seamlessly combining multiple cues with the DBN models. Multiple cues tracking is more robust in cluttered environments. Second, we present a prediction method based on online junction tree filtering algorithm for the models.

In section 2, we introduce some DBN models which have been used for visual tracking tasks, and design some DBN models with multiple observations cues under nonlinear, nonGaussian and multimodal assumptions for our visual tracking system, and in section 3 we describe the exact and approximate inference for the models, and present a prediction approach. In section 4, we demonstrate some experiment results on sampling data and real data. Section 5 is the summary.

DBN Models for Visual Tracking

Wu and Huang (2001), Murphy (1998), Murphy (2003), and Pavlovic, et al. (1999) describe some DBN models which have been used in visual tracking tasks. For example, Figure 1 shows a state space model (SSM) (Murphy, 2003a) and a factorial SSM (Wu & Huang, 2001).

Figure 1. DBN models with linear Gaussian. For all models, subscripts denote two time slices because the current state depends only on the previous state. Oval nodes are continuous and shaded nodes are observed.

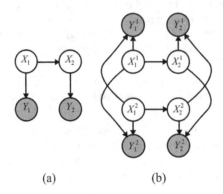

(a)   (b)

The DBN model in Figure 1(a) is a state space model (SSM) which looks identical to the graph structure of HMM. In Figure 1(b), the states of target can be decomposed into shape states and color states and the observation representation can also be separated into color and shape observations. All the nodes are continuous, and all the conditional probability distributions (CPDs) are linear-Gaussian. Shaded nodes are observed, and clear nodes are hidden.

In fact, the model in Figure 1(a) is a DBN representation of KFM, which is also called linear dynamic system (LDS). It can be defined as:

$$P(X_t = x_t \mid X_{t-1} = x_{t-1}) = N(x_t; Ax_{t-1}, Q)$$
$$P(Y_t = y \mid X_t = x) = N(y; Cx, R) \tag{1}$$

That is, the conditional probability distributions are just normal distributions with scaled means and fixed variances. To use multiple visual cues, Wu and Huang (2001) used the model in Figure 1(b). The factorial SSM in Figure 1(b) can be defined as:

$$P(X1t = x1t \mid X1t\text{-}1 = x1t\text{-}1) = N(x1t; A1 \; x1t\text{-}1, Q1)$$
$$P(X2t = x2t \mid X2t\text{-}1 = x2t\text{-}1) = N(x2t; a2 \; x2t\text{-}1, Q2)$$
$$P(Y1t = y1 \mid X1t = x1, X2t = x2) = N(y1; C1 \; x1 + C2 \; x2, R1)$$
$$P(Y2t = y2 \mid X1t = x1, X2t = x2) = N(y2; D1x1 + D2x2, R2) \tag{2}$$

The DBN model in Figure 2(a) (Murphy, 2003a) is a switching dynamic model. The model in Figure 2(b) (Murphy, 2002) is a switching dynamic model with switching observation for modeling nonGaussian observation noise. Square nodes are discrete, and oval ones are continuous. The dotted arcs are optional.

Figure 2. Switching DBN models with conditional Gaussian (CG) nodes. Square nodes are discrete.

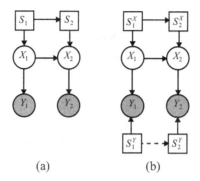

(a)　　　　　　(b)

The basic idea of the switching SSM in Figure 2(a) is that the model can switch between different kinds of dynamical "modes" or "regimes" (the resulting piece-wise linearity is one way to approximate nonlinear dynamics). The dynamics of the modes themselves are governed by a discrete-state Markov chain. After decoding, we can obtain the best sequence of switching states. The CPDs in Figure 2(a) are as follows (Murphy, 2003a):

$$P(X_t = x_t \mid X_{t-1} = x_{t-1}, S_t = i) = N(x_t; A_i x_{t-1}, Q_i)$$
$$P(Y_t = y \mid X_t = x) = N(y; Cx, R) \tag{3}$$
$$P(S_t = j \mid S_{t-1} = i) = M(i, j)$$

The basic idea of the switching SSM in Figure 2(b) is that the model can switch between different kinds of dynamical "modes" or "regimes." The image observations are corrupted by background clutter modeled by switched observations which make for a nonGaussian observation density. The CPDs for Figure 2(b) are as follows:

$$P(X_t = x_t \mid X_{t-1} = x_{t-1}, S_t^X = i) = N(x_t; A_i x_{t-1}, Q_i)$$
$$P(Y_t = y \mid X_t = x, S_t^Y = j) = N(y; C_j x, R_j) \tag{4}$$
$$P(S_t^X = j \mid S_{t-1}^X = i) = A^X(i, j)$$
$$P(S_t^Y = j \mid S_{t-1}^Y = i) = A^Y(i, j)$$

In our visual tracking system, we used the DBN switching SSMs in Figure 3, and experiment with single and multiple cues. Multiple feature representation for the target can be helpful for verifying various aspects of the image observations. For example, combining the color distribution of the target could enhance the robustness of contour tracking in a heavily cluttered background, and integrating shape and color feature representations could improve tracking against color distracters. If the target and the clutter become indistinguishable in terms of one stream of representation, the tracking has to be determined from the other streams. This problem motivates the research of tracking and integrating multiple visual cues (Wu & Huang, 2001).

Figure 3. DBN models for our visual tracking system

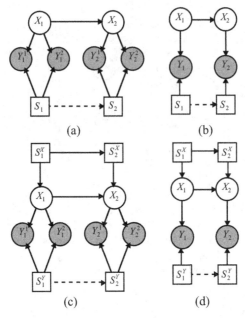

(a)   (b)

(c)   (d)

Figure 3(a) shows a model that allows for switched background clutter. It uses multiple cues such as color and shape observations. 3(b) is a switching observation model with single cue. 3(c) is a switching dynamic model with allowance for multiple cues of switching observation. 3(d) is the same as Figure 2(b).

The basic idea of using the switching SSM in Figure 3(a) is to model multiple nonGaussian observation noise. The CPDs of the model in Figure 3(a) are as follows:

$$P(X_t = x_t \mid X_{t-1} = x_{t-1}) = N(x_t; Ax_{t-1}, Q)$$
$$P(Y_t^1 = y^1 \mid X_t = x, S_t = i) = N(y^1; C_i x, R_i^1)$$
$$P(Y_t^2 = y^2 \mid X_t = x, S_t = i) = N(y^2; C_i x, R_i^2)$$
$$P(S_t = j \mid S_{t-1} = i) = A(i, j)$$

(5)

When the image observation is represented by a single cue and corrupted by background clutter, the resulting observation density is nonGaussian. Hence, we can use the DBN model in Figure 3(b) to model tracking with single cue by approximating the noise as a mixture of Gaussians. The CPDs are as follows:

$$P(X_t = x_t \mid X_{t-1} = x_{t-1}) = N(x_t; Ax_{t-1}, Q)$$
$$P(Y_t = y \mid X_t = x, S_t = i) = N(y^1; C_i x, R_i^1)$$
$$P(S_t = j \mid S_{t-1} = i) = A(i, j)$$

(6)

The basic idea of the switching SSM in Figure 3(c) is similar to 2(b), but it uses multiple observation cues. The CPDs in DBN model of Figure 3(c) are as follows:

$$P(X_t = x_t \mid X_{t-1} = x_{t-1}, S_t^X = i) = \text{N}(x_t; A_i x_{t-1}, Q_i)$$
$$P(Y_t^1 = y^1 \mid X_t = x, S_t^Y = j) = \text{N}(y^1; C_j x, R^1 j)$$
$$P(Y_t^2 = y^2 \mid X_t = x, S_t^Y = j) = \text{N}(y^2; C_j x, R^2 j) \qquad (7)$$
$$P(S_t^X = j \mid S_{t-1}^X = i) = A^X(i, j)$$
$$P(S_t^Y = j \mid S_{t-1}^Y = i) = A^Y(i, j)$$

After using the above models to express domain knowledge of visual tracking task, we try some DBN inference algorithms to make the tracking (filtering) and prediction.

Inference and Prediction

Here we overview some possible inference problems which appear in the visual tracking tasks, and give some analysis of time and space complexity for the inference algorithms involved, and then present a new DBN approach to make prediction in our visual tracking task.

Inference

In our tracking system, we used the models in Figure 3 with both exact and approximate inference algorithms for the DBNs. The exact inference algorithm is the junction tree algorithm, and we will discuss the details in the next section. The approximate algorithms are Boyen-Koller (BK) (Boyen & Koller, 1998), generalized pseudo Bayesian (GPB) (Kim, 1994) and particle filtering (PF) with likelihood weighting (importance sampling). PF is also known as sequential importance sampling (SIS), sequential Monte Carlo, the bootstrap filter (Gordon, 1993), or the condensation algorithm (Isard & Blake, 1996).

In practice, we implemented GPB and PF algorithms using the Bayesian networks toolkits (BNT) (Murphy, 2003b) and Intel's OpenPNL (Sysoyev, Bradski, Dash, Eruhimov, & Tarasov, 2003). There is a good description of PF using the likelihood weighting (LW) routine and GPB algorithms for DBNs, each with 2 variants we call 1 & 2 in Murphy (2002). It also includes pseudo code of PF and LW algorithms. BNT has an inference engine for LW approximate inference on static Bayesian networks, so we modified it for DBNs by using LW in a PF routine. The pseudo code of PF in a DBN is in Figure 4.

In the pseudo code of Figure 4, $[x_t^i, \hat{w}_t^i] = LW(x_{t-1}^i, y_i)$ is the process of likelihood weighting routine just as the pseudo code in Murphy (2002). $x_t^i = \text{LW}(x_{t-1}^i, y_i)$ is the likelihood weighing only containing sample x_t^i and without computing $\hat{w}_t^i$.

Figure 4. Pseudo code of the particle filtering in a DBN

function $[\{x_t^i, w_t^i\}_{i=1}^{N_s}] = PF(\{x_{t-1}^i, w_{t-1}^i\}_{i=1}^{N_s}, y_t)$

// Use LW to sample x_t^i and compute weights $\hat{w}_t^i$

if t is the first time slice

    for each node i in topological order

    $[x_t^i, \hat{w}_t^i] = LW(x_{t-1}^i, y_t)$

else

    Reshape the y_t to t and $t-1$ time slices

    for each node i in topology of first slice of DBN

        $x_t^i = LW(x_{t-1}^i, y_t)$

    for each node i in topology of second slice of

DBN

        $[x_t^i, \hat{w}_t^i] = LW(x_{t-1}^i, y_t)$

end

$w_t^i = \hat{w}_t^i \times w_{t-1}^i$

Normalize $w_t^i := w_t^i / \sum_{i=1}^{N_s} w_t^i$

//Resample step

    $N_{eff} = \dfrac{1}{\sum_{i=1}^{N_s}(w_t^i)^2}$

if $N_{eff} <$ threshold

    $\pi = resample(\{w_t^i\}_{i=1}^{N_s}$

    $x_t^i = x_t^{\pi}$

    $w_t^i = 1/N_s$

Inference Problems in Visual Tracking Tasks (Murphy, 2002, 2-4)

1. **Filtering:** Computing $P(X_t \mid y_{1:t})$, that is, monitoring (tracking) the state over time. This is used as a subroutine for online tracking. In some cases, the filtering output is the corrected value of the observations.

2. **Prediction:** Computing $P(X_{t+h} \mid y_{1:t})$ for some horizon $h > 0$ into the future. In visual tracking, the prediction output can assist feature extraction by making a hypothesis for the new observations.

3. **Fixed-interval smoothing (off-line):** Computing $P(X_t \mid y_{1:t})$. This is used as a subroutine for off-line training. Given the sequence of observation values, we use off-line smoothing for training.

4. **Viterbi decoding:** Computing arg $\max_{x_{1:t}} P(x_{1:t} \mid y_{1:t})$, that is, figuring out the most likely cause/ explanation/ state sequence of the observed data. For example, when tracking a hand gesture, the decoded result can be used to explain the meaning of the gesture.

5.   **Classification:** Computing $P(y_{1:t}) = \Sigma_{x_{1:t}} P(x_{1:t}, y_{1:t})$. This can be used to compute the likelihood of a sequence under different models. For example, when tracking a figure, the result is the recognition of different kinds of figure motions.

Time and Space Complexity

The models in Figure 1(a) and 1(b) are linear-Gaussian DBNs, and the time and space complexity of exact inference algorithm is $O((KD)^2)$ time per step, If we have D hidden continuous variables, each a vector of size K, the compound state-space will have size KD. Here a standard Kalman filter/smoother will usually be as efficient as using the junction tree algorithm. The switching SSMs in Figure 2(a), 2(b) and Figure 3 are conditional Gaussian (CG) models. If the belief state at time t is a mixture of K_t Gaussians, exact inference in a switching SSM takes $O(K_t)$ operations at the t'th time step.

Prediction

As mentioned in section 3.1, a prediction output can assist feature extraction parts by making a hypothesis for new observations. A prediction scheme may greatly improve the behavior of the tracker because it removes any restriction on the maximum lateral velocity of the subject, and only the amount of acceleration is limited (Birchfield, 1998). Hence, we design a DBN approach to make prediction in our visual tracking task.

Suppose the tracked object is modeled by an ellipse with a fixed vertical orientation and a fixed aspect ratio, then each time a new image becomes available, the ellipse's observation is: $y = (m, n, \sigma)$, (m, n) is the position in a 2D space and σ is the size (length of the minor axis), so in the DBN framework, a filtering process is computing $P(X_t | y_{1:t}) = P(X_t | (m^{1:t}, n^{1:t}, \sigma^{1:t}))$, which is monitoring (tracking) the state over time. A prediction process is computing $P(X_{t+h} | y_{1:t}) = P(X_{t+h} | (m^{1:t}, n^{1:t}, \sigma^{1:t}))$ for some horizon $h > 0$ into the future. That is, the predicted state X_{t+1} in the time slice $t + 1$ can be computed by the input of the observations in time slices $(1: t)$. The process is similar with the filtering process. Hence, we refer to a classical filtering algorithm in DBN framework, online junction tree filtering algorithm, to design our prediction method.

Online Junction Tree Filtering Algorithm

Junction tree algorithm is a very classical inference algorithm in DBN framework. Murphy (2002) has a good description of junction tree inference, so we will not discuss the detail of the algorithm here.

To hide the details from higher-level algorithm, we use abstract operators, Fwd 1, Fwd, and Back. The pseudo code of online junction tree filtering is shown in Figure 5.

Fwd 1, Fwd, and Back are the abstract forward and backward operators. Fwd1 is the forwards pass for the first time slice. Below is how to compute these operators.

Figure 5. Pseudo code of the online junction tree filtering algorithm

```
function Jtree_Filtering (y_t)
  if t = 1
      f_{1:1} = Fwd1(y_1)
  else
      f_{t:t} = Fwd (f_{t-1:t-1}, y_t)
  end
      b_{t:t} = Back (f_{t:t})
```

Suppose the DBN model is a KFM, then to compute the forward operator, $(x_{t|t}, V_{t|t}, L_t) = Fwd(x_{t-1|t-1}, V_{t-1|t-1}, y_t; A_t, C_t, Q_t, R_t)$, "First, we compute the predicted mean and variance, $x_{t|t-1} = Ax_{t-1|t-1}$ and $V_{t|t-1} = AV_{t-1|t-1}A' + Q$, then we First, we compute the predicted mean and variance, the variance of the error, the Kalman gain matrix, and the conditional log-likelihood of this observation:

$$e_t = y_t - Cx_{t|t-1} \quad\quad\quad K_t = V_{t|t-1}C'S_t^{-1}$$
$$\text{and}$$
$$S_t = CV_{t|t-1}C' + R \quad\quad\quad L_t = \log N(e_t; 0, S_t)$$

Finally, we update our estimates of the mean and variance:

$$x_{t|t} = x_{t|t-1} + K_t e_t$$
$$V_{t|t} = (I - K_t C)V_{t|t-1} = V_{t|t-1} - K_t S_t K_t'\text{''' (Murphy, 2002).}$$

To compute the backward operator, $(x_{t|T}, V_{t|T}, V_{t-1,t|T}) = Back(x_{t+1|T}, V_{t+1|T}, x_{t|t}, V_{t|t}; A_{t+1}, Q_{t+1})$, "First we compute the predicted quantities: $x_{t+1|t} = A_{t+1}x_{t|t}$ and $V_{t+1|t} = A_{t+1}V_{t|t}A_{t+1}' + Q_{t+1}$, then we compute the smoother gain matrix, $J_t = V_{t|t}A_{t+1}'V_{t+1|t}^{-1}$. Finally, we compute our estimates of the mean, variance, and cross variance:

$$V_{t,t-1|T} = Cov[X_{t-1}, X_t \mid y_{1:T}]$$

$$x_{t|T} = X_{t|t} + J_t(x_{t+1|T} - x_{t+1|t})$$
$$V_{t|T} = V_{t|t} + J_t(V_{t+1|T} - V_{t+1|t})J_t'\text{'''(Murphy, 2002).}$$
$$V_{t-1,t|T} = J_{t-1}V_{t|T}$$

Prediction Method

Considering the similarity between the filtering and prediction process for DBN models, we modify the online junction tree filtering algorithm to design the prediction method and

Figure 6. Pseudo code of the prediction method

```
function Prediction (y_t)
if t = 1
        f_{1:1} = Fwd1 (y_1)
        for j = 1:h // prediction step
                y_{1+j} = [y_{1+j-1} y^j_{null}]// new observation is null
                f_{1+j:1+j} = Fwd(f_{1+j-1:1+j-1}, y_{1+j})
        end
else
        f_{t:t} = Fwd (f_{t-1:t-1}, y_t)
        for j = 1 : h //prediction step
                y_{t+j} = [y_{t+j-1} y^j_{null}]// new observation is null
                f_{t+j:t+j} = Fwd(f_{t+j-1:t+j-1}, y_{t+j})
        end
end
        b_{t+h:t+h} = Back(f_{t+h:t+h})
```

implement it by Bayesian network toolkit (BNT) (Murphy, 2003b). The pseudo code is shown in Figure 6.

Compared with the pseudo codes in Figure 5, the prediction code has h more forward passes. The forward passes are similar with that in the filtering process. The only difference is that in the prediction step the new observation is null. That is, in the forward operator:

$$(x_{t+h|t+h}, V_{t+h|t+h}, L_{t+h}) =$$
$$Fwd(x_{t+h-1|t+h-1}, V_{t+h-1|t+h-1}, y_{t+h}; A_{t+h}, C_{t+h}, Q_{t+h}, R_{t+h}),$$
the observation is defined as: $y_{t+h} = [y_t \, y^1_{null} \, ... \, y^h_{null}]$.

Experiments

Our system contains two elements: the tracking engine and the observation stream. In experiments, we test both random sampled data from the DBN and real vision data as the observation source. For the tracking engine, we use models in Figure 2 to express nonlinear, nonGaussian and multimodal assumptions and test some approximate inference for these models. The approximate inference algorithms include expectation propagation (EP) and generalized pseudo Bayesian (GPB) algorithms. There is a good description of EP and GPB algorithm, each with two variants we call 1 & 2, in Murphy (2002). Hence, we will not discuss the details here.

In practice, we implement all the algorithms using the Bayesian networks toolkits (BNT) (Murphy, 2003b) and Intel's OpenPNL (Sysoyev et al., 2003).

Observations from Random Samples

To create ground truth data, we performed "random sampling" from the models by recording observations resulting from randomly generated state trajectories. The tracking result with different inference algorithms is shown in Figures 10 and 11. The tracking speed of different inference algorithms in different DBN models are shown in Table 1.

In Figure 10, Figure 11, and Table 1, we can see exact inference has the best performance, and BK tracks well. BK is in fact slower here than exact, but for more complex models, the computations in junction tree grow exponentially in maximum clique size so that junction tree would become much slower. GPB's approximation is too inaccurate here to track a random trajectory well.

Figure 12 shows that the prediction method can predict both observation and hidden state. When the DBN models support multiple observations, it can also predict multiple observations. But when the models become more complicated, as shown in Table 2, the speed is slower. Hence, in visual tracking system with real vision data, which may induce more complicated DBN models, we do not use the method.

Observations from Real Data

To test our DBN models on the real data, we follow the experiments of Birchfield (1997, 1998), trying to detect and track a person's head in some unmodified environments with a

Table 1. Tracking speed of different algorithms in DBN models with random sample observations

Speed (s/frame)	Model 3(a)	Model 3(b)	Model 3(c)	Model 3(d)
Junction tree	0.078	0.062	0.141	0.094
BK	0.468	0.313	0.547	0.531
PF1	1.797	1.375	2.25	1.891
PF2	0.8531	0.786	0.7838	0.7844
GPB1	0.0032	0.0031	0.0052	0.0032
GPB2	0.0047	0.0047	0.0053	0.0046

Table 2. Speed of online junction tree filtering and prediction with random sample observation

Speed (s/frame)	Model 1(b)	Model 2(a)	Model 1(a)
Filtering	0.015	0.078	0.015
Prediction	0.031	0.3	0.016

simple ellipse contour model (raw video data comes from Birchfield, 2003). In that system, when a new image comes in, a local search determines the location of the ellipse according to some evaluation function. In order to provide different evidence stream for the track engine, we use two matching evaluation functions based on head's shape and color, respectively.

The first image cue is based on shape information that uses the dot product of the intensity gradient vector and the ellipse normal around the ellipse perimeter, considering both the gradient magnitude and the gradient direction as follows (Birchfield, 1998):

$$\phi_g(s) = \frac{1}{N_\sigma} \sum_{i=1}^{N_\sigma} \left| n_\sigma(i) \cdot g_s(i) \right| \tag{8}$$

where $n_\sigma(i)$ is the unit vector normal to the ellipse at perimeter pixel i, $g_s(i)$ is the intensity gradient at the same pixel, N_σ is the number of pixels on the perimeter of the ellipse for an ellipse of size σ, and $(\cdot)$ denotes the dot product. In practice, this method runs well in uniform backgrounds, including moderate amounts of occlusions, but fails when distracted by heavily cluttered backgrounds in complex environments.

The other image cue is based on color histograms which can implicitly capture complex, multimodal patterns of color. We use this to represent the head's color distribution. When a candidate location is considered, pixels inside the contour are collected to build a histogram. The intersection of such a histogram and a predefined one reflects the match goodness, as follows (Birchfield, 1998):

$$\phi_c(s) = \frac{\sum_{i=1}^{N} \min(I_s(i), M(i))}{\sum_{i=1}^{N} I_s(i)} \tag{9}$$

where $I_s(i)$ and $M(i)$ are the numbers of pixels in the ith bin of the histograms, and N is the number of bins. In practice, this method demonstrates robust performance against some nonrigid and out-of-plane rotations. However, it suffers from lighting changes and from backgrounds which contain similar colors.

The DBN models in Figure 3(b) and 3(d) are switching SSMs using single cues where the target is solely represented by its color or shape. The DBN models in Figure 3(a) and 3(c) are switching SSMs using multiple cues, and the target is represented by both its color and shape.

Figure 7. Tracking results with shape alone using EP and GPB1 inference

(a) Model 2(b)   (b) Model 2(d)

Figure 8. Tracking results using GPB1 with shape and color cues

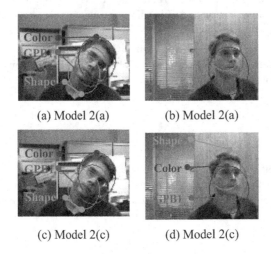

(a) Model 2(a)   (b) Model 2(a)

(c) Model 2(c)   (d) Model 2(c)

Figure 9. Tracking result of different DBN models in occlusion

(a) Tracking result of model 3(b), observation is shape alone (red circle)

(b) Tracking result of model 3(d), observation is shape alone (red circle)

(c) Tracking result of model 3(a), observations are shape (green circle) and color (blue circle)

(d) Tracking result of model 3(c), observations are shape (green circle) and color (blue circle)

Figure 7(b) shows the tracking result of model 2(d) using junction tree (EP) and GPB1 algorithms in DBN. The tracking speed of EP is about 0.078 s/frame, and the tracking speed of GPB1 is about 0.0015 s/frame.

In Figure 7, you can see that model 2(d) has better tracking performance than model 2(b), because it has more flexible assumptions. Both models 2(b) and 2(d) allow for nonGaussian observation densities in order to handle cluttered backgrounds, but model 2(d) allows different kinds of dynamical "modes" or "regimes" as a response, while model 2(b) allows only one mode of response.

Also, In Figure 7, although EP has better performance than GPB1 inference, its speed is far slower than GPB1.

Figure 8(a) and 8(b) are the tracking results of model 2(a) using GPB1. 8(c) and 8(d) are the tracking result of model 2(c) using GPB1. The tracking speed of GPB1 is about 0.0017s/frame.

In Figure 8, model 2(a) and 2(c) use both color and shape observations to track, and their results are similar. In Figure 8(a) and 8(c), when the background is cluttered, the observation is bad in terms of shape, but color is better, so models 2(a) and 2(c) still get good tracking results. In Figure 8(b) and 8(d), when the background has similar colors to the targets, the observation is bad in terms of color, but shape is better, so models 2(a) and 2(c) still get good tracking results.

Figure 9 shows the examples of our models and algorithms handling occlusion. Note that in all the figures, our models 3(c) and 3(d) always keep a consistent, generally tight bound and never lost tracking in any sequence.

Conclusion

In this chapter, firstly we describe DBN models with nonlinear, nonGaussian and multi-modal assumptions, and use exact and approximate inference algorithms for visual tracking. The models are able to fuse multiple cues for increased robustness. Our experiments show that these DBN models track robustly in complex environments in which the state of target becomes nonlinear, nonGaussian and multimodal. Second, we present a prediction method based on online junction tree filtering algorithm for the DBN models. We show the potential of DBNs to provide a general and flexible "tracking tool kit" for visual tracking in complex environments.

References

Birchfield, S. (1997). An elliptical head tracker. In *Proceedings of the 31st Asilomar Conference on Signals, Systems, and Computers* (pp. 1710-1714). Pacific Grove.

Birchfield, S. (1998). Elliptical head tracking using intensity gradients and color histograms. In *Proceedings Of the IEEE Conference on Computer Vision and Pattern Recognition* (pp. 232-237). IEEE.

Birchfield, S. (2003). Elliptical head tracking using intensity gradients and color histograms. Retrieved December 22, 2006, from http://vision.stanford.edu/~birch/headtracker/

Boyen, X., & Koller, D. (1998). Tractable inference for complex stochastic processes. In *Proceedings of the Conference on Uncertainty in AI* (pp. 33-42). Morgan Kauffmann.

Gordon, N. (1993). Novel approach to nonlinear/non-Gaussian Bayesian state estimation. *IEE Proceedings (F), 140*(2), 107-113.

Isard, M., & Blake, A. (1996). Contour tracking by stochastic propagation of conditional density. In B. Buxton & R. Cipolla (Eds.), *Proceedings of the European Conference on Computer Vision* (vol. 1) (pp. 343-356). New York: Springer-Verlag.

Kim, C.J. (1994). Dynamic linear models with Markov-switching. *Journal of Econometrics, 60*, 1-22.

Murphy, K.P. (1998). Switching Kalman filters (Tech. Rep.). University of California at Berkeley, Computer Science Division.

Murphy, K.P. (2002). *Dynamic Bayesian Networks: Representation, inference and learning.* Unpublished doctoral dissertation, University of California at Berkeley.

Murphy, K.P. (2003a). Dynamic Bayesian networks (Draft). In *Probabilistic graphical models*. Retrieved December 22, 2006, from http://www.cs.ubc.ca/~murphyk/Papers/dbnchapter.pdf

Murphy, K.P. (2003b). Bayes net toolbox. Retrieved December 22, 2006, from http://bnt.sourceforge.net/

Pavlovic, V., Rehg, J.M., Cham, T.J., & Murphy, K.P. (1999). A dynamic Bayesian network approach to figure tracking using learned dynamical models. In *Proceedings of the International Conference on Computer Vision* (pp. 94-101).

Rehg, J., Murphy, K.P., & Fieguth, P. (1999). Vision-based speaker detection using Bayesian networks. In *Proceedings of Computer Vision and Pattern Recognition* (pp. 110-116). Ft. Collins, CO.

Sysoyev, A., Bradski, G., Dash, D., Eruhimov, V., & Tarasov, V. (2003). Intel open source probabilistic networks library. Retrieved December 22, 2006, from https://sourceforge.net/projects/openpnl/

Wu, Y., & Huang, T.S. (2001). A co-inference approach to robust visual tracking. In *Proceedings of the IEEE International Conference on Computer Vision* (vol. II) (pp. 26-33).

Appendix: Additional Figures

Figure 10. Tracking result of different algorithms in DBN models, the single observation is random samples

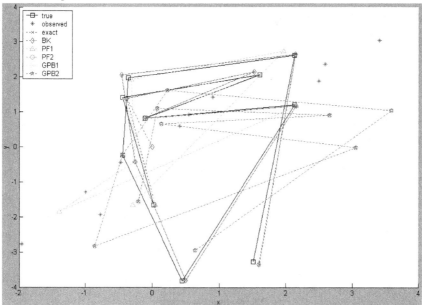

(a) DBN model in Figure 3(b)

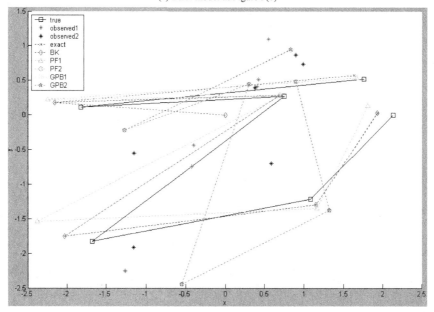

(b) DBN model in Figure 3(d)

Figure 11. Tracking result of different algorithms in DBN models, the multiple observations are random samples

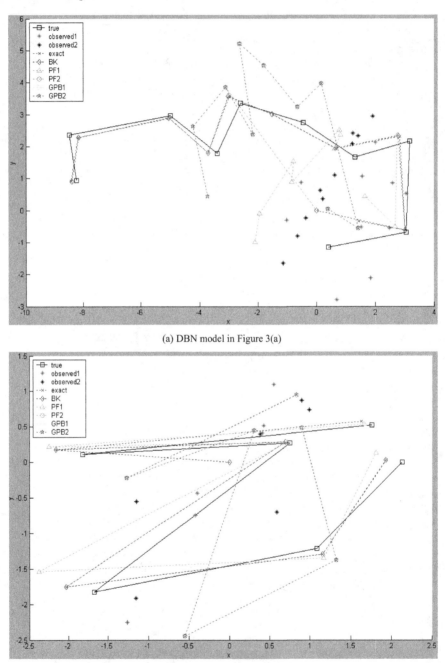

(a) DBN model in Figure 3(a)

(b) DBN model in Figure 3(c)

Figure 12. Prediction result of different DBN models

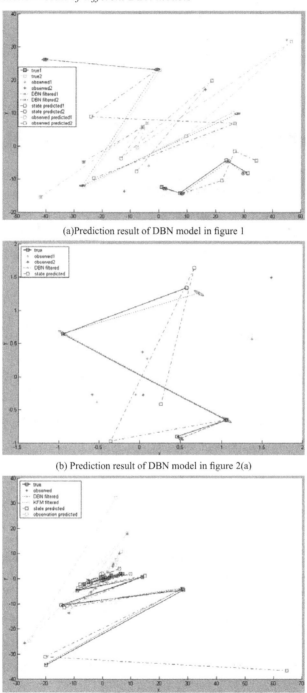

(a)Prediction result of DBN model in figure 1

(b) Prediction result of DBN model in figure 2(a)

(c) Prediction result of DBN model in figure 1(a)

Chapter X

Multimodal Human Localization Using Bayesian Network Sensor Fusion

David Lo, Carleton University, Canada

Abstract

In applications where the locations of human subjects are needed, for example, human-computer interface, video conferencing, and security surveillance applications, localizations are often performed using single sensing modalities. These mono localization modalities, such as beamforming microphone array and video-graphical localization techniques, are often prone to errors. In this chapter, a modular multimodal localization framework was constructed by combining multiple mono localization modalities using a Bayesian network. As a case study, a joint audio-video talker localization system for the video conferencing application was presented. Based on the results, the proposed multimodal localization method outperforms localization methods, in terms of accuracy and robustness, when compare with mono modal modalities that rely only on audio or video.

Introduction

Today's multisensor systems are becoming more complex with an increasing number of sensors, different types of sensors and increasing complexity of the sensor. Information gathered from multiple sensors often needs to be combined to form a more complete picture of the monitored environment. The dynamics of these modern sensor systems can be very complex. Sensors can be working cooperatively, competitively, or complimentarily (Tebo, 1997). Cooperative sensors work together to collect information of the environment that neither sensor alone can provide. Competitive sensors provide similar information, hence allowing informational redundancy. Complimentary sensors do not depend on each other, but can be combined to provide a more accurate picture of the environment. The complex nature of these sensor systems makes them difficult to combine coherently. Furthermore, the large amount of raw data these sensors generate also make them very difficult to combine. In recent years, the area of data fusion has gained research interest in multisensor applications because it provides a systematic approach to combine and extract useful information from the data. This chapter starts with the high level architectural view and the basic mechanics on how a Bayesian network and its improved variant can be used to fuse data from a multi-modal multisensor system. A multimodal human localization system and its implementation are given as an example in the later part of this chapter.

Multimodal Sensor Fusion

Often, a multimodal multisensor system is favored over a single sensor system. By adding more or different types of sensors, the overall system's accuracy and robustness is improved. For example, the system's temporal and spatial coverage can be extended by adding more sensors whereas, adding different types of sensors can improve the system's coverage in the measurement space (Waltz & Llinas, 1990). However, in order to realize these benefits, the system has to be able to take advantage of the extra information introduced by the extra sensors. Data fusion provides a mean for doing that (Waltz & Llinas, 1990). It allows information to be systematically combined from multiple sources while refining the states the system is trying to estimate (Steinberg, Bowman, & White, 1999). Data fusion has been successfully deployed in the field of robotics (Petriu, Ionescu, Petriu, Groen, Spoelder, Yeung et al., 1996; Yeung, McMath, Petriu, Trif, & Gal, 1994) and object tracking in a variety of environments (Strobel, Spors, & Rabenstein, 2001).

Figure 1 shows the general architecture of a multimodal sensor fusion system as block diagram. The *Sensor* block represents any single sensor modality using either a single sensor or a cluster of similar sensors. The *Data Processing* block processes the raw sensor data. Often, in a multimodal sensor system, fusion happens at both the raw data level and the information level (Lo, 2004a). Therefore, the type of processing performed by the *Data Processing* block can range from simple data filtering at the sensor level to complex statistical analyses and features extraction at the information level. The *Mapping* block transforms the processed data into a common space in which all processing modules can refer to; for example, a common coordinate system or common measuring unit. The *Data Fusion and*

Figure 1. General modular multimodal sensor fusion architecture

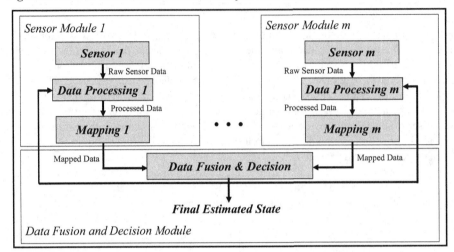

Decision block is responsible for performing the actual data fusion and contains the decision logic for the final output.

The architecture shown in Figure 1 is designed to be modular in nature. Data streams from each *Sensor* are kept separated at the beginning. Each *Sensor Module* represents a different sensor modality, and has its own associated *Sensor*, *Data Processing*, and *Mapping* blocks. The final estimate of the state, which the system is trying to approximate, is obtained by combining all the mapped data streams at the *Data Fusion and Decision* block. The modular nature of the architecture has the advantage of allowing high degrees of flexibility. The type of sensing device, number of sensing devices, the processing method, and the fusion method used can easily be changed without affecting the rest of the system. Furthermore, the architecture can easily accommodate an additional *Sensor Module* by simply duplicating the functional blocks and then just plugging it into the system. Because the modular design decouples the processing required by each sensor modality and the data fusion computation, this architecture is well suited for performing multiprocessor computing and distributed computing. The decoupling also allows sensing devices with different data rates to be used without blocking the computation of the *Final Estimated States*.

Multimodal Sensor Fusion Using Bayesian Network

More than one fusion method can be used (Lo, 2005b). In this chapter, we focus on the use of a Bayesian network to fuse high level information like extracted features. Consider a Bayesian network over universe U with observed evidence e expressed as the probability

$$P(U,e) = \prod_{A \in U} P(A|pa(A)) \cdot \prod_i e_i \qquad (1)$$

where *P(U,e)* is the joint probability of *U* and *e*, and *pa(A)* is the parent set of *A*.

Figure 2. Inference model for Bayesian network multimodal sensor fusion

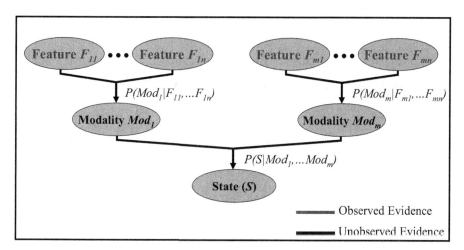

Assuming the *Data Processing* block of sensor modality m extracts n features from the raw data: $F_{m1}, \ldots, F_{mn}$, the inference modal of the Bayesian network fusion can be represented as direct acyclic graph (DAG) (Pearl, 1988, pp. 150-197) as shown in Figure 2. The nodes in the DAG represent the variables, both observed and unobserved, in the universe U, and the lines between the nodes represent probabilistic dependencies as conditional probabilities. The arrows represent the direction of information flow. Therefore, DAGs used in this chapter adopt the convention of putting the lowest level of information at the top. Informational fusion starts from the extracted features on the top, transversing down one level at a time with the final fused state at the bottom of the DAG.

The extracted features of each sensor modality are treated as observed evidences to support the modality's output in estimating state (S). With the observed evidences, equation (1) can be applied onto the inference modal shown in Figure 2 and the State node (S) can be found using:

$$P(S,e) = P(F_{11}, \ldots, F_{mn}, Mod_1, \ldots Mod_m)$$
$$= \prod_{i=1}^{m} P(Mod_i | F_{i1}, \ldots, F_{in}) \cdot P(S | Mod_1, \ldots, Mod_m) \qquad (2)$$

where S is the state the system is estimating, e are the evidences, and F_{mn} is the nth extracted feature of modality m.

There is more than one way to compute *P(S,e)*. In this chapter, we focus on the application of a Bayesian network on multimodal data fusion and how the components are built. How to solve a Bayesian network is left to the reader to look up references and learn how it is done. Also, there is public domain software, for example, the Microsoft MSBNx and the Bayes Net Toolbox for Matlab, which can be used to perform the mechanical aspect of solving a Bayesian network. In this particular example, the bucket elimination (Pearl, 1988, pp. 150-197) is used. Bucket elimination transverses the nodes in the inference model one by one. It marginalizes one nonobserved variable at a time and has it replaced with the simplified result. Only the nonobserved variables need to be marginalized (Pearl, 1988, pp. 150-197). Before the inference model can be used, each node is populated with its *a priori* knowledge.

Multimodal Sensor Fusion with Weights

The architecture shown in Figure 1 assumes each sensor module contributes equally in the fusion process. However, if the confidence level of one of the sensors is known to be lower than the others, less emphasis should be put on the data stream coming from this particular sensor. This can be accomplished by adding weights to the architecture. Figure 3 shows the modified fusion architecture. The architectural components are the same as Figure 1 with the exception of the added *Weight* block. The *Weight* block provides a mechanism to control how much each sensor contributes in the fusion process. By modulating the value of these weights, the system can be dynamically adjusted to adapt changes in the environment (Lo, 2004b), and accounted for failed sensors (Lo, 2005b).

Multimodal Sensor Fusion Using Bayesian Network with Weights

A simple modification of the Bayesian network inference equation shown in equation (1) and the inference model shown in Figure 2 are made to include weights. Each feature is

Figure 3. General architecture for multimodal data fusion with weights

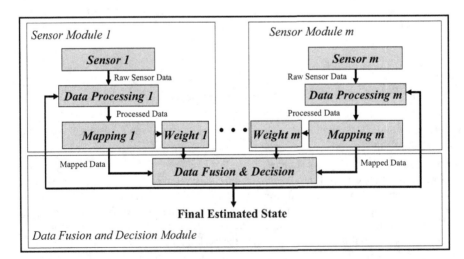

Figure 4. Inference model for Bayesian network multimodal sensor fusion with weights

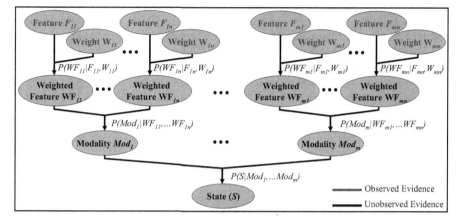

modified by its corresponding weight, and a new variable *Weighted Feature WF* is used to represent the result. Figure 4 shows the modified inference model, and the corresponding fusion equation becomes:

$$P(S,e) = P(F_{11},...,F_{mn},W_{11},...,W_{mn},Mod_1,...,Mod_m,S)$$
$$= \prod_{i=1}^{m}\prod_{j=1}^{n} P(F_{ij}) \cdot \prod_{i=1}^{m}\prod_{j=1}^{n} P(W_{ij}) \cdot \prod_{i=1}^{m}\prod_{j=1}^{n} P(WF_{ij}|W_{ij},F_{ij}) \cdot$$
$$\prod_{i=1}^{m} P(Mod_i|WF_{i1},...,WF_{in}) \cdot P(S|Mod_1,...,Mod_m) \qquad (3)$$

Application Example: Multimodal Talker Localization in Video Conferencing

In this section, we study how a Bayesian network is used to improve the overall accuracy and robustness of talker localization for a video conferencing system. We started off by building the architecture for the talker localization system using the developed multimodal architecture shown in Figure 3 and the Bayesian network inference model shown in 4. We then show how the individual single-modal localization methods, and the mechanics for the dynamic weight adjustment are built. These single-modal localizers are then combined to form the final multimodal system. Last but not least, the experimental results are presented.

In a video conferencing environment, it is desirable to isolate the active talker (Lo, 2004b; Lo, 2005b; Wang & Brandstein, 1998). Often, the isolation is done by means of audio or video localization (Lo, 2004b; Lo, 2005b; Messom, Demidenko, Subramaniam, & Gupta, 2002; Wang & Brandstein, 1998; Wang, griebel, & Brandstein, 2000; Zotkin, Duraiswami, Davis, & Haritaoglu, 2000). Most commercial systems use a beamforming microphone array to locate the active talker acoustically. Once the talker's location is found, the microphone array sends the talker's direction to the camera. The video camera is then pointed in the talkers' direction to capture their image. Although less popular, systems that rely on the video to perform localization are becoming more common as video equipment gets cheaper and computers become more powerful. Unfortunately, audio and video localization alone are prone to errors. For example, audio localization is very susceptible to acoustic reflections (Omologo & Svaizer, 1996), and video localization is susceptible to changes in lighting conditions (Hsu, Abdel-Mottaleb, & Jain, 2002) and complex backgrounds. Multimodal localization takes advantage of the complementing nature of multiple sources, giving a more robust localization (Strobel et al., 2001).

Multimodal Talker Localization Architecture

The general multimodal data fusion architecture shown in Figure 3 can be applied to a wide range of applications like surveillance (Davis, 1997), and robotics (Petriu et al., 1996; Yeung et al., 1994) . As an exploration platform and case study, the application of this architecture in video conferencing for the purpose of talker localization is studied. Figure 5 shows the architecture of the general multimodal talker localization. Detectable features of the talker, like speech, movements, and skin-color, trigger events that can be sensed by different localization modalities. The detection of these features maps well into the *Analysis* block in the general architecture. The *State* being estimated in this particular example is the talker's location.

Figure 5. Architecture of the general multimodal talker localization system

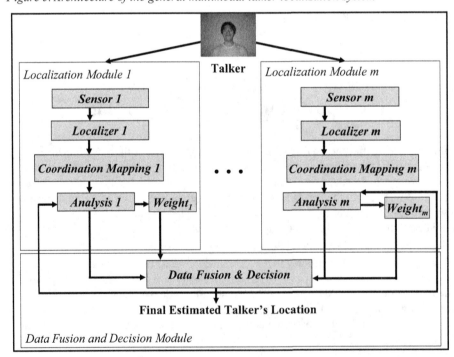

There are several approaches to perform multimodal talker localization in video conferencing. Some researchers approach it by cascading different localizers (Wang & Brandstein, 1998, 1999) while others might use one modality as the primary localization method with additional modalities as a means of confirmation (Fiala, Green, & Roth, 2004). The disadvantage of these approaches is that they are essentially "hard-wired" with limited flexibility or are still relying heavily on a particular localization method.

Taking advantage of the modular architecture, data streams are decoupled early in the beginning. Each stream feeds a different *Localization Module*. Each *Localization Module* is responsible for one localization modality, and a purpose specific localizer is used to locate the talker. Localization results from each *Localization Module* are then combined using the *Data Fusion and Decision Module* to form the final estimate of the talker's location. The multimodal nature of the architecture allows the system to use multiple localization modalities. Any one of these components can be changed without affecting the rest of the system. Also, the degree of influence from each localization modality in the final result is not fixed but controlled by a weighting function outlined as *Weight* in the block diagram. Consequently, how much the system relies on a particular modality can be dynamically adjusted according to the localization quality of each modality.

Each *Localization Module* contains a *Sensor* block which is any device that can sense the presence of the talker. The *Localizer* block is responsible for performing the localization. Because different sensors and localizers can have different coordinate systems, the *Coordinate Mapping* block is needed to transform the localizer's output into a common coordinate system that is used by the *Analysis* block, and the *Data Fusion and Decision* modules. Although localization results from different localizers can be contradicting at times, the *Data Fusion and Decision* module is responsible for drawing the best out of the available results from the individual localizers, and makes a collective output based on a predefined decision rule. The *Analysis* block performs statistical analysis on the localization data. Based on the results of the *Analysis* block, the *Weight* block provides an optional bias so that the data fusion engine can put different weights on the result from a specific localizer.

Single-Modal Talker Localization Methods

Three different localization methods, one audio and two video methods, are used in the talker localization system. Single-modal localizers are first constructed using each of these methods. These single-modal talker localizers are then combined to form the final multimodal system. In this section, we will look at the basics of constructing the single-modal localizers.

Beamforming Microphone Array

Traditionally, talker localization in video conferencing was done acoustically using a beamforming microphone array (Brandstein & Ward, 2001, pp. 3-16). A microphone array is a collection of two or more microphones distributed in space, working collectively as a single device. With a single microphone, the direction of an audio source cannot be determined (Johnson & Dudgeon, 1993, pp. 112-113). However, using two or more microphones, with the help of a beamforming technique, the spatial-temporal relationship can be used to recover

Figure 6. Localization sectors of the microphone array

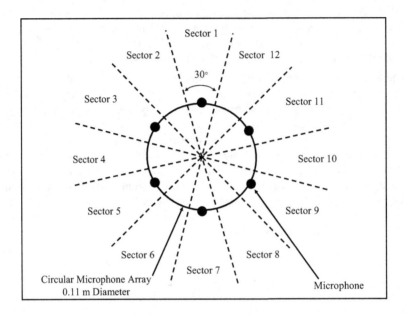

directional information about the source (Johnson & Dudgeon, 1993, pp. 112-113). Audio beamforming is a signal processing technique that is used to enhance the audio signal in the incoming direction and at the same time attenuates the signal in all other directions. The microphone array used in this particular localization example has six microphone elements. Through delay-and-sum beamforming, the microphone array is capable of segmenting the space around it into 12 sectors with each sector spanning 30°, as shown in Figure 6. These sectors are labeled from 1 to 12.

The beamforming algorithm combines the signals from the various microphones to enhance the audio signal originating from a desired location and attenuates the audio signals originating from all other locations. Given a microphone array with any number of microphones and beamforming algorithm capable of detecting audio signals originating from N different directions (sectors), the N beamforming algorithms have N output signals $B_1(t)$, $B_2(t)$, ..., $B_N(t)$. The delay-and-sum algorithm is a commonly used beamforming technique (Johnson & Dudgeon, 1993, pp. 112-113) and it is chosen for this example because of its simplicity. The required delays are calculated based on the physical layout of the microphone array with the assumption that the source is in the far field. The outputs of the microphone array are the windowed power signals $P_i(t)$, $i = 1,...,N$, for each sector which are calculated over the time window $[t - \Delta_t, t]$ from the beamformed signals $B_i(t)$ using:

$$P_i(t) = \frac{1}{\Delta_t} \int_{t-\Delta_t}^{t} B_i^2(t)dt \qquad i \in [1, N] \qquad (4)$$

where Δ_t is the width of the time window. Using the sampling notation $B_i[n] \stackrel{\Delta}{=} B_i(nf_s)$, where $n \in \mathbb{Z}$ and f_s is the sampling frequency, then for the numeric implementation we used:

$$P_i^{(k)} = \frac{1}{M} \sum_{n=0}^{M-1} B_i^2[n + (k-1)D_B] \qquad\qquad i \in [1, N] \qquad\qquad (5)$$

where $M = [\Delta_t f_s]$ samples is the width of the window and D_B controls the spacing of the windows in $B_i[n]$ for the kth window forming $P_i^{(k)}$. Notice that if $D_B = M$, then the windows extracted from $B_i[n]$ are nonoverlapping. In this particular study $D_B = M$, $\Delta_t = 1$ ms, $f_s = 8000$ Hz, $N=12$ sectors, and $M = [(0.001)(8000)] = 8$ samples.

Once the windowed power signals $P_i^{(k)}$ are computed for the kth window, then a decision must be made as to which sector $i = i_{active}$ is *active* (i.e., enough sound to be identified as voice activities). The approach used in this study is to set a predetermined power threshold T_{active} and take the sector with the maximum power that is greater than this threshold such that:

$$i_{active} = \arg\max_i \left\{ P_i^{(k)} \right\} > T_{active} \qquad\qquad (6)$$

We assume that the background noise power is small compared to the speech signals. If the noise levels are higher, then extensions to this approach will be needed to distinguish speech from background noise (Lo, 2005a). If multiple talkers are speaking, then the one with the greatest windowed power is considered active. Note that this approach to determine the active sector can produce undesirable results when steering a camera because it may erroneously swap back and forth between a talker and an acoustic reflection.

Motion Detection Using Video

The motion detection localizer identifies movements of the talker. There is more than one way in motion detection, and these methods can vary widely. Frame subtraction (Pingali, Tunali, & Carlbom, 1999; Toyama & Horvitz, 2000) and optical flow (Meier & Ngan, 1999) are two of the well-established methods used in performing motion detection. Frame subtraction operates based on the assumption that if a camera is perfectly stationary, changes between subsequent image frames can only be caused by the motions of objects. Optical flow operates based on the assumption that if an object is moving with constant velocity, the path and the direction (i.e., motion vector) of the image pixels reveals information about the object's distance from the camera (Archibald & Kwok, 1995). Frame subtraction has the advantages of being simple and easy to implement. However, it requires the camera to be perfectly stationary, and has low accuracy in measuring motions that are moving directly toward or away from the camera. Optical flow has the advantage of allowing the camera to move, and can measure motions in all directions. Because the experimental setup in this example used a fixed camera, background subtraction is chosen because of its simplicity.

To perform background subtraction, 24-bit RGB color video frames are first converted to 8-bit grayscale video frames according to ITU-R BT.709 standard using

Grey = 0.2125 * Red + 0.7154 * Green + 0.0721 * Blue $\qquad$ (7)

The ith grayscale frame is then subtracted from the $(i+k)^{th}$ grayscale frame, where k is used to control the time interval between frame comparisons which will, in part, depend on the video frame rate. The resulting difference frame is pixels that have changed.

$$D_{(x,y)} = F(i)_{(x,y)} - F(i+k)_{(x,y)}; x = 1...width; y = 1...height \qquad (8)$$

where $D_{(x,y)}$ is the resulting difference frame, $F(i)_{(x,y)}$ is video frame at time index i, $F(i+k)_{(x,y)}$ is video frame at time index $(i+k)$, (x,y) is the location of the pixel, and *width* and *height* are the respective width and height of the video image. Binary thresholding is then applied to the resulting difference frame. In order to eliminate unnecessary computations during image processing, images often need to be segmented so that the area of interest (AOI) can be isolated. Again, there is more than one way to identify AOIs in an image. These methods vary widely and they are still an active area of research in the image processing field. Two of the more popular methods are defining the AOIs manually on the first video frame and then letting the system track the AOIs in the subsequent video frames (Lo, 1994, pp. 14-21), and defining the AOIs automatically using a human visual system (HVS) model (Agarwal, Anbu, & Sinha, 2003; Osberger & Maeder, 1998). In a video conferencing system, user intervention decreases the usability of the system; therefore, defining the AOIs manually is not desirable. In this talker localization example, a simple HVS method (Lo, 2004b, 2005b) is used.

When more than one object is moving in the video scene, multiple AOIs will be detected. Motion detection can identify where motions happen, but it cannot distinguish whether the source of the motions is a talker or something else. Therefore, using just motion detection alone is not sufficient to localize the talker accurately.

Skin-Color Detection Using Video

Using color images, skin-color detection can be used to identify objects with skin-like color (Hsu et al., 2002; Terrillon, Shirazi, Fukamachi, & Akamatsu, 2000). Color can be represented using different color spaces. The most popular color space used by digital storage is the red-green-blue (RGB) color space. Although variations in the RGB space, such as the R-G space, has the advantage of reducing the sensitivity of segmentation to the changes in amount of light (Terrillon et al., 2000), RGB color space spreads skin-color pixels over a large range, making the detection difficult (Terrillon et al., 2000). It has been shown that color analysis done in luma-chroma space, such as the YCrCb, concentrates the skin-color pixels in a tight range (Terrillon et al., 2000) as shown in Figure 7. Therefore, a luma-chroma space is well-suited for detecting skin color pixel.

Hsu et al. (2002) used 137 images from nine subjects in the Heinrich-Hertz-Institute image database to define the skin tone cluster in the YCrCb space. They used a nonlinear model to compensate the luminance in low light and then fitted an ellipse to the skin tone cluster (Hsu et al., 2002). To reduce computational complexity, a system of eight linear equations, equation (9), is used to enclose the skin tone cluster and the fitted ellipse as shown in Figure 7.

Figure 7. A system of 8 equations enclosing the skin pixel area in Cr-Cb color domain (Hsu et al., 2002))

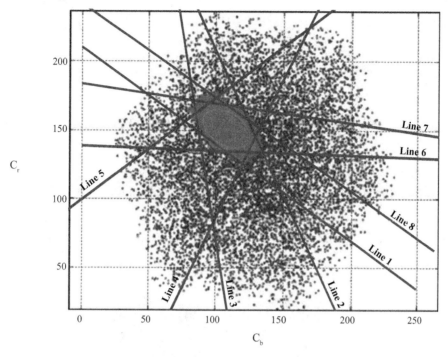

Line 1: $Cr \geq -0.702 \cdot Cb + 209.945$;

Line 2: $Cr \leq -2.12 \cdot Cb + 420.184$;

Line 3: $Cr \geq -5.984 \cdot Cb + 669.481$;

Line 4: $Cr \geq 2.012 \cdot Cb - 115.329$;   (9)

Line 5: $Cr \leq 0.7389 \cdot Cb + 99.171$;

Line 6: $Cr \geq -0.0333 \cdot Cb + 138.122$;

Line 7: $Cr \leq -0.142 \cdot Cb + 183.425$;

Line 8: $Cr \leq -0.681 \cdot Cb + 241.713$;

To perform skin-color detection, the 24-bit RGB color video frame is first transformed into the CCIR601-4 YCrCb color space (Poynton, 1996, pp. 176-177) using:

$$\begin{bmatrix} Y \\ Cr \\ Cb \end{bmatrix} = \begin{bmatrix} 16 \\ 128 \\ 128 \end{bmatrix} + \frac{1}{256} \begin{bmatrix} 65.738 & 129.057 & 25.064 \\ -37.945 & -74.494 & 112.439 \\ 112.439 & -94.154 & -18.285 \end{bmatrix} \begin{bmatrix} Red \\ Green \\ Blue \end{bmatrix} \qquad (10)$$

equation (9) is then used to determine the thresholding values for detecting skin-color pixels. Each pixel is checked using:

$$\begin{cases} if\,(Cr_{(x,y)} \geq TestCr1)\,\&\,(Cr_{(x,y)} \leq TestCr2)\,\&\,(Cr_{(x,y)} \geq TestCr3)\,\&\,(Cr_{(x,y)} \geq TestCr4)\,\&\,(Cr_{(x,y)} \leq TestCr5) \\ \&\,(Cr_{(x,y)} \geq TestCr6)\,\&\,(Cr_{(x,y)} \leq TestCr7)\,\&\,(Cr_{(x,y)} \leq TestCr8) = True \Rightarrow pixel_{(x,y)} = 1 \\ \qquad\qquad\qquad\qquad else\,pixel_{(x,y)} = 0 \end{cases}$$

$$(11)$$

where $Cr_{(x,y)}$ is the r-chrominance value of the pixel located at (x,y), $pixel_{(x,y)}$ is the resulting skin-color mask, $TestCr1$ is the r-chrominance value computed using the equation of Line 1 in equation (9), $TestCr2$ is using the equation of Line 2 in equation (9), and so forth.

Figure 8 demonstrates the skin-color detection process. Figure 8(a) shows the original image. The resulting image is a skin-color pixel mask (Figure 8(b)). To clean up the mask, morphological closing is applied to emphasize large groups of pixels such as faces (Figure 8(c)). Often, small holes exist within a large group of pixels, such as the eyes and the mouth. Therefore, a flood fill operation is used to fill out any small holes in it (Figure 8(d)). Morpho-

Figure 8. An example of skin-color detection

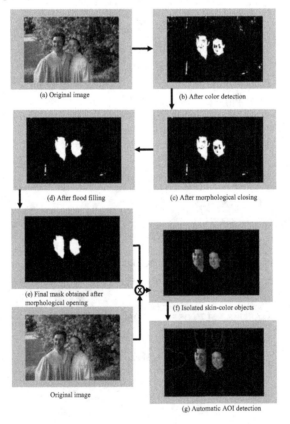

(a) Original image

(b) After color detection

(d) After flood filling

(c) After morphological closing

(e) Final mask obtained after morphological opening

(f) Isolated skin-color objects

Original image

(g) Automatic AOI detection

logical opening is then used to eliminate any small cluster of pixels and background noises (Figure 8(e)). The resulting mask represents large skin-color objects such as faces. The mask is then multiplied with the original image giving only objects with skin-color (Figure 8(f)). AOIs are then identified using an automatic AOI identifier (Figure 8(g)).

The outlined skin-color detection method is robust and works well in most well illuminated images of the upper body and full body that occupied big portion of the frame. However, localization methods based on skin-color can only identify the human faces in the image; it has no ability to distinguish who is the active talker. Furthermore, if there are pictures or posters with human faces in the video scene, the skin-color detection method will treat them just as another potential human talker.

Using Occupancy Estimates as Weights

The fusion architecture shown in Figure 5 assumes the accuracy and reliability of each localizer are equal. However, if the temporal correctness of the output of each localizer can be estimated, the *Weight* block can be used to bias the less reliable localizers away from the fusion process so that they contribute less in the final fused output.

In this section, we investigate the use of the occupancy information as weights. The confidence level of each localizer's output is estimated using the occupancy grid mapping technique. The occupancy grid mapping technique is widely used in robotics, especially for the purpose of navigation (Elfes, 1989; Petriu et al., 1996; Yeung et al., 1994). The technique divides the environment into a discrete grid and assigns each grid location a value related to the probability that the location is occupied by an object. Initially, the entire grid is assigned with equal value. Sensor readings are then used to modify the grid value to reflect the probability that a specific grid location is being occupied.

In order to compute the occupancy information, the grid is set up so that it coincides with the activation sectors of the microphone array, as shown in Figure 6. As the localizers locate the talker in the conferencing environment, we estimate the probability of a talker occupying a particular sector. The occupancy estimates are derived based on known physical properties of each individual localizer and the current measurement of that localizer. Occupancy estimates allow including the unique physical characteristics of each localizer as part of the fusion process, and therefore further improve the overall localization performance. In order to achieve better localization performance, the occupancy estimates are introduced into the fusion engines to influence the weights, which in turn control how much individuals can contribute in the data fusion process. Also, when one or more localizers fail, the persistent erroneous data streams from the failed localizers can negatively affect a statistically based data fusion method, like the Bayesian network, resulting in poor localization accuracy (Chaodhury, Rehg, Pavlovic, & Pentland, 2002). The occupancy estimates provide a means to automatically stop the failed devices from contributing in the data fusion process, hence improving the overall robustness of the system. In this talker localization example, the impact of adding occupancy estimates into the fusion engine, and how occupancy estimates can be used to eliminate the failed localizers from the fusion process, are investigated.

Talker's Occupancy Estimates $G_{(m,n)}$ and Correctness Probability $P_{(m,n)}$for Grid Location n and Localization Modality m

The video conferencing space is divided into a discrete two-dimensional polar grid which coincides with the activation sectors used by microphone array, as shown in Figure 6. The occupancy estimates for each detection modality are derived and computed based on the specific physical properties of the sensors and their current output. The following section outlines how the occupancy information is estimated and why.

Occupancy Estimates for Audio Localization

In a video conferencing environment, acoustic reflections and multiple talkers often confuse the microphone array and cause the microphone array to locate the active talker incorrectly (Omologo & Svaizer, 1996). The occupancy measurement $G_{(audio,n)}$ of the audio localizer is designed to discriminate localization errors from these sources.

The main concept for deriving the occupancy estimates for the audio detection is based on the averaged power profile method developed in Lo (2004b, 2005b). Because of the use of a delay-and-sum beamformer, a single talker gives a unique power profile. If the averaged power profile is collected for one active sector at a time in an ideal condition, such as the anechoic chamber, these averaged power profiles can be normalized and stored as a set of reference profiles. When the averaged power profile of the current detection is cross-correlated with the reference profile, the amount of deviation can be used to estimate the likelihood that the current detected sector is occupied by a talker.

After audio localization is performed, the output is used to calculate its occupancy $G_{(audio,n)}$ and the associated correctness probability $P_{(audio,n)}$. First, the average power of each sector is computed, and normalized by dividing by its root-mean-square (RMS) value using:

$$\overline{\alpha[k]} = \frac{\alpha[k]}{RMS}; \qquad RMS = \sqrt{\frac{\sum_{k=1}^{N}\alpha[k]^2}{N}} \qquad k \in [1,N] \qquad (11)$$

where $a[k]$ is the averaged power profile, $\overline{\alpha[k]}$ is the RMS normalized averaged power profile, and N is the number of sectors, which is 12 in this example.

The RMS normalized power profile is then cross-correlated with the corresponding N reference profile. Because the maximum cross-correlation result between the two RMS normalized series is N, the cross-correlation result is first divided by N so that it ranges from zero to one. The maximum value of the scaled cross-correlation result is then used as $G_{(audio,n)}$.

$$R_{(\overline{\alpha}\overline{\rho},n)}(i) = \sum_{k=1}^{N-i}\overline{\alpha}_n[k+i]\cdot\overline{\rho}_n[k] \qquad i = 1,2,3,...2N-1; k \in [1,N]$$

$$G(audio,n) = \frac{1}{N}\max_i(R_{(\overline{\alpha}\overline{\rho},n)}(i)) \qquad (13)$$

where $R_{\overline{(\alpha\rho,n)}}(i)$ is the cross-correlation between $\overline{\alpha}_n[k]$ and $\overline{\rho}_n[k]$ and N is the dimension of the profile, which is also the total number of sectors in this case. $\overline{\alpha}_n[k]$ is the RMS normalized averaged power profile for sector n, and $\overline{\rho}_n[k]$ is the reference averaged power profile for sector n.

The reference averaged power profile $\overline{\rho}_n[k]$ is generated through controlled experiments done in an anechoic chamber where audio source is presented from the same distance to only one sector at a time. The averaged sector power is RMS normalized and subsequently stored as the reference averaged power profile. There are a few situations where an averaged power profile can deviate from its reference profile, which will result in a low cross-correlation value. For example, the current sector is not the active sector at all, and the microphone array is picking up reflections instead of the active talker, or multiple talkers are speaking simultaneously.

Occupancy Estimates for Video Localization

In this localization example, the occupancy of the motion detection $G_{(motion,n)}$ and the occupancy of the skin-color detection $G_{(skin-color,n)}$ are derived from the changes of the foreground-to-background ratio (f-b ratio) within an area-of-interest (AOI) (Toyama & Horvitz, 2000). The f-b ratio is computed as the ratio of black pixels (foreground) to white pixels (background) within a binary thresholded AOI. Changes in the f-b ratio should be gradual. Any sudden jumps in the f-b ratio indicate questionable localization result.

Similar to its audio counterpart, video localization results are used to compute the reliabilities and the correctness probabilities for both the motion and skin-color detection. Because the degree of motion should be limited in finite time, large changes of the f-b ratio suggest questionable localization results. Based on the changes in f-b ratio, a detection quality, Q, is assigned. In order to allow the occupancy calculation to have better stability in a highly

Table 1. Foreground-to-background ratio to detection quality assignment

Changes In Foreground-to-Background Ratio (%)	Assigned Detection Quality Q
0-9.99	1
10-19.99	$\sqrt{0.9} \approx 0.95$
20-29.99	$\sqrt{0.8} \approx 0.89$
30-39.99	$\sqrt{0.7} \approx 0.84$
40-49.99	$\sqrt{0.6} \approx 0.77$
50-59.99	$\sqrt{0.5} \approx 0.71$
60-69.99	$\sqrt{0.4} \approx 0.63$
70-79.99	$\sqrt{0.3} \approx 0.55$
80-89.99	$\sqrt{0.2} \approx 0.45$
90->100	$\sqrt{0.01} = 0.1$

dynamic conferencing environment, the detection quality assignments are set up in a way that small fluctuations of the change of f-b ratio do not affect the assigned value of the detection quality significantly. However, when the change in f-b ratio is large, it is heavily penalized. Consequently, an inverted power curve like distribution, power of square root, is used to assign the detection quality to the corresponding changes in f-b ratio. Table 1 shows the assignment values used in this example. The occupancy of the active sectors is then computed using equation (14) and sectors which are not reported as active are assumed to have equal occupancy and are computed using equation (15)

$$G_{(video, n)} \text{ for the active sector} = Q \tag{14}$$

$$G_{(video, n)} \text{ for the inactive sector} = \frac{J_s - \displaystyle\sum_{i=\text{active sector}} G_{(video,i)}}{N - J_s} \qquad N < J_s \tag{15}$$

where Q is the assigned detection quality based on the mapped grading scale in Table 7-1, J_s is the total number of detected active sectors, N is the number of sectors, and *video* can be either motion or skin-color detection.

Correctness Probability for Audio and Video Localization

The probability of correctness for the current audio and video localization output are statistical measurements of how often the output sector was detected in the past.

$$P_{(m,n)}[i] = \frac{\displaystyle\sum_{k=i-td}^{i} D_n[k]}{\displaystyle\sum_{s=1}^{N} \sum_{k=i-td}^{i} D_s[k]} \tag{16}$$

where $D_n[k]$ is the number of detections in sector n at time, k and td is the width of the window of time to look back to from the current data point, N is the number of sectors, and m is the detection method which can be the audio beamforming, motion, or skin-color detection for this talker localization example.

Motion detection identifies people, as well as any periodic movements like fan blades and monitors flicker. Similarly, skin-color detection identifies people as well as any objects that have skin-like color. Therefore, additional steps are necessary to reduce the chance of detecting artifacts. Periodic motions give little averaged change over a long period of time; therefore, active sectors with small averaged change in the f-b ratio over a long period of time are treated as static background objects in the experiment. In this talker localization example, a simple method is developed to check for periodic or static objects. AOIs containing the objects are first found using an automatic AOI identifying algorithm. A sliding window is then used to compute the running average of the changes of the f-b ratio in each AOI. Only AOIs with the averaged change above a predefined threshold are identified as valid AOIs.

Device Failure Detection

When a localizer fails, its output should be considered erroneous. Because the output of a failed localizer is usually persistent, statistically based fusion methods, such as a Bayesian network, often have no choice but to fuse the failed output along with the other outputs, causing significant degradation on the overall localization accuracy (Chaodhury et al., 2002). For example, when the lights are dimmed to give a presentation, the skin-color video localizers produce erroneous outputs in establishing the AOI. Therefore, it is important to eliminate any contribution from the failed localizers. As an improvement to the Bayesian network, the occupancy estimates are used to bias the Bayesian network away from fusing the erroneous data from the failed localizers, hence eliminating their contribution. For motion and skin-color detection, if all the pixels in the video scene are black, the localizers will assume that there is a device failure and force the corresponding occupancy estimate to zero, as shown in equation (17). Similarly, if there is no detectable audio signal from the microphones within a time window, the microphone array will assume that there is a device failure and force its occupancy estimate to zero, as shown in (18).

$$If\, (\sum_{row=1}^{x} \sum_{column=1}^{y} P_{(row,column)}) < T_{video} \Rightarrow G_{(video,n)} = 0; \qquad n = 1...12 \qquad (17)$$

$$If \sum_{i=1}^{6} Mic_i < T_{audio} \Rightarrow G_{(audio,n)} = 0; \qquad n = 1...12 \qquad (18)$$

where $P_{(row,column)}$ is a video pixel located at (row, column) in the video image, X and Y are the respective width and height of the video image, T_{video} and T_{audio} are predefined threshold values, which are zero in this study, Mic_i is the microphone number of the microphone array, $G_{(video,n)}$ is the occupancy estimates of the motion detection and skin-color detection, and $G_{(audio,n)}$ is the occupancy estimates of the microphone array.

If the failed device is repaired and comes back to life, or conditions are improved (i.e., light levels improve for video), the corresponding $G_{(video,n)}$ or $G_{(audio,n)}$ will no longer trigger the device failure detection mechanism and, hence, will not be forced to zero. As a result, the output of the repaired device will be included in the fusion process automatically. How often the device failure check is performed will determine how fast the system responds to a device failure or after the fault has been repaired. Also, as the number of devices used in the system increases, the computational load imposed by the device failure checking will also increase.

Talker Localization Using Multimodal Methods

Audio localization using beamforming generally works flawlessly when the talker speaks directly toward the microphone array and no other interfering sounds exist. However, microphone array often fails to locate the talker correctly due to acoustic reflections (Omologo & Svaizer, 1996). Video localization does not suffer from acoustic reflections, but does fail when the lighting conditions in the scene change drastically (Hsu, 2002), or when other people enter and leave the video scene in the background. Because using only audio or only video for localization is prone to failure, researchers are now exploring multimodal approaches by combing audio and video localization methods (Brandstein & Ward, 2001, pp. 3-16; Hsu et al., 2002; Lo, 2004a, 2004b; Messom et al., 2002; Toyama & Horvitz, 2000; Wang & Brandstein, 1998; Wang et al., 2000; Wu, Siegel, Stiefelhagen, & Yang, 2002). Joint audio-video localization takes advantage of the complementary nature of the two methods, giving a more robust localization (Wu et al., 2002). In this talker localization example, the single modal localization methods are combined using the fusion architecture shown in Figure 5 to perform multimodal talker localization.

Joint Audio-Video Talker Localization using Occupancy Assisted Bayesian Network Fusion

The Bayesian network, Figure 4, and the fusion equation, equation (3), are modified to accommodate the specifics for the talker localization system. Figure 9 shows the Bayesian inference model for performing data fusion on the localization results and the occupancy information. The observed evidence e is the localization outputs from the microphone array, the motion detection localizer, and skin-color detection localizer, as well as their corresponding occupancy estimates. The localizers are represented by the nodes Microphone Array (MA), Motion Detection (MD), Skin-color Detection (CD) and their corresponding weight is represented by node $G_{(audio,n)}$, $G_{(motion,n)}$, and $G_{(skin-color,n)}$, respectively. Motion (M), Color (C), Voice (V), and Image (I) are the unobserved random variables. The Talker node (T) is the talker's location which we are trying to find. Each arrow represents a conditional probability. The values of the observed evidence are represented by $MA=ma$, $MD=md$, $CD=cd$, $G_{(audio,n)}=g1$, $G_{(motion,n)}=g2$, and $G_{(skin-color,n)}=g3$, respectively. With the observed evidence, equation (3) can be applied into the inference model and the Talker node (T) can be found using:

$$P(T \mid V, I) = P(ma, md, cd, g1, g2, g3, M, C, V, I, T)$$
$$=P(ma) \cdot P(md) \cdot P(cd) \cdot P(g1) \cdot P(g2) \cdot P(g3) \cdot P(V \mid g1, ma) \cdot \qquad (19)$$
$$P(M \mid g2, md) \cdot P(C \mid g3, cd) \cdot P(I \mid M,C)$$

Bucket elimination (Pearl, 1988, pp. 150-197) is used to marginalize the nonobserved variables. The values of MA, MD, CD, $G_{(audio,n)}$, $G_{(motion,n)}$, and $G_{(skin-color,n)}$ are observed variables and M, C, V, and I are nonobserved variables. Before the inference model can be used, each node is populated with its *a priori* knowledge. The *a priori* knowledge can be obtained during initialization runs before the start of an experiment and from other standalone experiments.

Camera's Field of View to Active Sector Mapping

In a video conferencing system, the camera and the microphone array use a different frame of reference to localize objects. The camera usually uses the room or a fixed point in the

Figure 9. Bayesian inference model with occupancy estimates for joint audio-video localization

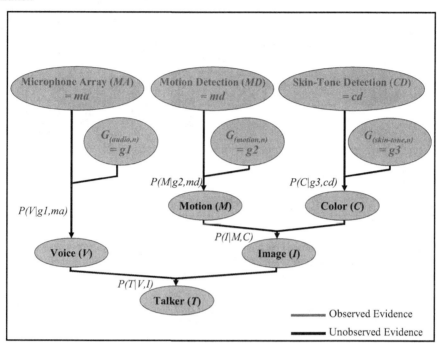

room as the reference point (Lo, 1994, pp. 14-21). A video localizer that uses the camera will then report the relative position of an object with respect to the reference point. On the other hand, the microphone array uses itself as a point of reference and reports all acoustic localizations relative to the locations of the microphone array. Therefore, localization results from each of the localizer will need to be mapped to a common frame of reference, which is the function of the *Coordination Mapping* block in the multimodal talker localization architecture shown in Figure 5. If the video and the microphone array are co-located, using two different frames of reference causes little problem because the relative location between the two is fixed and is known. Locations from one reference frame can be mapped to the other one or vice versa. For example, the simplest way to co-locate the camera and the microphone array is to set them up in such a way that the principle axis for the camera's pan is aligned with the center of the microphone array, so that every 30° of the camera's pan is mapped to a microphone array sector.

In this talker localization example, the camera and the microphone array are placed separately in the conference room. Because the spatial resolution of the microphone array is less than the camera, the field of view of the camera is mapped to the regions defined by the microphone array sectors, as shown in Figure 10, so that the locations of the active talker are reported using a common frame of reference. The sectors in which the AOIs fall on are identified as the active sectors. A calibration run performed before the start of the experiment provides the locations of these sectors.

Figure 10. Camera's field of view to microphone array active sector mapping

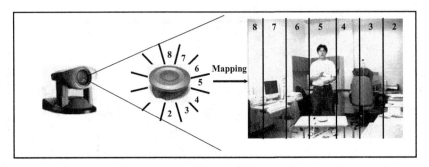

Experimental Results

Experiments were done in a similar manner as in Lo (2004b). Recordings were done in a 3.3 m x 6.3 m x 3 m high reverberant room with concrete walls, concrete floor, and suspended acoustic tiled ceiling. A six-element circular microphone array was placed on a table. A Canon VC-C4 video camera was placed two meters away from the microphone array, as shown in Figure 11. Acoustic data was sampled at 8 kHz and source localization was done using delay-and-sum beamformer running on a DSP board (BTPC-4062-2) equipped with a 40 MHz ADI DSP processor. The video data was digitized at 320×240 pixels, 15 frame/s with a Belkin F5U208 USB frame grabber. The experiments were done with the talker standing at 1 m in front of the microphone array giving a presentation. Because the range of the talker's motion was limited, a fixed camera was used to simplify the experiment. The camera was set up so that the field-of-view captured motion in sectors 4 – 10 (see Figure 11). The Bayes Net Toolbox for Matlab is used to perform inference on the Bayesian network. The experiments are set up so that if the talker is talking directly toward the microphone, audio localization will always give sector 7 as the active sector. However, when the talker turns toward the sidewalls, reflections will cause the microphone array to localize incorrectly. Before the experiments were started, initialization runs were done to populate the inference model with *a priori* knowledge, and to calibrate the mapping required for relating the locations of the sectors and the camera's field of view. The *a priori* knowledge of each localizer is computed using the histogram of its localization output for every four video frames.

Six different scenarios, as outlined in Table 2, are considered in the experiments. These six scenarios represent different permutations of the audio and video localization disturbances the localization system can potentially face. In order to compare the performance between different sensor fusion techniques, the total localization error rate for scenarios (1) – (6) and the error rate for just scenario (6) are computed. The error rate for scenario (6) is especially of interest because it represents the tracking error rate, and it reflects the dynamic behavior of the system. The error rate for a given time frame t_{start} to t_{end} is computed as:

Figure 11. Experimental setup for camera and microphone array

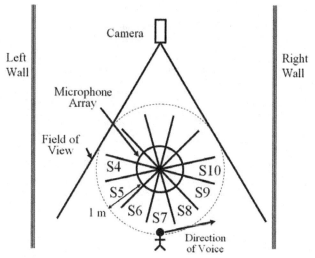

$$Error\ Rate = \frac{\sum_{i=t_{start}}^{t_{end}} t_{error}(i)}{(t_{end} - t_{start})} \qquad t_{end} > t_{start} \qquad (20)$$

where t_{error} is the duration of the localization error.

Figure 12 shows the localization results for the occupancy assisted Bayesian network fusion engine. Figure 12(a) shows the localization output using only the microphone array. Figure 12(b) shows the localization output using only the motion detection. Figure 12(c) shows the localization output using only skin-color detection. These three cases represent the localization performance if only one of the localizers is used. Figure 12(d) shows the fused localization results and Figure 12(e) shows the hypothetical ideal localization result for comparison.

In order to study the effect of device failure, a new set of experiments was conducted using the same experiment. Device failure was simulated by turning off the camera during the experiment 7.1 s after the experiment was started. Figure 13(a) and Figure 14(a) show the microphone array location output. However, without any video input, both the motion detection (Figure 13(b) and Figure 14(b)) and the skin-color detection (Figure 13(c) and Figure 14(c)) malfunctioned, and reported sector 5 as the active sector, which is their default AOI location. Figure 13(d) and Figure 14(d) show the Bayesian network fused results with and without occupancy estimates added in the case of devices failure. Without the help of the occupancy estimates, the fused localization output (Figure 13(d)) was incorrectly reporting sector 5 as the active sector. However, with the occupancy estimates added, the Bayesian network was biased away from the motion detection and the skin-color detection localizers. The fused localization output (Figure 14(d)) was correctly reporting sector 7 as the active sector.

Table 2. Scenarios for audio and video disturbances

	Scenario
(1)	Talker giving a presentation in front of the camera and directing his voice toward the microphone array.
(2)	Talker giving a presentation in front of the camera and directing his voice toward sidewalls causing strong acoustic reflections.
(3)	Scenario (2) + Another person sitting in the background at sector 10 facing the camera.
(4)	Scenario (1) + Lights were dimmed.
(5)	Scenario (2) + another person, facing the camera, conducting tasks in the background at sector 10.
(6)	Talker walk around the microphone array in the following sequence: sector 5, sector 4, sector 5, sector 6, sector 7, sector 8

The results show that adding occupancy estimates to the Bayesian network fusion engine significantly improves the accuracy of the overall localization performance with total error rate of 3.2% and tracking error rate of 4.3%. The use of the occupancy estimates with the Bayesian network is important, because without the occupancy estimates adjusting how much the system relies on each modality, the Bayesian network will by default rely more on the audio localizer than the other two. In the inference model, Figure 9, the inference of the talker's localization is derived from its two immediate parent nodes Voice (V) and Image (I). The V node is directly affected by the microphone array, whereas I is the combined effect of both the motion detection and the skin-color detection node. Nodes V, I are placed in the network as anchor points for adding the occupancy estimates into the network. Without the occupancy estimates controlling how much each localization modality contributes to the overall fusion, the Bayesian network is putting roughly twice as much weight on the microphone array localizer than the other two video localizers.

In the case of a device failure, its output should be considered erroneous (Figure 13). The simulated results show that the occupancy information automatically biases the Bayesian fusion engine away from failed localizers, thus making the overall system less sensitive to device failure and resulting in improved overall robustness (Figure 14). For this to function correctly, the occupancy estimator or the localizers themselves have to be capable of detecting device failure. In essence, the occupancy information effectively controls how the statistical distribution (*a priori* knowledge) places inference on the Bayesian fusion process.

Conclusion

Bayesian network is a powerful tool for performing data fusion. In this chapter, we presented a modular multimodal localization architecture using a Bayesian network as the fusion engine. The developed multimodal architecture is very flexible and yet allows individual

Figure 12. Results for joint audio-video localization using Bayesian network fusion with occupancy estimates

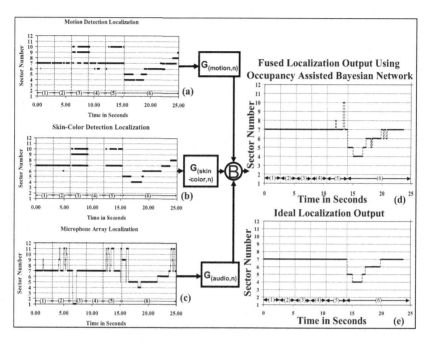

Figure 13. Results for joint audio-video localization using Bayesian network fusion estimates in the case of device failure

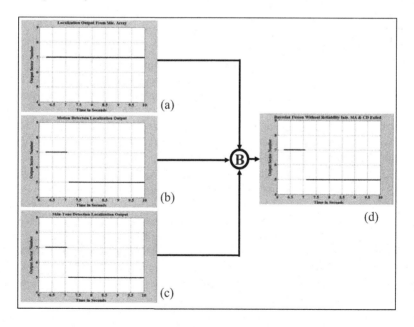

Figure 14. Results for joint audio-video localization using Bayesian network fusion with occupancy estimates in the case of device failure

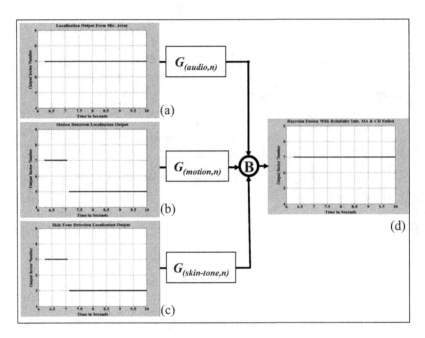

localizers to be kept relatively simple. With the flexibility of the modular architecture, specific refinements can easily be implemented without affecting the operation of other parts in the architecture. As a case study, the deployment of this modular architecture in the area of video conferencing applications is studied.

Video conferencing allows users to communicate more naturally using both sight and sound. Most commercially available video conferencing systems rely only on audio or video to locate the active talker. Challenges in the conferencing environment like acoustic reflections, changes in lighting condition, and complex backgrounds often make single-modal audio and video localizers unrealizable. In this chapter, we investigate how the Bayesian network based multimodal architecture can be used to combine three traditional single-modal localizers, audio and video, to form a more accurate one.

As a refinement to the basic Bayesian network fusion method, the occupancy information is used to improve the localization accuracy and robustness. The occupancy information uses known physical properties of the localizers to estimate the temporal trustworthiness of the localization results. These estimates are then used to dynamically bias the fusion engine away from erroneous data resulting in better overall localization accuracy. Also, with the help of simple device failure detection, the occupancy estimates provide a means for the fusion engine to handle failed localizers automatically by biasing the fusion engine away from the failed localizers. This method reduces the system sensitivity to device failure, thus improving the overall robustness.

The talker localization example shown in this chapter, although realistic, is still relatively simple. The purpose of this example is to show the reader how a Bayesian network can be used to fuse data in the outlined multimodal fusion architecture, Figure 3, and how each of the components in the architecture can be built. The multimodal fusion architecture and the methods developed can be equally valuable to other applications like surveillance and mobile robotics. With the flexibility and modularity of the architecture, how this architecture can be applied is really an open-ended question.

References

Agarwal, G., Anbu, A., & Sinha, A. (2003). A fast algorithm to find the region-of-interest in the compressed MPEG domain. In *Proceedings of the International Conference on Multimedia and Expo* (vol. *2*) (pp. 133-136).

Archibald, C., & Kwok, P. (1995). *Research in computer and robot vision*. Singapore: World Scientific Publishing Cooperation.

Brandstein, M., & Ward, D. (Eds.). (2001). *Microphone arrays. Signal processing techniques and applications*. New York: Springer-Verlag.

Chaodhury, T., Rehg, J.M., Pavlovic, V., & Pentland, A. (2002). Boosted learning in dynamic Bayesian networks for multimodal detection. In *Proceedings of the Fifth International Conference on Information Fusion* (vol.1) (pp. 550-556).

Davis, A.L. (1997). An integrated solution for effective video alarm verification. In *Proceedings of the IEEE International Conference on Security Technology* (pp. 154-157).

Elfes, A. (1989, June). Using occupancy grids for mobile robot perception and navigation. *Computer, 22*(6), 46-57.

Fiala, M., Green, D., & Roth, G. (2004, October). A panoramic video and acoustic beamforming sensor for videoconferencing. In *Proceedings of the IEEE International Workshop on Haptic, Audio and Visual Environments and their Applications* (pp. 47-52).

Hsu, R., Abdel-Mottaleb, M., & Jain, A. (2002, May). Face detection in color images. *IEEE Transactions on Pattern Analysis and Machine Intelligence, 24*(5), 696-706.

Johnson, D., & Dudgeon, D. (1993). *Array signal processing*. NJ: Prentice Hall.

Lo, C.L. (1994). *Biaxial strain study of porcine aortic valve using stereographic technique*. Master thesis, University of Western Ontario, London, Ontario, Canada.

Lo, D., Goubran, R.A., & Dansereau, R.M. (2004). Multimodal talker localization in video conferencing environment. In *Proceedings of the IEEE International Workshop on Haptic, Audio Visual Environments and Their Applications* (pp. 195-200).

Lo, D., Goubran, R.A., & Dansereau, R.M. (2005, May). Acoustic reflections detection for microphone array applications. In *Proceedings of the IEEE Instrumentation and Measurement Technology Conference* (vol. 2) (pp. 1139-1143).

Lo, D., Goubran, R.A., & Dansereau, R.M. (2005, August). Robust joint audio-video localization in video conferencing using reliability information II: Bayesian network fusion. *IEEE Transactions on Instrumentation and Measurement, 54*(4), 1541-1547.

Lo, D., Goubran, R.A., Dansereau, R.M., Thompson, G., & Schulz, D. (2004, August). Robust joint audio-video localization in video conferencing using reliability information.
IEEE Transactions on Instrumentation and Measurement, 53(4), 1132-1139.

Meier, T., & Ngan, K.N. (1999, December). Video segmentation for content-based coding.
IEEE Transactions on Circuits and Systems for Video Technology, 9, 1190-1203.

Messom, C., Demidenko, S., Subramaniam, K., & Gupta, G. (2002). Size/position identification in real-time image processing using run length encoding. In *Proceedings
of the 19th IEEE Instrumentation and Measurement Technology Conference* (vol. 2)
(pp. 1055-1059).

Omologo, M., & Svaizer, P. (1996). Acoustic source location in noisy and reverberant environment using CSP analysis. In *Proceedings of the IEEE International Conference
on Acoustics, Speech, and Signal Processing* (vol. 2) (pp. 921-924).

Osberger, W., & Maeder, A.J. (1998). Automatic identification of perceptually important
regions in an image. In *Proceedings of the International Conference on Pattern Recognition* (vol. 1) (pp. 701-704).

Pearl, J. (1988). *Probabilistic reasoning in intelligent systems: Networks of plausible inference.* CA: Morgan Kaufmann.

Petriu, E.M., Ionescu, D., Petriu, D.C., Groen, F.C.A., Spoelder, H., Yeung, S.K. et al.
(1996). Multisensor system for mobile robot navigation. In *Proceedings of the IEEE
Instrumentation and Measurement Technology* (vol. 1) (pp. 388-392).

Pingali, G., Tunali, G., & Carlbom, I. (1999). Audio-visual tracking for natural interactiv-
ity. In *Proceedings of the Seventh ACM International Conference on Multimedia* (pp.
373-382).

Poynton, C.A. (1996). *A technical introduction to digital video.* New York: John Wiley.

Steinberg, A.N., Bowman, C.L., & White, F.E. (1999). Revisions to the JDL data fusion
model. In *Proceedings of the SPIE AreoSense* (pp. 430-441). Orlando, FL, USA.

Strobel, N., Spors, S., & Rabenstein, R. (2001, January). Joint audio-video object localization and tracking. *IEEE Signal Processing Magazine, 18*(1), 22-31.

Tebo, A. (1997, August). Sensor fusion employs a variety of architecture, algorithms, and
application. *OE Magazine, 164.* Retrieved December 22, 2006, from http://www.spie.
org/web/oer/august/aug97/sensor.html

Terrillon, J.C., Shirazi, M.N., Fukamachi, H., & Akamatsu, S. (2000). Comparative performance of different skin chrominance models and chrominance spaces for the automatic
detection of human faces in color images. In *Proceedings of the IEEE International
Conference on Face and Gesture Recognition* (pp. 54-61).

Toyama, K., & Horvitz, E. (2000, January). Bayesian modality fusion: Probabilistic integration of multiple vision algorithms for head tracking. In *Proceedings of the Fourth Asian
Conference on Computer Vision.* Retrieved December 22, 2006, from http://research.
microsoft.com/~horvitz/modfusion.htm

Waltz, E., & Llinas, J. (1990). *Multisensor data fusion.* Norwood, MA: Artech House.

Wang, C., & Brandstein, M. (1998). A hybrid real-time face tracking system. In *Proceedings
of the IEEE International Conference on Acoustics, Speech and Signal Processing*
(vol. 6) (pp. 3737-3740).

Wang, C., & Brandstein, M. (1999). Multi-source face tracking with audio and visual data. In *Proceedings of the IEEE 3rd Workshop on Multimedia Signal Processing* (pp. 169-174).

Wang, C., Griebel, S., & Brandstein, M. (2000). Robust automatic video-conferencing with multiple cameras and microphones. In *Proceedings of the IEEE International Conference on Multimedia and Expo* (vol. 3) (pp. 1585-1588).

Wu, H., Siegel, M., Stiefelhagen, R., & Yang, J. (2002). Sensor fusion using Dempster-Shafer theory. In *Proceedings of the IEEE Instrumentation and Measurement Technology Conference* (vol. 1) (pp. 7-12).

Yeung, S. K., McMath, W.S., Petriu, E.M., Trif, N., & Gal, C. (1994). Teleoperator-aided multi-sensor data fusion for mobile robot navigation. In *Proceedings of the IEEE International Conference on Multisensor Fusion and Integration for Intelligent Systems* (pp. 470-476).

Zotkin, D., Duraiswami, R., Davis, L., & Haritaoglu, I. (2000). An audio-video front-end for multimedia applications. In *Proceedings of the IEEE International Conference on Systems, Man, and Cybernetics* (vol. 2) (pp. 786-791).

Chapter XI

Retrieval of Bio-Geophysical Parameters from Remotely Sensing Data by Using Bayesian Methodology

C. Notarnicola, University of Bari, Italy

Abstract

This chapter introduces the use of Bayesian methodology for inversion purposes: the extraction of bio-geophysical parameters from remotely sensed data. Multisources information, such as different polarizations, frequencies, and sensors are fundamental to the development of operationally useful inversion systems. In this context, Bayesian methodologies offer a convenient tool of combining two or more disparate sources of information, models, and data. The chapter describes the development of a general model starting from a theoretical model, including the sensor noise and the model errors, by using a Bayesian approach. Furthermore, the developed procedure is applied to some experimental data sets. The author hopes that considering theoretical models and experimental data in many different configurations can give an idea of the versatility and robustness of the Bayesian framework.

Introduction

During the last years, remote sensing has become an important method for the areal and temporal derivation of Earth surface parameters. In this context, the evaluation of the spatial and temporal soil and vegetation moisture changes is of primary importance.

The prediction of soil moisture variations is equally important at mesoscale and smaller scales. Mesoscale atmospheric models have demonstrated sensitivity to spatial gradients (Fast & McMorcle, 1991). Furthermore, the initialization of the global climate model weather forecast (GCMWF) with current soil moisture values can lead to improved rainfall predictions.

In addition to the role of soil moisture in the interactions between land surface and the atmosphere, soil moisture is storage of water between rainfalls and evaporations that acts as a regulator to a fundamental hydrologic process, infiltration, and runoff production from rainfall (Delworth & Manabe, 1988).

The vegetation water content yields information about the physiological condition of the plants and system losses due to mowing or harvesting of agricultural fields. Furthermore, estimation of vegetation water content from local to global scales is central to the understanding of biomass burning processes.

Ground measurements are time consuming and they cannot take into account the great variability of soil and vegetation moisture from one point to the other of the same field. Due to high resolution combined with an extensive coverage, spaceborne and airborne sensors can provide a unique perspective on the spatial and temporal variation in soil and vegetation moisture both at a relatively high resolution (e.g., gradient of moisture within a field or along the slope of a hill) and at a global scale (feature of the order of 10 km).

Spaceborne and airborne sensors that operate in the microwave domain are best suited for the detection of water content. These sensors are classified as active and passive systems. Active systems, synthetic aperture radars, and scatterometers (Ulaby, Moore, & Fung, 1986) transmit short bursts or "pulses" of electromagnetic energy in the direction of interest and record the strength of the backscatter received from objects within the system's field of view. Passive systems, and radiometers (Ulaby et al., 1986), sense low level microwave radiation given off by all objects in the natural environment. Active and passive microwave data has been shown to depend on several natural surface parameters such as soil and vegetation dielectric constant and surface roughness (Ulaby et al., 1986). Among surface features, the dielectric constant, ε, is highly dependent on soil moisture due to the large difference between dry conditions (ε of 2-3) and water (approximately 80).

This chapter discusses the application of Bayesian techniques for the estimation of surface features, soil, and vegetation water content, starting with the acquisitions of remotely sensed data.

The retrieval of bio-geophysical parameters from remotely sensed data falls within the category of inverse problems where, from a vector of measured values, m, one wishes to infer the set of ground parameters, x, that gave rise to them. The inverse problem is a typically ill-posed problem. It presents many difficulties due to the nonlinearity between remote sensing measurements and ground parameters, and generally because more than one value of x could produce the same measured vector m (Satalino, Pasquariello, Mattia, Le Toan, Davidson, & Borgeaud, 1999).

Even if many theoretical models have been developed describing the interaction between the electromagnetic radiation and natural surfaces, parameter estimation is always a difficult task. Noise corruption and lack of extensive in situ measurements are only two of many problems that make the work hard. Moreover, the effect of different parameters on radar response is not easy to disentangle.

In this view, the use of multisources information, such as different polarizations, frequencies, and sensors, are fundamental to the development of operationally useful inversion systems in which the interference among different parameters in the microwave system response can be disentangled.

Bayesian methodologies offer a convenient tool of combining two or more disparate sources of information, models and data (Haddad & Dubois, 1995). Furthermore, it can be used to combine prior information on an arbitrary number of parameters, with the information content of related data, to obtain parameter estimates.

This methodology is particularly useful when one would like to extract target characteristics from remotely sensed data. The efficacy of conventional parameter estimation techniques drops sharply as the number of parameters to be estimated increases, particularly if the model representing the sensor responses is nonlinear. In contrast, procedures based on Bayesian methodologies can generate full probability distributions for an arbitrary number of parameters. Conceptually, probability distributions may represent the lack of knowledge regarding the "true" value of a parameter, the natural variability of a parameter, or a combination of both (Roy & Georgopoulos, 1998).

Taking into account all these considerations, this chapter describes an algorithm development based on an experimental/modeling scheme aimed at extracting bio-geophysical parameters, soil, and vegetation water content from remotely sensed data. The algorithm that uses the synergy of experimental data of different microwave sensors and simulated data is based on a Bayesian approach.

The inversion procedure has been tested in numerous situations that illustrate the method versatility:

- Microwave measurements of a radiometer and a scatterometer over bare fields
- synthetic aperture radar (SAR) acquisitions on bare and vegetated fields

The chapter is organized as follows.

In part I, the background on inversion methodologies for both active and passive systems is illustrated. This part also introduces some background information about the theoretical models whose simulated data are used in synergy with the experimental measurements. The last section is dedicated to a brief description of inversion algorithms that are based on Bayesian techniques.

Part II is completely dedicated to the description of the three experimental data sets to be used in the proposed inversion procedure.

Part III describes the inversion procedure that is based on a Bayesian approach. The results of the application of this procedure to three datasets are illustrated in Part IV.

Part V lists the advantages and disadvantages of the inversion approach and exploits the feasibility of the approach for the inversion of remotely sensed data. Future developments are also indicated.

Background

Background on Inversion Methodologies

The use of remotely sensed data to retrieve soil moisture and other surface characteristics is fundamental in many disciplines. The retrieval of surface parameters can be considered as a mapping problem from the domain of measured signals to the range of surface characteristics that quantify the observed portion of earth (Fung, 1994). This mapping is not always unique. In some circumstances, equivalent sensor responses can be generated from distinct media that have very dissimilar characteristics.

One of the common approaches for soil moisture retrieval is the development of direct models by simulating the radar observations in terms of the soil attributes, such as the dielectric constant and the surface roughness, for an area with known characteristics. Dielectric constant and roughness are the main features that govern the interaction of electromagnetic radiation with a bare natural surface:

- The dielectric constant is directly dependent on soil moisture and soil texture constituents
- The roughness description is mainly based on two parameters: the standard deviation of heights, s, and the correlation length, l. The standard deviation of height is an estimate of the variance of the surface profile vertical dimension, while its correlation function relates the statistical correlation between any two points on a given surface. If the surface statistics are assumed to remain constant across the horizontal plane (wide-sense stationary), then the correlation function is dependent only on the distance between any two points. The surface correlation length, l, is usually defined as the displacement for which the correlation function is equal to $1/e$ (Ulaby et al., 1986)

These direct models are subsequently used in the inverse mode to estimate the surface parameters, given the sensor measurements. Several empirical and theoretical models have been introduced in order to link microwave remote sensing measurements to soil features. At the same time several inversion techniques have been exploited: simple and multiple regressions, iterative methods and statistical approaches. Among these methods, the Bayesian approaches and neural networks are widely applied. In all the cases, the use of a specific model and the application of the relative inversion technique present advantages and disadvantages.

As in this chapter, active and passive sensor data are considered, and a review of the inversion methodologies for both these kinds of data are briefly illustrated.

Active Sensors

The development of empirical models has been studied both as a first approach in order to study the relationship between backscatter and soil moisture and to obtain a simple inversion model in itself. The frequently used linear approach is based on regression coefficients generated by the observations over a specific site (Lin, Wood, Bevan, & Saatchi, 1994; Prevot & Dechambre, 1993). As a result, they may not be suitable for the features estimation applied to data that are acquired on other sites. Some empirical approaches have been developed, and are based on the knowledge of scattering behavior of experimental observations. For example, one of the first empirical models was proposed by Oh, Sarabandi, and Ulaby (1992) on bare soils. In this model, the copolarized and cross-polarized ratios of the backscattering coefficients are expressed in terms of the surface parameters. Subsequently Dubois, van Zyl, and Engman (1995) developed an empirical that described only the copolarized backscatter coefficients of bare surfaces as a function of surface roughness, dielectric constant, incidence angle, and frequency. The model originally derived from scatterometer data and was subsequently applied to SAR data in the case of bare soils. Oh et al.'s model, developed from multipolarization radar data, was revealed to be poorly effective when tested on SAR data. In contrast, Dubois et al.'s model was revealed to be applicable to different forms of data measured, and tended to be quite accurate. The results indicate values of soil moisture with a rms error of 4.2 %. Although the model performed highly, it is however, site specific and is valid under the conditions in which the measurements were taken.

As a result, the conclusive effect of development of empirical models and their relative inversion procedure is that they have a limited range of applicability. The complexity and the nonlinearity of the problems cannot be taken into account in empirical formulations, thus leading to the necessity of considering theoretical backscattering models.

Theoretical models can represent a great variety of situations and still have the possibility to consider situations that have not been taken into account by the empirical models. However, the theoretical models are developed under several hypotheses that may not be completely verified in field conditions. As an example, the description of the surface morphology is considered a limitation of a theoretical model. One of the most widely used descriptions is based on two parameters: the standard deviation of heights, s, and the correlation length, l. This parametrization is often considered critical because they do not describe completely the variability of natural surfaces (Mattia & Le Toan, 1999).While the standard deviation of height can be accurate on the order of 10%, the correlation length measurements vary as much as an order of magnitude (Dubois et al., 1995; Notarnicola, D'Alessio, Casarano, Posa, & Sabatelli, 2003).

Theoretical scattering forward models are of a certain complexity and sometimes are difficult to invert due to the requirement of several parameters in the computations. This is the reason that typical inversion techniques are iterative methods and statistical approaches. Bindlish and Barros(2000) used the integral equation model (IEM) with the Jacobian method, an iterative scheme, to perform the inversion on multifrequency, multipolarizarion SAR data. In this case, the retrieval can be performed on all the surface parameters, as they are included in the IEM model. This algorithm, tested only with one data set in a single sensor configuration, produces soil moisture estimates with an average error of 3.4%.

A theoretical model can be also used to train a system that, after such training, will represent the inverse model. A suitable method for this kind of multidimensional retrieval is the neural network. In particular, it can be trained to extract surface parameters from remotely sensed data and so can perform the same function as a statistical inversion method. The training data for the neural networks can be obtained from theoretical forward scattering models, thus allowing the control of the range of parameters with which the network is trained. The main drawback of neural networks is that the inverse empirical mapping established between remotely sensed data and surface parameters cannot be explicitly written down. In this way, the neural network can be sometimes considered as a "close system" where the user can generally only act on some configuration parameters but not on the analytical expression that lead to the results.

Once more, the accuracy of the system relies on the accuracy of the data or models used during the training phase. To overcome this difficulty, the used models should be previously validated in a wide range of experimental situations.

Validation is another critical problem, because soil moisture measurements are acquired in some points and are generally not representative of the whole area observed by the radar; this makes the comparison between extracted values of soil moisture from remote sensed data and those measured on the fields somewhat difficult.

Passive Sensors

Many approaches have also been developed to retrieve soil moisture from microwave radiometric measurements where each of the various effects (i.e., vegetation and soil surface roughness) contributing to the surface microwave emission can be taken into account. The first generation of the soil moisture retrieval method has been developed from airborne observations with a single sensor configuration sensor (Jackson, Le Vine, Swift, Schmugge, & Schiebe, 1995; Schmugge & Jackson, 1994; Wang, Shiue, Schmugge, & Engman, 1990). Generally, when a single measurement is available, only soil moisture can be retrieved from microwave measurements. In most recent methods (Kerr, Waldteufem, Wigneron, Font, & Berger, 2001; Njoku & Li, 1999) based on multiconfiguration measurements, other parameters such as vegetation attenuation and surface temperature can be retrieved along with soil moisture.

On the other hand, in order to extract some soil parameters, such as soil dielectric constant, roughness, and vegetation, a single sensor configuration model could also be used but should be implemented into a more complex inversion system than regression techniques or iterative schemes, that is, Bayesian methods or neural networks. However, it is necessary that such inversion systems provide for a good parameterization of all the parameters to be extracted. In this application, a simple semiempirical approach, the Wang and Choudhury model (1995) can be considered adequate.

Background on Inversion Methodologies with Bayesian Approach

Statistically based inversion methods, such as the Bayesian approach, have been in existence for a long time and are based on probabilities that a given set of measurements come from certain surface parameter values. The Bayesian methodology obtains much of its power from the ability to incorporate new information derived from measurements as conditional probabilities.

The probability density functions are estimated by training, where examples of sensor and surface measurements are presented to the algorithm. Another important aspect is that, in order to derive these general probability density functions as performed with Bayesian methodology, a large amount of experimental data is requested. The experimental data should cover a wide spectrum of real situations in order to obtain reliable statistical functions.

One of the first examples is the algorithm developed by Haddad and Dubois (1994) where they exploited a Bayesian estimation method of soil standard deviation of heights and soil moisture. Their procedure does not take into account an important soil parameter, that of the correlation length. Even though this parameter is highly variable, it is fundamental if in the inversion process one wishes to consider some theoretical models. These models mainly characterize the surface with two parameters: the standard deviations of heights and the correlation length.

Although this built-in limitation, the methodology presents a drastic simplification of the inversion process and potentially more accurate estimation of soil physical properties, based on Bayesian theorem to calculate the posterior probability density function. This function is useful for the calculation of the probability to obtain surface parameters, given some remotely sensor data. In another paper, Haddad and Dubois (1995), starting from the forward model proposed by Oh et al. (1992), used a Bayesian approach to determine the inverse model. Because the model was based on a data set with low correlation length, it failed to be applicable to data sets that do not verify this condition.

The proposed algorithm is based on experimental data and theoretical models. The approach is justified by two important observations. First, an algorithm based only on measurements could be of limited applicability, as it represents a specific situation. It requires a large number of experimental measurements in order to derive empirical models (Oh et al., 1992), which are dependent on the site and surface type where they were developed and tested. Second, on the other hand, when adopting theoretical models, the inversion procedure might be general purpose, in which the data can be simulated for different sensor parameters (frequency, polarization, and incidence angle) and surface conditions (surface roughness and soil moisture). Theoretical models are excellent tools for studying the effect of soil parameter variations on measured responses; however, the physical approximations introduced in these models should be verified (Remond, 1997; Zribi, Taconet, Le Hegarat-Mascle, Vidar-Madjar, Emblanch, Loumagne, & Normand, 1994). The development of the algorithm follows the guidelines of the Haddad and Dubois (1994) methodology, but tries to extend the applicability of the algorithm to more sources of information and to include as many experimental situations as possible.

The adopted Bayesian procedure takes advantage of several remotely sensed data configurations, such as active and passive data, multifrequency and multipolarization active data, optical and radar data, and the corresponding simulated data, in order to extract dielectric constant values.

Theoretical Models for Emissivity and Backscattering Coefficients in the Microwave Domain

As the proposed approach also considers simulated data, theoretical models for emissivity and backscattering coefficients are briefly introduced. Active and passive microwave instruments are both sensitive to soil moisture changes, but they also markedly differ with regard to the quantities they detect and the responses they generate. Active sensors measure the backscattering coefficients of soil surfaces that depend on both roughness and dielectric characteristics.

Their responses were modeled by means of the integral equation model (IEM) (Fung, 1994). The cited model has the advantage of being applicable to a wide range of roughness scales. For the IEM, the input parameters are the real part of the dielectric constant, the standard deviation of height, and the correlation length.

In the IEM formulation, the like polarized backscattering coefficients for surfaces with small or medium size roughness are given by:

$$\sigma_{pp}^0 = \frac{k^2}{2} \exp(-2k_z^2 s^2) \sum_{k=1}^{\infty} \left| I_{pp}^n \right| \frac{W^{(n)}(-2k_x, 0)}{n!} \tag{1}$$

where k is the wave number, θ is the incidence angle, $k_z = k\cos\theta$, $k_x = k\,sen\theta$, and pp refers to the horizontal (HH) or vertical (VV) polarization state and s is the standard deviation of terrain heights. The term I_{pp}^n depends on k, s, and R_H, R_V, the Fresnel reflection coefficients in horizontal and vertical polarizations. The Fresnel coefficients depend directly on the dielectric constant. The symbol $W(-2k_x, 0)$ is the Fourier transform of the nth power of the surface correlation coefficient. In this context, an exponential correlation function has been adopted that seems to better describe the properties of natural surfaces (Fung, 1994).

Passive sensors measure the natural thermal emission of land surfaces at microwave wavelengths using extremely sensitive radiometers.

When the radiometer response is analyzed, the simplest soil-emission configuration is represented by a homogeneous isothermal soil medium with a plain air-soil boundary. In this case, the brightness temperature of the soil surface when viewed from the air at a nadir angle θ_0 is:

$$T_B(\theta_0, p) = e^{sp}(\theta_0, p) T_s \tag{2}$$

where T_s is the soil temperature and $e^{sp}(\theta_0, p)$ is the soil emissivity evaluated at θ_0 with polarization p. For the evaluation of emissivity, a semiempirical expression proposed by Wang and Choudhury (1995) including the effect of roughness, has been introduced:

$$e_H = 1 - [(1 - Q)r_H + Qr_V] \exp(-4\,k^2 s^2 \cos^2\theta)$$
$$e_V = 1 - [(1 - Q)r_V + Qr_H] \exp(-4\,k^2 s^2 \cos^2\theta) \tag{3}$$

where r_H and r_V are the smooth surface reflectivities for the horizontal and vertical polarization and depend on soil dielectric constant values. Q is a mixing polarization parameter depending on the operating frequency and s.

Both models have been extensively analyzed and validated with many data sets (Fung, 1994, Ruf & Zhang, 2001; Wang & Choudhury, 1995) including those analyzed in this chapter.

Experimental Data Sets

Active and Passive Data on Bare Soils

The experimental data sets were acquired by the University of Bern's truck-mounted radiometer-scatterometer operating with the following frequencies: 2.5, 3.1, 4.6, 7.2, 10.2, and 11 GHz over the incidence angle range from 10° to 70° (Wegmueller, Maetzler, Hueppi, & Schanda, 1994). The same antennae were used for the active and passive instrument in order to ensure that they observed the target under identical spatial conditions. The bare fields analyzed in this study were essentially smooth. For the collection of the ground truth data, the researchers at the University of Bern followed the guidelines given by Cihlar, Dobson, Schmugge, Hoogeboom, Janse, Baret et al. (1987), as indicated in Wegmueller et al. (1994). The volumetric soil moisture is the average water content of the top 4 cm of the soil and was measured by taking five soil samples of a known volume and drying them at 105°. The percentage error is around 10%. A special effort was made in order to characterize the surface roughness of bare soils and fields with little vegetation cover.

A laser surface height profiler was used to determine 1-m-long height profiles with a horizontal spacing of 0.5 mm and a vertical accuracy of 0.1 mm. For each surface height profile, the azimuth angle between the direction of the height profile and the row direction caused by mechanical cultivation (0 being parallel and 90 perpendicular to the cultivation direction) was indicated. The soil temperature is the average temperature of the top 3 cm of soil. The prevailing soil composition was 45% loam, 18% clay, and 37% sand. In this analysis, only bare soils, whose parameters were within the limits of the IEM (Fung, 1994) and Wang models (Wang & Choudhury, 1995), were selected. Their characteristics are listed in Table 1. With regard to sensor data, the experimental accuracy, as indicated in the dataset, is approximately 1 dB for backscattering coefficients and 1–2 K for brightness temperatures, which determines an error of 0.01 for emissivity.

The considered inversion configurations are the following:

1. Backscattering coefficients HH polarization and emissivity H polarization both at 4.6 GHz and at an incidence angle of 20° (indicated as 1f1p);

2. Backscattering coefficients HH polarization at 4.6 GHz and emissivity H polarization at 2.5 GHz both at an incidence angle of 20° (indicated as 2f1p);

3. Backscattering coefficients HH and VV polarizations and emissivity H and V polarizations at 4.6 GHz and an incidence angle of 20° (indicated as 1f2p).

Table 1. Main characteristics of the fields analyzed for active and passive data inversion

Field type	Roughness, s and l, range	Soil moisture, mv, range
3 bare or lightly vegetated fields with sensor acquisitions in 12 different dates	$0.50 \text{ cm} \leq s \leq 1.20 \text{ cm}$ $2.00 \text{ cm} \leq l \leq 5.00 \text{ cm}$	$6\% \leq mv \leq 38\%$

The choice of 20° for testing the algorithm has been driven by the possible comparison with satellite sensors such as ERS and ENVISAT data. Furthermore, the effect of roughness is minimised for data acquired at low incidence angles (Ulaby et al., 1986) and the discrepancy between models and measured data generally increases with incidence angle (Boisvert, Gwyn, Chanzy, Major, Brisco, & Brown, 1997; Oh et al., 1992; Rakotoarivony, 1995).

C-Band Scatterometer Data on Bare Soils

Five experiments were carried out with a C-band scatterometer from 1998 to 2004. They acquired backscattering coefficients for HH and VV polarizations at an incidence angle of 23° and 40° (Mattia, Le Toan, Picard, Posa, D'Alessio, Notarnicola et al., 2003; Notarnicola et al., 2003) and ground data, namely soil moisture and roughness. The acquisitions were run on bare fields with various roughness conditions. Main field characteristics are reported in Table 2. The mean rms error for volumetric soil moisture values is 10%. The roughness parameters were computed from digitized photos of a three-meter long profile-meter placed at different points in the area. Because a row structure was present in the test fields due to the ploughing practice, which was more evident for the smoother field, the soil profiles were taken in three directions, namely "range," "azimuth," and "diagonal." Also, the correlation lengths were calculated from the digitized photos. This parameter showed an extreme variability (from 1.5 to 21 cm), even within the same field (Notarnicola et al., 2003).

The analyzed configurations are as follows:

1.   Backscattering coefficients for HH and VV polarizations at incidence angle of 23°
2.   Backscattering coefficients for HH and VV polarizations at incidence angles of 23° and 40°

The experimental error on scatterometer backscattering coefficients is around 1dB.

Washita '92 Data on Bare Soils

Washita '92 experiment (Jackson & Shiebe, 1993) was designed to provide ground truth soil moisture data and the supporting hydrological data for microwave remote sensing algorithm development and hydrological studies, with a focus on remotely sensed soil moisture. The USDA ARS Little Washita Watershed was selected for these efforts because of the extensive hydrological research that has been conducted there in the past, and the ongoing hydrological data collection efforts.

Table 2. Main characteristics of the fields analyzed for scatterometer data inversion

Field type	Roughness, s and l, range	Soil moisture, mv, range
2 bare fields with acquisitions in different dates	1.31 cm ≤ s ≤ 2.49 cm 6.50 cm ≤ l ≤ 21.00 cm	8 % ≤ mv ≤ 32%

Table 3. AIRSAR calibration accuracy

Absolute/relative	C-BAND	L-BAND
AIRSAR	±1.0 dB / ± 0.4 dB	±1.2 dB / ± 0.5 dB

The Little Washita Watershed is a 610 km^2 drainage basin situated in the southern part of the Great Plains in southwest Oklahoma. The climate is classified as moist or sub humid with an average annual rainfall of about 640 mm. During the field experiments, extensive soil moisture measurements were taken, surface roughness data obtained, and vegetation cover was characterised and sampled. Washita '92 was a multisensor aircraft campaign conducted from June 10 to June 18, 1992. The observations followed a period of heavy rain so that the conditions on June 10 were very wet with standing water and saturated soils fairly common. No further rain fell during the following nine days and so it has been possible to follow a drying pattern. SAR data (AirSAR) and extensive field data were collected each day during this period. The data of this experiment are available online at the site: http://hydrolab. arsusda.gov/washita92/airsar.htm.

The area covered is around 8 km by 10 km. It was imaged by the AIRSAR system on five different days on June 10, 13, 14, 16, and 18, 1992, with incidence angles respectively of 19.2°, 18.4°, 18.4°, 15.2°, and 14.8°. The pixel spacing is 10 x 10 m^2. The five L- and C-band images were processed by the AirSAR operational processor providing calibrated data sets. The absolute and relative calibration accuracy obtained for each sensor, as reported in the literature (van Zyl, Carande, Lou, Miller, & Wheeler, 1992), are listed in Table 3.

Table 4. Field AG002 characteristics

Field AG002 (bare)	
Surface roughness	Standard deviation of height s = 1.82 cm Correlation length l = 17.75 cm
Soil texture	Sand = 45.5 %, silt = 41.1 %, clay = 13.4 %
Bulk density	1.33 g/cm^3
Comments	Western ploughed section (on the right in AIRSAR images)
Site dimensions	700 by 1400 m^2

From sensitivity studies (Dubois et al., 1995), in order to avoid errors in the soil moisture estimation larger than 4.2%, the relative calibration error should be less than 0.5 dB and the absolute calibration error should be less than 2.0 dB, because the inversion is also more sensitive to relative than absolute calibration errors.

The bare field denominated AG002 was extensively characterised during the experiment and it is the object of the present algorithm test. Table 4 illustrates its characteristics. There was no indication of where the ground data was collected within the field.

SMEX'02 Data on Vegetated Soils

The inversion procedure has been applied to a subset of data acquired during the SMEX'02 Experiment (*http://nsidc.org/data/amsr_validation/soil_moisture/smex02/*). The SMEX'02 experiment took place in Iowa from June 24 - July 12, 2002. The study area was chosen in order to obtain microwave and optical observations over a range of soil moisture conditions with moderate to high vegetation biomass conditions.

The main site chosen for intensive sampling was the Walnut Creek watershed, where 32 field sites were identified and sampled intensively. The fields were mainly cultivated with soybean and corn.

Table 5 provides information about the remote sensing and ground data utilized in this analysis, while Table 6 gives some important information about the fields analyzed in this inversion procedure.

Volumetric soil moisture values are calculated by using gravimetric soil moisture and bulk density that are the parameters directly measured in the fields. Furthermore, soil texture is of the utmost importance in physical models for estimation of soil dielectric properties due to the fact that in the Hallikainen empirical formula, soil dielectric constant is derived from soil moisture using soil texture values (Hallikainen, Ulaby, Dobson, El-Rayes, & Wu, 1985). The values of the real part of the dielectric constant, along with the roughness parameters, are the inputs to the theoretical models used in this inversion approach. This part is described in the following section.

Table 5. Remote sensing and ground data from SMEX'02 used in this analysis

Remote sensing data	
Sensor	**Acquisition date**
AirSAR(microwave, res. 8-12 m ground range)	1, 5, 7, 8, 9 July 2002
Landsat (optical, res. 30 m)	1, 8 July 2002
Ground data	
Parameter	**Acquisition date**
Soil moisture	1, 5, 7, 8, 9 July 2002
Soil roughness	1, 5, 7, 8, 9 July 2002
Vegetation water content	Few days during the acquisition period

Table 6. Some characteristics of the SMEX'02 fields analysed in the inversion procedure

Fields	Roughness range	Volumetric soil moisture range	Vegetation	Biomass range (kg/m2)
WC03	0.34 cm $\leq$ s $\leq$ 0.72 cm 1.40 cm $\leq$ l $\leq$ 13.05 cm	11 % $\leq$ mv $\leq$ 29%	Soybean	0.13 – 0.41
WC05	0.45 cm $\leq$ s $\leq$ 1.80 cm 3.48 cm $\leq$ l $\leq$ 5.92 cm	10 % $\leq$ mv $\leq$ 16%	Corn	1.14 – 2.36
WC06	0.37 cm $\leq$ s $\leq$ 0.73 cm 3.06 cm $\leq$ l $\leq$ 10.55 cm	9 % $\leq$ mv $\leq$ 24%	Corn	0.35 – 2.23
WC08	0.85 cm $\leq$ s $\leq$ 2.56 cm 2.32 cm $\leq$ l $\leq$ 19.19 cm	9 % $\leq$ mv $\leq$ 24%	Corn	1.06 – 1.62
WC09	0.41 cm $\leq$ s $\leq$ 1.10 cm 1.91 cm $\leq$ l $\leq$ 14.74 cm	9 % $\leq$ mv $\leq$ 25%	Soybean	0.28 – 0.60
WC010	0.41 cm $\leq$ s $\leq$ 1.10 cm 5.15 cm $\leq$ l $\leq$ 16.06 cm	7 % $\leq$ mv $\leq$ 27%	Soybean	0.21 – 0.75
WC012	0.64 cm $\leq$ s $\leq$ 1.65 cm 8.17 cm $\leq$ l $\leq$ 16.94 cm	7 % $\leq$ mv $\leq$ 14%	Soybean	1.06 – 2.32
WC013	0.33 cm $\leq$ s $\leq$ 1.35cm 0.47 cm $\leq$ l $\leq$ 11.17 cm	10 % $\leq$ mv $\leq$ 24%	Soybean	0.10 – 0.42

Bayesian Approach for Inversion of Remotely Sensed Data (Bare Soil Approach)

Bayesian Methodology

The main aim is to infer the soil parameter values, S_i, that for bare soils can be the dielectric constant ε, the standard deviations of heights, s, and the correlation length, l, by measuring features f_1, f_2, ..., in this case backscattering coefficients or emissivities acquired by the sensors such as those considered in this work scatterometer, radiometer, and AirSAR data. The procedure is divided into the training and test phase.

Training Phase

The conditional probability density function (PDF) $P(f_1, f_2, ..., | S_i)$ can be estimated from training data. This is the probability of finding that particular vector of features, given specific values of S_i. The conditional PDF is supposed to be normal (Nezry, Yakam-Simen, Supit, & Zagolsky, 1997). To evaluate the conditional PDF, the half part of acquired data is used as training data. For these data, both the sensor responses and the ground truth information are utilized. This is necessary in order to build the PDF that represents the "forward" model between sensor responses and soil parameters. Using theoretical models, in this case the integral equation model (IEM) (Fung, 1994), for backscattering coefficients and the Wang model for emissivities (Wang & Choudhury, 1995), theoretical values of the sensors responses, in correspondence to ground truth, are obtained.

The theoretical values calculated with (1) and (3) are compared to the experimental values introducing random variables, N_i, not depending on ε, s, and l and representing a function that takes into account the sensor noise and model errors (Haddad & Dubois, 1995):

$$f_{im} = N_i f_{ith} \qquad (4)$$

where f_{im} and f_{ith} are respectively the measured and theoretical values of sensor responses. The problem consists in finding an estimate of the $P(f_1, f_2, ..., | S_i)$ taking into account the presence of a noise factor N_i. Pdf parameters, namely mean and standard deviation, are determined by using the Maximum Likelihood Principle (MLP). Subsequently, the joint PDF is tested for goodness-of-fit with a χ^2 test (Notarnicola & Posa, 2004). The Bayes' theorem allows for the calculation of the posterior probability from the above conditional probability and the prior probability. It is stated formally as:

$$P(S_i | f_1, f_2, ...) = \frac{P(S_i)P(f_1, f_2, ... | S_i)}{\sum_i P(S_i)P(f_1, f_2, ... | S_i)} \qquad (5)$$

where the denominator is the normalisation factor. The posterior PDF $P(S_i | f_1, f_2, ...)$ is the probability about parameters S_i after measuring the feature vector $f_1, f_2, ..., $.

$P(S_i)$ is the prior joint density probability about parameters S_i in which one includes all the prior information about these parameters, such as estimates based on other instruments. In case one does not know anything "a priori" about them except its physical range of values, this would be a uniform density function over the length of the corresponding interval.

In the calculation, it is more convenient to express $P(f_1, f_2, ... | S_i)$ in terms of the variables N_i, that is in terms of the probability density function $P(N_i)$. In order to transform the probability density from one pair of variables to another, a Jacobian is used (Stuart & Ord, 1996):

$$P(N_1, N_2, ... | S_i) = P(f_1, f_2, ... | S_i) \cdot J \qquad (6)$$

where

$$J = \frac{\partial(f_1, f_2, ...)}{\partial(N_1, N_2, ...)} \qquad (7)$$

As an example, we can consider one of the cases that will be illustrated in the next section:

- Backscattering coefficients HH polarization and emissivity H polarization both at 4.6 GHz and at an incidence angle of 20° (indicated as 1f1p).

The joint density function $P(N_1, N_2)$ is determined by calculating the ratios:

$$N_1 = \frac{e_{Hm}}{e_{Hth}} \quad N_2 = \frac{\sigma_{HHm}}{\sigma_{Hth}} \tag{8}$$

where e_{Hm} and e_{Hth} are the measured and theoretical emissivity values, respectively, and σ_{HHm} and σ_{HHth} are the measured and theoretical backscattering coefficient values, respectively.

The ratios N_1 and N_2 are computed using the experimental data set and the corresponding simulated values. It is well known that the family of gamma density functions is a suitable solution for representation of the statistical properties of a natural scene. However, a Gaussian probability density function is introduced, being commonly used to describe natural scenes and more convenient as mathematical approach (Nezry et al., 1997). In this case, the joint distribution function can be written as:

$$P(N_1, N_2) = \frac{e^{-(N_1-\mu_1)^2/2\sigma_1^2}}{\sqrt{2\pi\sigma_1}} \frac{e^{-(N_2-\mu_2)^2/2\sigma_2^2}}{\sqrt{2\pi\sigma_2}} \tag{9}$$

The hypothesis underlying the use of this expression is that N_1 and N_2 are independent gaussian distributed random variables. In fact, N_1 and N_2 represent the noise element in measurements obtained from different sensors, sensible to different soil processes. To evaluate the conditional probability, the principle of the maximum likelihood (MLP) is applied, so the parameters μ_1, μ_2, σ_1, σ_2 are those that maximize the joint distribution function. The parameter values at which the maximum is achieved are the following: $\mu_1 = 0.96$, $\mu_2 = 1.14$, $\sigma_1 = 0.04$, $\sigma_2 = 0.25$. Figure 1 illustrates the joint distribution of N_1 and N_2 obtained with the MAP principle. Now, the joint density function obtained can be tested for goodness-of-fit, by integrating (9) directly. So all the ratios between experimental and theoretical values are computed and then the χ^2 test is applied to verify that these ratio values are consistent with the assumption that the joint distribution of N_1 and N_2 is as equation (9). The data are segmented into nine disjoint events, and using the integral of equation (9), the predicted frequencies for each event are computed. The ratio of predicted to observed counts is summarised in Table 7.

The χ^2 statistic for these counts is 1.03 and for χ variable with five degrees of freedom, the cut-off value for the critical region of size 0.05 is 11.1. Thus this value is well within the acceptable region and it is reasonable to assume that the expression (9) is indeed the joint density function for N_1 and N_2 in the case of our data.

Figure 1. Joint probability density $P(N_1, N_2)$

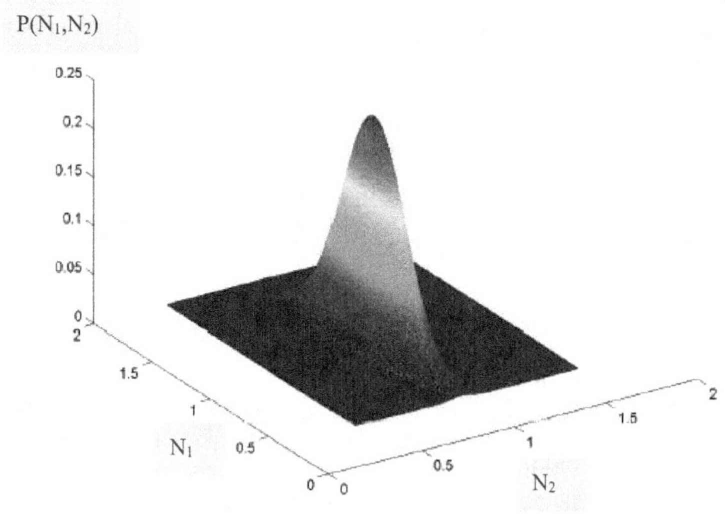

Table 7. Comparison between observed and predicted counts for N_1 and N_2

	$0.8 < N_1 < 0.9$	$0.9 < N_1 < 1.0$	$1.0 < N_1 < 1.1$
$0.5 < N_2 < 1.0$	0/1.77	11/11.67	3/3.38
$1.0 < N_2 < 1.5$	3/3.77	26/24.8	5/5.72
$1.5 < N_2 < 2.0$	0/0.4	6/3	0/0.75

Test Phase

The aim of the training phase is to evaluate the PDF $P(S_i | f_1, f_2, \ldots)$ while in the test phase the expression (5) is applied on the second half of the acquired data in order to verify the prediction capability of this methodology. In the case of bare soils, the parameters S_i are ε, s, l, and f_1, f_2,...are backscattering coefficients or emissivities. As the main interest was to extract dielectric constant values, a first integration over the PDF $P(\varepsilon, s, l | f_1, f_2, \ldots)$ is performed with respect to the roughness parameters, s and l, over their range of values in order to obtain a marginal distribution:

$$P(\varepsilon | f_1, f_2, \ldots) = \frac{\iint\limits_{s,l} P(\varepsilon, s, l) P(f_1, f_2, \ldots | \varepsilon, s, l) ds dl}{\iiint\limits_{\varepsilon, s, l} P(\varepsilon, s, l) P(f_1, f_2, \ldots | \varepsilon, s, l) ds dl} \qquad (10)$$

(with respect to (5), we use integral formulation, because we deal with continuous functions). This distribution represents the probability of the different dielectric constant values for the possible combination of measured backscattering coefficients or emissivities f_1, f_2,...(Notarnicola & Posa, 2004). From this distribution the mean value and the variance of the estimator can be extracted (Gelman, Carlin, Stern, & Rubin, 1995) as follows:

$$\bar{\varepsilon} = \int_\varepsilon \varepsilon \cdot f(\varepsilon \mid f_1, f_2,...)d\varepsilon \tag{11}$$

$$\sigma^2(\varepsilon) = \int_\varepsilon (\varepsilon - \bar{\varepsilon})^2 \cdot f(\varepsilon \mid f_1, f_2,...)d\varepsilon \tag{12}$$

In all these calculations, the prior PDF for the parameters, over which an integration is performed, is to be specified. In the integration for the calculation of the marginal distribution, the prior PDF for roughness parameters has been considered uniform across the whole possible range of values. This means that no supplementary information about these parameters were considered apart from their range of values. The dielectric constant has been integrated in the range from 2 to 20. The integration window for s is [0.1 cm, 3.0 cm] and for l is [0.1 cm, 21.0 cm]; they cover most of the surface measurements. The purpose was to verify the capability to extract dielectric constant values independently from roughness levels.

Result Analysis

For each configuration and approach three figures of merit have been calculated (Barreto & Andreade, 2000):

Mean Squared Error (MSE)= $\dfrac{1}{k}\sum\limits_{i=1}^{k}(\varepsilon_i^m - \varepsilon_i^p)^2$ (13)

Mean Absolute Deviation (MAD)= $\dfrac{1}{k}\sum\limits_{i=1}^{k}\left|\varepsilon_i^m - \varepsilon_i^p\right|$ (14)

Mean Relative Error (MRE)= $\dfrac{100}{k}\sum\limits_{i=1}^{k}\dfrac{\left|\varepsilon_i^m - \varepsilon_i^p\right|}{\varepsilon_i^p}$ (15)

where ε_i^p and ε_i^m are the predicted and the measured dielectric constant values, respectively.

The comparison among the results for different techniques have been verified through a Student's t-test with 95% level of confidence (Stuart & Ord, 1996). In this test, the values of the figure of merit have been compared, considering that each figure of merit derives from a mean over the k number of extracted dielectric constant values as expressed in (13), (14), and (15). The mean values have been compared under the null hypothesis that they were equal. In the tables, the results that are underlined indicate a significant difference among the configurations.

Active and Passive Data on Bare Soils

The results of the three figures of merit are listed in Table 8.

With respect to the dielectric constant levels, a particular behaviour is found for the figure MRE: the best configurations are 1f1p and 2f1p for the extraction of ε values higher than 10 (wet soils), and the configuration 1f2p performs better for ε values lower than 10 (dry soils) (Notarnicola & Posa, 2004). Dielectric constant values are separated into two regimes, above and below 10, due to the relationship between the dielectric constant and the volumetric soil moisture, which shows a marked change in its slope at approximately ε =10 (Hallikainen et al., 1985) corresponding to volumetric soil moisture between 18% and 20% according to different soil types.

The analysis is also confirmed by the behaviour of the marginal PDF. In fact, the distribution shape depends on the soil moisture level. Figure 2 represents three marginal distributions obtained from three cases:

1.   Measured dielectric constant 8.78, predicted 7.36
2.   Measured dielectric constant 13.51, predicted 13.69
3.   Measured dielectric constant 10.89, predicted 11.32

During the integration, the presence of long tails introduces the contribution of the dielectric constant higher values. In order to reduce this effect, prior information should be available. In fact, in this case, no prior information on roughness or soil moisture, apart from their range of values, was available. The introduction of prior information regarding soil rough-

Table 8. Results of the Bayesian approach for active and passive data

Configurations	4.6 GHz, Horiz. pol. (1f1p)			2.5/4.6 GHz, Horiz. pol. (2f1p)			4.6 GHz, Horiz./Vert.pol (1f2p)		
Figures of merit	MSE	MAD	MRE	MSE	MAD	MRE	MSE	MAD	MRE
Bayes	3.30	1.41	12.62%	2.34	1.30	12.25%	3.55	1.52	14.29%
Dielectric constant > 10									
Bayes	2.01	1.15	9.0%	2.04	1.20	9.52%	4.68	1.80	13.13%
Dielectric constant < 10									
Bayes	5.45	1.86	18.82%	2.84	1.46	16.62%	2.07	1.17	15.80%

Figure 2. Comparison among the marginal distributions for different level of dielectric constant. The indicated values are the corresponding measured values of the dielectric constant.

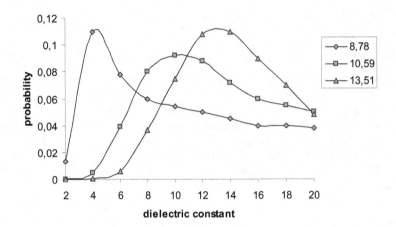

ness (Davidson, Le Toan, Mattia, Satalino, Verhoest, & Boreaud, 2001) and soil moisture (Notarnicola & Posa, 2002) can determine a corresponding improvement in the inversion process.

Active Scatterometer Data

The results of the three figures of merit are listed in Table 9.

The Bayesian method performance does not change significantly through the two configurations.

For these two data sets, the errors for the Bayesian method increase with the number of input. This could be due to the Bayesian methodology, where every source of information brings its own PDF whose width quantifies the source errors. In fact, the width of the PDF

Table 9. Results of the Bayesian approach for active scatterometer data

Configurations	23°, HH/VV Pol.			23°/40°, HH/VV Pol.		
Figures of merit	MSE	MAD	MRE	MSE	MAD	MRE
Bayes	8.17	2.28	18.93%	10.20	2.71	21.96%
Dielectric constant > 10						
Bayes	8.45	2.41	17.35%	16.16	3.75	25.76%
Dielectric constant < 10						
Bayes	7.93	2.17	20.33%	4.91	1.78	18.58%

represents the spreading of the measured data around the theoretical ones. As the parameter estimates are based on these PDFs, both PDF mean and variance (width) influence the results. The errors on estimates are limited by the PDF variance and the estimates cannot be more precise than how much is established in the PDF during the training phase, when the posterior PDF is calculated (Gelman et al., 1995).

The mean relative errors are relatively high but they are comparable with the errors on soil moisture ground measurements that were around 20%.

Washita'92 Data

Before commenting on the results of the application of the Bayesian methodology to Washita'92 data, some more hints about processing are indicated, because now we are dealing with images and not with point data. According to the general scheme of the Bayesian algorithm, the application to the AirSAR images has proceeded as follows during the training phase:

1.   On the images acquired on field AG002 on 10/06/1992 in L- and C-band at HH and VV polarisation, respectively, already coregistered, an averaging filter has been applied for noise removal (Curlander & McDonough, 1991). This filter has also been applied to the images in the test phase.

2.   After a scaling in dB values (Jackson & Shiebe, 1993), a mean value of the backscattering coefficient for both polarisations on the field AG002 has been calculated and compared with the theoretical values obtained from the IEM model. The experimental and theoretical values of the backscattering coefficients are useful to derive the noise factor N_i, and subsequently the likelihood function.

For the testing phase, the procedure has been as follows:

3.   For the application of the Bayes' theorem, the prior PDF is assumed uniform for all the parameters ε, s, and l. This eliminates personal subjectivity (Gelman et al., 1995). After the integrations (eq. (11)), it is possible to associate to each pixel a dielectric constant value starting with backscattering coefficient values.

4.   This procedure has been applied for all the images from 13 to 18 June for which it is possible to make a comparison with ground measurements.

The listed steps have been applied in order to obtain a dielectric constant map of the field AG002, by using the following combinations of AIRSAR data:

1.   C-band images at HH and VV polarisations
2.   L-band images at HH and VV polarisations

Table 10. Results of the Bayesian approach for Washita'92 AirSAR data

Configurations	C band, HH/VV Pol.			L band, HH/VV Pol.		
Figures of merit	MSE	MAD	MRE	MSE	MAD	MRE
Field AG002	3.18	1.31	12.30%	5.31	2.21	15.67%

Figure 3. The temporal variation of the dieletric constant values for field AG002 (indicated by the arrow) as extracted from C-band data. The map for the 10/06/1992 has been used for the training and has been reported for comparison with the other dates.

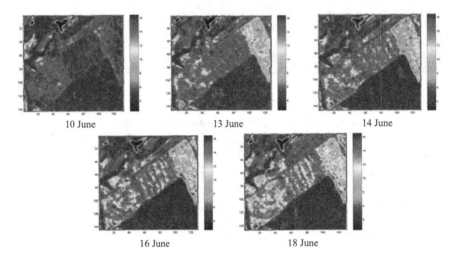

The variation of the dielectric constant values within AG002 field is illustrated in Figure 3, while Table 10 reports the comparison with measured values in terms of the three figures of merit.

The results indicate a good capability of retrieving dielectric constant values with errors that vary from 12% to 16% for C and L-band, respectively. The higher errors for L-band can be due to the fact that the wavelength for L band is longer than for C band and then can penetrate deeply in the soil. The ground truth measurements were taken in the first few centimetres of the soil layers and then are more comparable to the estimates that are derived from the inversion with C-band data.

Anyway, according to t-Student test, the difference between C- and L-band results are not found significant with 95% level of confidence.

SMEX'02 Data

The same procedure that has been described before for Washita'92 data has been also applied to the case of vegetated fields. In this case some more considerations have to be added. In

Table 11. Pdf mean and std ranges for the application of the bare soil model

Polarization and frequency	Pdf parameters	
	mean	std
L_{HH}	0.4 – 0.7	0.05 – 0.08
L_{VV}	0.3 – 0.7	0.04 – 0.08
C_{HH}	0.2 – 0.5	0.04 – 0.08
C_{VV}	0.3 – 0.5	0.05 – 0.07

fact, the retrieval of soil moisture over vegetated fields is a more complicated task. On one side, the contribution from soil is masked by the presence of vegetation. On the other side, the vegetation itself contributes with its water content to the radar signal. Consequently, the approach is modified to take into account these two contributions.

When using a theoretical model such as IEM suitable for bare soils and comparing the simulated values with those acquired on vegetated fields, the resulting PDF means should quantify the different behavior of radar signal for bare and vegetated fields. In the case of bare fields, the theoretical values calculated by the IEM model should be as close as possible to the measured ones and then the PDF mean should be close to the value of 1 with a standard deviation that represents the field variability as well as the sensor error. For vegetated areas, the mean is less than 1 because the backscattering coefficients for vegetation are generally higher than those for bare soils (Table 11).

Thus, PDFs should contain information on some vegetation parameters that influence the radar signal. Particularly, a good correlation has been found between PDF means and vegetation water content (Notarnicola, Angiulli, & Posa, 2006).

Instead of correlating PDF means directly to measured vegetation water content, the estimates of this parameter, obtained from an optical image, LANDSAT image, have been considered. The purpose is to verify whether the PDF mean variations can be predicted using vegetation water content derived from other remote sensed data. The methodology for the calculation of vegetation water content (VWC) from LANDSAT images has been derived and tested in Jackson, Chen, Cosh, Li, Anderson, and Walthall et al. (2004). VWC was estimated from the normalized difference water index (NDWI) which is a ratio of bands 4 and 5 available from the LANDSAT sensor. These values have been found in very good correlation with measured values of vegetation water content (Jackson et al., 2004).

With these formulae, the values of VWC for soybean varies between 0.10 and 0.98 kg/m² and for corn between 0.10 and 7.50 kg/m². The PDF means have been correlated to these Landsat derived VWC. A linear relationship has been presumed among PDF means and vegetation water content. In Table 12, the found correlation coefficients are listed. The bold values are those found significant with a confidence level of 95% according to an F-test (Dowdy & Wearden, 1991). The analysis has been carried out on all the 32 fields.

The found relationships between PDF means and vegetation water, expressed as follows:

$$PDF_{HH} = a\ VWC + b \tag{16}$$

$$PDF_{VV} = c\ VWC + d \tag{17}$$

have been used in two ways:

- As the PDF mean changes according to the found linear relationship with vegetation water content extracted from the LANDSAT image, this procedure has been inserted in the inversion procedure for the extraction of dielectric constant values; the posterior density function is then expressed as follows:

$$P(\varepsilon,s,1|\sigma_{HH},\sigma_{VV}) = \frac{P_{prior}(\varepsilon,s,1)P(\sigma_{HH},\sigma_{VV}|\ \varepsilon s,1)}{\iiint\limits_{\varepsilon,s,1}P(\varepsilon,s,1)P(\sigma_{HH},\sigma_{VV}|\ \varepsilon s,1)d\ \varepsilon ds d1} \tag{18}$$

where σ_{HH}, σ_{VV} are the backscattering coefficients for HH and VV polarizations, respectively.

- As the dependence of the PDF mean on the amount of vegetation water content introduces a new variable in the inversion problem that uses a model for bare soils, it can be used to extract the vegetation water content itself from the radar signal. With the introduction of the vegetation water content as a new variable k, the posterior PDF (18) changes as follows:

$$P(\varepsilon,s,1,k|\sigma_{HH},\sigma_{VV}) = \frac{P_{prior}(\varepsilon,s,1,k)P(\sigma_{HH},\sigma_{VV}|\ \varepsilon s,1,k)}{\iiint\limits_{\varepsilon,s,1}\int P(\varepsilon,s,1,k)P(\sigma_{HH},\sigma_{VV}|\ \varepsilon s,1,k)d\ \varepsilon ds d1 dk} \tag{19}$$

Table 12. Correlation coefficients between the pdf means and vegetation water content (WVC) for different polarization and frequency (indicated with C_{HH} C_{VV} L_{HH} L_{VV} C_{HH}/C_{VV} L_{HH}/L_{VV})

Polarization/frequency	WVC All fields	WVC Soybean	WVC Corn
Pdf mean for CHH	0.43	**0.68**	0.20
Pdf mean for CVV	0.20	0.46	0.24
Pdf mean for LHH	**0.63**	0.05	0.04
Pdf mean for LVV	0.20	0.19	0.23
Pdf mean for CHH/CVV	**0.68**	0.46	**0.75**
Pdf mean for LHH/LVV	**0.91**	**0.84**	**0.87**

Figure 4. Block diagram of the inversion procedure for vegetated fields

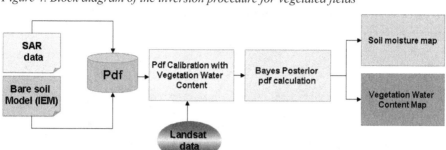

Table 13. Results of the Bayesian approach for SMEX'02 AirSAR data

Configurations	C band, HH/VV Pol.			L band, HH/VV Pol.		
Figures of merit	MSE	MAD	MRE	MSE	MAD	MRE
Dielectric constant estimates	2.79	1.30	13.75%	3.52	1.60	16.30%
Vegetation water content estimates	0.98	0.67	22.61%	2.40	1.01	25.45%

This procedure implies that the expression (19) should be integrated over the whole range of dielectric constant values and roughness parameters in order to obtain a marginal PDF that retains exclusively information on the vegetation water content. The whole procedure is sketched in Figure 4.

The results for the application of this procedure to vegetated fields are indicated in Table 13.

This new approach, that takes into account the presence of vegetation, determines soil dielectric constant estimates with figures of merit values comparable to those obtained with the bare fields approach of Little Washita'92 (Table 10).

The retrieval of vegetation water content indicates errors that are around 25%. As the WVC ground measurements were available only on few dates, for the comparison with satellite retrieved values, the estimates have been averaged on two or three dates that were closest to the ground truth acquisition dates. For the measured values it has been assumed an error of 30%. As for each field a mean value of VWC has been considered, the error includes both the within field variability and the variation from one day to another one.

Figure 5 is an example of soil moisture maps obtained from AirSAR images during four days of acquisition (Notarnicola et al., 2006). On July 7, there was a heavy rainfall, so it is possible during the following days (July 8 and 9) to capture the dry-down phase.

Extension of the Approach: The Vegetated Field Model

As a further development of the procedure proposed, instead of considering a bare soil model and subsequently calibrating the PDFs on vegetated fields, a simple model for vegetation

Figure 5. Soil moisture (cm³/cm³) map for field WC03 (soybean) from AIRSAR C-band data (top) and L band data (bottom). The Hallikainen formula has been used to trasform soil dielectric constant to volumetric soil moisture (Hallikainen et al., 1995).

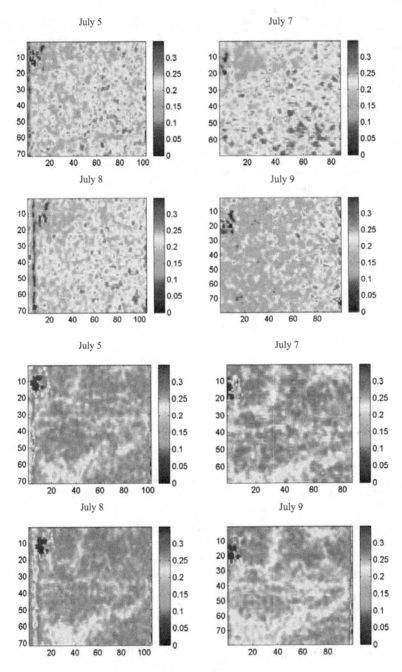

and soil backscatter can be considered. In this paragraph, the procedure is only outlined but not applied to the remotely sensed data. The consideration of this new model is to show how the proposed approach can be extended to other models.

The simple approach, based on the so-called water-cloud model, was developed by Attema and Ulaby (1978), who proposed to represent, in a radiative transfer model, the vegetation canopy as a uniform cloud whose spherical droplets are held in place structurally by dry matter. The water-cloud models represent the power backscattered by the whole canopy σ_0 as the incoherent sum of the contribution of the vegetation σ_{0veg} and the contribution of the underlying soil σ_{0soil}, which is attenuated by the vegetation layer through the vegetation trasmissivity τ^2. For a given incidence angle, the backscatter coefficient is represented by the general form:

$$\sigma_0 = \sigma_{0veg} + \tau^2 \sigma_{0soil} . \tag{20}$$

This expression can be written in more detailed way:

$$\sigma_0 = A\, m_v \cos\theta (1-\tau^2) + \tau^2 \sigma_{0soil} . \tag{21}$$

where

m_v = vegetation water content (kg/m^2);

θ = incidence angle;

σ_{0soil} = backscattering coefficient of bare soil in this case calculated by using the IEM model;

τ^2 = two-way vegetation trasmissivity that can be expressed as $\tau^2 = \exp(-2B\, m_v / \cos\theta)$;

A and B = two parameters depending on the canopy type.

The procedure is divided in the following steps:

1. The model has to be calibrated, that is, parameters A and B have to be determined based on the actual vegetation. To this purpose some fields, corn and soybean, for different days were chosen randomly in the dataset. The maximum likelihood procedure can be used.

2. Once the values of A and B are obtained, the model is ready to be used after a suitable validation.

3. From now on, the procedure is the same followed in the case of bare soils. In this case, however, the Ni represents the sensor noise and the model error and they should be centred around the value of 1 because the model is pertinent to vegetated fields. In Table 14, the PDF means and standard deviations have been indicated for C and L-band determined by applying this procedure.

Table 14. Pdf mean and std ranges for the application of the vegetated model

Polarization and frequency	Pdf parameters	
	mean	std
L_{HH}	0.8 – 1.2	0.2 – 0.3
L_{VV}	0.7 – 1.2	0.2 – 0.3
C_{HH}	1.0 – 1.5	0.1 – 0.2
C_{VV}	1.0 – 1.5	0.1 – 0.2

4.   Inserting these PDFs in the calculation of the posterior probability, we will determine a function which depends on four variables: the real part of the dielectric constant, the roughness parameters, s and l, and the vegetation water content.

5.   Integrating on all the possible values of the dielectric constant and roughness parameters, we obtain a function which retains exclusively the dependence on vegetation water content.

Conclusion

The principal aim of this chapter is to illustrate the application of Bayesian methodologies to experimental data. The context is that of the inversion of remotely sensed data for soil and vegetation water content retrieval. The Bayesian approach offers the possibility to build a more general model starting from a theoretical model including the sensor noise and the model errors.

The built PDF can be considered as a tool to be tuned according to the particular situations. This is illustrated when the PDFs that have been obtained for bare soils, and that have been subsequently adapted for vegetated fields by integrating data of other remotely sensed data.

Some considerations emerge about the inversion results; some of them are due to the data themselves and some of them to the considered inversion procedures.

With respect to the data sets, the following features have been found:

•   Difficulties in retrieving dielectric constant values lower than 10, because in this case the signal due to soil moisture is low with respect to that due to roughness or vegetation (Ulaby et al., 1986).

•   The errors on estimates are reduced, especially for $\varepsilon < 10$ by using two polarizations (1f2p) or two incidence angles (23°/ 40° HH-VV). In fact, the backscattering coefficients vary with the incidence angle and this variation depends on the soil roughness level (Ulaby et al., 1986). Then the information of two incidence angles is useful to individuate the correct level of roughness and consequently more reliable dielectric constant values.

- For active and passive data, the algorithm performances markedly change according to the soil moisture level and the selected data configuration. The different behavior of ε for values below and above 10 can be due to the relationships between volumetric soil moisture and dielectric constant values, whose slope greatly increases at approximately ε = 10 (Hallikainen et al., 1995).

- For vegetated fields (SMEX'02 data), the PDF variations, as derived from a correlation with optical images, are able to take into account the contribute of vegetation and then determine dielectric constant estimates with the same level of errors of the bare field case (Little Washita'92 data).

With respect to the inversion procedure, main considerations are:

- The PDFs have to be calculated in the initial training phase. If the PDF values have been calculated in previous similar cases considering large data set statistics, they may be used directly without a training phase. Anyway, the PDFs should be firstly validated on a subset of data in order to verify their applicability to the present experimental case.

- One main advantage is that the procedure does not require specific roughness values, but for the integration, it is necessary to introduce only the roughness parameter ranges.

- The PDF relationship with VWC should be supported by data sets which contain a wider range of VWC values. This is necessary to determine a more general relationship between PDF parameters and VWC values.

- One main advantage of the procedure is the possibility to include easily as many sources of information as available.

From the above consideration, the main drawback of this methodology is that it requires an extended dataset because a part of the data set has to be used to build the posterior PDFs. In some cases, as for the water cloud model, the model has to be calibrated on the specific data sets. This prevents the methodologies from being applicable in other data sets. In this case, it could be better to use a general model that does not need any validation on specific sites.

In this context, when the procedure has been applied to different kinds of experimental data, one effort is to create global PDFs that could be applicable to general experimental contexts rather than to one single data set.

In this direction, Monte Carlo simulations can be performed in order to build remotely sensed databases from which robust PDFs can be calculated. The main advantage of these PDFs should be their applicability in many experimental situations.

References

Attema, E.P.W., & Ulaby, F.T. (1978). Vegetation modelled as a water cloud. *Radio Science, 13,* 357-364.

Barreto, G.A., & Andreade, M.G. (2000). Bayesian inference and Markov chain Monte Carlo methods applied to streamflow forecasting. In *Proeedings of the. 6th Conference on Probabilistic Methods Applied Power Systems (PMAPS)* (vol. 2), Funchal, Portugal. FOR-034.

Bindlish, R., & Barros, A.P. (2000). Multifrequency soil moisture inversion from SAR measurements with the use of IEM. *Remote Sensing of Environment, 71*(1), 67-88.

Boisvert, J., Gwyn, Q., Chanzy, A., Major, D., Brisco, B., & Brown, R. (1997). Effect of surface soil moisture gradients on modeling radar backscattering from bare fields. *International Journal of Remote Sensing, 18,* 153-170.

Cihlar, J., Dobson, M.C., Schmugge, T., Hoogeboom, P., Janse, A.R.P., Baret, F. et al. (1987). Procedures for the description of agricultural crops and soils in optical and microwave remote sensing studies. *International Journal of Remote Sensing, 8*(3), 427-439.

Curlander, J.C., & McDonough, R.N. (1991). *Synthetic aperture radar* (pp. 216-220). John Wiley & Sons.

Davidson, M.W.J., Le Toan, T., Mattia, F., Satalino, G., Verhoest, N.E.C., & Borgeaud, M. (2001, July 9-13). Improving soil moisture retrieval by incorporating a prior information on roughness parameters. In *Proceedings of the IGARSS 2001* (vol. 3) (pp. 1421-1423). Sydney, Australia.

Delworth, T.L., & Manabe, S. (1988). The influence of potential evaporation on the variabilities of the simulated soil wetness and climate. *Journal of Climate, 1*(5), 523-547.

Dowdy, S., & Wearden, S. (1991). *Statistics for research* (pp. 213-216). John Wiley & Sons.

Dubois, P.C., van Zyl, J., & Engman T. (1995). Measuring soil moisture with imaging radars. *IEEE Transaction on Geoscience and Remote Sensing, 33*(4), 915-926.

Fast, J.D., & McCorcle, M.D. (1991). The effect of heterogeneous soil moisture on a summer baroclinic circulation in the central United States. *Monthly Weather Review, 119*(9), 2140-2167.

Fung, A.K. (1994). *Microwave scattering and emission models and their application.* Boston: Artech House.

Gelman, R., Carlin, J.B., Stern, H.S., & Rubin, D.B. (1995). *Bayesian data analysis.* Chapman & Hall.

Haddad, Z.S., & Dubois, P. (1994). Bayesian estimation of soil parameters from remote sensing data. In *Proceedings of the International Geoscience and Remote Sensing Symposium (IGARSS'94),* (vol.3, pp. 1421-1423).

Haddad, Z.S., & Dubois, P. (1995). *Bayesian estimation of soil parameters from radar backscatter data* (Internal JPL Rep.).

Hallikainen, M.T., Ulaby, F.T., Dobson, M.C., El-Rayes, M.A., & Wu, L. (1985). Microwave dielectric behavior of wet soil—Part I: Empirical models and experimental observations. *IEEE Transaction on Geoscience and Remote Sensing, GE-23,* 25-34.

Jackson, T.J., Chen, D., Cosh, M., Li, F., Anderson, M. , Walthall, C. et al. (2004). Vegetation water content mapping using Landsat data derived normalized difference water index for corn and soybeans. *Remote Sensing of Environment, 92*, 475-482.

Jackson, T.J., Le Vine, D.M., Swift, C.T., Schmugge, T.J., & Schiebe, F.R. (1995). Large area mapping of soil moisture using the ESTAR passive microwave radiometer in Washita '92. *Remote Sensing of Environment, 53*, 27-37.

Jackson, T.J., & Shiebe, F.R. (1993). *Washita '92 data report*. NAWQL Report 101. Durant, OK: USDA National Agricultural Water Quality Lab.

Kerr, Y.H., Waldteufem, P., Wigneron, J.P., Font, J., & Berger, M. (2001). Soil moisture retrieval from space: The Soil Moisture and Ocean Salinity (SMOS) mission. *IEEE Transaction on Geoscience and Remote Sensing, 39*(8), 1729-1735.

Lin, D.S., Wood, E.F., Bevan, K., & Saatchi, S. (1994). Soil moisture estimation over grass-covered areas using AIRSAR. *International Journal of Remote Sensing, 15*(11), 2323-2343.

Mattia, F., & Le Toan, T. (1999). Backscattering properties of multi-scale rough surfaces. *Journal of Electromagnetic Waves and Applications, 13*, 491-526.

Mattia, F., Le Toan, T., Picard, G., Posa, F., D'Alessio, A.C., Notarnicola, C. et al. (2003). Multitemporal C-band radar measurements on wheat field. *IEEE Transactions on Geoscience and Remote Sensing, 41*(7), 1551-1560.

Nezry, E., Yakam-Simen, F., Supit, I., & Zagolsky, V. (1997). Retrieval of environmental and geophysical parameters through bayesian fusion of ERS and RADARSAT data. In *Proceedings of the 3rd ERS Symposium (ESA)*, Florence, Italy.

Njoku, E.G., & Li, l. (1999). Retrieval of land surface parameters using passive microwave measurements at 6-8 GHz. *IEEE Transaction on Geoscience and Remote Sensing, 37*(1), 79-93.

Notarnicola, C., Angiulli, M., & Posa, F. (2006). Use of radar and optical remotely sensed data for soil moisture retrieval over vegetated areas. *IEEE Transaction on Geoscience and Remote Sensing, 44*(4), 925-935.

Notarnicola, C., D'Alessio, A.C., Casarano, D., Posa, F., & Sabatelli, V. (2003). Use of a C-band ground-based scatterometer to monitor surface roughness and soil moisture changes. *Subsurface Sensing Technologies and Applications: An International Journal, Kluwer Academic/Plenum Publishers, 4*(2), 187-206.

Notarnicola, C., & Posa, F. (2002, June 24-28). Extraction of soil parameters: Two case studies using Bayesian fusion of multiple sources data. In *Proceedings of the International Geoscience and Remote Sensing Symposium 2002* (vol. 2, pp. 905-907). Toronto, Ontario, Canada.

Notarnicola, C., & Posa, F. (2004). Bayesian algorithm for the estimation of the dielectric constant from active and passive remotely sensed data. *IEEE Geoscience and Remote Sensing Letters, 1*(3), 179-203.

Oh, Y., Sarabandi, K., & Ulaby, F.T. (1992). An empirical model and an inversion technique for radar scattering from bare soil surfaces. *IEEE Transaction on Geoscience and Remote Sensing, 30*(2), 378-381.

Prevot, L., & Dechambre, M., (1993). Estimating the characteristics of vegetation canopies with airborne radar measurements. *International Journal of Remote Sensing, 14*(15), 2803-2818.

Rakotoarivony, L. (1995). *Validation de modèles de diffusion électromagnétique: Comparaison entre simulations et mesures radar hélipoté sur des surfaces agricoles de sol nu.* Unpublished doctoral thesis,University of Caen, France.

Remond, A. (1997). *Image SAR: Potentialities d'extraction d'un parameter physique du ruissellement, la rugosité (modélization et experimentation).* Unpublished doctoral thesis, University of Bourgogne, Orléans, France.

Roy, A., & Georgopoulos, P.G. (1998). Data and model assimilation using a Bayesian methodology: Markov chain monte carlo simulation. In *Proceedings of the 3rd CRESP Annual Meeting.*

Ruf, C.S., & Zhang, H. (2001). Performance evaluation of a single and multichannel microwave radiometers for soil moisture retrieval. *Remote Sensing of Environment, 75*, 86-99.

Satalino, G., Pasquariello, G., Mattia, F., Le Toan, T., Davidson, M., & Borgeaud, M. (1999). The potential of multi-angle C-band SAR data for soil moisture retrieval. In *Proceedings of the International Geoscience and Remote Sensing Symposium, IGARSS 1999* (G.E.-18) (pp. 288-295).

Schmugge, T.J., & Jackson, T.J. (1994). Mapping soil moisture with microwave radiometers. *Meteorology and Atmospheric Physics, 54*, 213-223.

Stuart, A., & Ord, J.K. (1996). *Advanced theory of statistics* (vol. 1, 5th ed.). London: Charles Griffin.

Ulaby, F.T., Moore, R.K., & Fung, A.K. (1986). *Microwave remote sensing: Active and passive* (vol. II). Artech House.

van Zyl, J., Carande, R., Lou, Y., Miller, T., & Wheeler, K. (1992). The NASA/JPL three-frequency polarimetric AIRSAR system. *IEEE International Geoscience and Remote Sensing Symposium Dig., 1,* 649-651.

Wang, J.R., & Choudhury, B.J. (1995). Passive microwave radiation from soil: Examples of emission model and observations. *Passive microwave remote sensing of land-atmosphere interactions.* VSP Publishing.

Wang, J.R., Shiue, J.C., Schmugge, T.J., & Engman, E.T. (1990). The L-band PBMR measurements of surface soil moisture in FIFE. *IEEE Transaction on Geoscience and Remote Sensing, 28*, 906-913.

Wegmueller, U., Maetzler, C., Hueppi, R., & Schanda, E. (1994). Active and Passive Microwave Signature Catalog on Bare Soil (2-12 GHz). *IEEE Transaction on Geoscience and Remote Sensing, 32*(3), 698-702.

Zribi, M., Taconet, O., Le Hegarat-Mascle, S., Vidar-Madjar, D., Emblanch, C., Loumagne, C., & Normand, M. (1994). Backscattering behavior and simulation: Comparison over bare soils using SIR-C/X-SAR and ERASME 1994 data over orgeval. *Remote Sensing of Environment, 59*, 256-266.

Section III:

Bayesian Networks for Bioinformatics Applications

Chapter XII

Application of Bayesian Network in Drug Discovery and Development Process

Arunkumar Chinnasamy, Bioinformatics Institute, Singapore

Sudhanshu Patwardhan, Bioinformatics Institute, Singapore

Wing-Kin Sung, National University of Singapore, Singapore

Abstract

The end of the 20th century and the advent of the new millennium have brought in a true merger of sciences for the benefit of mankind. The biggest promise it holds is that of improving the quality of human life by the discovery of newer medicines and better cures for diseases such as cancer and heart disease. Pharmaceutical companies and academic institutions alike have not failed to deliver on part of the promise by bringing out technologies and products that have significantly decreased mortality and morbidity associated with these diseases. An increase in the scale and complexity of the technologies has made it increasingly important to develop intelligent tools to analyze their output, and numerous mathematical and statistical techniques have been explored and exploited to do exactly this. Bayesian networks (BN) and similar graphical models for multivariate analysis are being used for analyzing these data with great success. They have made possible a high resolution insight into disease mechanisms like never before. These insights into the biological processes of health and disease have helped identify the appropriate targets for drug discovery and aided in the process of bringing better drugs faster to the market for patients in need. This chapter briefly explains the application and contribution of Bayesian networks to the drug discovery and development process.

Introduction

The end of the 20th century and the advent of the new millennium have brought in a true merger of sciences for the benefit of mankind. One field to benefit from this strong interdisciplinary synergy is biotechnology. It is often said that the 21st century belongs to biotechnology. The biggest promise it holds is that of improving the quality of human life by the discovery of newer medicines and better cures for diseases such as cancer and heart disease. Pharmaceutical companies and academic institutions alike have not failed to deliver on part of the promise by bringing out technologies and products that have significantly decreased mortality and morbidity associated with these diseases. These successes owe a lot to technologies such as genomics, proteomics, and metabonomics, to name a few, that have evolved in the past decade or so (see Figure 1).

Despite the availability of hyper-dimensional data from disparate technologies and different levels of organismal organization, the real challenge has been to integrate them to make biological sense. An increase in the scale and complexity of the technologies has made it increasingly important to develop intelligent tools to analyze their output, and numerous mathematical and statistical techniques have been explored and exploited to do exactly this. Bayesian networks (BN) and similar graphical models for multivariate analysis are being used for analyzing these data with great success. They have made possible a high resolution insight into disease mechanisms like never before. These insights into the biological processes of health and disease have helped identify the appropriate targets for drug discovery and aided in the process of bringing better drugs faster to the market for patients in need. This chapter briefly explains the application and contribution of Bayesian networks to the drug discovery and development process.

Figure 1. Advent of the era of high-throughput technologies and hyper dimensional data in biology

Biology and Technology

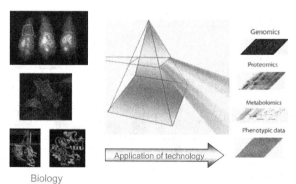

Drug Discovery Process

Current drug discovery and development process has come a long way from the earlier hit-and-miss approach (Reichert, 2003) (see Figure 2). Now, with the advent of tools and technologies to probe biological systems at the molecular level, more emphasis is given on understanding the target better. **A target** is a biological entity that supposedly has a role in the disease process either directly or indirectly. For example, a particular protein (say "protein x") could be playing a pivotal role in causing a particular type of cancer. "Blocking" this protein from doing its function would logically (and ideally) be enough to treat and cure the cancer. Thus, potentially, protein x could be a good target for the industry to start looking for chemicals that could modulate it.

Once a target is known using a combination of target discovery techniques, it is validated using biological experiments to determine how effective it would be to modulate it and treat a disease.

Following this, a search begins for the right chemical entity that can act on this target. This process is refined from an initial high-throughput screening of millions of structurally diverse compounds to medium-to-low throughput screening of specific hits from the earlier screens. This process yields a few **lead molecules** that are then taken through a process of **lead optimization**. This is essentially a medicinal chemistry process where the lead compounds are tweaked to yield the desired physico-chemical properties of effective drugs, but is also complemented by in-vivo experiments for toxicity and pharmacokinetics studies. Thus, at the end of this oft iterative process, **a candidate compound** is chosen. This compound, depending on market forces and health outcomes research, is then taken through **three phases of human clinical trials**. These phases test the compound for safety and efficacy and are used to determine the most appropriate dose. At the end of this almost decade-long process, the data is sent to the administrative agency (Food and Drug Administration for the USA) for approval. Following approval, the drug finally enters the market.

Figure 2. Drug discovery and development process, a time perspective

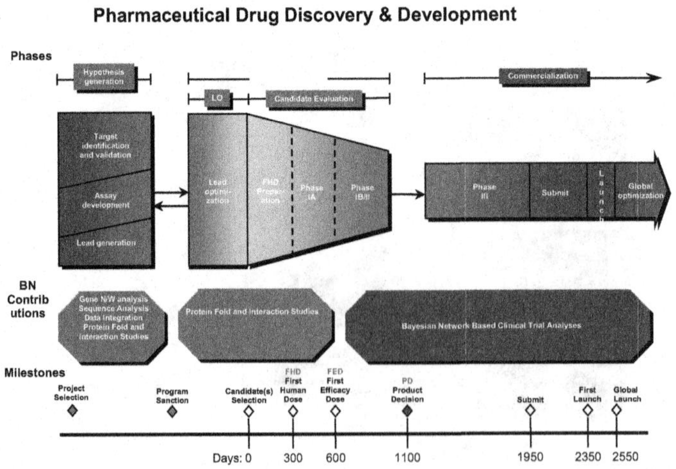

After years of research and development and about a billion dollars spent on a successful drug, pharmaceutical companies usually seek to recover the R&D costs within a period of exclusivity of about another decade before the generic versions of the drug hit the market. Among other factors, whether the drug and its target prove effective in treating and curing a disease determines the blockbuster status of a drug. Failure of drugs and withdrawal from the market are not uncommon, and are usually a result of side effects not observed or deemed insignificant in clinical trials only later to be found unacceptable in larger populations. Many times, this failure is a result of an inappropriately chosen target, and scientists have to go back to the drawing board to rework the networks of physiological and pathological pathways and reevaluate check points for pharmaceutical intervention (Butcher, 2005).

In the drug discovery and development process, Bayesian network contributes in each phase which is summarized in Figure 2. The first major challenge in the whole process is integrating all heterogeneous data from various sources (Stein, 2003). Abstraction and details of all the databases are represented in meta data. Increasing complexity of these meta data itself leads to another layer of meta data which is meta data's meta data. Organizations like NCBI and EBI took initiative in integrating all these data sources. These systems provide an interlinked framework of all data rather than consolidating into single sources of information for complex biological queries. Several intelligent techniques are required for intelligent system integration for incorporating data filtration and aggregation processes. In these processes, encoding human knowledge and prioritizing the data are very important. Pavlovic, Garg, and Kasif (2000) designed a Bayesian based approach for specialized gene function analysis from various heterogeneous data sources. This model incorporates expert knowledge and provides a belief level with its output which has several advantages over other methods.

The real challenge begins with the processing of these integrated data. In post integration analysis, Bayesian network contributes significantly in gene network, protein structure, and interaction studies and in clinical trials. In gene expression analysis, Bayesian network dominates significantly over other techniques, which we will discuss in detail in Section 3. The protein structure prediction problem gives better results with Bayesian network over other learning techniques which help scientists in better understanding with probability values. Bayesian network has a big contribution in protein interaction analysis and clinical trial studies, which we will discuss in last two sections.

In praise of Bayes (2000), Economist summarizes the importance of Bayesian analysis in clinical trial with a cartoon showing new drugs going to *Bayesville* of 1 Km compared to *Frequentistown* of 95 Km. Jansen, Yu, Greenbaum, Kluger, Krogan, Chung et al. (2003) reviews benefits of BN when applying it to life science data analysis. Bayesian networks have several advantages: they allow for combining highly dissimilar types of data (i.e., numerical and categorical), converting them to a common probabilistic framework, without unnecessary simplification; they readily accommodate missing data; and they naturally weigh each information source according to its reliability. In contrast to "black-box" predictors, Bayesian networks are readily interpretable, as they represent conditional probability relationships among information sources. Expressing scientific results in Bayesian terms makes scientists easier to understand and makes borderline or inconclusive results less prone to misinterpretation. Bayesian methods can also be used to decide between several competing hypotheses, by seeing which is most consistent with the available data. The rest of this chapter explains in detail how BN supports the drug discovery pipeline.

Gene Network Analysis

Target identification is the first step in the pipeline. How good a target is depends on many factors and is the crux of the challenge the pharmaceutical industry faces currently. Using high-throughput technologies, that is, technologies that give huge information on thousands of genes and proteins in just a few experiments, it is now possible to find out more than one "player" in the game of disease causation and progression. Deciding on which one of these players is an optimal target is hinged on the granularity in which the biological network of DNA and protein interactions is understood in various states of health and disease.

Molecular biology is based on the dogma of DNA→ RNA→ Protein. In simple words, this points to a flow of information from the genomic material of DNA through RNA intermediates to finally form proteins. Proteins constitute everything from building blocks to the workhorses of any biological system and control each other and the DNA through complex feedback loops. Overall, this network of signaling and biochemically interacting molecules runs the ultimate complex machinery that is a human body. Finding control points in these biological networks is essentially an optimization problem. Even though we now have tools for an elaborate inquiry into the molecular machinery of an organism, we are far from sure about the meaning of the observations if taken in isolation. There is too much noise in biological systems that can confound an untrained eye. Although redundancy and feedback loops introduce an element of robustness in the biological system, they also make it difficult to pinpoint the exact drug target for effective intervention.

Over the past few years, the use of microarray technology and the resultant generation of gene expression data have resulted in a data deluge (see Figure 3). The initial emphasis on looking at lists of a select few genes from a superset of a few thousand did not yield the desired understanding of disease mechanisms that these data intensive methods promised.

Figure 3. Data analysis and integration: Technological and experimental challenges

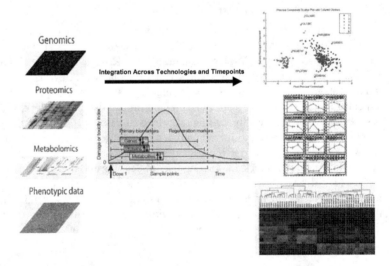

Robust techniques for mapping gene/protein expression and reverse engineering of the pathways in time-series experiments are now needed to extract maximum value out of these information-rich datasets.

Numerous statistical methods have been used for analyzing the data with varying degrees of success. Bayesian network can be applied to these data for reverse engineering and deciphering of the gene regulatory networks that could potentially make the biological system amenable to tracking and possible intervention. Numerous groups across the scientific community are now increasingly employing graphical models for deriving causal networks from such data.

Friedman's group in Israel has done some fundamental work in collaboration with scientists at Stanford and Harvard in the application of probabilistic graphical models for inferring regulatory modules from gene expression data (Friedman, 2003). Regulatory modules are a set of genes that are regulated in concert by a shared regulation program. The regulation program specifies the behavior of the genes in the module as a function of the expression level of a small set of regulators. These regulators are either promoters or transcription factors under whose common control a multiple number of genes are co-regulated. In the analysis set-up, the expression level of each gene is modeled as a random variable. Also, other attributes of the experiment, such as temporal indicators, experimental conditions, sample details, and so forth, are modeled as random variables. Then they learn a Bayesian network based on statistical dependencies between these variables. The outputs of the network serve as models of causal influence, thus reverse engineering the network connections and indicating the direction of influence. Usually, there are thousands of genes per chip per experiment, but the same scale is not available for the number of experiments or time points for which the data is collected. Thus, issues arising out of the heterogeneity of the population, small sample size and insufficient power for statistical inference, make application of Bayesian network to gene expression data erroneous and unsatisfactory.

Newer techniques with finer resolution are evolving with the hope that the statistical shortcomings of microarrays will make way for robust experimental platforms. One such example is the use of multidimensional flow cytometry analysis of single cells. Garry Nolan's group at Stanford have recently come out with a revolutionary technique for deriving causal protein signaling networks from such multiparameter single cell data (Sachs, Perez, Pe'er, Lauffenburger, & Nolan, 2005). They use flow cytometry to record levels of 11 phosphoproteins and phospholipids in individual human T cells. Thus, thousands of cells can be individually assayed in their native state one by one, allowing for a statistically large sample that could enable Bayesian network inference to accurately predict pathway structure.

Despite its apparent advantages in reverse engineering genetic networks using data obtained from such high throughput technologies, Bayesian networks come with a major limitation in the context of biological systems. Bayesian networks are restricted to being acyclic graphs, while signaling pathways are known to be rich in feedback loops. This is evident in Figure 6, where two of the three missed connections are feedback loops. One way around this problem would be to use dynamic Bayesian network (Husmeier, 2003) on time series data.

Protein Structure Analysis

The next step in drug discovery following target discovery is to understand the target as much as possible. The target is usually a protein. Knowing the structure of the protein can be a good starting point to design new drugs that could potentially modulate the protein's activity. Given the difficulty in getting good protein structure information from x-ray crystallography and NMR studies, in-silico approaches have been developed to supplement the structure analysis process. The protein structure problem can be defined in numerous ways and layers. The essence of the analysis is in knowing the **sequence** of the protein (primary structure), understanding how it **folds** in **three-dimension** (tertiary structure), mapping out its various **modifications** (called post-translational modifications), understanding "how it works" and finding out how and where can it be acted upon to modulate its behavior. Also important is to understand the **repertoire of proteins that this protein interacts** with to predict the outcome of an intervention. Studying protein-protein interaction is not only a part of target discovery and validation, but also an ongoing process for designing target-specific drugs and minimizing toxicity. Thus, having chosen a protein as a target for drug discovery essentially means that a pharmaceutical company has to understand the protein in-and-out and then use that information to make the best chemical to alter its behavior.

In the remaining chapter, we will be reviewing a few applications of Bayesian network in understanding protein structures and the interaction network of proteins to better characterize them as drug targets. hidden Markov models (HMMs) have found an immediate application in this field by their ability to build a probabilistic model to align and analyze sequence datasets by generalization from a protein sequence profile (Krogh, Brown, Mian, Sjolander, & Haussler, 1994). hidden Markov models (HMMs) are a formal foundation for making probabilistic models of linear sequence "labeling" problems. They provide a conceptual toolkit for building complex models just by drawing an intuitive picture. They are at the heart of a diverse range of programs, including gene finding, profile searches, multiple sequence alignment, and regulatory site identification. HMMs are the Legos™ of computational sequence analysis.

Fold Class Prediction

The next application in protein sequence analysis is by tree augmented naïve Bayesian classifier for structure class prediction. In proteomics, finding the structure and the fold of a protein is important because it helps to understand the functions, the catalytic, and the structural roles of proteins. Protein structure can be determined experimentally by X-ray diffraction and NMR techniques. These methods are expensive, which limits researchers to lead to get all protein structures. The number of solved structures is in the ten thousands compared to available millions of available unsolved protein sequences. Hence, researchers are interested in getting approximate inference of protein structure based on the given sequence. (Chinnasamy, Sung, & Mittal, 2004, 2005) used a TAN-based approach (BAYESPROT, See Figure 4) for the prediction and showed how it is superior to other models both experimentally and

Figure 4. Overview of BAYESPROT

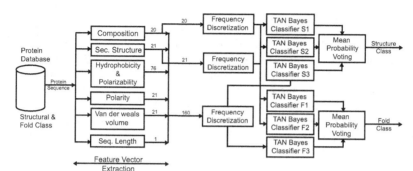

theoretically. The major challenges in this prediction are handling multidimensional data and the large number of fold classes.

The best result from Previous study (Ding & Dubchalk, 2001) is 56% by SVM AvA method using 2106 binary SVM classifiers. BAYESPROT achieves the highest accuracy of 62.86%. In 10-fold cross-validation studies, accuracy of 63.33% is achieved by BAYESPROT, which is 39.49% higher than the SVM AvA method. The number of classifiers used for this cross validation study is 10*3 (=30) TAN Bayesian Classifiers, which is substantially less than the number of classifiers in SVM AvA, where 84,240 binary SVM classifiers were employed.

Learning complexity of SVM depends on the number of iterations and the learning complexity is quite high. The conventional approach suffers from large complexity, approaching $O(N^3)$ where N represents the number of training samples. But in BAYESPROT, because the dataset is complete and structure is known, the time required to learn the parameters is much less $O(N)$. In addition, the number of classifiers used in Bayesian network is substantially less than that in SVM.

Cross validation is a method to estimate the generalization error of a given model. From this study, it is also clearly evident that after performing cross validation, accuracy of BAYESPROT increases or remains almost the same while that of SVM decreases significantly.

Interpreting the classification results is very important for solving biological problems. The biologists need to know the confidence level of the resultant classes given as output by the classifiers so that they can do further analysis. Understanding the marginal differences between top predicted classes is also important in further confirming the structure class of the protein. BAYESPROT classification approach supports this type of interpretation, as it gives the probability for each class as the output. This kind of interpretation is not possible in neural networks and SVM. Neural networks contain many hidden nodes and final output is based on threshold value. In SVM, as the number of classifiers is high, reading the distances between hyper plane and the classes is very difficult.

Protein Side Chain Prediction

Side chain conformation is another protein structure analysis problem given its backbone structure. Many heuristic approaches (Desmet, Maeyer, Hazes, & Lasters, 1992) helped, but failed to predict the global minima. Recently, Yanover and Weiss (2002) have shown that predicting a minimum energy side chain is equivalent to performing inference in an undirected graphical model. The success rates of the conformations, inferred by a Bayesian-based approach, outperformed well known algorithm SCWRL's. Increasing the weight of side-chain to backbone interactions over side-chain to side-chain interactions resulted in better success rates.

Protein-Protein Interaction Analysis

Protein-protein interaction studies the interactions among proteins. Understanding the interactions provides us insight on the gene functions, facilitates the reconstruction of the normal and tumor cells signal transduction pathways. Through this process, we can expand our knowledge of genes and proteins which are associated with disease or drug response. Below, we describe methods for predicting protein-protein interactions.

Prediction of Protein-Protein Interactions

To analyze the interactions, the traditional way is to rely on X-ray crystallography to study whether two proteins can form complex. Such an approach can only study the interaction one by one. Later, scientists applied the two-hybrid system (Ito, Chiba, Ozawa, Yoshida, Hattori, & Sakaki, 2001; Uetz, Giot, Cagney, Mansfield, Judson, Knight et al., 2002) to study protein-protein interaction in high-throughput. Recently, they have also turned to high-throughput mass spectrometry (Ho, Gruhler, Heilbut, Bader, Moore, Adams et al., 2002).

Although high-throughput experimental methods are available now, they suffer from high rates of both false positives and false negatives. To confirm whether a pair of proteins can interact, we may still need to rely on X-ray crystallography. However, most of the complexes in the cell are transitional. It is difficult to get a crystallographic picture of a transitional complex. The results of in silico methods can increase our confidence on the protein-protein interaction results. Hence, in silico methods are getting more and more popular.

There are a number of computational approaches for predicting protein-protein interaction. The traditional approaches include the Rosetta stone method (Marcotte, Pelligrini, Ng, Rice, Yeates, & Eisenberg, 1999), the Phylogenetic profiling method (Pellegrini, Marcotte, Thompson, Eisenberg, & Yeates, 1999), the gene neighbor method (Overbeek, Fonstein, D'Souza, Pusch, & Maltsev, 1999), and the gene cluster method (Strong, Mallick, Pelligrini, Thompson, & Eisenberg, 2003).

The Rosetta stone method is based on the observation that a pair of proteins in some organisms are interacting when they have homolog with a fused protein in another organism. A comparison of sequence homologs from multiple organisms can reveal these fused sequences, called Rosetta stone sequences because they decipher the interactions between the protein pairs.

The phylogenetic profile method was developed by Pellegrini et al. (1999). Two proteins with similar inheritance patterns tend to be "functionally linked" and may participate in the same structural complex or biochemical pathway. In other words, two proteins are linked if they co-occur (that is, they are always both present or absent in the genome).

Gene neighbor, developed by Peer Bork of the European Molecular Biology Laboratory, Heidelberg, Germany, relies on monitoring the distance between two genes in the genomes of different organisms. If that distance is constant, the two genes may encode proteins that work together. In similar fashion the gene cluster method (Strong et al., 2003) uses the physical proximity of genes to infer functional relatedness. When two genes are encoded next to each other, they tend to be working together.

Below, we describe two advance graphical methods for predicting protein-protein interactions. One is based on Bayesian network (Jansen et al., 2003) while another one is based on the relational probabilistic model (Jaimovich, Elidan, Margalit, & Friedman, 2005).

Predicting Protein-Protein Interactions Using Bayesian Network

Recently, Jansen et al. (2003) proposed a method to predict protein-protein interactions using Bayesian networks. Their idea is to assess each source of evidence for interactions by comparing it against a good-standard positive and negative datasets, yielding a statistical reliability, and then to extrapolate the statistics to genome-wide and predict the chance of possible interactions for every protein pair by combining each independent evidence source according to its reliability.

More precisely, they proposed a Bayesian method to use the MIPS (Mewes, Frishman, Guldener, Mannhaupt, Mayer, Mokrejs et al., 2002) complex data as the gold-standard positive dataset while the lists of proteins in separate subcellular compartments (Kumar, Agarwal, Heyman, Matson, Heidtman, Piccirillo et al., 2002) as the gold-standard negative dataset. Then, for each genomic feature f, a likelihood ratio $L(f)$ is defined as the fraction of gold-standard positives having feature f divided by the fraction of negatives having feature f. The bigger the value $L(f)$ implies the more reliable the feature f in predicting the protein-protein interaction. By means of Bayesian network, the relationships among multiple features can be learned. Then, the chance that two proteins can interact can be estimated from the Bayesian network.

The next question is what types of genomic features should be included. In the paper of Jansen et al. (2003), first, they include the high-throughput experimental interaction data, which include the in-vivo pull-down data by Gavin, Bosche, Krause, Grandi, Marzioch, Bauer et al. (2002) and Ho et al. (2002) and the yeast two-hybrid data by Uetz et al. (2002) and Ito et al. (2001). Then, they observed that two proteins often have coregulated mRNA expression and similar biological functions and are more likely to be either essential or nonessential for survival. Hence, in addition to the experimental interaction data, they included two sets of mRNA expression data, two sets of information of biological function, MIPS functional annotation data, and the information about whether proteins are essential for survival.

From the gold standard dataset, Jansen et al. (2003) found that the information sources, taken alone, are only weak predictors of interactions, can yield reliable predictions when combined. This means that combining different data sources is a good approach in computational biology. Then, they perform the prediction in two settings: (a) use just the high-throughput experimental interaction data and (b) use the rest of the data. They found that the prediction sensitivity for setting (b) is better than that for setting (a) under a comparable error level. This suggests that the high-throughput experimental interaction datasets are noisy. Prediction by combining other data sources using Bayesian network can give a better result. Finally, they also check if simpler voting procedures can match the performance of more complicated machine-learning methods such as Bayesian network. Their results imply that Bayesian network can really improve the accuracy.

Therefore, combining different data sources for predicting protein-protein interaction is a promising direction. Follow-up on the work of Jansen et al. (2003) and Lin, Wu, Jansen, Gerstein, and Zhao (2004) showed that, by using multiple logistic regression or random forest to combine information, the prediction accuracy can be further improved. Moreover, we should be careful in choosing data sources. Choosing noisy data sources may reduce the prediction accuracy. For instance, Lin et al. (2004) showed that, by applying random forest and just using the information of biological function (MIPS functional annotation data and gene Ontology data), we can improve the prediction accuracy.

Predicting Protein-Protein Interaction Using the Relational Probabilistic Model

Though the previous solutions combine different data sources to predict the protein-protein interaction, they still ignore possible dependencies between different data sources. Jaimovich et al. (2005) argued that by explicitly modeling such dependencies in the model, we can leverage observations from varied sources to produce better joint predictions of the protein interaction network as a whole.

To demonstrate the idea, they gave the following example. Consider the budding yeast proteins Pre7 and Pre9. These proteins were predicted to be interacting by computational method. However, by large-scale localization assay, Pre9 is observed in the cytoplasm and in the nucleus, while Pre7 is not observed in either of those compartments. Thus, a naïve examination of this interaction might assign it a low probability. Jaimovich et al. (2005) try to gain more confidence by looking at related interactions. Note that, by experimental assays, Pre9 interacts with Pre5, while Pre7 interacts with Pup3 and Pre5. Also, by computational assay, both Pre9 and Pre7 interact with Pup3. These observations suggest that these proteins might form a complex. Moreover, both Pre5 and Pup3 were found both in the nucleus and in the cytoplasm. This implies that Pre7 might be also localized in these two compartments. Hence, it increases our belief that there exists an interaction between Pre9 and Pre7.

By the language of relational probabilistic model (Friedman, Getoor, Koller, & Pfeffer, 1999; Taskar, Pieter, Abbeel, & Koller, 2002), they explicitly define probabilistic dependencies between related protein-protein interactions and protein attributes (e.g., localization information). They apply their model on budding yeast S. cerevisiae and find that the new model improves the accuracy.

Bayesian networks can also be applied to later stages of drug discovery. Predictive toxicology is an upcoming field with huge implications on the way drugs are tested for toxicity and approved for testing in humans for clinical trials. Knowing the toxicology profile of all the different classes of compounds can be used to train decision systems to predict toxicity profile of a test compound. This application to toxicology can dramatically alter the time and accuracy of toxicology studies in the drug discovery process, thus potentially saving millions of dollars and also cutting research time drastically. Presently, the sensitivity and specificity of such tools is being tested to establish reliability criteria for decision making, and we can expect their substantial contribution in moving safer compounds quicker to the clinical trials.

Clinical Trials

Clinical trials are the last part of the drug discovery process. The objective is to study the effectiveness of a candidate drug on a sample set of population in three phases: to test safety, dosing, and efficacy of a drug.

Given the duration of the trials and the resources required to conduct them, clinical trials are the most expensive component of the discovery pipeline. A major challenge in these studies is to generalize the results from small samples to an entire population. And this is where Bayesian statistics has begun to play a very significant role in recent times (Economist.com, 2000).

There is a considerable amount of risk involved in testing different doses of a trial drug to deduce the most effective dose. This titration is done by administering different doses to different people in the earlier phases of clinical trials. An immediate application of Bayesian network is in studying the cause-effect relationship between treatment and observed outcome and using that information to modify the dose of the drug that is being administered. Being able to do so in real-time *during* the clinical trials will naturally lead to faster, cheaper trials with smaller sample size without compromising the quality and rigor of the decision-making process.

Another related application to the medical field is in disease diagnosis and prognosis. Most diseases have a multifactorial etiology. Being able to train systems on available historical data and using them for providing a weighted differential diagnosis is a promising area of research and application for Bayesian networks in clinical medicine. Much work is being done at both the extremes of the disease process, that is, in epidemiological studies and in predicting disease outcomes. In epidemiology, the role and contribution of various factors in any disease process is being studied and understood by building networks of causality. In predicting outcomes, a similar application of Bayesian statistics can make a great impact not only on the quality of healthcare delivery to individuals but also in health care management and health economics.

Conclusion

Given the complex and often parallel nature of the drug discovery and development process, the major challenges faced are in integrating and analyzing huge volumes of interdisciplinary data. Bayesian network holds promise and often solutions at every step of the process from data integration to clinical trials. Bayesian networks have several advantages: they allow for combining highly dissimilar types of data (i.e., numerical and categorical), converting them to a common probabilistic framework, without unnecessary simplification; they readily accommodate missing data; and they naturally weigh each information source according to its reliability. In contrast to "black-box" predictors, Bayesian networks are readily interpretable as they represent conditional probability relationships among information sources. Overall, the application of Bayesian networks, to the drug discovery process in particular and life sciences in general, is revolutionizing the speed, quality, and effectiveness of these sciences to bring benefit to mankind.

References

Butcher, E.C. (2005). Can cell systems biology rescue drug discovery?. *Nature Review: Drug Discovery, 4*(6), 461-467.

Chinnasamy, A., Sung, W.-K., & Mittal, A. (2004). Protein structure and fold prediction using tree-augmented Bayesian classifier. In *Proceedings of the Pacific Symposium on Biocomputing* (pp. 387-398).

Chinnasamy, A., Sung, W.-K., & Mittal, A. (2005). Protein structure and fold prediction using tree-augmented Bayesian classifier. *Journal of Bioinformatics and Computational Biology, 3*(4), 803-819.

Desmet, J., Maeyer, M.-D., Hazes, B., & Lasters, I. (1992). The dead-end elimination theorem and its use in protein side-chain positioning. *Nature, 356*, 539-542.

Ding, C.H., & Dubchak, I. (2001, April). Multi-class protein fold recognition using support vector machines and neural networks. *Bioinformatics, 17*(4), 349-58.

Economist.com, (2000). In praise of Bayes. *Economist.com.* Retrieved March 13, 2007, from http://www.economist.com/displayStory.cfm?Story_ID=382968&CFID=2426 50&CFTOKEN=90644500

Friedman, N. (2003). Probabilistic models for identifying regulation networks. *Bioinformatics, 19*(2), II57.

Friedman, N., Getoor, L., Koller, D., & Pfeffer, A. (1999). Learning probabilistic relational models. In *Proceedings of the International Joint Conference in Artificial Intelligence* (pp. 1300-1309).

Gavin, A.C., Bosche, M., Krause, R., Grandi, P., Marzioch, M., Bauer, A. et al. (2002). Functional organization of the yeast proteome by systematic analysis of protein complexes. *Nature, 415*, 141-147.

Ho, Y., Gruhler, A., Heilbut, A., Bader, G.D., Moore, L., Adams, S.L. et al. (2002). Systematic identification of protein complexes in Saccharomyces cerevisiae by mass spectrometry. *Nature, 415,* 180-193.

Husmeier, D. (2003). Sensitivity and specificity of inferring genetic regulatory interactions from microarray experiments with dynamic Bayesian networks. *Bioinformatics, 19*(17), 2271-2282.

In praise of Bayes. (2000). Science & Technology, Economist. Retrieved December 29, 2006, from http://www.economist.com/displayStory.cfm?Story_ID=382968&CFID =242650&CFTOKEN=90644500

Ito, T., Chiba, T., Ozawa, R., Yoshida, M., Hattori, M., & Sakaki, Y. (2001). A comprehensive two-hybrid analysis to explore the yeast protein interactome. In *Proceedings of the National Academy of Sciences* (vol. 64) (pp. 4569-4574), USA.

Jaimovich, A., Elidan, G., Margalit, H., & Friedman, N. (2005). Towards an Integrated Protein-Protein Interaction Network. *Research in Computational Molecular Biology*, 14-30.

Jansen, R., Yu, H., Greenbaum, D., Kluger, Y., Krogan, N. J., Chung, S. et al. (2003). A Bayesian network approach for predicting protein-protein interactions from genomic data. *Science, 302,* 449-453.

Krogh, A., Brown, M., Mian, I. S., Sjolander, K., & Haussler, D. (1994). Hidden Markov models in computational biology: Applications to protein modeling. *Journal of Molecular Biology, 235,* 1501-1531.

Kumar, A., Agarwal, S., Heyman, J.A., Matson, S., Heidtman, M., Piccirillo, S. et al. (2002). Subcellular localization of the yeast proteome. *Genes and Development, 16,* 707-719.

Lin, N., Wu, B., Jansen, R., Gerstein, M., & Zhao, H. (2004). Information assessment on predicting protein-protein interactions. *BMC Bioinformatics, 5,* 154.

Marcotte, E.M., Pellegrini, M., Ng, H.-L, Rice, D.W., Yeates, T., & Eisenberg, D. (1999). Detecting Protein Function and Protein-Protein Interactions from Genome Sequences. *Science, 285,* 751-753.

Mewes, H.W., Frishman, D., Guldener, U., Mannhaupt, G., Mayer, K., Mokrejs, M. et al. (2002). MIPS: A database for genomes and protein sequences. *Nucleic Acids Research, 30,* 31-34.

Overbeek, R., Fonstein, M., D'Souza, M., Pusch, G.D., & Maltsev, N. (1999). The use of gene clusters to infer functional coupling. In *Proceedings of the National Academy of Sciences* (vol. 96) (pp. 2896-2901).

Pavlovic, V., Garg, A., & Kasif, S., (2002). A Bayesian framework for combining gene predictions. *Bioinformatics, 18*(1) 19-27.

Pellegrini, M., Marcotte, E.M., Thompson, M.J., Eisenberg, D., & Yeates, T.O. (1999). Assigning protein functions by comparative genome analysis: Protein phylogenetic profiles. In *Proceedings of the National Academy of Sciences* (vol. 96) (pp. 4285-4288).

Reichert, J.-M. (2003). Trends in development and approval times for new therapeutics in the United States. *Nature Review: Drug Discovery, 2*(9), 695-702.

Sachs, K., Perez, O., Pe'er, D., Lauffenburger, D.A., & Nolan, G.P. (2005). Causal protein-signaling networks derived from multiparameter single-cell data. *Science, 308*(5721), 523-529.

Stein, L.D. (2003). Integrating biological databases. *Nature Review genetics*, *4*(5), 337-45.

Strong, M., Mallick, P., Pellegrini, M., Thompson, M.J., & Eisenberg, D. (2003). Inference of protein function and protein linkages in Mycobacterium tuberculosis based on prokaryotic genome organization: A combined computational approach. *Genome Biology, 4*, R59.

Taskar, B., Pieter, A., & Koller, D. (2002). Discriminative probabilistic models for relational data. In *Proceedings of Uncertainty in Artificial Intelligence* (pp. 485-492).

Uetz, P., Giot, L., Cagney, G., Mansfield, T.A., Judson, R.S., Knight, J.R. et al. (2002). In D. Eisenberg, DIP: The Database of Interacting Proteins: A research tool for studying cellular networks of protein interactions. *Nucleic Acids Research, 30*, 303-305.

Yanover, C., & Weiss, Y. (2002). Approximate Inference and Protein Folding. *Neural Information Processing Systems, 15*, 1457-1464.

Chapter XIII

Bayesian Network Approach to Estimate Gene Networks

Seiya Imoto, University of Tokyo, Japan

Satoru Miyano, University of Tokyo, Japan

Abstract

In cells, genes interact with each other and this system can be viewed as directed graphs. A gene network is a graphical representation of transcriptional relations between genes and the problem of estimation of gene networks from genome-wide data, such as DNA microarray gene expression data, is one of the important issues in bioinformatics and systems biology. Here, we present a statistical method based on Bayesian networks to estimate gene networks from microarray data and other biological data. Because microarray data are measured as continuous variables and the relationship between genes are usually nonlinear, we combine Bayesian networks and nonparametric regression to handle continuous variables and nonlinear relations. Most parts of gene networks are still unknown, and we need to estimate them from observational data. This problem is equivalent to the structural learning of Bayesian networks, and we solve it from a Bayes approach. The main difficulty of gene network estimation is due to the number of genes involved in the network. Therefore, it leads to model overfitting to the observational data like microarray data. Hence, a combination of various kinds of biological data is a key technique to estimate accurate gene networks. We show a general framework to combine microarray data and other biological information to estimate gene networks.

Introduction

The microarray technology has produced a huge amount of gene expression data under various conditions such as gene knock-down, overexpression, experimental stressors, transformation, exposure to a chemical compound, and so forth. Along with this new data production, there have been considerable attempts to infer gene networks from such gene expression profile data, and several computational methods have been proposed together with gene network models such as Boolean networks, differential equation models, and Bayesian networks.

A Bayesian network is an effective method in modeling phenomena through the joint distribution of a large number of random variables. In recent years, some interesting works have been established in constructing gene networks from microarray gene expression data by using Bayesian networks. Friedman and Goldszmidt (1998) discretized the expression values and assumed multinomial distributions as the candidate statistical models. Pe'er, Regev, Elidan, and Friedman (2001) investigated the threshold value for discretizing. On the other hand, Friedman, Linial, Nachman, and Pe'er (2000) pointed out that the discretizing probably loses information of the data. In addition, the number of discretizing values and the thresholds are unknown parameters, which have to be estimated from the data. The resulted network strongly depends on their values. Then Friedman et al. (2000) considered fitting linear regression models, which analyze the data in the continuous variables (see also Heckerman & Geiger, 1995). However, the assumption that the parent genes depend linearly on the objective gene is not always guaranteed. Imoto et al. (2002) proposed the use of nonparametric additive regression models (see also Green & Silvermn, 1994; Hastie & Tibshirani, 1990) for capturing not only linear dependencies but also nonlinear structures between genes. In this chapter, we introduce a method for constructing the gene network by using Bayesian networks and the nonparametric regression, which is more suitable for estimating gene networks from microarray gene expression data than discrete type Bayesian networks.

Once we set the graph, we have to evaluate its goodness or closeness to the true graph, which is usually unknown. Hence, the construction of a suitable criterion becomes the center of attention of statistical genetic network modeling. Friedman and Goldszmidt (1998), used the BDe criterion, which was originally derived by Cooper and Herskovits (1992) for choosing a graph (see also Heckerman, Geiger, & Chickering, 1995). The BDe criterion only evaluates the Bayesian network model based on the multinomial distributions and Dirichlet priors. However, Friedman and Goldszmidt (1998) kept the unknown hyperparameters in Dirichlet priors and we only set up the values experimentally. We investigate the graph selection problem as a statistical model selection or evaluation problem and theoretically derive a new criterion for choosing a graph using the Bayes approach (see Berger, 1985). The proposed criterion automatically optimizes all parameters in the model and gives the optimal graph when we can score all candidate graphs.

The problem of finding an optimal Bayesian network is known to be NP-hard. The brute force method employing all computing resources in the world would even require time exceeding the lifetime of the solar system for finding an optimal Bayesian network of 30 genes from 100 microarray datasets. Our approach has made it possible to find optimal and near optimal Bayesian networks with respect to the score of the network in a reasonable time and has provided an evidence of the biological rationality in this computational approach (Ott & Miyano, 2003; Ott, Imoto, & Miyano, 2004; Ott, Hansen, Kim, & Miyano, 2005). For larger networks, we carefully employ the greedy hill-climbing algorithm for finding better gene networks.

The main drawback for the gene network construction from microarray data is that, while the gene network contains a large number of genes, the information contained in gene expression data is limited by the number of microarrays, their quality, the experimental design, noise, and measurement errors. Therefore, estimated gene networks contain some incorrect gene regulations, which cannot be evaluated from a biological viewpoint. In particular, it is difficult to determine the direction of gene regulation using gene expression data only. Hence, the use of biological knowledge, including protein-protein and protein-DNA interactions (Bader, Donaldson, Wolting, Ouellette, Pawson, & Hogue, 2001; Ideker, Ozier, Schwikowski, & Siegel, 2002; Ito, Chiba, Ozawa, Yoshida, Hattori, & Sakaki, 2001) sequences of the binding site of the genes controlled by transcription regulators (Lee, Rinaldi, Robert, Odom, Bar-Joseph, Gerber et al., 2002), literature, and so forth, are considered to be a key for microarray data analysis. The use of biological knowledge has previously received considerable attention for extracting more information from microarray data (Bannai, Inenaga, Shinohara, Takeda, & Miyano, 2002; Bussemaker, Li, & Siggia, 2001; Hartemink, Gifford, Jaakkola, & Young, 2002; Masys, 2001; Ong, Glasner, & Page, 2002; Pilpel, Sudarsanam, & Church, 2001; Segal, Barash, Simon, Friedman, & Koller, 2002; Segal et al., 2003a, Segal et al., 2003b). In this chapter, we also provide a general framework for combining microarray data and biological knowledge aimed at estimating a gene network by using a Bayesian network model.

We show the effectiveness of our approach by the analysis of *Saccharomyces cerevisiae* gene expression data obtained by singly disrupting 100 genes, which are almost all transcription factors together with binding site information. We also apply the method to the estimation of human endothelial cell gene networks by using 270 novel gene knock-downs and time-course of gene expression following treatment with the drug fenofibrate.

Modeling of Gene Networks

In gene network estimation, we regard a gene as a random variable representing the abundance of a specific RNA species, shown as a node in a graph, and the interaction between genes is represented by the direct edge between nodes. In this section, we show our basic model for constructing gene networks from microarray gene expression data. More precisely, we introduce a combination of Bayesian network and nonparametric regression to model gene networks.

Bayesian Networks with Continuous Variables

Suppose that $\{X_1, ..., X_p\}$ is the set of p random variables, and that the dependency among these p random variables is shown as a directed graph G. When the random variables X_j

take discrete values, we can decompose the joint probability of $\{X_1, ..., X_p\}$ into the product of conditional probabilities as:

$$\Pr(X_1, ..., X_p) = \prod_{j=1}^{p} \Pr(X_j | Pa(X_j)) \tag{1}$$

where $Pa(X_j)$ is the set of random variables corresponding to the direct parents of X_j in G. Because gene expression data take continuous variables, some discretization methods are required for using the Bayesian networks based on the discrete random variables described above. However, the discretization lead to information loss, and the number of categories and the threshold values are parameters to be optimized. To avoid the discretization, we rewrite the decomposition of joint probability given in (1) by using densities.

Suppose that we have the observational data $X = (x_1, ..., x_n)'$ of the set of p random variables $\{X_1, ..., X_p\}$, where $x_i = (x_{i1}, ..., x_{ip})'$ and x_{ij} is the gene expression value of jth gene from ith microarray. That is, we measure p genes' expression values by n microarrays. We then rewrite the decomposition (1) by:

$$f(X | \Theta, G) = \prod_{i=1}^{n} \prod_{j=1}^{p} f_j(x_{ij} | pa_{ij}, \theta_j) \tag{2}$$

where $\Theta = (\theta'_1, ..., \theta'_p)'$ is a parameter vector, and pa_{ij} is the expression value vector of $Pa(X_j)$ measured by ith microarray. Hence, the construction of the graph G is equivalent to model the conditional probabilities f_j ($j = 1, ..., p$), that is essentially the same as the regression problem. A possible and simple solution of the construction of conditional density is given by using the linear regression as:

$$x_{ij} = \beta_0 + \beta_1 p_{i,1}^{(j)} + \cdots + \beta_{q_j} p_{i,q_j}^{(j)} + \varepsilon_{ij}$$

where β_j ($j = 1, ..., q_j$) are parameters, ε_{ij} ($i = 1, ..., n$) are independently and normally distributed with mean 0 and variance σ_j^2, and $pa_{ij} = (p_{i,1}^{(j)}, ..., p_{i,q_j}^{(j)})'$ with $q_j = |Pa(X_j)|$. This model assumes the relationships between genes are linear, and it is unsuitable to extract effective information from the data with complex structure. Also, the assumption that the parent genes depend linearly on the objective gene is not always guaranteed. To capture even nonlinear dependencies, (Imoto, Goto, & Miyano, 2002) proposed the use of the nonparametric additive regression model (Hastie & Tibshirani, 1990) of the form:

$$x_{ij} = m_{j1}(p_{i,1}^{(j)}) + \cdots + m_{jq_j}(p_{i,q_j}^{(j)}) + \varepsilon_{ij} \tag{3}$$

where $m_{jk}(\cdot)(k = 1, ..., q_j)$ are smooth functions from $\Re$ to $\Re$. We construct $m_{jk}(\cdot)$ by the basis function expansion method with B-splines (De Boor, 1978; Imoto et al., 2003):

$$m_{jk}(p) = \sum_{s=1}^{M_{jk}} \gamma_{sk}^{(j)} b_{sk}^{(j)}(p)$$

where $\gamma_{sk}^{(j)}$ $(s=1,...,M_{jk})$ are parameters, $\{b_{1k}^{(j)}(\cdot),...,b_{M_{jk}k}^{(j)}(\cdot)\}$ is the prescribed set of B-splines, and M_{jk} is the number of B-splines. We then have the Bayesian network and nonparametric regression model:

$$f_j(x_{ij} \mid pa_{ij}, \theta_j) = \frac{1}{\sqrt{2\pi\sigma_j^2}} \exp\left[-\frac{\{x_{ij} - \sum_k \sum_s \gamma_{sk}^{(j)} b_{sk}^{(j)}(p_{ik}^{(j)})\}^2}{2\sigma_j^2}\right]$$

Note that the Bayesian network model based on the linear regression is included in this model as a special case. To extend from the additive regression model to a general regression, (Imoto, Higuchi, Kim, Jeong, & Miyano, 2005) proposed a Bayesian network with moving boxcel median filtering to capture such interactions.

Information Criterion for Structural Learning

Once we set a graph, the statistical model based on the Bayesian network and nonparametric regression can be constructed and estimated by a suitable procedure. However, the problem that still remains to be solved is how we can choose the optimal graph which gives a best approximation of the system underlying the data. Notice that we cannot use the likelihood function as a model selection criterion, because the value of likelihood becomes large in a more complicated model. Hence, we need to consider the statistical approach based on the generalized or predictive error, Kullback-Leibler information, Bayes approach, and so forth (see e.g., Akaike, 1973; Burnham & Anderson 1998; Konishi, 1996; Konishi & Kitagawa, 1996, for the statistical model selection problem). In this section, we construct a criterion for evaluating a graph based on our model from Bayes approach.

The posterior probability of the graph $p(G \mid X)$ is given by:

$$p(G \mid X) = \frac{p(G)p(X \mid G)}{p(X)} \propto p(G)p(X \mid G)$$

where $p(G)$ is the prior probability of the graph, $p(X \mid G)$ is the likelihood of the data X conditional on G, and $p(X)$ is the normalizing constant and does not depend on the selection of G. The likelihood $p(X \mid G)$ is computed by the marginization:

$$p(X \mid G) = \int f(X \mid \Theta, G)\, p(\Theta \mid \lambda, G)\, d\Theta \tag{4}$$

where $p(\boldsymbol{\Theta} \mid \lambda, G)$ is the prior distribution on the parameter $\boldsymbol{\Theta}$ specified by the hyperparameter λ. We now suppose the decomposition:

$$p(\boldsymbol{\Theta} \mid \lambda, G) \prod_{j=1}^{p} p_j(\theta_j \mid \lambda_j)$$

We also assume that the prior distribution on the parameter vector θ_j is decomposed as:

$$p_j(\theta_j \mid \lambda_j) = \prod_{k=1}^{q_j} p_{jk}(\gamma_{jk} \mid \lambda_{jk})$$

with $\gamma_{jk} = (\gamma_{1k}^{(j)}, ..., \gamma_{M_{jk}k}^{(j)})'$. Each prior distribution $p_{jk}(\gamma_{jk} \mid \lambda_{jk})$ is a singular M_{jk} variate normal distribution given by:

$$p_{jk}(\gamma_{jk} \mid \lambda_{jk}) = \left(\frac{2\pi}{n\lambda_{jk}}\right)^{-(M_{jk}-2)/2} |K_{jk}|_+^{1/2} \exp\left(-\frac{n\lambda_{jk}}{2} \gamma'_{jk} K_{jk} \gamma_{jk}\right) \tag{5}$$

where λ_{jk} is a hyper parameter, K_{jk} is an $M_{jk} \times M_{jk}$ matrix that holds:

$$\gamma'_{jk} K_{jk} \gamma_{jk} = \sum_{l=3}^{M_{jk}} (\gamma_{lk}^{(j)} - 2\gamma_{l-1k}^{(j)} + 2\gamma_{l-2k}^{(j)})^2$$

and $|K_{jk}|_+$ is the product of $M_{jk}-2$ nonzero eigenvalues of K_{jk}. Under the decomposition of the prior of parameters $p(\boldsymbol{\Theta} \mid \lambda, G)$ and the decomposition of the joint density by the Bayesian network given in (2), the marginal likelihood (4) can be rewritten as:

$$p(\boldsymbol{X} \mid G) = \int f(\boldsymbol{X} \mid \boldsymbol{\Theta}, G) p(\boldsymbol{\Theta} \mid \lambda, G) d\boldsymbol{\Theta} = \prod_{j=1}^{p}\left\{\prod_{i=1}^{n} f(x_{ij} \mid \boldsymbol{pa}_{ij}, \theta_j) \, p_j(\theta_j \mid \lambda_j) d\theta_j\right\}$$

$$\equiv \prod_{j=1}^{p} p_j(\text{sub}.G_j \mid \boldsymbol{X}),$$

where sub.G_j is a subgraph of G consisting of jth gene and its direct parents as the node and edges from these parents to jth gene.

The high-dimensional integral in $p_j(\text{sub}.G_j \mid \boldsymbol{X})$ can be asymptotically approximated with an analytical form by the Laplace approximation:

$$p_j(\text{sub.}G_j \mid X) = \int \exp\{nl_\lambda(\theta_j \mid X)\} d\theta_j \tag{6}$$

$$= \frac{(2\pi/n)^{r_j/2}}{\left| J_\lambda(\hat{\theta}_j) \right|^{1/2}} \exp\{nl_\lambda(\hat{\theta}_j \mid X)\} \{1 + O_p(n^{-1})\}$$

where r_j is the dimension of θ_j,

$$l_\lambda(\theta_j \mid X) = \frac{1}{n} \sum_{i=1}^{n} \log f_j(x_{ij} \mid pa_{ij}, \theta_j) + \frac{1}{n} \log p_j(\theta_j \mid \lambda_j),$$

$$J_\lambda(\theta_j) = -\frac{\partial l_\lambda(\theta_j \mid X)}{\partial \theta_j \, \partial \theta_j'}$$

and $\hat{\theta}_j$ is the mode of $l_\lambda(\theta_j \mid X)$. We also decompose the prior probability of the graph $p(G)$ as $\prod_j p(\text{sub.}G_j)$. By taking minus twice logarithm of $p(\text{sub.}G_j) \times$ (6), we then define:

$$\mathbf{BNRC}_j = -2 \log p(\text{sub.}G_j) - r_j \log(2\pi/n) + \log|J_\lambda(\hat{\theta}_j)| - 2nl_\lambda(\hat{\theta}_j \mid X)$$

$$= 2(q_j - 1) - \left(\sum_{k=1}^{q_j} M_{jk} + 1 \right) \log\left(\frac{2\pi}{n} \right) + n \log(2\pi \hat{\sigma}_j^2) + n$$

$$+ \sum_{k=1}^{q_j} \{\log|\Lambda_{jk}| - M_{jk} \log(n\hat{\sigma}_j^2)\} - \log(2\hat{\sigma}_j^2)$$

$$+ \sum_{k=1}^{q_j} \left\{ (M_{jk} - 2) \log\left(\frac{2\pi \hat{\sigma}_j^2}{n\beta_{jk}} \right) - \log|K_{jk}| + \frac{n\beta_{jk}}{\hat{\sigma}_j^2} \hat{\gamma}'_{jk} K_{jk} \hat{\gamma}_{jk} \right\}$$

with

$$\Lambda_{jk} = B'_{jk} B_{jk} + n\beta_{jk} K_{jk}, \qquad \beta_{jk} = \hat{\sigma}_j^2 \lambda_{jk},$$

$$B_{jk} = (b_{jk}(p_{1k}^{(j)}), ..., b_{jk}(p_{nk}^{(j)}))',$$

$$b_{jk}(p_{ik}^{(j)}) = (b_{1k}^{(j)}(p_{ik}^{(j)}), ..., b_{M_{jk}k}^{(j)}(p_{ik}^{(j)}))',$$

$$\hat{\sigma}_j^2 = \frac{1}{n} \sum_{i=1}^{n} \left\{ x_{ij} - \sum_{k=1}^{q_j} \hat{\gamma}'_{jk} b_{jk}(p_{ik}^{(j)}) \right\}^2.$$

Here we approximate the Hessian matrix by:

$$l_\lambda(\boldsymbol{\theta}_j | X) = \frac{1}{n} \sum_{i=1}^{n} \log f_j(x_{ij} | \boldsymbol{pa}_{ij}, \boldsymbol{\theta}_j) + \frac{1}{n} \log p_j(\boldsymbol{\theta}_j | \lambda_j),$$

$$\log|J_\lambda(\hat{\boldsymbol{\theta}}_j)| \approx \sum_{k=1}^{q_j} \log\left| -\frac{\partial^2 l_\lambda(\hat{\boldsymbol{\theta}}_j | X)}{\partial \gamma_{jk} \partial \gamma'_{jk}} \right| + \log\left| -\frac{\partial^2 l_\lambda(\hat{\boldsymbol{\theta}}_j | X)}{\partial (\sigma_j^2)^2} \right|$$

Then, we define an information criterion, named BNRC, for the Bayesian network and nonparametric regression model in order to select a graph structure:

$$\mathrm{BNRC}(G) = \sum_{j=1}^{p} \mathrm{BNRC}_j$$

The optimal graph is chosen such that the criterion BNRC is minimal.

Algorithms

Learning Parameters

Consider the nonparametric regression model defined in (3). The estimate $\hat{\boldsymbol{\theta}}_j$ is a mode of $l_\lambda(\boldsymbol{\theta}_j | X)$ and depends on the hyperparameters. In fact, the hyperparameter plays an essential role in estimating the smoothed curve.

In our model, we construct the nonparametric regression model by 20 B-splines. We confirmed that the differences of the smoothed estimates against the various number of the basis functions cannot be found visually. Because when we use a somewhat large number of the basis functions, the hyperparameters control the smoothness of the fitted curves. The algorithm for obtaining $\hat{\boldsymbol{\theta}}_j$ and selection of β_{jk} is summarized as follows:

Step 1: Set j and initialize: $\gamma_{jk} = \boldsymbol{0}(k = 1, ..., q_j)$.
Step 2: Set k and find the optimal β_{jk} by repeating the following steps:

    A. Compute:

$$\gamma_{jk} = (\boldsymbol{B}'_{jk} \boldsymbol{B}_{jk} + n\beta_{jk} \boldsymbol{K}_{jk})^{-1} \boldsymbol{B}'_{jk}(\boldsymbol{x}_{(j)} - \sum_{k' \neq k} \boldsymbol{B}_{jk'} \gamma_{jk'}),$$

    for fixed β_{jk}. Here $\boldsymbol{x}_{(j)} = (x_{1j}, ..., x_{nj})'$
    B. Evaluate: Repeat Step 2-A against the candidate value of β_{jk}, and choose the optimal value of β_{jk}, which minimizes the BNRC_j.

Step 3: Convergence: Repeat Step 2 for $k = 1, ..., q_j, 1, ..., q_j, 1,...$ until a suitable convergence criterion is satisfied.

The mode $\hat{\sigma}_j^2$ is given by:

$$\hat{\sigma}_j^2 = \frac{1}{n} \left\| x_{(j)} - \sum_{k=1}^{q_j} B_{jk} \hat{\gamma}_{jk} \right\|^2$$

Learning Graph Structure

Finding optimal Bayesian networks is computationally hard. Potentially, we need to search the space of directed acyclic graphs of p vertices whose size c_p is approximately:

$$c_p = \frac{p! \times 2^{p(p-1)/2}}{r \times z^p}$$

where $r \sim 0.57436$ and $z \sim 1.17881$ (Robinson, 1973). From this formula we can see that there are roughly 2.34×10^{72} networks with 20 vertices and 2.71×10^{158} for 30 vertices. This complexity does not allow us any brute force approach even with a supercomputer system. Furthermore, without obtaining the optimal Bayesian networks, we cannot have any right insight that the Bayesian network model can really extract biologically meaningful regulatory information from microarray gene expression data. Thus, we are faced with two issues. The first issue is how to cope with this complexity and the second is the search for optimal Bayesian networks and their biological evaluation.

Greedy Heuristics for Searching Bayesian Networks

Some heuristic approaches have been employed for this search problem, for example, greedy algorithms (Friedman et al., 2000; Heckerman et al., 1995; Imoto et al., 2002), simulated annealing (Hartemink et al., 2002), and genetic algorithms (Somereren et al., 2002).

The greedy hill-climbing algorithm due to Heckerman et al. (1995) is shown below as a typical example, where n is the number of repeats. The greedy hill-climbing algorithm assumes a score function for solutions. It starts from some initial solution and successively improves the solution by selecting the modification from the space of possible modifications which yields the best score. When no improvement is found, then the algorithm terminates with the currently best solution. Some ideas should be employed for the choice of the initial solution and for the choice of the space of possible modifications. Biologically reasonable locally optimal Bayesian networks of several hundred genes are reported (Imoto et al., 2002; Imoto et al., 2003; Nariai, Kim, Imoto, & Miyano, 2004; Tamada, Kim, Bannai, Imoto, Tashiro, Kuhara, & Miyano, 2003). The following algorithm is a greedy hill-climbing algorithm provided by Heckerman et al. (1995):

Step 1: Initialize the network as the empty network.

Step 2: Randomly select a permutation π: $\{1, ..., |X|\} \rightarrow X$, where X is the set of vertices.

Step 3: For all $i = 1, ..., p$ do the following two steps:

    A. Compute the changes of the score when adding a new parent for $\pi(i)$ or removing or reversing the edge of a parent gene of $\pi(i)$.

    B. Select the modification among the modifications which improve the score most without violating the acyclicity condition.

Step 4: Repeat Step 3 until their score does not improve.

Step 5: Repeat Steps 1 through Step 4 for T times and return the best solution found in these iterations.

Search Algorithm for Optimal Bayesian Networks

BNRC score can be decomposed to an additive form $\mathrm{BNRC}(G) = \sum_{j=1}^{p} \mathrm{BNRC}_j$ as shown in Section 2.2. We will formulate this optimization problem in an abstract way: For a finite set X (of genes), we call a function $s: X \times 2^X \rightarrow R$ a score function for X. Then for a DAG $G = (X, E)$ we define the score of X by $\mathrm{score}(G) = \Sigma_{g \in X} s(g, Pa(g))$. The problem is to find the best network $G = (X, E)$ which attains the optimal score. In the case of the BNRC score, the problem is defined as a minimization problem. Furthermore, it is noted in Ott et al. (2004) that the case for the MDL score (Friedman & Goldszmidt, 1998) is also formulated as a minimization problem while the case for the BDe score (Cooper & Herskovits, 1992; Friedman & Goldszmidt, 1998; Heckerman et al., 1995) is defined as a maximization problem.

Ott et al. (2004), have devised an algorithm which can find optimal Bayesian networks of size up to 35 if a supercomputer such as SUN FIRE 15K with 96CPUs 900MHz each is used. The algorithm decomposes the search space into subspaces and employs the dynamic programming technique for finding the right subspace as well as for determining the optimal solution in the subspace. In order to describe the algorithm, several notations shall be introduced as follows: For a gene g in X and a subset $A \subseteq X$:

$$F(g, A) = \min_{B \subseteq A} s(g, B)$$

gives the optimal choice of parents for g if the parents are selected from A. An order on a subset $A \subseteq X$ is given as a permutation π: $\{1, ..., |A|\} \rightarrow A$. We denote by Π^A the set of all permutations on A. We denote the subnetwork of $G = (X, E)$, restricted to A by $G(A) = (A, E(A))$. For a permutation $\pi \in \Pi^A$, we say that G is π-*linear* if $\pi^{-1}(g) < \pi^{-1}(h)$ holds for all $(g, h) \in E(A)$. The idea of the algorithm is to decompose the set of all DAGs on A into subsets of π-linear DAGs for all $\pi \in \Pi^A$. Then, we divide the problem into (i) to find the subspace of the search space that contains the optimal network and (ii) to find the optimal network within the selected subspace. We denote:

$$Q^A(\pi) = \sum_{g \in A} F(g, \{h \in A \mid \pi^{-1}(h) < \pi^{-1}(g)\})$$

Then we find the best π-linear network for any given permutation by F and Q. The optimal network can be found by finding the optimal permutation which yields the global minimum, which is given by:

$$M(A) = \arg\max_{\pi \in \Pi^A} Q^A(\pi)$$

Then, the whole algorithm derived in Ott et al. (2004) is described as follows:

Step 1: Compute $F(g, \phi) = s(g, \phi)$ for all $g \in X$.

Step 2: For all $g \in X$ and all $A \subseteq X - \{g\}$ with $A \neq \phi$, compute $F(g, A)$ as

$$\min\{s(g, A), \min_{a \in A} F(g, A - \{a\})\}$$

Step 3: Set $M(\phi) = \phi$.

Step 4: For all $A \subseteq X$ with $A \neq \phi$, execute the following steps:

  A. Compute

$$g^* = \arg\max_{g \in A}\{F(g, A - \{g\}) + Q^{A-\{g\}}(M(A - \{g\}))\}$$

  B. For all $1 \leq i \leq |A|$, set $M(A)(i) \equiv M(A - \{g^*\})(i)$ and $M(A)(|A|) \equiv g^*$.

Step 5: Return $Q^G(M(G))$.

Here we have the following theorem:

Theorem (Ott et al., 2004)

Optimal Bayesian networks can be found using $(|X| / 2 + 1) \times 2^{|X|}$ dynamic programming steps, where X is a set of genes.

A rigorous proof is required to show the correctness of this algorithm that can be found in Ott et al. (2004). Furthermore, with some biologically reasonable constraints on the networks, we can obtain a much faster algorithm (Ott & Miyano, 2003). By computing optimal Bayesian networks of small size and evaluating them, it is reported that optimal Bayesian networks are not necessarily biologically optimal. However, by combining optimal to near optimal Bayesian networks thoroughly, we can extract biologically more accurate information from microarray gene expression data (Ott & Miyano, 2003; Ott et al., 2004; Ott et al., 2005).

Combining Biological Knowledge with Microarray Data

Discrete Information

The criterion BNRC(G), introduced in Section 2.2, contains two quantities: the prior probability $p(G)$ of the network, and the marginal likelihood of the data. The marginal likelihood shows the fitness of the model to the microarray data. The biological knowledge can then be added into the prior probability of the network $p(G)$. Let U_{ij} be the interaction energy of the edge from gene$_i$ to gene$_j$ and let U_{ij} be categorized into I values, H_1, ..., H_I, based on biological knowledge. For example, if we know a priori that gene$_i$ regulates gene$_j$, we set $U_{ij} = H_1$. However, if we do not know whether gene$_k$ regulates gene$_l$ or not, we set $U_{kl} = H_2$. We treat the prior information of each edge independently. Note that in $0 < H_1 < H_2$, it is more natural to choose the network with a large number of H_1 edges rather than H_2 edges in the sense of prior information. Our setting, $H_1 < H_2$, gives a higher prior probability to the graph with a lot of H_1 edges than to the graph with a lot of H_2 edges.

The total energy of the network G can then be defined as:

$$E(G) = \sum_{\{i,j\} \in G} U_{ij}$$

where the sum is taken over the existing edges in the network G. Under the Bayesian network framework, the total energy can be decomposed into the sum of the local energies:

$$E(G) = \sum_{j=1}^{p} \sum_{i \in L_j} U_{ij} = \sum_{j=1}^{p} E_j \tag{7}$$

where L_j is the index set of parents of gene$_j$ and $E_j = \Sigma_{i \in L_j} U_{ij}$ is the local energy defined by gene$_j$ and its parents.

The probability of a network G, $p(G)$, is modeled by the Gibbs distribution (Geman & Geman, 1984):

$$p(G) = Z^{-1} \exp\{-\zeta E(G)\}, \tag{8}$$

where $\zeta (> 0)$ is a hyperparameter and Z is a normalizing constant called the partition function

$$Z = \sum_{G} \exp\{-\zeta E(G)\}$$

Here the sum is taken over the set of possible networks. By replacing ζH_1, ..., ζH_l with ζ_1, ..., ζ_p, respectively, the normalizing constant Z is a function of ζ_1, ..., ζ_l. We call ζ_j an inverse normalized temperature. By substituting (7) into (8), we have:

$$p(G) = Z^{-1} \exp\{-\zeta E_j\} = Z^{-1} \prod_{j=1}^{p} \prod_{i \in L_j} \exp\{-\zeta_{\alpha(i,j)}\}$$

with $\alpha(i,j) = k$ for $U_{ij} = H_k$. Hence, by adding biological knowledge into the prior probability of the network, BNRC can be rewritten as:

$$\mathrm{BNRC}(G, \zeta_1, ..., \zeta_l) = 2\log Z + \sum_{j=1}^{p} \left\{ 2\sum_{i \in Lj} \zeta_{\alpha(i,j)} + \mathrm{BNRC}_j \right\} \qquad (9)$$

We can choose an optimal network under the given ζ_1, ..., ζ_l. Also the optimal values of ζ_1, ..., ζ_l are obtained as the minimizer of (9). Therefore, we can represent an algorithm for estimating a gene network from microarray data and biological knowledge as follows:

Step 1: Set the values ζ_1, ..., ζ_l.

Step 2: Estimate a gene network by minimizing BNRC(G) under the given ζ_1, ..., ζ_l.

Step 3: Repeat Step 1 and Step 2 against the candidate values of ζ_1, ..., ζ_l.

Step 4: An optimal gene network is obtained from the candidate networks obtained in Step 3.

In Step 2, we use the greedy hill-climbing algorithm for learning networks.

The computation of normalizing constant, Z, is intractable even for moderately sized gene networks. To avoid this problem, we compute upper and lower bounds of the partial function and use them to choose the optimal value of inverse normalized temperature. An upper bound is obtained by directed graphs that are allowed to contain cyclic graphs. The number of graphs that has b_1, b_2, ..., b_l edges of ζ_1, ζ_2, ..., ζ_l out of a_1, a_2, ..., a_l edges, respectively, is obtained by:

$$S(b_1, ..., b_l) = \prod_{i=1}^{l} \frac{a_i!}{b_i!(a_i - b_i)!}$$

The upper bound of Z is then:

$$\sum_{b_1, ..., b_l} S(b_1, ..., b_l) \exp\left(-\sum_{i=l}^{l} b_i \zeta_i \right)$$

Thus, the true value of the partition function is not greater than the upper bound. A lower bound is computed by multilevel directed graphs with following assumptions: (A1) There is one top gene and (A2) Genes at the same level have a common direct parent gene. We also consider joined graphs of some multilevel directed graphs satisfying (A1) and (A2). Because the number of possible graphs is much larger than those included in the computation, the true value of the partition function should be greater than the lower bound. Because the optimization of the network structure for fixed $\zeta_1, ..., \zeta_l$ does not depend on the value of the partition function, our method works well in practice. Of course, when the number of genes is small, we can perform an exhaustive search and compute the partition function completely. However, we think that the development of an effective algorithm to enumerate all possible networks or approximate the partition function is an important problem.

As a related work, Segal et al. (2003a) proposed an interesting method for combining protein-protein interaction data with microarray gene expression data. They modeled protein-protein interaction data based on Markov networks (Kindeman & Snell, 1980) and considered the joint probability of microarray data and protein-protein data for estimating molecular pathways. Although our model is different from their model, their model contains a hyperparameter, denoted by α, that plays a quite similar role of ζ_1 and ζ_2. Similar to our criterion, their joint probability contains the normalizing constant, which is a function of the hyperparameter, α. While we optimize the hyperparameters by our criterion, they did not compute the normalizing constant and chose the value of α heuristically.

Discrete and Continuous Information

Imoto, Higuchi, Goto, Tashiro, Kuhara, and Miyano (2004), proposed a general framework for combining biological knowledge with expression data aimed at estimating more accurate gene networks. In Imoto et al. (2004), the biological knowledge is represented as the binary values, for example, known or unknown, and is used for constructing $p(G)$. In reality, there are, however, various confidence in biological knowledge in practice. Bernard and Hartemink (2005) constructed $p(G)$ using the binding location data (Lee et al., 2002) that is a collection of p-values (continuous information). In this section, we construct $p(G)$ by using multisource information including continuous and discrete prior information.

Let Z_k be the matrix representation of k-th prior information, where (i, j)-th element $z_{ij}^{(k)}$ represents the information of gene$_i \rightarrow$ gene$_j$. For example, (1) If we use a prior network G_{prior} for Z_k, $z_{ij}^{(k)}$ takes 1 if $e(i, j) \in G_{prior}$ or 0 for otherwise. Here $e(i, j)$ denotes the direct edge from gene$_i$ to gene$_j$. (2) By using the gene knock-down data for Z_k, $z_{ij}^{(k)}$ represents the value that indicates how gene$_j$ changes by knocking down gene$_i$. We can use the absolute value of the log-ratio of gene$_j$ for gene$_i$ knock-down data as $z_{ij}^{(k)}$. Using the adjacent matrix $E = (e_{ij})_{1 \le i, j \le p}$ of G, where $e_{ij} = 1$ for $e(i, j) \in G$ or 0 for otherwise, we assume the Bernoulli distribution on e_{ij} having probabilistic function:

$$p(e_{ij}) = \pi_{ij}^{e_{ij}} (1 - \pi_{ij})^{e_{ij}}$$

where $\pi_{ij} = \Pr(e_{ij} = 1)$ For constructing π_{ij}, we use the logistic model with linear predictor

$$\eta_{ij} = \sum_{k=1}^{K} w_k (z_{ij}^{(k)} - c_k)$$

as $\pi_{ij} = \{1 + \exp(-\eta_{ij})\}^{-1}$, where w_k and c_k ($k = 1, ..., K$) are weight and baseline parameters, respectively. We then define a prior probability of the graph based on prior information $\mathbf{Z}_k (k = 1, ..., K)$ by:

$$p(G) = \prod_i \prod_j p(e_{ij})$$

This prior probability of the graph assumes that edges $e(i,j)(i,j = 1, ..., p)$ are independent of each other. In reality, there are several dependencies among e_{ij}'s such as $p(e_{ij} = 1) < p(e_{ij} = 1 \mid e_{ki} = 1)$, and so forth, and we consider that adding such information into $p(G)$ is premature by the quality of such information.

Computational Experiments

Monte Carlo Simulations

Before analyzing real gene expression data, we perform Monte Carlo simulations to examine the properties of the proposed method. We assume an artificial network with 20 nodes shown in Figure 1 (a). The functional relationships between nodes are listed in Figure 1 (b). The data were generated from the artificial network of Figure 1 (a) with the functional structures between nodes shown in Figure 1 (b). Then, the observations of the child variable are generated after transforming the observations of the parent variables to mean 0 and variance 1. A network was rebuilt from simulated data consisting of 50 or 100 observations, which corresponds to 50 or 100 microarrays, because, recently more microarray data have become available and it is often the case that we can use more than 100 microarrays. While at the starting point of the analysis, we have over 6000 genes for yeast, after some pretreatments of the data or using some prior knowledge, the number of target genes is typically less than 50 or so. We consider such a case in this simulation. As for the biological knowledge, we tried the following situations: (**Case 1**) we know some gene regulations (100%, 75%, 50%, or 25% out of 19 edges shown in Figure 1 (a)) and (**Case 2**) we know some gene regulations, but some (1, 2, or 3) incorrect edges are kept in the database. We set $\{0.5, 1.0\}$ and $\{\zeta_1, 2.5, 5.0, 7.5, 10.0\}$ as the candidate values of ζ_1 and ζ_2, respectively.

Figure 1. Artificial gene network and functional structures between nodes

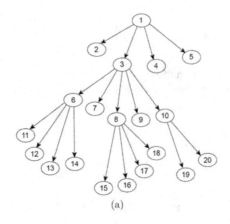

(a)

$$g_1 = \varepsilon_1, \quad g_2 = .7g_1 + \varepsilon_2 \quad g_5 = .7g_1 + \varepsilon_5, \quad g_{10} = 1/\{1 + \exp(-4g_3)\} + \varepsilon_{10}$$

$$g_3 = \begin{cases} -1 + \varepsilon_3 \ (g_1 \leq -.5) \\ g_1 + \varepsilon_3 \ (|g_1| < .5) \\ 1 + \varepsilon_3 \ (g_1 \geq .5) \end{cases} \qquad g_6 = \begin{cases} .8g_3 + \varepsilon_6 \ (g_3 \leq -1) \\ (g_3 + 1)^{1.5} + \varepsilon_6 \ (-1 < |g_3| < 0) \\ 1 + \varepsilon_6 \ (g_3 \geq 1) \end{cases}$$

$$g_4 = \begin{cases} .4g_1 + 1 + \varepsilon_4 \ (|g_1| \leq .3) \\ (g_1 + 1)^2 + \varepsilon_4 \ (|g_1| < .3) \end{cases} \qquad g_8 = \begin{cases} .2g_3 - 1 + \varepsilon_8 \ (g_3 \leq .2) \\ 1.4g_3 + \varepsilon_8 \ (g_3 > .2) \end{cases}$$

$$g_{11} = .7g_6 + \varepsilon_{11}, \quad g_{14} = .7g_6 + \varepsilon_{14}, \quad g_{15} = 1/\{1 + \exp(-4g_8)\} + \varepsilon_{15}$$

$$g_9 = \begin{cases} .4g_3 + 1 + \varepsilon_9 \ (|g_3| \leq .3) \\ (g_3 + 1)^{1.2} + \varepsilon_9 \ (|g_3| < .3) \end{cases} \qquad g_{13} = \begin{cases} .4g_6 + 1 + \varepsilon_{13} \ (|g_6| \leq .3) \\ (g_6 + 1)^2 + \varepsilon_{13} \ (|g_6| < .3) \end{cases}$$

$$g_{12} = \begin{cases} -1 + \varepsilon_{12} \ (g_6 < -.5) \\ g_6 + \varepsilon_{12} \ (|g_6| \leq .5) \\ 1 + \varepsilon_{12} \ (|g_6| > .5) \end{cases} \qquad \begin{array}{l} g_{16} = .8g_8 + \varepsilon_{16} \\ g_{19} = 1/\{1 + \exp(-4g_{10})\} + \varepsilon_{19} \\ g_{20} = 1.1g_{10} + \varepsilon_{20} \end{array}$$

$$g_{17} = \begin{cases} .2g_8 - 1 + \varepsilon_{17} \ (g_8 \leq .2) \\ 1.4g_8 + \varepsilon_{17} \ (g_8 > .2) \end{cases} \qquad g_{18} = \begin{cases} .4g_8 + 1 \ (|g_8| > .3) \\ (g_8 + 1)^{1.2} \ (g_8 \leq .3) \end{cases}$$

(b)

Figure 2 shows two estimated networks: One is estimated by 100 observations (microarrays) alone. We use $\zeta_1 = \zeta_2 = 0.5$, that is, we did not use any prior knowledge (we denote this network by N_0 for convenience). The other is estimated by 100 observations and prior information of 75% gene regulations, that is, we know 14 correct relations out of the all 19 correct edges (we denote this network by N_1). Edges appearing in both networks are colored green, while edges appearing in N_0 or N_1 only are colored blue and red, respectively. By adding prior knowledge, it is clear that we succeeded in reducing the number of false positives. We also find four additional correct relationships. Figure 3 shows the behavior of BNRC, when $\zeta_1 = 0.5$. We find that the optimal value of ζ_2 is 5.0. From the Monte Carlo simulations, we observed that ζ_2 can be selected by using middle values (depicted by a blue line) of upper and lower bounds or upper bounds in practice. For the selection of ζ_1, we use the middle value of the upper and lower bounds of the score of our criterion.

Figure 2. An example of resulting networks based on 100 samples. We used $\zeta_1 = 0.5$ and $\zeta_2 = 5.0$ that are selected by our criterion (see Figure 3).

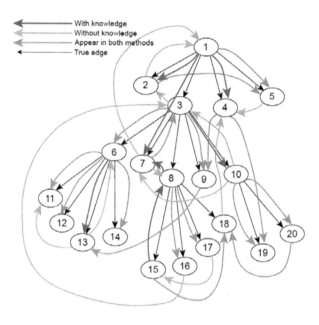

Figure 3. The behavior of BNRC when $\zeta_1 = 0.5$. We can find out the optimal inverse normalized temperature ζ_2 is 5.0.

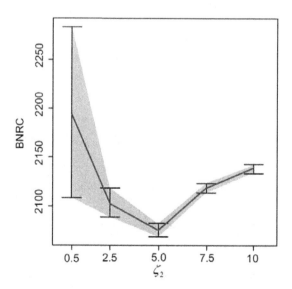

Figure 4. Boxplots of the average squared errors

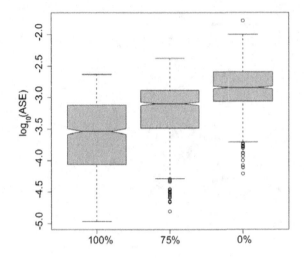

Figure 5. Distribution of the number of true positives and false positives of the estimated networks. The left three figures show the number of true positives when we use 100%, 75%, and 0% prior information, respectively. The right three figures show the number of false positives with respect to 100%, 75%, and 0%. Note that because there are 19 edges in the true network, the maximum number of true positives is 19.

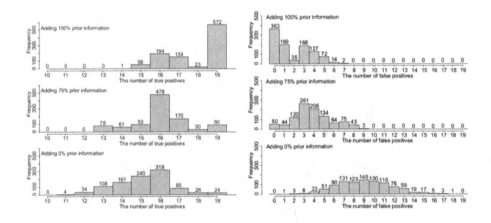

Figure 4 shows the boxplots of the average squared errors (ASEs) that are defined by:

$$ASE = \sum_{i=1}^{100} \sum_{j=1}^{20} (x_{ij}^* - \hat{x}_{ij})^2$$

where x_{ij}^* is the true value of x_{ij}, that is, x_{i2}^* is given by $0.7x_{i1}$, and $\hat{x}_{ij}$ is the estimate of x_{ij} based on the estimated network. Because we repeated the Monte Carlo simulation 1000 times, each boxplot is obtained from 1000 ASEs. Smaller ASE means a more accurate estimated network. From Figure 4, it is clear that by adding prior information we succeeded in reducing the ASE. The distributions of the number of true positives and false positives of the estimate networks are shown in Figure 5. While the estimated networks without prior information contain many correct edges, we observe that the proposed method could reduce the number of false positives even if we added only a part of the true relations.

The results of the Monte Carlo simulations are summarized as follows:

In (**Case 1**), we obtained networks more accurately as long as we add correct knowledge. We observed that the number of false positives decreased drastically. We presume the reason is the nature of directed acyclic graphs. Because a Bayesian network model is a directed acyclic graph, one incorrect estimate may affect the relations in its neighborhood. However, by adding some correct knowledge, we can restrict the search space of the Bayesian network model learning effectively.

In (**Case 2**), the results depend on the type of incorrect knowledge:

1. If we use misdirected relations, for example, $gene_8 \rightarrow gene_3$, as prior knowledge, serious problems occur. Because microarray data to some degree support the misdirected relations, they tend to receive a better criterion score.

2. If we add indirect relations such as $gene_1 \rightarrow gene_8$, we observed that our method controlled the balance between this prior information and microarray data and could decide whether the prior relation is true.

3. If irrelevant relations such as $gene_{20} \rightarrow gene_5$ are added as prior information, our method could reject these prior information because the microarray data do not support these relations.

Table 1. Five transcription factors and their regulating genes

MCM1 :	transcription factor of the MADS box family
	MET14, CDC6, MET2, CDC5, MET6, SIC1, STE6, CLN2, PCL2, STE2,
	ACE2, MET16,MET3, MET4, CAR1, SWI5, PCL9, CLB1, MET17, EGT2,
	ARG5,6, PMA1, RME1, CLB2
SWI5 :	transcription factor
	CDC6, SIC1, CLN2, PCL2, PCL9, EGT2, RME1, CTS1, HO
ACE2 :	metallothionein expression activator
	CLN2, EGT2, HO, CTS1, RME1
SNF2 :	component of SWI/SNF global transcription activator complex
	CTS1, HO
STE12:	transcriptional activator
	STE6, FAR1, KAR3, SST2, FUS1, STE2, BAR1, AGA1, AFR1, CIK1

Example Using Experimental Data of Yeast

In this section, we demonstrate our method by analyzing *Saccharomyces cerevisiae* gene expression data obtained by disrupting 100 genes, which are almost all transcription factors. We used the BY4741 (*MATa, HIS3D1, LEU2D0, MET15D0, URA3D0*) as the wild type strain and purchased gene disruptions from Research Genetics, Inc. We focus on five genes, *MCM1, SWI5, ACE2, SNF2,* and *STE12* (see Table 1) and extract genes that are regulated by these 5 genes from the Yeast proteome database. Thus, we construct a prior network, shown in Figure 6, based on the database information. We include the prior network in our Bayesian network estimation method. That is, the purpose of this analysis is to estimate the gene network containing above 36 genes from microarray data together with the prior network. For constructing a Bayesian network with prior knowledge, the simplest way is to fix the prior edges and learn the other parts of the network based on the observed data. However, we observed that the score of our criterion, BNRC, of the estimated network learned with fixed prior edges cannot decrease compared with the optimal one. Figure 7 shows the estimated gene network using microarray data only. There are many nonprior edges and many of them are probably false positives. In addition, we find three misdirected relations: "*SWI5 → MCM1*," "*HO → ACE2*," and "*STE6 → STE12*." By adding the prior network, we obtain the gene network shown in Figure 9. As for the inverse normalized temperatures ζ_1 and ζ_2, we set $\zeta_1 = 0.5$ and choose the optimal value of ζ_2. We also estimated a gene network based on $\zeta_1 = 1$ and found the results described below to be essentially unchanged.

Figure 6. Prior knowledge network. The genes that are in each shadowed circle are regulated by the parent genes.

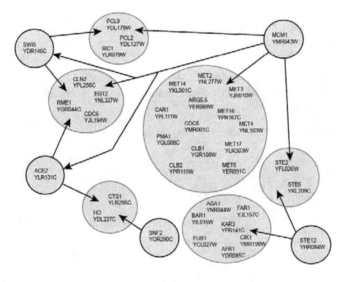

Figure 7. Resulting network based on microarray only

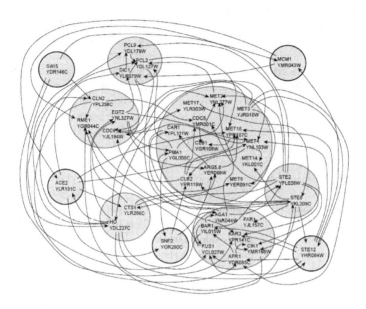

Figure 8. Optimization of ζ_2. We can find out that the optimal value of ζ_2 is 2.5.

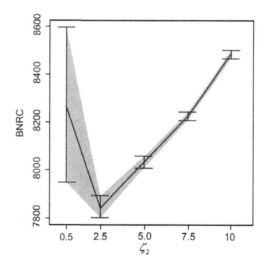

Figure 8 shows the behavior of BNRC with respect to ζ_2. We find that the optimal value of ζ_2 is 2.5. Figure 9 shows the resulting network based on microarray data and the biological knowledge represented by the prior network in Figure 6. We show the edges that correspond to the prior knowledge in black. The edges between genes that are regulated by the same transcription factor in the prior network are shown in blue. The red edges do not correspond to the prior knowledge. In particular, we find that the relationships around *MCM1* improve drastically. The network based on microarray only shown in Figure 7 indicates that only *SIC1* and *ACE2* are regulated by *MCM1*. Note that the underlined genes correspond to the prior network information. After adding the prior knowledge and optimizing the inverse normalized temperatures, we find that 10 genes out of 24 genes that are listed as coregulated genes of *MCM1* in Table 1 are extracted. Also, the relationships around *STE12* become clearer. Before adding prior knowledge, the estimated network in Figure 7 suggests that *FUS1*, *AFR1*, *KAR3*, *BAR1*, *MET4*, *MET16*, and *MCM1* are regulated by *STE12*, while *STE12* is controlled by *HO*, *STE6*, and *MET3*. On the other hand, the network in Figure 9 shows that *STE12* regulates *FUS1*, *AFR1*, *KAR3*, *CIK1*, *STE2*, *STE6*, *HO*, and *MCM1*. Note that the three misdirected relations described above are corrected in Figure 9. The difference between the inverse normalized temperatures $\zeta_1 = 0.5$ and $\zeta_2 = 2.5$ is small because the score of the criterion is added as $2\zeta_1$ or $2\zeta_2$, when we add an edge that is listed or not listed in the prior network, respectively. Therefore, microarray data contain this information and we succeeded in extracting this information with the slight help of the prior network.

Figure 9. Resulting network based on microarray data and biological knowledge. The inverse normalized temperatures are selected by our criterion ($\zeta_1 = 0.5$, $\zeta_2 = 2.5$).

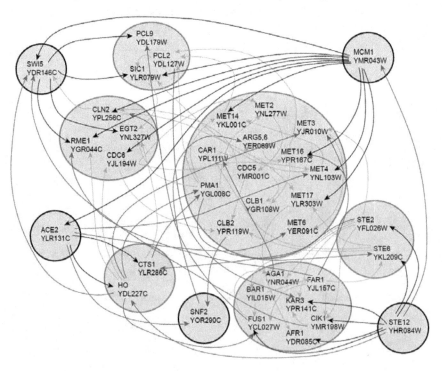

Table 2. Significant GO annotations of selected fenofibrate-related genes from 18 hours microarray

		GO Function	p-value	#genes
＼	GO:0007049	cell cycle	1.0E-08	35
＼	GO:0000278	mitotic cell cycle	3.7E-07	19
＼	GO:0000279	M phase	5.0E-06	17
／	GO:0006629	lipid metabolism	1.3E-05	25
＼	GO:0007067	mitosis	1.3E-05	15
＼	GO:0000087	M phase of mitotic cell cycle	1.6E-05	15
＼	GO:0000074	regulation of cell cycle	2.7E-05	22
／	GO:0044255	cellular lipid metabolism	4.4E-05	21
／	GO:0016126	sterol biosynthesis	4.3E-04	6
／	GO:0016125	sterol metabolism	4.5E-04	8
／	GO:0008203	cholesterol metabolism	1.5E-03	7
／	GO:0006695	cholesterol biosynthesis	2.4E-03	5
／	GO:0008202	steroid metabolism	3.6E-03	10
＼	GO:0000375	RNA splicing, via transesterification reactions	4.1E-03	9
＼	GO:0000377	RNA splicing, via transesterification reactions with bulged adenosine as nucleophile	4.1E-03	9
＼	GO:0000398	nuclear mRNA splicing, via spliceosome	4.1E-03	9
／	GO:0006694	steroid biosynthesis	6.0E-03	7
＼	GO:0016071	mRNA metabolism	6.3E-03	13

We optimized the inverse normalized temperature ζ_2 based on the proposed criterion. From the network based on the optimal inverse normalized temperatures, we can find the difference between microarray data and biological knowledge. By comparing Figure 7 with Figure 9, we find that the microarray data reflect the relationship between seven genes (*CLN2*, *RME1*, *CDC6*, *EGT2*, *PCL2*, *PCL9*, and *SIC1*) and two transcription factors (*MCM1* and *SWI5*). On the other hand, we find that there are somewhat large differences between microarray data and the prior network for the relationship between *MCM1* and the 13 genes that are in the biggest circle.

Application to Human Endothelial Cells' Gene Network

Fenofibrate Time-Course Data

We measure the time-responses of human endothelial cell genes to 25mM fenofibrate. The expression levels of 20,469 probes are measured by CodeLinkTM Human Uniset I 20K at six time-points (0, 2, 4, 6, 8, and 18 hours). Here, time 0 means the start point of this observation and just before exposure to the fenofibrate. In addition, we measure this time-course data as the duplicated data in order to confirm the quality of experiments.

Because our fenofibrate time-course data are duplicated data and contain six time-points, there are $2^6 = 64$ possible combinations to create a time-course dataset. We should fit the same regression function to a parent-child relationship in the 64 datasets. Under this constrain, we consider fitting nonparametric regression model to the connected data of 64 datasets. That is, if we consider gene $i \rightarrow$ gene j, we will fit the model $x_j^{(c)}(t) - m_j(x_i^{(c)}(t-1) + e_j^{(c)}(t)$, where $x_j^{(c)}(t)$ is the expression data of gene j at time t in the c-th dataset for $c = 1, ..., 64$. In the Bayesian networks, the reliability of estimated edges can be measured by using the bootstrap method. For time-course data, several modifications of the bootstrap method are proposed, such as block resampling, but it is difficult to apply these methods to the small number of data points generated by short time-courses. However, by using above time-course modeling, we can define a method based on the bootstrap as follows: Let $D = \{D(1), ..., D(64)\}$ be the combinatorial time-course data of all genes. We randomly resample $D(c)$ with replacement and define a bootstrap sample $D^* = \{D^*(1), ..., D^*(64)\}$. We then re-estimate a gene network based on D^*. We repeat 1000 times bootstrap replications and obtain $\hat{G}_T^{*1}, ..., \hat{G}_T^{*1000}$, where $\hat{G}_T^{*B}$ is the estimated graph based on the B-th bootstrap sample. The estimated reliability of edge can be used as the matrix representation of the first prior information $\mathbf{Z}_1$ as:

$$z_{ij}^{(1)} = \#\{B | e(i,j) \in \hat{G}_T^{*B}, B = 1,...,1000\}/1000$$

Gene Knock-Down Data by siRNA

For estimating gene networks, we newly created 270 gene knock-down data by using siRNA. We measure 20,469 probes by CodeLinkTM Human Uniset I 20K for each knock-down microarray after 24 hours of siRNA transfection. The knock-down genes are mainly transcription factors and signaling molecules. Let $\tilde{x}_{D_i} = (\tilde{x}_{1|D_i}, ..., \tilde{x}_{p|D_i})'$ be the raw intensity vector of i-th knock-down microarray. For normalizing expression values of each microarray, we compute the median expression value vector $v = (v_1, ..., v_p)'$ as the control data, where $vj = \text{median}_i(\tilde{x}_{j|D_i})$ We apply the loess normalization method to the MA transformed data and the normalized intensity $x_{j|D_i}$ is obtained by applying the inverse transformation to the normalized $\log(\tilde{x}_{j|D_i}/V_j)$ We refer to the normalized $\log(\tilde{x}_{j|D_i}/V_j)$ as the log-ratio.

In 270 gene knock-down microarray data, we know which gene is knocked-down for each microarray. Thus, when we knock-down gene D_i, genes that significantly change their expression levels can be considered as the direct regulatees of gene D_i. We measure this information by computing corrected log-ratio as follows: The fluctuations of the log-ratios depend on their sum of sample's and control's intensities. From the normalized MA transformed data, we can obtain the conditional variance $s_j = \text{Var}[\log(x_{j|D_i}/v_j) | \log(x_{j|D_i} \cdot v_j)]$ and the log-ratios can be corrected $z_{ij}^{(2)} = \log(x_{j|D_i}/v_j)/s_j$, satisfying $\text{Var}(z_{ij}^{(2)}) = 1$.

Results

For estimating fenofibrate-related gene networks from fenofibrate time-course data and 270 gene knock-down data, we first define the set of genes that are possibly related to fenofibrate as follows: First, we extract the set of genes whose variance-corrected log-ratios, $|\log(x_{j|D_i}/v_j)/s_j|$, are greater than 1.5 from each time point. We then find significant clusters of selected genes using GO Term Finder. Table 2 shows the significant clusters of genes at

Figure 10. Down-stream of PPAR-α

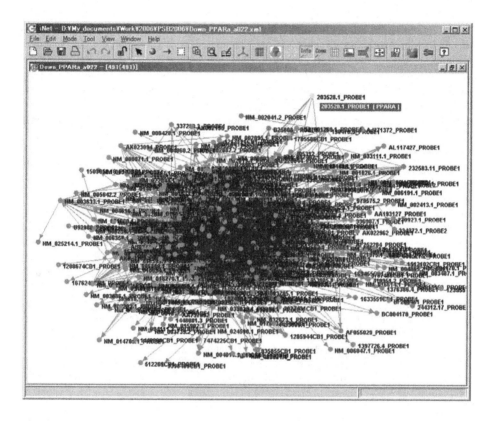

18 hours. The first column indicates how expression values are changed, that is, right-up-arrow and right-down-arrow mean "overexpressed" and "suppressed," respectively. The GO annotations of clusters with right-down-arrow are mainly related to cell cycle, the genes in these clusters are expressed ubiquitously and this is a common biological function. On the other hand, the GO annotations of clusters with right-up-arrow are mainly related to lipid metabolism. In biology, it is reported that the fenofibrate acts around 12 hours after exposure (Goya, Sumitani, Xu, Kitamura, Yamamoto, Kurebayashi et al., 2004; Hayashida, Kume, Minami, Inui-Hayashida, Mukai, Toyohara, & Kita, 2004). Our first analysis for gene selection suggests that fenofibrate affects genes related to lipid metabolism, and this is consistent with biological facts. We also focus on the genes from the 8 hour time-point microarray. Unfortunately, no cluster with specific function could be found in the selected genes from the 8 hour time-point microarray However, there also exist some genes related to lipid metabolism. Therefore we use the genes from the 8 and 18 hour time-point microarrays. Finally, we add the 267 knock-down genes (three genes are not spotted on our chips) to the selected genes above, total 1192 genes are defined as possible fenofibrate-related genes and used for the next network analysis.

By converting the estimated dynamic network and knock-down gene information into the matrix representations of the first and second prior information Z_1 and Z_2, respectively, we estimate the gene network $\hat{G}_k$ based on Z_1, Z_2 and the knock-down data matrix X_K. For extracting biological information from the estimated gene network, we first focus on lipid metabolism-related genes, because the clusters related to this function are significantly changed at 18 hours microarray. In the estimated gene network, there are 42 lipid metabolism-related genes and *PPAR-α* (*Homo sapiens* peroxisome proliferative activated receptor, alpha) is the only transcriptionfactor among them. Actually, *PPAR-α* is a known target of fenofibrate. Therefore, we next focus on the node down-stream of *PPAR-α*. In Figure 10, the node down-stream of *PPAR-α* (491 genes). Here, we consider that genes in the four steps down-stream of *PPAR-α* are candidate regulatees of *PPAR-α*. Among the candidate regulatees of *PPAR-α*, there are 21 lipid metabolism-related genes and 11 molecules previously identified experimentally to be related to *PPAR-α*. Actually, *PPAR-α* is known to be activated by fenofibrate. We show one subnetwork having *PPAR-α* as a root node in Figure 11. One of the drug efficacies of fenofibrate whose target is *PPAR-α* is to reduce LDL cholesterol. LDLR and VLDLR mainly contribute the transporting of cholesterol and they are children of *PPAR-α*, namely candidate regulatees of *PPAR-α*, in our estimated network. As for LDLR, its relationship with *PPAR-α* has been reported (Islam, Knight, Frayn, Patel, & Gibbons, 2005). Moreover, several genes related to cholesterol metabolism are children of *PPAR-α* in our network. We also could extract STAT5B and GLS that are children of *PPAR-α* and have been reported their regulation-relationships with *PPAR-α* (Kersten, Mandard, Escher, Gonzalez, Tafuri, Desvergne, & Wahli, 2001; Shipley & Waxman, 2003). Therefore, it is not surprising that our network shows that many direct and indirect relationships involving known *PPAR-α* regulates are triggered in endothelial cells by fenofibrate treatment. In the node up-stream of *PPAR-α*, *PPAR-α*, and RXR-α, which form a heterodimer, share a parent. We could extract fenofibrate-related gene network and estimate that *PPAR-α* is the one of the key molecules of fenofibrate regulations without previous biological knowledge.

Figure 11. A sub-network related to PPAR-α

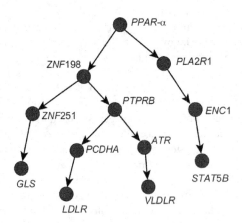

Discussion

In this chapter, we illustrate a statistical method for estimating gene networks from microarray gene expression data. The use of Bayesian networks and nonparametric regression is a key of our method to capture nonlinear relationships between genes. An information criterion we call BNRC, derived from the Bayesian point of view in Section 2, is powerful to evaluate candidate networks and to choose one as the best one. Also, the framework we used to derive BNRC is flexible to combine other biological knowledge. We have conceptually shown the capability of our framework to use protein-protein interaction, binding site information, and other types of information to estimate gene networks. In fact, research has been done using this framework. Tamada, et al. (2003) combined the promoter element detection method with Bayesian networks to find binding sites of transcription factors and to estimate gene networks simultaneously. Nariai et al. (2004) used protein-protein interaction data observed by yeast two hybrid and TAP experiments together with microarray data to estimate gene networks. More recently, Tamada et al. (2005) used protein sequence similarity as evolutionary information of two distinct organisms and estimate gene networks of two organisms, simultaneously. As we described above, combination of multiple types of genomic data is a key to estimate accurate gene networks.

The next step of gene network research is to understand mode-of-action of a chemical compound when we do it to cells by using estimated gene networks. In reality, the affected genes by a chemical compound, or drug, form subgraphs in the whole gene network. Therefore, it is possible to consider estimating subnetworks affected by a drug as a next challenge. This network enables us to know not only genes that are directly affected by the drug (Imoto et al., 2003), but also the drug affected pathways (Tamada et al., 2005). Imoto, Tamada, Araki, Yasuda, Print, Charnock-Jones et al. (2006) provides a concept druggable gene networks to understand mode-of-action of a chemical compound. The druggable gene networks contain known drug target gene and novel drug target candidate genes. They show that several known drug target genes are hubs in the druggable gene network, computationally.

Statistical estimation approach is a way to know gene networks in bioinformatics. This has a background that we do not know or partially know the true gene network and estimate unknown parts by using observational data like microarray gene expression data. However, there is another approach to understand networks in cells. This is based on the known facts and builds a simulation model like Petri net (Matsuno, Tanaka, Aoshima, Doi, Matsui, & Miyano, 2003; Nagasaki, Doi, Matsuno, & Miyano, 2004a, 2004b). We consider that the combination of these two approaches will become a key technology to understanding cellular networks.

Acknowledgment

We wish to thank our colleagues and collaborators Hideo Bannai, Yoshinori Tamada, Ryo Yoshida, Takao Goto, Sunyong Kim, Naoki Nariai, Sascha Ott, Tomoyuki Higuchi, Sachiyo Aburatani, Kousuke Tashiro, Satoru Kuhara, Ben Dunmore, Sally Humphries, Muna Affara, Kaori Yasuda, Hiromitu Araki, Cristpher J. Savoie, Stephen D. Charnock-Jones, Yuki Tomiyasu, Deborah Sanders, and Cristin G. Print. Computation time was provided by the Super Computer System, Human Genome Center, Institute of Medical Science, University of Tokyo.

References

Akaike, H. (1973). Information theory and an extension of the maximum likelihood principle (pp. 267-281). In B.N. Petrov & F. Csaki (Eds.). Akademiai Kiad'o, Budapest.

Bader, G.D., Donaldson, I., Wolting, C., Ouellette, B.F.F., Pawson, T., & Hogue, C.W.V. (2001). BIND: The biomolecular interaction network database. *Nucleic Acids Research, 29*, 242-245.

Bannai, H., Inenaga, S., Shinohara, A., Takeda, M., & Miyano, S. (2002). A string pattern regression algorithm and its application to pattern discovery in long introns. *Genome Informatics, 13*, 3-1.

Berger, J.O. (1985). *Statistical decision theory and Bayesian analysis*. New York: Springer-Verlag.

Bernard, A., & Hartemink, A. (2005). Informative structure priors: Joint learning of dynamic regulatory networks from multiple types of data. In *Proceedings of the Pacific Symposium on Biocomputing* (vol. 10, pp. 459-470).

Burnham, K.P., & Anderson, D.R. (1998). *Model selection and inference: A practical information-theoretical approach*. New York: Springer-Verlag.

Bussemaker, H.J., Li, H., & Siggia, E.D. (2001). Regulatory element detection using correlation with expression. *Nature Genetics, 27*, 167-171.

Cooper, G.F., & Herskovits, E. (1992). A Bayesian method for the induction of probabilistic networks from data. *Machine Learning, 9*, 309-347.

De Boor, C. (1978). *A practical guide to splines*. Berlin: Springer-Verlag.

Friedman, N., & Goldszmidt, M. (1998). Learning Bayesian networks with local structure. In M.I. Jordan (Ed.). Kluwer Academic Publisher.

Friedman, N., Linial, M., Nachman, I., & Pe'er, D. (2000). Using Bayesian network to analyze expression data. *Journal of Computational Biology, 7*, 601-620.

Geman, S., & Geman, D. (1984). Stochastic relaxation, Gibbs distribution and the Bayesian restorations. *IEEE Transactions on Pattern Analysis and Machine Intelligence, 6*, 721-741.

Goya, K., Sumitani, S., Xu, X., Kitamura, T., Yamamoto, H., Kurebayashi, S. et al. (2004). Peroxisome proliferator-activated receptor α agonists increase nitric oxide synthase expression in vascular endothelial cells. *Arteriosclerosis, Thrombosis, and Vascular Biology, 24*, 658-663.

Green, P.J., & Silverman, B.W. (1994). *Nonparametric regression and generalized linear models*. Chapman & Hall.

Hartemink, A.J., Gifford, D.K., Jaakkola, T.S., & Young, R.A. (2002). Combining location and expression data for principled discovery of genetic regulatory network models. In *Proceedings of the Pacific Symposium on Biocomputing* (vol. 7, pp. 437-449).

Hastie, T., & Tibshirani, R. (1990). *Generalized additive models*. Chapman & Hall.

Hayashida, K., Kume, N., Minami, M., Inui-Hayashida, A., Mukai, E., Toyohara, M., & Kita, T. (2004). Peroxisome proliferator-activated receptor α ligands activate transcription of lectin-like oxidized low density lipoprotein receptor-1 gene through GC box motif. *Biochemical and Biophysical Research Communications, 323*, 1116-1123.

Heckerman, D., & Geiger, D. (1995). Learning Bayesian networks: A unification for discrete and Gaussian domains. In *Proceedings of the Eleventh Conference on Uncertainty in Artificial Intelligence* (pp. 274-284).

Heckerman, D., Geiger, D., & Chickering, D.M. (1995). Learning Bayesian networks: The combination of knowledge and statistical data. *Machine Learning, 20*, 197-243.

Ideker, T., Ozier, O., Schwikowski, B., & Siegel, A.F. (2002). Discovering regulatory and signaling circuits in molecular interaction networks. *Bioinformatics, 18*, S233-S240.

Imoto, S., Goto, T., & Miyano, S. (2002). Estimation of genetic networks and functional structures between genes by using Bayesian networks and nonparametric regression. In *Proceedings of the Pacific Symposium on Biocomputing* (vol. 7, pp. 175-186).

Imoto, S., Higuchi, T., Goto, T., Tashiro, K., Kuhara, S., & Miyano, S. (2004). Combining microarrays and biological knowledge for estimating gene networks via Bayesian networks. *Journal of Bioinformatics and Computational Biology, 2*, 77-98.

Imoto, S., Higuchi, T., Kim, S., Jeong, E., & Miyano, S. (2005). Residual bootstrapping and median filtering for robust estimation of gene networks from microarray data. In *Proceedings of the 2nd Computational Methods in Systems Biology* (LNIB 3082, pp. 149-160). Springer-Verlag.

Imoto, S., Kim, S.-Y., Goto, T., Aburatani, S., Tashiro, K., Kuhara, S., & Miyano, S. (2003). Bayesian network and nonparametric heteroscedastic regression for nonlinear modeling of genetic network. *Journal of Bioinformatics and Computational Biology, 1*, 231-252.

Imoto, S., & Konishi, S. (2003). Selection of smoothing parameters in B-spline nonparametric regression models using information criteria. *Annals of the Institute of Statistical Mathematics, 55*, 671-687.

Imoto, S., Savoie, C.J., Aburatani, S., Kim, S., Tashiro, K., Kuhara, S., & Miyano, S. (2003). Use of gene networks for identifying and validating drug targets. *Journal of Bioinformatics and Computational Biology, 1*, 459-474.

Imoto, S., Tamada, Y., Araki, H., Yasuda, K., Print, C.G., Charnock-Jones, S.D. et al. (2006). Computational strategy for discovering druggable gene networks from genome-wide RNA expression profiles. In *Proceedings of the Pacific Symposium on Biocomputing* (vol. 11, pp. 559-571).

Islam, K.K., Knight, B.L., Frayn, K.N., Patel, D.D., & Gibbons, G.F. (2005). Deficiency of PPARα disturbs the response of lipogenic flux and of lipogenic and cholesterogenic gene expression to dietary cholesterol in mouse white adipose tissue. *Biochimica et Biophysica Acta*, 1734, 259-268.

Ito, T., Chiba, T., Ozawa, R., Yoshida, M., Hattori, M., & Sakaki, Y. (2001). A comprehensive two-hybrid analysis to explore the yeast protein interactome. *Proceedings of the National Academy of Science, 97,* pp. 4569-4574).

Kersten, S., Mandard, S., Escher, P., Gonzalez, F.J., Tafuri, S., Desvergne, B., & Wahli, W. (2001). The peroxisome proliferator-activated receptor α regulates amino acid metabolism. *Federation of American Societies for Experimental Biology Journal, 15*, 1971-1978.

Kindeman, R., & Snell, J. (1980). *Markov random fields and their applications*. Providence, RI: American Mathematical Society.

Konishi, S. (1996). Statistical model evaluation and information criteria. In S. Ghosh (Ed.). Marcel Dekker.

Konishi, S., & Kitagawa, G. (1996). Generalised information criteria in model selection. *Biometrika, 83*, 875-890.

Lee, T.I., Rinaldi, N.J., Robert, F., Odom, D.T., Bar-Joseph, Z., Gerber, G.K. et al. (2002). Transcriptional regulatory networks in Saccharomyces cerevisiae. *Science, 298*, 799-804.

Masys, D.R. (2001). Linking microarray data to the literature. *Nature Genetics, 28*, 9-10.

Matsuno, H., Tanaka, Y., Aoshima, H., Doi, A., Matsui, M., & Miyano, S. (2003). Biopathways representation and simulation on hybrid functional Petri net. *In Silico Biology, 3*, 389-404.

Nagasaki, M., Doi, A., Matsuno, H., & Miyano, S. (2004a). Integrating biopathway databases for largescale modeling and simulation. In *Proceedings of the Second Asia-Pacific Bioinformatics Conference* (vol. 29, pp. 43-52). Australian Computer Society.

Nagasaki, M., Doi, A., Matsuno, H., & Miyano, S. (2004b). A versatile petri net based architecture for modeling and simulation of complex biological processes. *Genome Informatics, 15*, 180-197.

Nariai, N., Kim, S.-Y., Imoto, S., & Miyano, S. (2004). Using protein-protein interactions for refining gene networks estimated from microarray data by Bayesian networks. In *Proceedings of the Pacific Symposium on Biocomputing* (vol. 9, pp. 336-347).

Ong, I.M., Glasner, J.D., & Page, D. (2002). Modelling regulatory pathways in E. coli from time series expression profiles. *Bioinformatics, 18*, S241-S248.

Ott, S., Hansen, A., Kim, S.-Y., & Miyano, S. (2005). Superiority of network motifs over optimal networks and an application to the revelation of gene network evolution. *Bioinformatics, 21*, 227-238.

Ott, S., Imoto, S., & Miyano, S. (2004). Finding optimal models for small gene networks. In *Proceedings of the Pacific Symposium on Biocomputing, 9*, 557-567.

Ott, S., & Miyano, S. (2003). Finding optimal gene networks using biological constraints. *Genome Informatics, 14*, 124-133.

Pe'er, D, Regev, A., Elidan, G., & Friedman, N. (2001). Inferring subnetworks from perturbed expression profiles. *Bioinformatics, 17*, S215-S224.

Pilpel, Y., Sudarsanam, P., & Church, G.M. (2001). Identifying regulatory networks by combinatorial analysis of promoter elements. *Nature Genetics, 29*, 153-159.

Robinson, R.W. (1973). Counting labeled acyclic diagraphs. In F. Harary (Ed.), *New directions in the theory of graphs* (pp. 239-273). New York: Academic Press.

Segal, E., Barash, Y., Simon, I., Friedman, N., & Koller, D. (2002). From promoter sequence to expression: A probabilistic framework. In *Proceedings of the 6th Annual International Conference on Research in Computational Molecular Biology* (pp. 263-272).

Segal, E., Wang, H., & Koller, D. (2003). Discovering molecular pathways from protein interaction and gene expression data. *Bioinformatics, 19*, i264-i272.

Segal, E., Yelensky, R., & Koller, D. (2003). Genome-wide discovery of transcriptional modules from DNA sequence and gene expression. *Bioinformatics, 19*, i273-i282.

Shipley, J.M., & Waxman, D.J. (2003). Down-regulation of STAT5b transcriptional activity by ligand-activated peroxisome proliferator-activated receptor (PPAR) α and PPAR γ. *Mol. Pharmacol., 64*, 355-364.

Tamada, Y., Bannai, H., Imoto, S., Katayama, T., Kanehisa, M., & Miyano, S. (2005). Utilizing evolutionary information and gene expression data for estimating gene regulations with Bayesian network models. *Journal of Bioinformatics and Computational Biology, 3*, 1295-1313.

Tamada, Y., Imoto, S., Tashiro, K., Kuhara, S., & Miyano, S. (2005). Identifying drug active pathways from gene networks estimated by gene expression data. *Genome Informatics, 16*, 182-191.

Tamada, Y., Kim, S.-Y., Bannai, H., Imoto, S., Tashiro, K., Kuhara, S., & Miyano, S. (2003). Estimating gene networks from gene expression data by combining Bayesian network model with promoter element detection. *Bioinformatics, 19*, ii227-ii236.

Van Someren, E.P., Wessels, L.F.A., Backer, E., & Reinders, M.J.T. (2002). Genetic network modeling. *Pharmacogenomics, 3*, 507-525.

Chapter XIV

Bayesian Network Modeling of Transcription Factor Binding Sites:
A Tutorial

Vipin Narang, National University of Singapore, Singapore

Rajesh Chowdhary, National University of Singapore, Singapore

Ankush Mittal, Indian Institute of Technology, India

Wing-Kin Sung, National University of Singapore, Singapore

Abstract

A predicament that engineers who wish to employ Bayesian networks to solve practical problems often face is the depth of study required in order to obtain a workable understanding of this tool. This chapter is intended as a tutorial material to assist the reader in efficiently understanding the fundamental concepts involved in Bayesian network applications. It presents a complete step by step solution of a bioinformatics problem using Bayesian network models, with detailed illustration of modeling, parameter estimation, and inference mechanisms. Considerations in determining an appropriate Bayesian network model representation of a physical problem are also discussed.

Introduction

Although there is considerable literature on the diverse applications of Bayesian networks in the bioinformatics domain, its highly technical nature makes it difficult for a beginner in the field to clearly understand the concept of applying Bayesian networks to practical problems. In this chapter, we have addressed this concern by presenting a complete step by step solution to a bioinformatics problem using Bayesian networks. The presentation has been kept simple and self-explanatory, assuming that the reader does not have much exposure to either Bayesian networks or bioinformatics.

Problem Background

All organisms are made up of basic structural and functional units called cells. Most activities in a cell are carried out by proteins, which are complex macromolecules of amino acids. Proteins are manufactured whenever required within the cell itself. The blueprint for the manufacture of proteins is contained in the genetic code, which exists in the form of DNA. The DNA is present in the cell nucleus as chromosomes, and it contains information of both how and when a protein is manufactured within the cell. A gene is a segment of DNA on a chromosome that encodes a protein.

The process of forming a protein from a gene is called gene expression. It is a strictly controlled process. The control mechanism involves regulatory DNA sequences called *promoters* and proteins called *transcription factors*. The promoter sequence is located just adjacent to the gene sequence. Gene expression begins when a group of transcription factors bind to the promoter sequence. The transcription factors subsequently induce the recruitment of the enzyme RNA polymerase, which starts the process of gene expression. A transcription factor (TF) binds to the promoter sequence at a small DNA segment of length 6 to 20 nucleotides, known as *transcription factor binding site* (TFBS), as shown in Figure 1.

To understand the mechanism of gene expression control, it is important to know the TFBS present in the promoter region. TFBS can be identified either experimentally or computationally. Though experimental techniques give reliable results, they are not suited for large volumes of data because of being costly and time consuming. The computational approach is thus preferred for a preliminary analysis, which can be followed by experimental validation.

Figure 1. Binding of transcription factors to a promoter sequence

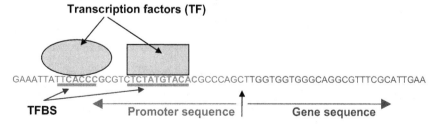

Figure 2. A collection of experimentally verified TFBS (CAAT box) for the transcription factor NF-Y

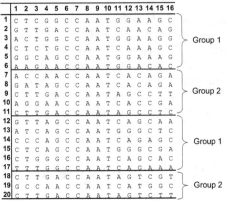

The computational technique uses examples of experimentally verified TFBS and aims to find similar sites in the promoter sequence to be analyzed. For example, Figure 2 shows a set of experimentally verified TFBS to which the transcription factor called NF-Y (Nuclear Factor – Y) binds. It can be observed that the TFBS sequences are not the same, even though they bind to the same TF. This is because a transcription factor can interact with DNA through a variety of physical mechanisms, each of which may prefer a different TFBS sequence. In addition, variations in the TFBS sequence are used in the cell as a mechanism to vary the affinity of TF binding and in turn vary the level of gene expression. The computational technique to detect TFBS must therefore capture the probabilistic nature of TF binding. Note that it is not sufficient to just find the exact occurrences of experimentally known sites in the target promoter sequence; the probabilistic nature of TF binding has to be understood. The essential component of the computational technique is to thus develop a probabilistic model for TF binding using known TFBS data (Benos, Lapedes, & Stormo, 2002).

The most commonly used computational model for TF binding is the positional weight matrix (PWM) (Stormo, Schneider, & Gold, 1982; Stormo, 2000). A PWM records the preference for each DNA nucleotide at each binding site position. Its entries are the frequencies, $f_{b,i}$, of the nucleotides, $b \in \{A, C, G, T\}$, in the positions, $i \in \{1, 2, ..., N\}$, among known TFBS sequences. Here N is the length of a TFBS sequence. For example, Figure 3 shows the PWM for the TFBS data shown in Figure 2.

Figure 3. Positional weight matrix developed from the collection of NF-Y TFBS in Figure 2

Base	Position 1	2	3	4	5	6	7	8	9	10	11	12	13	14	15	16
A	5	2	0	10	9	0	0	20	20	0	4	10	6	8	6	6
C	9	4	8	0	0	20	20	0	0	0	10	0	5	11	0	8
G	5	2	3	9	11	0	0	0	0	0	6	10	6	1	10	3
T	1	12	9	1	0	0	0	0	0	20	0	0	3	0	4	3

Base	Position 1	2	3	4	5	6	7	8	9	10	11	12	13	14	15	16
A	0.25	0.10	0.00	0.50	0.45	0.00	0.00	1.00	1.00	0.00	0.20	0.50	0.30	0.40	0.30	0.30
C	0.45	0.20	0.40	0.00	0.00	1.00	1.00	0.00	0.00	0.00	0.50	0.00	0.25	0.55	0.00	0.40
G	0.25	0.10	0.15	0.45	0.55	0.00	0.00	0.00	0.00	0.00	0.30	0.50	0.30	0.05	0.50	0.15
T	0.05	0.60	0.45	0.05	0.00	0.00	0.00	0.00	0.00	1.00	0.00	0.00	0.15	0.00	0.20	0.15

Figure 4. Scanning an uncharacterized promoter sequence for potential TFBS

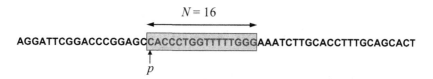

The PWM is used to search for potential TFBS in an uncharacterized promoter sequence. As shown in Figure 4, at each position, p, of the uncharacterized sequence, a window of length N = number of columns in the PWM is selected. Let the currently selected sequence window be denoted by $S = S_1 S_2 \ldots S_N$, $S_i \in \{A, C, G, T\}$. Using the PWM, the "matrix score" for this window is calculated by the formula (Bucher, 1990):

$$\text{Matrix score} = \frac{\sum_{i=1}^{N} \ln(f_{S_i,i}) - \sum_{i=1}^{N} \ln(f_{\min_i,i})}{\sum_{i=1}^{N} \ln(f_{\max_i,i}) - \sum_{i=1}^{N} \ln(f_{\min_i,i})}, \tag{1}$$

where, $f_{b,i}$ is the value at row $b \in \{A, C, G, T\}$ and column $i \in \{1, 2, \ldots, N\}$ of the PWM, and $\max_i$ and $\min_i$ represent the rows for which $f_{b,i}$ is maximum and minimum, respectively, in the column i. The matrix score is a real number within the range [0, 1]. If the matrix score for the window S exceeds a chosen threshold value, it is marked as a potential TFBS.

The PWM representation makes certain assumptions which limit its accuracy. Firstly, the frequencies $f_{b,i}$ are computed by pooling together all known TFBS sequences and weighting them equally. This implies the assumption that all TFBS belong to a single class and are equally effective in binding to the TF. The PWM model therefore cannot accommodate differences in TFBS sequences arising due to different physical mechanisms of TF binding. Secondly, the contributions $\ln(f_{b,i})$ at each position i are summed up while computing the matrix score in equation (1). This assumes that each position in the TFBS contributes independently and equally to the binding of the TF to TFBS. It may not be a good approximation for the physical nature of TF binding to DNA.

For example, consider some example binding site sequences for the TF NF-Y, shown in Figure 2, and observe the nucleotides at positions 11, 12, and 13. The sequences have been grouped according to the nucleotide at position 13. Distinct characteristics of TFBS sequences can be recognized in each group. When the nucleotide A or G is present at position 13, either GG or CA occurs at positions 11 and 12. Similarly, when C or T is present at position 13, only AG or CA occurs at positions 11 and 12. Such relationships or correlations cannot be specifically addressed in the PWM model.

Bayesian network models can easily and intuitively accommodate flexibility which the PWM representation cannot allow. The rest of this chapter describes how Bayesian networks can be applied for improved modeling of TFBS. We illustrate the usage of Bayesian networks in this context step by step, including model building, training of the parameters using EM algorithm, and application of the trained model for detection of TFBS in an uncharacterized

DNA sequence.

Bayesian Networks

A Bayesian network is a formalism to represent and reason about probabilistic cause-and-effect relationships among a set of entities or events in an intuitive manner. It has two components: (i) a graphical map of the cause-and-effect relationships among the entities or events in the domain, and (ii) a numerical measurement of the extent of this dependence.

In the graph, each entity or event is represented as a *node*, and the cause-effect relationships among the nodes are shown by *directed edges* linking causes to effects. This is technically called a directed acyclic graph (DAG). For example, consider a Bayesian network model of the causes of heart disease as shown in Figure 5. The different events or causes associated with heart disease such as diet, obesity, blood pressure, smoking, and so forth, are shown in oval shaped nodes. The causal relationships are shown as edges, for example, because exercise directly affects obesity, blood pressure and arteriosclerosis, it is the parent of these three nodes.

In the numerical representation, each entity or event (from now onward referred to as a node in the Bayesian network) is represented by a variable which can take a set of possible values or *states* for the event. For example, the set of possible states of each node are shown alongside the nodes in Figure 5 in rectangular captions. A *conditional probability table* (CPT) is associated with each variable to quantify the extent to which the variable is likely to be affected by other variables. For example, the CPT of obesity is illustrated in Figure 6, showing the probabilistic dependence of an individual's obesity on his diet and exercise habits. Each row of the CPT shows how obesity is affected by a particular combination of its parent variables diet and exercise. For example, a fatty diet with low exercise is likely to produce obesity in 35% of the cases (row 3 of the CPT) Note that the sum of probabilities in each row of the CPT is always 1.

In the Bayesian network structure as shown in Figure 5, a node from which there is an edge

Figure 5. A Bayesian network for modeling the causes of heart disease

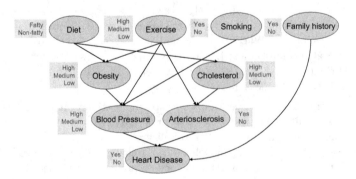

Figure 6. Conditional probability table (CPT) for the node "obesity" in the Bayesian network of Figure 5

Diet	Exercise	Obesity=High	Obesity=Medium	Obesity=Low
Fatty	High	0.2	0.4	0.4
Fatty	Medium	0.25	0.5	0.25
Fatty	Low	0.35	0.5	0.15
Non-fatty	High	0.1	0.2	0.7
Non-fatty	Medium	0.15	0.25	0.6
Non-fatty	Low	0.2	0.3	0.5

to another node is called a parent of that child node, for example, the node "diet" is a parent of the node "obesity." Similarly, there is an ancestor-dependent relationship between nodes that are linked in a chain, for example, "diet" is an ancestor of "blood pressure." These relationships describe how one variable influences the state of another variable. The parent nodes directly influence the child node, while the ancestor nodes have an indirect influence upon their descendants. There exists a *conditional independence* relationship in the network, which is stated as follows: a node is independent of its ancestors given its parents. For example since diet affects blood pressure not directly but through obesity, once the state of a person's obesity is known, the knowledge of his diet does not give any additional information about his blood pressure.

In mathematical terms, the concept of conditional independence is explained as follows. Each node in the Bayesian network is a random variable. The complete *joint distribution* of this set of N random variables $X_1, X_2, ..., X_N$ is given by the *chain rule* as

$$\Pr(X_1, X_2, ..., X_N) = \prod_{i=1}^{N} \Pr(X_i | X_{i-1}, X_{i-2}, ..., X_1).$$

(2)

Note that the variable X_i is conditioned on the variables $X_{i-1}, X_{i-2}, ..., X_1$ which precede it in the topological ordering. The conditional independence between the variables allows this joint distribution to be simplified. Thus in the simplified expression,

$$\Pr(X_1, X_2, ..., X_N) = \prod_{i=1}^{N} \Pr(X_i | \mathrm{Pa}(X_i)),$$

(3)

where $\mathrm{Pa}(X_i)$ denotes the set of parents of the node X_i in the Bayesian network. Instead of being conditioned on all its predecessors, the node X_i is conditioned only on its parents.

If each variable X_i has m possible states, the full joint distribution would require $O(m^\wedge N)$ parameters, whereas the factored form of the Bayesian network would require only $O((m^\wedge k)*N)$ parameters, where k is the maximum number of parents for any node. Thus the Bayesian network formalism makes mathematical modeling much simpler.

The purpose of a Bayesian network is to estimate certainties of events that are not directly observable. For example, whether or not a patient has heart disease cannot be directly known; however, a doctor can *infer* about it using knowledge of associated symptoms. As information regarding the symptoms accumulates, the doctor's belief about the existence of heart disease changes accordingly. For example, if the doctor comes to know that the patient smokes, his belief about the patient's chances of having heart disease increases. The Bayesian network can be used to make intelligent inferences similar to the medical expert. After representing the problem domain in terms of a Bayesian network, one can use it to reason how information about states of certain nodes in the network changes the belief about states of other nodes. This is called *inference* using a Bayesian network.

An interesting aspect of Bayesian network modeling is that both the network's structure and parameters (CPTs) can be determined from a known set of data automatically using algorithms such as expectation-maximization (EM). Estimation of the parameters is called *parameter learning* and estimation of the structure is called *structure learning*, and the complete process of learning from given data is called *training* of the Bayesian network. How parameter learning and inference are performed in a Bayesian network will be shown in the course of this chapter through the modeling of TFBS.

Bayesian Network Model for TFBS

Defining a Bayesian network model for a given problem involves specifying (a) the variables or nodes in the graph, (b) the set of possible states for each node, (c) the edges connecting the nodes in the graph, and (d) the probability distributions or CPTs associated with each node. The former three, that is, the nodes, states, and the edges, comprise the Bayesian network *structure*, and the latter comprises the *parameters*. The structure represents modeler's understanding or beliefs about the problem domain, and there is a fair bit of flexibility possible in choosing the structure.

A Bayesian network model for TFBS is thus defined in this section. Refer to the set of TFBS for the factor NF-Y, as shown in Figure 2. A Bayesian network graph for this TFBS is shown in Figure 7. The length of the TFBS is $N = 16$. Each position in the TFBS sequence is a node X_i in the network. Thus there are 16 nodes, X_1, ..., X_{16}. Each node X_i has four states corresponding to the four nucleotides A, C, G, and T, any of which may be present at position i in the TFBS. The node C is a class variable having states $1,2,...,c$. The first $c-1$ states correspond to the different TFBS classes, while the state c corresponds to the nonTFBS sequence class. The different TFBS classes account for the different types of mechanisms of TF-TFBS interaction. For example, as discussed previously, the NF-Y data has at least two distinct classes of TFBS. The node C may therefore have $c = 3$ states in this case, with states 1 and 2 representing the two TFBS classes and state 3 representing a nonTFBS class.

The edges in the network are determined as follows. Because the TFBS class directly affects the TFBS sequence, the state of the variable C directly affects the states of each of the variables X_i. Conversely, each of the attributes X_i contributes to the classification variable C. Thus there is an edge linking C to each X_i. Additionally, the presence of a particular nucleotide at some

Figure 7. Bayesian network model structure for NF-Y TFBS

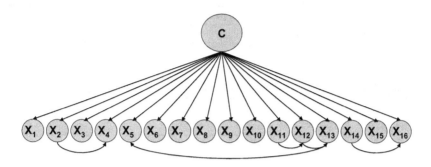

position X_j may influence the distribution of nucleotides at another position X_i. In this case there is an edge linking X_j to X_i. For example, in the NF-Y data, the nucleotides at positions 11 and 12 depend upon which nucleotide is present at position 13. Thus X_{11}, X_{12} and X_{13} are linked. With similar observations, other edges among the nodes X_i are created.

The network configuration, shown in Figure 7, is technically called a tree-augmented network (TAN) (Friedman, Geiger, & Goldszmidt, 1997). In a TAN Bayesian network, a node X_i can have at most one X_j: $j \neq i$, as its parent apart from the common parent node C.

The parameters that quantitatively describe the Bayesian network model in Figure 7 are defined as follows. First we write the joint probability distribution encoded by the network:

$$\Pr(X_1,...,X_{16},C) = \Pr(C)\prod_{i=1}^{16}\Pr(X_i|C,Pa(X_i)), \qquad (4)$$

where Pa (X_i) is the set of parents of the node X_i. That is, Pa $(X_i) = C$ if C is the only parent of X_i, or Pa$(X_i) = \{C, X_j\}$ if there is an edge linking some node X_j to the node X_i. There are 17 different terms in equation (4), viz. Pr(C), Pr $(X_1 \mid C)$, ..., Pr($X_{12} \mid C, X_{11}$), ..., Pr($X_{16} \mid C$). Each of these terms actually expands as a conditional probability table (CPT). The CPT formed by expanding the term Pr($X_1 \mid C$), for example, is illustrated in Figure 8. It is called the CPT for node X_1. Here the probabilities in row $C = 1$ have been calculated from the twelve TFBS data in Figure 2 that have nucleotide A or G in position 13. Similarly, in the row $C = 2$, the probabilities are calculated from the eight TFBS data that have nucleotide C or T in position 13. In row $C = 3$, equal distribution of nucleotides has been assumed to represent nonTFBS sequences.

Figure 8. Conditional probability table (CPT) for the node X_1 in the Bayesian network model of Figure 7. The CPT is expansion of the term Pr($X_1 \mid C$) in equation (4).

	$X_1 = $ 'A'	$X_1 = $ 'C'	$X_1 = $ 'G'	$X_1 = $ 'T'
C=1	3/12	5/12	3/12	1/12
C=2	2/8	4/8	2/8	0
C=3	0.25	0.25	0.25	0.25

Table 1. Parameters of the Bayesian network model shown in Figure 7

Node	Associated parameters (CPTs)
C	Pr (C = 1), Pr(C = 2), ..., Pr(C = c)
X1	The c×4 CPT table Pr(X1 = σ | C = x) where σ ∈ {A, C, G, T} and x ∈ {1, 2, ..., c}
...	...
X12	The (4c) × 4 CPT table Pr(X12 = σ1 | C = x, X11 = σ2) where σ1, σ2 ∈ {A, C, G, T} and x ∈ {1, 2, ..., c}
...	...
XN	The c×4 CPT table Pr(XN = σ | C = x) where σ ∈ {A, C, G, T} and x ∈ {1, 2, ..., c}

The 12 cells in the CPT table of Figure 8 are the parameters associated with node X_1. Similarly, the CPTs for all the nodes in the network together comprise the parameters of the Bayesian network. The complete set of parameters for the Bayesian network of Figure 7 is thus listed in Table 1.

The PWM representation can be understood as a special case of the Bayesian network model. The PWM joint distribution is given by the equation:

$$Pr(X_1,...,X_N) = \prod_{i=1}^{N} Pr(X_i).$$

(5)

This is a special case of the distribution in equation (4) when there is only one class of TFBS data and the X_i are all independent. Thus Bayesian network is a more powerful and general representation.

Learning and Inference

This section describes how the Bayesian network model for TFBS is used for inference and how its parameters (CPTs) are learned using expectation maximization (EM) algorithm.

Inference With Complete Evidence

As stated above, inference refers to determining how information about the states of some variables (such as "smoking," "diet," etc.) changes our belief about the states of other variables (such as "heart disease") for which direct information is not available. The set of nodes for which information is available are called *evidence nodes* and the available information is called *evidence*. For example, the available evidence **e** about a patient may be {Smoking=Yes, Diet=Fatty, Family History=No, Exercise=Medium}, and the inference required may be Pr(Heart disease).

In the TFBS modeling problem, the inference required is whether or not a sequence of length N, $S = S_1 S_2 \ldots S_N$, $S_i \in \{A, C, G, T\}$, is a TFBS. The nucleotides S_1, S_2, ..., S_N serve as evidence $\mathbf{e}$ for the nodes X_1, X_2, ..., X_N, respectively, in the Bayesian network model shown in Figure 7. That is, $e = \langle X_1 = S_1, X_2 = S_2, \ldots, X_N = S_N \rangle$. Given this evidence, the Bayesian network provides belief about the state of the node C, that is, $\Pr(C \mid \mathbf{e})$. Recall that the states $1, 2, \ldots, c$ of node C represent the TFBS / nonTFBS classes. The inference procedure assigns a probability value to each of the states $1, 2, \ldots, c$ of the node C. The probability value indicates the degree of belief with which the sequence window S belongs to a particular TFBS class or the nonTFBS class.

The computation of the beliefs $\Pr(C \mid \mathbf{e})$ is described as follows. The available evidence is written in its expanded form as:

$$\Pr(C \mid \mathbf{e}) = \Pr(C \mid X_1 = S_1, X_2 = S_2, \ldots, X_N = S_N). \tag{6}$$

Using the Bayesian formula $\Pr(A \mid B) = \dfrac{\Pr(B \mid A)\Pr(A)}{\sum\limits_A \Pr(B \mid A)\Pr(A)}$, we can write:

$$\Pr(C \mid \mathbf{e}) = \frac{\Pr(X_1 = S_1, \ldots, X_N = S_N \mid C)\Pr(C)}{\sum\limits_C \Pr(X_1 = S_1, \ldots, X_N = S_N \mid C)\Pr(C)} \tag{7}$$

This expression can be simplified using the conditional probability assumptions encoded in the Bayesian network. Thus, using equation (4),

$$\Pr(C \mid \mathbf{e}) = \frac{\prod\limits_{i=1}^{N} \Pr(X_i = S_i \mid C, X_j = S_j)\Pr(C)}{\sum\limits_C \left[\prod\limits_{i=1}^{N} \Pr(X_i = S_i \mid C, X_j = S_j)\Pr(C) \right]}, \tag{8}$$

where X_j is present in the conditional probability term if an edge exists from X_j to X_i. All the required probabilities in equation (8) are readily available in the parameters (CPTs) of the Bayesian network, such as those listed in Table 1.

Example 1

We take a simpler version of the TFBS modeling problem in this example. Consider the Bayesian network model as shown in Figure 9 for a TF known as CAAT enhancer binding protein (c-EBP) with length 5 TFBS. The CPTs for all the nodes are shown alongside. There are only two sequence classes in this model, TFBS and non-TFBS, that is, there are only two states of the node C. It is required to infer using this model whether or not an observed sequence "GTAAC" is a TFBS for c-EBP.

Solution: The available evidence in this case is $\mathbf{e} = \langle\ X_1 = G, X_2 = T, X_3 = A, X_4 = A, X_5 = C \rangle$. In equation (8), the terms in the numerator for $\Pr(C = TFBS \mid \mathbf{e})$ and $\Pr(\ C = \text{non} - TFBS \mid \mathbf{e})$ are:

	$C = TFBS$	$C = non - TFBS$
$\Pr(C)$	0.32	0.68
$\Pr(X_1 = G \mid C)$	0.34	0.25
$\Pr(X_2 = T \mid C)$	0.11	0.25
$\Pr(X_3 = A \mid C)$	1.00	0.25
$\Pr(X_4 = A \mid C)$	1.00	0.25
$\Pr(X_5 = C \mid X_1 = G, C)$	0.52	0.25
	$- - - - -$	$- - - - -$
Product	6.22×10^{-3}	6.64×10^{-4}

Thus, we have:

$$\Pr(C = TFBS \mid \mathbf{e}) = \frac{6.22 \times 10^{-3}}{6.22 \times 10^{-3} + 6.64 \times 10^{-4}} = 0.903, \quad \Pr(C = non - TFBS \mid \mathbf{e}) = \frac{6.64 \times 10^{-4}}{6.22 \times 10^{-3} + 6.64 \times 10^{-4}} = 0.097$$

Figure 9. Bayesian network model for TFBS of transcription factor c-EBP

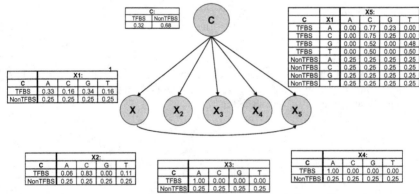

Because $\Pr(C = TFBS \mid \mathbf{e})$ is close to 1.0, we can conclude that the sequence "GTAAC" belongs to the TFBS class. Thus, it is a TFBS for c-EBP, according to the Bayesian network model.

Inference With Partial Evidence

In the case of complete evidence, the values of all the nodes X_i are available as $X_i = S_i$, $i = 1, 2, ..., N$. However, in some cases only partial information is available, that is, the available evidence specifies values of only some of the nodes X_i, with the values of other nodes unknown. Inference using partial evidence is possible in the Bayesian network using a technique called *marginalization*. Marginalization refers to eliminating the unknown variable in a joint probability distribution by summing over all its possible states. For example, the equation, $\sum_B \Pr(A, B) = \Pr(A)$, with the summation performed over all states of B, is an example of marginalizing out the variable B. The following example illustrates how inference using partial evidence is performed.

Example 2

Consider again the Bayesian network model of Example 1. Can we infer whether the sequence "*CAAT" is a TFBS (where * denotes a wildcard, that is, any nucleotide can be present at that position)?

Solution: The available evidence in this case is $\mathbf{e} = \langle X_2 = C, X_3 = A, X_4 = A, X_5 = T \rangle$. Though X_1 is not available, the inference is possible by marginalizing out X_1. We can write:

$$\Pr(C \mid \mathbf{e}) = \sum_{X_1} \Pr(C \mid \mathbf{e}, X_1) \Pr(X_1),$$

where the first term, $\Pr(C \mid \mathbf{e}, X_1)$, can be directly obtained from the CPT, while the second term, $\Pr(X_1)$, can be calculated as:

$$\Pr(X_1) = \sum_C \Pr(X_1 \mid C) \Pr(C).$$

As in example 1, we can compute (refer to Figure 9):

$$\Pr(C = TFBS \mid \mathbf{e}, X_1 = A) = 0.00, \qquad \Pr(X_1 = A) = 0.28$$
$$\Pr(C = TFBS \mid \mathbf{e}, X_1 = C) = 0.00, \qquad \Pr(X_1 = C) = 0.22$$
$$\Pr(C = TFBS \mid \mathbf{e}, X_1 = G) = 0.00, \qquad \Pr(X_1 = G) = 0.28$$
$$\Pr(C = TFBS \mid \mathbf{e}, X_1 = T) = 0.00, \qquad \Pr(X_1 = T) = 0.22$$
$$\Pr(C = TFBS \mid \mathbf{e}) = 0 \times 0.28 + 0 \times 0.22 + 0.985 \times 0.28 + 0.97 \times 0.22 = 0.49$$

Because the probability is about 0.5, "*CAAT" may or may not be a TFBS, according to the model. The reader can try to show similarly that $\Pr(C = non - TFBS \mid \mathbf{e}) = 0.51$.

Parameter Learning

As a machine learning tool, a Bayesian network can learn from examples to simulate the real world phenomenon. Learning, in this context, refers to the procedure of updating the parameter values (CPTs) of the Bayesian network model to make it representative of the known examples. The known examples are referred to as training data. The measure of how well the model fits the training data is provided by the *likelihood function*, which indicates how likely the Bayesian network is to produce this data, that is,

Likelihood function = Pr(Data | Model).

The learning algorithm updates the model parameters so as to maximize the value of the likelihood function, and the parameter values thus obtained are known as maximum likelihood estimates. The basic idea therefore is to find a model configuration which is more likely than any other to produce the given data.

The *expectation-maximization (EM) algorithm* is a general method which can be used to obtain maximum likelihood estimates of the parameters of a Bayesian network for a given training dataset. The EM algorithm works even when the dataset is incomplete or has missing values. Missing values are encountered not only in problems where there are limitations in the data gathering process, but rather they occur more frequently in situations where there are hidden or unobserved variables in the system. The TFBS modeling problem is an example of incomplete data problem because the value of the class variable, C, is unknown for the TFBS data (at least when there are multiple TFBS states).

The EM is an iterative algorithm with two steps, expectation step (E-step) and maximization step (M-step). In the E-step, the current parameters are used to estimate the missing data

Figure 10. The c-EBP TFBS data for learning parameters of the Bayesian network model

Sno	X1	X2	X3	X4	X5	C
1	G	C	A	A	T	?
2	G	C	A	A	C	?
3	A	C	A	A	T	?
4	A	C	A	A	T	?
5	A	C	A	A	T	?
6	C	C	A	A	C	?
7	G	C	A	A	T	?
8	A	C	A	A	C	?
9	G	C	A	A	T	?
10	T	C	A	A	T	?
11	G	C	A	A	G	?
12	T	C	A	A	C	?
13	G	C	A	A	G	?
14	G	T	A	A	T	?
15	G	A	A	A	T	?
16	G	C	A	A	C	?
17	C	C	A	A	C	?
18	G	A	A	A	T	?

using the inference procedure as was described above. In the M-step, the filled-in data is used to perform maximum likelihood estimation of the parameters. The updated parameter values obtained in the M-step are again used in the next E-step to make a new (improved) estimate of the missing data. An M-step again follows to update the parameter values. In this way, the E-M steps are repeated iteratively until convergence.

The EM steps are explained in detail below in the context of Bayesian network model for c-EBP TFBS, shown in Figure 9. The TFBS data used for learning the model parameters is shown in Figure 10. Note that the class variable C is the missing data. The number of states for C is set to 3, with two different TFBS classes and one nonTFBS class.

1.   **Initialization:** The first step in the EM algorithm is to give some initial values to all the parameters (CPTs) of the Bayesian network model. The initial values can be random real numbers in the range (0,1), or can be uniform probabilities giving equal values to all the states. The sum of values in each row of the CPT must be equal to 1. In the present example, random probabilities have been chosen for initialization as shown in Figure 11.

2.   **E-step:** The E-step involves inferring the missing/hidden data using the observed data and the current parameter values. The missing data is predicted using the inference procedure described in section 5.1. For example, filling a missing value of node C in the c-EBP TFBS data involves computing $\Pr(C \mid \mathbf{e})$ using equation (8), where the evidence $\mathbf{e}$ is the known states of the variables X_i for that data point. The estimate of missing data is not a discrete value but a probability distribution over its possible states. To illustrate, estimates of the unknown variable C in the first and hundredth E-steps of the EM iterations are shown in Figure 12.

3.   **M-step:** From the predictions of missing data made in the E-step, the completed training data is made available. Using this completed training data, new parameter estimates (CPTs) for the Bayesian network are computed in the M-step. The maximum

Figure 11. Random initialization of the parameters (CPTs) of c-EBP TFBS Bayesian network model

C	X1:				C	X2:			
	A	C	G	T		A	C	G	T
TFBS1	0.27	0.25	0.24	0.24	TFBS1	0.23	0.26	0.24	0.28
TFBS2	0.27	0.25	0.24	0.24	TFBS2	0.23	0.26	0.26	0.24
NonTFBS	0.25	0.25	0.25	0.25	NonTFBS	0.25	0.25	0.25	0.25

C	X1	X5:				C	X3:			
		A	C	G	T		A	C	G	T
TFBS1	A	0.25	0.24	0.26	0.25	TFBS1	0.25	0.23	0.27	0.24
TFBS1	C	0.25	0.22	0.27	0.25	TFBS2	0.24	0.26	0.24	0.25
TFBS1	G	0.25	0.25	0.26	0.24	NonTFBS	0.25	0.25	0.25	0.25
TFBS1	T	0.25	0.24	0.26	0.25					
TFBS2	A	0.25	0.23	0.26	0.26	C	X4:			
TFBS2	C	0.27	0.25	0.23	0.25		A	C	G	T
TFBS2	G	0.26	0.25	0.23	0.25	TFBS1	0.24	0.25	0.27	0.24
TFBS2	T	0.24	0.24	0.26	0.26	TFBS2	0.27	0.24	0.25	0.23
NonTFBS	A	0.25	0.25	0.25	0.25	NonTFBS	0.25	0.25	0.25	0.25
NonTFBS	C	0.25	0.25	0.25	0.25					
NonTFBS	G	0.25	0.25	0.25	0.25	TFBS1	C:			
NonTFBS	T	0.25	0.25	0.25	0.25	TFBS1	TFBS2	NonTFBS		

C:		
TFBS1	TFBS2	NonTFBS
0.326	0.340	0.333

Figure 12. EM iterations for learning the parameters of the c-EBP TFBS Bayesian network model. The missing values are predicted in the E-step and used to update the parameters in the M-step.

After 1st Iteration

Sno	X1	X2	X3	X4	X5	C TFBS1	TFBS2	non-TFBS
1	G	C	A	A	T	0.309	0.357	0.333
2	G	C	A	A	C	0.320	0.346	0.333
3	A	C	A	A	T	0.309	0.357	0.333
4	A	C	A	A	T	0.309	0.357	0.333
5	A	C	A	A	T	0.309	0.357	0.333
6	C	C	A	A	C	0.291	0.375	0.333
7	G	C	A	A	T	0.309	0.357	0.333
8	A	C	A	A	C	0.320	0.346	0.333
9	G	C	A	A	T	0.309	0.357	0.333
10	T	C	A	A	T	0.311	0.355	0.333
11	G	C	A	A	G	0.343	0.323	0.333
12	T	C	A	A	C	0.319	0.347	0.333
13	G	C	A	A	G	0.343	0.323	0.333
14	G	T	A	A	T	0.332	0.334	0.333
15	G	A	A	A	T	0.308	0.358	0.333
16	A	C	A	A	C	0.320	0.346	0.333
17	C	C	A	A	C	0.291	0.375	0.333
18	G	A	A	A	T	0.308	0.358	0.333

After 100 Iterations

Sno	X1	X2	X3	X4	X5	C TFBS1	TFBS2	non-TFBS
1	G	C	A	A	T	0.059	0.607	0.333
2	G	C	A	A	C	0.666	0.000	0.333
3	A	C	A	A	T	0.666	0.000	0.333
4	A	C	A	A	T	0.666	0.000	0.333
5	A	C	A	A	T	0.666	0.000	0.333
6	C	C	A	A	C	0.666	0.000	0.333
7	G	C	A	A	T	0.059	0.607	0.333
8	A	C	A	A	C	0.666	0.000	0.333
9	G	C	A	A	T	0.059	0.607	0.333
10	T	C	A	A	T	0.666	0.000	0.333
11	G	C	A	A	G	0.666	0.000	0.333
12	G	C	A	A	C	0.666	0.000	0.333
13	G	C	A	A	G	0.666	0.000	0.333
14	G	T	A	A	T	0.000	0.666	0.333
15	G	A	A	A	T	0.000	0.666	0.333
16	G	C	A	A	C	0.666	0.000	0.333
17	C	C	A	A	C	0.666	0.000	0.333
18	G	A	A	A	T	0.000	0.666	0.333

E-step → — **M-step**   **E-step** → — **M-step**

After 1st Iteration — E-step

C:

TFBS1	TFBS2	nTFBS
0.314	0.352	0.333

X1:

C	A	C	G	T
TFBS1	0.22	0.10	0.57	0.11
TFBS2	0.22	0.12	0.55	0.11
nTFBS	0.25	0.25	0.25	0.25

X2:

C	A	C	G	T
TFBS1	0.11	0.83	0.00	0.06
TFBS2	0.11	0.83	0.00	0.05
nTFBS	0.25	0.25	0.25	0.25

X3:

C	A	C	G	T
TFBS1	1.00	0.00	0.00	0.00
TFBS2	1.00	0.00	0.00	0.00
nTFBS	0.25	0.25	0.25	0.25

After 1st Iteration — M-step

X4:

C	A	C	G	T
TFBS1	1.00	0.00	0.00	0.00
TFBS2	1.00	0.00	0.00	0.00
nTFBS	0.25	0.25	0.25	0.25

X5:

C	X1	A	C	G	T
TFBS1	A	0.00	0.26	0.00	0.74
TFBS1	C	0.00	1.00	0.00	0.00
TFBS1	G	0.00	0.20	0.21	0.59
TFBS1	T	0.00	0.51	0.00	0.49
TFBS2	A	0.00	0.24	0.00	0.76
TFBS2	C	0.00	1.00	0.00	0.00
TFBS2	G	0.00	0.20	0.19	0.61
TFBS2	T	0.00	0.49	0.00	0.51
nTFBS	A	0.25	0.25	0.25	0.25
nTFBS	C	0.25	0.25	0.25	0.25
nTFBS	G	0.25	0.25	0.25	0.25
nTFBS	T	0.25	0.25	0.25	0.25

After 100 Iterations — E-step

C:

TFBS1	TFBS2	nTFBS
0.454	0.212	0.333

X1:

C	A	C	G	T
TFBS1	0.33	0.16	0.35	0.16
TFBS2	0.00	0.00	1.00	0.00
nTFBS	0.25	0.25	0.25	0.25

X2:

C	A	C	G	T
TFBS1	0.00	1.00	0.00	0.00
TFBS2	0.35	0.48	0.00	0.17
nTFBS	0.25	0.25	0.25	0.25

X3:

C	A	C	G	T
TFBS1	1.00	0.00	0.00	0.00
TFBS2	1.00	0.00	0.00	0.00
nTFBS	0.25	0.25	0.25	0.25

After 100 Iterations — M-step

X4:

C	A	C	G	T
TFBS1	1.00	0.00	0.00	0.00
TFBS2	1.00	0.00	0.00	0.00
nTFBS	0.25	0.25	0.25	0.25

X5:

C	X1	A	C	G	T
TFBS1	A	0.00	0.25	0.00	0.75
TFBS1	C	0.00	1.00	0.00	0.00
TFBS1	G	0.00	0.47	0.47	0.06
TFBS1	T	0.00	0.50	0.00	0.50
TFBS2	A	0.00	0.24	0.00	0.76
TFBS2	C	0.00	1.00	0.00	0.00
TFBS2	T	0.00	0.49	0.00	0.51
nTFBS	C	0.25	0.25	0.25	0.25
nTFBS	G	0.25	0.25	0.25	0.25
nTFBS	T	0.25	0.25	0.25	0.25

likelihood estimate, in general, for any discrete random variable X that takes n possible states $x_1, x_2, ..., x_n$ is given as:

$$MLE : \Pr(X = x_i) = \frac{N_{X=x_i}}{\sum_{j=1}^{n} N_{X=x_j}},$$ (9)

where $N_{X=x_j}$ represents the number of training data points in which the variable X assumes the state x_j. Note that the denominator of equation (9) is equal to the total number of data points. So the MLE for $\Pr(X = x_i)$ is equal to the percentage of data points in which the state of variable X is x_i.

In the c-EPB TFBS problem, consider the CPT of the variable X_1. Consider one of the parameters in this CPT, $\Pr(X_1 = A \mid C = TFBS1)$, which may also be written as:

$$\Pr(X_1 = A \mid C = TFBS1) = \frac{\Pr(X_1 = A, C = TFBS1)}{\Pr(C = TFBS1)}.$$

The number of data points for which $C = TFBS1$ cannot be exactly determined because C is a missing data variable. But the estimates of C obtained in the E-step can be used to compute a sort of count. The data points for which $X_1 = A$ are no. 3, 4, 5, and 8 in Figure 10. We note down the values of $\Pr(C = TFBS1)$ for each of these data points after the E-step of the first iteration (refer in Figure 12 the same rows no. 3, 4, 5, and 8). Then the count for $(X_1 = A, C = TFBS1)$ is given by $0.309 + 0.309 + 0.309 + 0.320 = 1.246$. In the same manner, the total count for $(C = TFBS1)$ from Table 9 is 5.660. Therefore, the estimate for the parameter $\Pr(X_1 = A \mid C = TFBS1)$ is $1.246 / 5.660 = 0.2201$ in the M-step of the first EM iteration.

Similarly, for each cell in each of the CPTs, the count of data points corresponding to that cell is calculated, and using this count the updated parameter value is calculated.

Sometimes in place of MLE, another type of estimate called maximum a posteriori (MAP) is used in the literature. Omitting the technical details, the formula for the MAP estimate corresponding to equation (9) for MLE is given as:

$$MAP : \Pr(X = x_i) = \frac{\alpha_i + N_{X = x_i}}{\alpha_i + \sum_{j=1}^{n} N_{X = x_j}}, \tag{10}$$

where α_i is a fixed constant known as *Dirichlet prior* for the state x_i. The values of α_i for different states x_i are decided by the researcher. If α_i are all equal, it is called a uniform prior. Prior helps in adding the researcher's knowledge in the computation of Bayesian network parameters. It biases the parameter values according to the researcher's belief about them. The use of priors in MAP estimation is also found useful in problems where training data are less in number. It helps assign informative values to parameters which cannot be reliably estimated due to lack of sufficient data concerning them.

Results

Experiments conducted to compare the performance of Bayesian network model and positional weight matrix (PWM) in predicting TFBS in uncharacterized promoter sequences are

Figure 13. Positional weight matrix (PWM) for the NF-Y TFBS

		Position														
		1	2	3	4	5	6	7	8	9	10	11	12	13	14	15	16
Base	A	34	16	7	58	51	0	2	112	116	0	14	66	13	39	36	25
	C	37	33	51	14	4	116	113	0	0	1	65	6	20	43	9	35
	G	27	26	25	41	56	0	1	1	0	0	33	42	73	22	47	29
	T	18	41	33	3	5	0	0	3	0	115	4	2	10	12	24	27

		Position														
		1	2	3	4	5	6	7	8	9	10	11	12	13	14	15	16
Base	A	0.293	0.139	0.062	0.498	0.438	0.002	0.019	0.959	0.994	0.002	0.122	0.566	0.113	0.335	0.310	0.216
	C	0.318	0.284	0.438	0.122	0.036	0.994	0.968	0.002	0.002	0.011	0.558	0.053	0.173	0.370	0.079	0.301
	G	0.233	0.224	0.216	0.353	0.481	0.002	0.011	0.011	0.002	0.002	0.284	0.361	0.626	0.190	0.404	0.250
	T	0.156	0.353	0.284	0.028	0.045	0.002	0.002	0.028	0.002	0.985	0.036	0.019	0.088	0.105	0.207	0.233

reported in this section. The study concerns NF-Y, a ubiquitous transcription factor whose binding sites are present in the promoters of several genes. The Bayesian network model for NF-Y TFBS, as shown in Figure 7, was compared with the corresponding PWM model shown in Figure 13. The training data for both models was a set of 116 known high-quality NF-Y TFBS obtained from JASPAR database (Sandelin, Alkema, Engstrom, Wasserman, & Lenhard, 2004).

Test sequences were obtained from experimental evidences of NF-Y TFBS that have appeared in the recent literature. These TFBS are not included in the training data obtained from JASPAR. The sequence set, described in Figure 14, contains a total of 18 NF-Y sites. The -1000 to +200 region around the transcription start site (TSS) was extracted in each sequence.

The procedure for using a PWM to scan test sequences for potential TFBS was described in section 2. A similar procedure is used for discovering TFBS using the Bayesian network model. At each position p in the test sequence, as shown in Figure 4, a window of length $N = 16$ is selected. Let the current sequence window be $S = S_1, S_2, ..., S_{16}$, where $S_i \in \{A, C, G, T\}$. This is provided as evidence to the Bayesian network, that is, $\mathbf{e} = \langle X_1 = S_1, X_2 = S_2, ..., X_{16} = S_{16} \rangle$ and is used to compute $\Pr(C \mid \mathbf{e})$. If the distribution of the class variable C shows higher probability for the TFBS classes as compared to the nonTFBS class, it can be concluded that the current window is a TFBS.

Table 2 shows the quality of TFBS predictions obtained using a Bayesian network model, as well as a PWM model. The PWM assigns a match score to each window of the test sequence, and a threshold must be fixed by the user above which the window can be classified as a TFBS. The value of this threshold was varied over a broad range to obtain a fair range of the sensitivity-selectivity tradeoff. Bayesian network, on the other hand, provides a definitive prediction of whether or not a window is a TFBS. The results show that both PWM and Bayesian network can achieve a high level of sensitivity (89%) in predicting the NF-Y TFBS. However, for comparable sensitivity (89%), the PWM reports 4 times as many false positives (257) as compared to the Bayesian network (65). Although for nearly half of the binding sites (7 to 8 out of 18) the selectivity of the PWM is high (>50% PPV), and the false positives increase drastically while predicting the rest of the binding sites. The Bayesian network automatically yields the best sensitivity with an acceptable level of selectivity.

Table 2. Results of TFBS predictions on test data using Bayesian network and PWM

Model		True positives	False positives	Sensitivity	PPV
Bayesian network model		16	65	89%	20%
PWM model	Threshold = 0.90	7	2	39%	78%
	Threshold = 0.85	8	8	44%	50%
	Threshold = 0.80	9	26	50%	26%
	Threshold = 0.75	15	81	83%	16%
	Threshold = 0.70	16	257	89%	6%

Figure 14. Test sequences used to evaluate the performance of NF-Y TFBS prediction using Bayesian network model and PWM model

Gene	Orga-nism	GeneID	Refseq ID	Chr.	TSS	Strand	No. of NFY sites	PubMed ID	Pub. Year
Amelx	MM	11704	NM_009666	X	159299889	+	2	16595692	2006
STMN1	HS	3925	NM_005563	1	25917062	-	4	16757134	2006
PADI3	HS	51702	NM_016233	1	17320899	+	2	16671893	2006
TP73L	HS	8626	NM_003722	3	190990151	+	2	16645595	2006
EDF1	HS	8721	NM_003792	9	137036597	-	1	16567061	2006
IL10	HS	3586	NM_000572	1	203334206	-	1	16256199	2006
PTH	HS	5741	NM_000315	11	13474143	+	1	15890770	2005
ZNF267	HS	10308	NM_003414	16	3179261	+	1	15890770	2005
SOX3	HS	6658	NM_005634	X	139312772	-	1	15656994	2005
Adipoq	MM	11450	NM_009605	16	22990606	+	3	15504955	2004

Thus, Bayesian network models have the advantages of reducing the number of false positives and automatically yielding the highest sensitivity in predicting TFBS. This is because Bayesian network allows much greater flexibility of modeling as compared to the simplistic PWM approach, and so it can model the phenomenon of TF-TFBS interaction in a manner which is more representative of the actual physical mechanism.

Conclusion

Bayesian networks are a powerful formalism for mathematical modeling of real world phenomena. It has great scope of application in a number of engineering and bioinformatics problems due to its being a logical and intuitive way of representing physical objects / attributes and their interactions in the language of probability. However, this versatile tool has remained inaccessible to a large number of potential users due to being obscured by terse manner of presentation and mathematical notations. We attempted to explain the working and application of Bayesian networks in a simpler manner through a practical bioinformatics problem. Only a basic background of undergraduate level probability theory was expected of the reader. The following concepts were discussed in this chapter:

- What a Bayesian network is and how it represents a physical phenomenon in terms of a graphical model (nodes, states, and edges) and probabilities (parameters).

- How a physical problem is translated into a Bayesian network model, with an example of how a suitable network structure is designed.

- How to perform inference using the Bayesian network, given either full or partial evidence or observations.

- How the parameters of a Bayesian network are learned from training data using expectation maximization (EM) algorithm.

- Demonstrating the advantage of using Bayesian networks over a modeling approach that enforces simplistic assumptions.

References

Benos, P.V., Lapedes, A.S., & Stormo, G.D. (2002). Is there a code for protein-DNA recognition? Probab(ilistical)ly... *Bioessays, 24*(5), 466-475.

Bucher, P. (1990). Weight matrix descriptions of four eukaryotic RNA polymerase II promoter elements derived from 502 unrelated promoter sequences. *Journal of Molecular Biology, 212*(4), 563-578.

Friedman, N., Geiger, D., & Goldszmidt, M. (1997). Bayesian network classifiers. *Machine Learning, 29*, 131-163.

Sandelin, A., Alkema, W., Engstrom, P., Wasserman, W.W., & Lenhard, B. (2004). JASPAR: An open-access database for eukaryotic transcription factor binding profiles. *Nucleic Acids Research, 32* (Database Issue), D91-94.

Stormo, G.D. (2000). DNA binding sites: Representation and discovery. *bioinformatics, 16*(1), 16-23.

Stormo, G.D., Schneider, T.D., & Gold, L. (1982). Characterization of translational initiation sites in E. coli. *Nucleic Acids Research, 10*(9), 2971-2996.

Chapter XV

Application of Bayesian Network in Learning Gene Network

Tie-Fei Liu, National University of Singapore, Singapore

Wing-Kin Sung, National University of Singapore, Singapore

Ankush Mittal, Indian Institute of Technology, India

Abstract

Exact determination of a gene network is required to discover the higher-order structures of an organism and to interpret its behavior. Currently, learning gene network is one of the central themes of the post genome era. A lot of mathematical models are applied to learn gene networks. Among them, Bayesian network has shown its advantages over other methods because of its abilities to handle stochastic events, control noise, and handle dataset with a few replicates. In this chapter, we will introduce how Bayesian network has been applied to learn gene networks and how we integrated the important biological factors into the framework of Bayesian network to improve the learning performance.

Introduction

Although a cell is the fundamental unit of all living organisms, it is complicated in terms of both structure and function. The information of such complexities are stored in genes. The whole set of the genes in a cell, called genome, defines the structure and the function of the cell. The expression of a gene is controlled by some other genes. This process is called gene regulation, which is an essential part of life (Goldsbrough, 2001). It is estimated that each gene on average interacts with 4 to 8 other genes, and is involved in 10 biological functions (D'haeseleer, Liang, & Somogyi, 2000). The complexity of a living cell is achieved by the concerted activity of many genes and their products. This activity is often coordinated by the organization of the genome into regulatory modules, or sets of coregulated genes that share a common function (Segal, Shapira, Regev, Pe'er, Botstein, & Koller, 2003). The global gene expression pattern is therefore the result of the collective behavior of individual regulatory pathways. In such highly interconnected cellular signaling networks, gene function depends on its cellular context. These genes (proteins) work together as a team to accomplish certain processes that no single protein can do alone, such as metabolism, detoxification, and various responses to the environment. Without such information, it has been nearly impossible to manipulate the genes as a team. Thus, understanding the network as a whole is essential, and learning the gene network is an important central theme in post genomic research (D'haeseleer et al., 2000; Friedman, 2004; Hasty, McMillen, Isaacs, & Collins, 2001). There are several applications and advantages to studying gene networks:

- Gene networks provide a large-scale, coarse-grained view of the physiological state of an organism at the mRNA level (Brazhnik, Fuente, & Mendes, 2002). Gene networks describe a large number of interactions in a concise way. They also present the dynamic properties of the gene regulatory system. They are capable of being the annotation of genomics and functional genomics data.

- It is an important step to uncover the complete biochemical networks of cells (Brazhnik et al., 2002).

- Knowledge about gene networks might provide valuable clues and lead to new ideas for treating complex diseases (Brazhnik et al., 2002; Friedman, 2004).

- As most phenotypes are the result of a collective response of a group of genes, gene networks help to realize how the complex traits arise and which groups of genes are responsible for them (Brazhnik et al., 2002; Friedman, 2004).

- Gene networks are well suited for comparative genomics. Comparing the gene networks from different genomes is helpful to discover the evolutions (Brazhnik et al., 2002).

Identifying gene networks from experimental data is now an extremely active research area (Chen, Filkov, & Skiena, 1999; Friedman, Linial, Nachman, & Peer, 2000; Imoto, Goto, & Miyano, 2002). The aim of this chapter is to study such complex system by the Bayesian network frame.

Background

Considering the large number of genes in a genome (tens to tens of thousands in deferent genomes), it is unrealistic to understand the global regulation profile by analyzing the regulation pathway one by one manually (D'haeseleer, 2000; Dutilh, 1999). With the development of high-throughput technology microarray, massive gene expression data on thousands of cellular species are being gathered. Computer science shows that inferring a logical regulatory network is possible with the genome wide gene expression data solely (D'haeseleer, 2000). The early computational approaches were based on learning the relationships among genes either by studying the mutual information or the correlation among their expression values. The representatives of such approaches are Pair-wise interaction (Arkin, Shen, & Ross, 1997) and clustering (Wahde & Hertz, 2000), which directly find the correlations between genes. After that, Boolean networks (Akutsu, Miyano, & Kuhara, 1999; Liang, Fuhrman, & Somogyi, 1998) are used in several works, which assume the gene expression levels are represented by Boolean values and the gene regulatory relationship are represented by a set of Boolean functions. Linear and nonlinear models are followed, which assume the regulatory relationships are represented by linear functions and nonlincar functions, respectively. In a famous paper by Friedman et al. (2000), an algorithm to learn gene network using Bayesian network is presented. Since then, several extensions of Bayesian network are proposed, such as Bayesian network integrated with nonparametric regression (Imoto et al., 2002), dynamic Bayesian network (DBN) (Murphy & Mian, 1999), and so forth.

Considering the data problem of microarray dataset (a lot of genes with a few data replicates, noisy, stochastic, etc.), Bayesian networks are more suitable to learning gene networks compared to other methods:

- Bayesian networks are particularly useful for describing processes composed of locally interacting components (Friedman et al., 2000). That is, the value of each component directly depends on the values of a relatively small number of components.

- Statistical foundations for learning Bayesian networks from observations, and computational algorithms to do so, are well understood and have been used successfully in many applications (Friedman et al., 2000).

- Bayesian networks provide models of causal influence (Friedman et al., 2000). Although Bayesian networks are mathematically defined strictly in terms of probabilities and conditional independence statements, a connection can be make between this characterization and the notion of direct causal influence.

- Because of its solid statistic basis, Bayesian network can deal with the stochastic aspects of gene expression and noisy measurements of microarray data in a natural way (Friedman et al., 2000; Hasty et al., 2001).

- Bayesian networks are able to handle a large number of variables with only a few replicates (Murphy & Mian, 1999; Friedman et al., 2000). It is especially useful when learning gene networks, because the microarray data generally have thousands, even tens of thousands, of genes while only tens of replicates. Besides, Bayesian network is capable of estimating the confidence in the different features of the network (Friedman et al., 2000). The absence of the data often lead to the consequence that a lot of networks explain the data equally well. The confidence is useful to measure whether a statistic feature of the network is likely to be true.

- Learning gene networks are NP-Hard (Chen et al., 1999). The decomposability (Friedman et al., 2000) of Bayesian network ensures the local searches can get the global optimization, thus making the learning easier.

- Hidden variables in the network and missing values of the gene expression data are easy to handle using Bayesian networks. Many methods have been set up in learning Bayesian networks with hidden variable and missing values (Elidan, Lotner, Friedman, & Koller, 2000; Murphy & Mian, 1999).

Friedman proposed to model a gene network as a Bayesian network (Friedman et al., 2000). Each gene is a vertex and each regulatory relationship is a edge in the Bayesian network. As learning a sparse network is technically diffcult, Friedman proposed a two steps algorithm, sparse candidate algorithm, to learn the structure and parameter: for each gene, (1) some candidate parents who are likely to be the parents of the target gene are selected; and (2) the search of parents based on Bayesian score is performed in the candidate parent set. For the first step, a general method is using the pair-wise correlation, such as mutual information (MI), to find the genes with high dependence with the target genes. However, some dependence cannot be measured by MI. Thus, some weak parents are generated. Weak parents are the parents to the target gene but do not have high dependence to the target gene. A Kullback-Leibler (KL) divergence is used in the work, which can be improved iteratively using the learned network as the prior knowledge in the iterated learning process, to find the better dependence between gene pairs. The second step can be done by some heuristic method like hill climbing (Friedman et al., 2000). Some biologically meaningful results are obtained and examined by a set of statistic measurements (Friedman et al., 2000): robust test, order relation, Markov relation, and so forth.

Since then, many works based on Bayesian network framework ahave been proposed and some more biological relevant results are obtained. Hartemink (Hartemink, Gifford, Jaakkola, & Young, 2001) extended Friedman's work by adding the annotations to the edges: "+," "-," or "+/-" which represent the positive, negative, or unknown regulation. Murphy and Mian (1999) and Gransson and Koski (2002) used dynamic Bayesian network (DBN), which is an extension of Bayesian network, to model gene networks. In this model, a gene at a time point is regulated by its parent in the previous time point. Thus, the acyclic limitation of Bayesian network is broken in DBN. Murphy and Mian (1999) and gave a thorough report in (Murphy & Mian, 1999) of the application of DBN in learning gene network. Imoto et al. (2002) and Kim (Kim, Imoto, & Miyano, 2004) further extended Bayesian networks and DBN by integrating the nonparametric regression, so that their methods can use the continuous gene expression values instead of the discrete values used in general Bayesian network approaches. Their method can grasp the nonlinear relationships among genes. In this approach, they proposed to use density which integrates nonparametric regression instead of probability measurements. A new criterion is used in the work for model selection which employs Laplace approximation of integral to compute the maximum likelihood.

With more and more works using Bayesian networks as the framework to tackle the gene network reconstruction problem (Friedman, 2004; Hasty et al., 2001; Pe'er, Regev, Elidan, & Friedman, 2001; Segal et al., 2003), nowadays, Bayesian network is becoming one of the widely used approaches in learning gene networks.

However, when learning gene network using time series gene expression data, biologically significant results are only obtained when the gene network is learned from some small datasets. Scientists fail to learn a gene network for medium or large datasets because they overlook some important biological factors, including the variable time delay in the gene regulatory system, the effect of proteins in the regulatory system, and so forth.

In the rest of the chapter, we introduce some new methods which incorporate the important biological information into Bayesian network to learn gene network. Section *Time-Delayed Bayesian Network* models a gene network as a time delayed network and describes a time delayed network learning algorithm to learn the model. Section *Semi-Fixed Bayesian Network* describes a semifix model with hidden variables, as well as a SemiFix Structure EM algorithm.

Time-Delayed Bayesian Network

Most research work in learning gene networks either assumes that there is no time delay in gene expression or that there is a constant time delay. However, gene expression literature (Lee, Sung, Kim, & Kim, 2003) shows that different gene pairs have different time delays for gene regulation. To the best of our understanding, Chen, He, and Church (1999) is the only group who attempted to incorporate the variable time delay factor into the gene network learning process. They proposed to model the regulation process and the variable time delay using differential equations. However, their algorithm has a high computational complexity and no real experiment has been done based on their model.

To address the issue, a learning framework based on Bayesian network enhanced with a variable time delay model is proposed (Liu, Sung, & Mittal, 2004b). A Bayesian network represents probabilistic multivariate statistical dependencies among variables in a compact and easy-to-decipher way. Because it can handle stochastic events, control noise, and handle dataset with a few replicates (Friedman et al., 2000; Murphy & Mian, 1999), it has been applied to discover gene networks and has been shown to have advantages over the other methods (Friedman et al., 2000; Imoto et al., 2002; Murphy & Mian, 1999). However, no work has been done to apply Bayesian networks to address the variable time delay issue of the gene networks. One possible explanation is that learning time-delay models introduce too many variables and thus makes the learning intractable. In order to deal with variable time delay problem, a number of improvements are proposed to make the learning process more effcient and accurate: (1) an improved mutual information calculation method for measuring the dependency between two genes; (2) random sampling to give all weak parents the chance to be selected; and (3) a new structure learning algorithm which is suited to learn the sparse network such as the gene network. In addition, unlike traditional Bayesian networks, the framework can represent and detect directed loops that commonly occur in gene network.

The rest of the section is organized as follows: The time-delayed Bayesian network and its suitability in modeling a gene network is discussed in Section *Time-Delayed Network and its Transformation to Traditional Bayesian Network*. Section *Time delayed network Learning Algorithm* describes the learning algorithm for the time-delayed network.

Time-Delayed Network and its Transformation to Traditional Bayesian Network

Time-Delayed Network

It is well known that for a pair of genes G_i and G_j (suppose G_i regulates G_j), the change of expression level of G_i affects the expression level of G_j after a certain time interval. For example, in Yeast, a gene MCM1 regulates another gene CLN3. Based on the gene expression microarray dataset by Spellman (Spellman, Sherlock, & Futcher, 1998), each time the expression level of MCM1 changes, the expression level of CLN3 correspondingly changes around 30 minutes later.

Time delay intervals are different for different gene regulatory pairs. For example, human TNF-α and iNOS genes are regulated by AP-1 and NF-κB. Their delays in expression after the activation of AP-1 and NF-κB are 3 and 6 hours, respectively (Lee et al., 2003). It is further known that there should be an upper limit for the time delay in a gene network because the length of a cell cycle is limited.

The regulation of genes can form feedback loops (for example, $G_1 \rightarrow G_2 \rightarrow ... \rightarrow G_1$), which exist in many metabolism pathways and are critical in maintaining the stability of a gene network. However, the traditional Bayesian network framework fails to represent and learn the feedback loops.

To model a gene network, we propose the time-delayed network that can capture the variable time delay relationships as well as discover the directed loops spanning over at least one time slice[1]. Time-delayed network is an extension of Bayesian network. It is defined as follows:

Let k be the maximum time delay allowed for each regulation. A Time-delayed network can be described by $N = < G, \theta, \delta >$:

- $G = < V, E >$ is a directed graph, where $V = \{V_1, V_2, ..., V_n\}$ is the set of variables of G and E is the set of directed edges of G. Each variable V_i represents a gene and each edge (V_i, V_j) represents the regulation process from V_i to V_j.

- For every edge $(V_i, V_j) \in E$, $\delta(V_i, V_j)$ represents the unique time delay for the edge (V_i, V_j). Note that $k \geq \delta(V_i, V_j) \geq 0$.

- θ is the parameter set of G that stores conditional probability distribution $Pr(V_i|Pa(V_i))$ for every $V_i \in V$, where $Pa(V_i)$ is the parent set of V_i in G.

- Directed cycle is allowed if at least one of its edges has the time delay ≥ 1. Figure 1(a) shows an example of directed cycle with four genes in the time-delayed network.

Relationship Between Traditional Network and Time-Delayed Network.

Given a maximum time delay k (k is smaller than the time of a cell cycle), a variable at a time slice can only be affected by variables in the current time slice and the previous k time slices. For each variable V_i, let $V_{i,0}$, $V_{i,1}$,..., $V_{i,k-1}$, $V_{i,k}$ be its states in the previous k time slices and the current time slice. Learning whether the edge (V_j, V_i) has a time delay Δ is equivalent to learning whether $(V_{j,k-\Delta}, V_{i,k})$ is an edge. The formal transformation is described as follows. Given a time-delayed network $N =< G, \theta, \delta >$ where $G =< V, E >$, with the maximum time delay k, N can be represented using a traditional network $M =<H, \theta >$ such that:

- $H =< V, E >$, where V is the vertex set and E is the edge set.
- $V = \{V_{i,t} | V_i \in V, t = 0, 1,..., k\}$. Thus, each vertex $V_i \in V$ is transformed to k + 1 vertices $\{V_{i,0},..., V_{i,k}\}$.
- Consider a variable $V_i \in V$ with $Pa(V_i) = \{V_{i1},..., V_{is}\}$ being the parent set of Vi in G. In H, the variable $V_{i,k}$ has s parents $V_{i1,(k-\Delta 1)}$, $V_{i2,(k-\Delta 2)}$,..., Vis,$(k-\Delta s)$ where Δj is the time delay $\delta(V_i, V_{ij})$ associated with the edge between Vi and V_{ij}. In the parameter set θ, the conditional probability distribution $P r(V_{i,k}|V_{i1,(k-\Delta 1)},..., V_{is,(k-\Delta s)})$ of M is the same as the conditional probability distribution $P r(V_i|V_{i1},..., V_{is})$ of N.

Figure 1 shows an example of the transformation. It can be easily verified that the transformed network M is a directed acyclic graph and that the network M contains all the parameters of N. Once the network M is learned, the parameters of the network N can be easily recovered. It is obvious that if the time delay k = 0, the time delayed network is indeed a traditional Bayesian network, and if k = 1 the time delayed network is a dynamic Bayesian network (DBN). Thus, the learning algorithm discussed later is also applicable to the learning of traditional Bayesian network and DBN.

Dataset Transformation

Following the network transformation, the original training dataset D_N for the time-delayed Bayesian network N needs to be transformed. D_N is a time-series dataset with n variables V_1,..., V_n. Each variable V_i is described by its states in m time slices, that is, $v_{i,1}$, $v_{i,2}$,..., $v_{i,m}$.

Recall that M is a Bayesian network with (k + 1)n variables, namely, $V_{1,0}$,..., $V_{n,0}$, $V_{1,1}$,..., $V_{n,1}$,..., $V_{1,k}$,..., $V_{n,k}$. Its training data can be expressed as a set of (k + 1) n-dimensional vectors. Given DN with m time slices, we transformed it into (m − k) training samples for M. The (m − k)'s training samples for M are denoted as D_M. Precisely, for t = 1, 2,..., m − k, the t-th sample for D_M is $(v_{1,t},..., v_{n,t}, v_{1,t+1},..., v_{n,t+1},..., v_{1,t+k},..., v_{n,t+k})$. Figure 2 gives an example of the transformation from D_N to D_M.

Figure 1. An example of network transformation is shown here. (a)The time delayed network contains 4 variables & 4 edges. The integer on each edge indicates the time delay and the maximum time delay k is assumed to be 2. This network has one cycle: $V_1 \to V_2 \to V_3 \to V_4 \to V_1$. (b) The transformed network contains 12 variables and 4 edges. Each variable Vi is transformed to 3 variables: Vi,0, Vi,1, and Vi,2. The edge (V_i, V_j), with time delay Δ, is transformed to edge $(V_{i,k-\Delta}, V_{j,k})$. For example, the edge (V_1, V_2) with time delay 1 is transformed to the edge $(V_{1,1}, V_{2,2})$. After the transformation, no cycle exists.

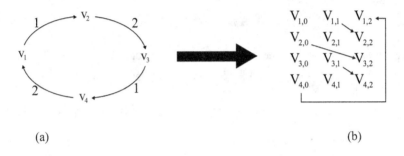

(a)   (b)

Figure 2. An example of dataset transformation. (a) is the original dataset with n variables and m time slices. $v_{i,t}$ represents the state of the variable V_i at time slices t. Suppose the max delay k is 2. (b) is the transformed dataset. The new dataset contains $n \times 3$ variables. Each variable V_i is transformed to 3 variables.

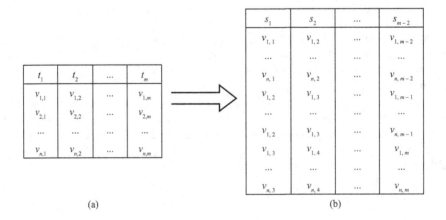

(a)   (b)

Time-Delayed Network Learning Algorithm

Given the transformed dataset, the problem of learning the gene network N (which is a time-delayed network) is reduced to the problem of learning a traditional Bayesian network M. As the gene network N is sparse (Someren, Wessels, & Reinders, 2000) and the transformation makes it more sparse, learning the transformed network M could be more time-consuming. This section presents an algorithm which speeds up the learning process.

A Bayesian network is normally represented by $M = <G, \theta>$ where $G = (V, E)$ is a directed acyclic graph and θ is the parameter set of G. An essential point of Bayesian network is the decomposition of the joint probability of the random variables into the conditional probabilities as shown below:

$$P(V_1, ..., V_n) = \prod_i P(V_i | Pa(V_i)) \tag{1}$$

where V_i is a variable and $Pa(V_i)$ is the set of parents of Vi in the network (Friedman et al., 2000). Learning Bayesian network structure is often an optimization problem. A general approach is to define a score that describes the closeness of a possible structure to the observed data (Friedman, Nachman, & Peer, 1999) and then to find a structure that maximizes the score. Bayesian score (Cooper & Herskovits, 1992) is one of the often used score functions because of its important property of decomposability in the presence of full data (Friedman, Murphy, & Russell, 1998), as shown below:

$$Score(G : D) = \sum_i Score(Vi | Pa(Vi)) \tag{2}$$

With the property of decomposability, the learning procedure can be decomposed into a number of local search procedures to search the parents for each variable independently. A technique used frequently is to divide the learning procedure into two steps. The first step finds a small candidate parent set for each variable based on the dependency between two variables. The second step selects the parent set $Pa(V_i)$ for every variable V_i that maximizes $Score(V_i|Pa(V_i))$ from the candidate parent set. $Score(V_i|Pa(V_i) : D)$ is the measurement of the fitness that $Pa(V_i)$ is the parent set of V_i given the dataset D. In general, greedy or heuristic algorithms are used to accomplish this step (Cooper & Herskovits, 1992; Friedman et al., 2000).

We propose a learning algorithm, time-delayed network learning (TDNL) algorithm, which transforms the time delayed network to traditional network and recovers the time delayed network by learning the transformed network. The learning procedure is based on the framework of sparse candidate algorithm (SCA) (Friedman et al., 1999). SCA improves the first step by selecting a set of candidate parent for every variable V_i and enhancing the candidate parent set iteratively based on the network learned from previous iteration. We perform further improvements for the first step using the following: (1) a modified mutual information to measure the dependence between two genes. This measurement considers common structures that repeatedly appear over several iterations instead of only considering the structure appearing in a single iteration; (2) random sampling to ensure each variable has the chance to be a candidate parent of some gene; and (3) a novel learning method, learning by modification, to effciently select parents from a candidate parent set in the second step.

Choosing Candidate Parent Sets

A general method for generating a small candidate parent set for a variable is based on the dependencies between the variable and its possible parents. One commonly used measurement for dependency between variables is the mutual information (MI), defined below:

$$MI(X;Y) = \sum_{x,y} \overline{P}(x,y) \log \frac{\overline{P}(x,y)}{\overline{P}(x)\overline{P}(y)} \tag{3}$$

where X and Y are some variables and P represents the observed frequency of samples in the dataset. If X and Y have child-parent relationship, MI(X; Y) is expected to have a high value. However, because of the noise in the data and the combined effect of parents, some child-parent pairs sometimes have low MI values and may be excluded from the corresponding candidate parent sets.

To solve the problem, Friedman (Friedman et al., 1999) proposed to employ Kullback-Leibler (KL) divergency to measure the dependency, which uses the structure learned from previous iteration as the prior knowledge to calculate the mutual information. This measurement is expected to be more noise-resistant and is defined as follows:

$$M_{Disc}(X,Y|M) = \sum_{x,y} \overline{P}(x,y) \log \frac{\overline{P}(x,y)}{P_M(x,y)} \tag{4}$$

where $M_{Disc}(X, Y|M)$ is the correlation of X and Y with respect to the network M and P_M is the estimated joint probability given M. However, some true parents of a variable X may have small MI value and KL divergence value. Those parents of X are denoted as the weak parents of X. Such weak parents of variables may not be considered in the candidate parent set in the SCA algorithm. In order to overcome this problem, we propose the following: In each iteration, the following steps are executed: (1) the parents of X in previous iteration become the candidate parents of X in current iteration automatically; (2) the genes with high mutual information to X are selected to be the candidate parents of X; and finally (3) we randomly include some extra genes into the candidate parent set of X. Steps (1) and (2) select the genes with high dependencies to X to be the candidate parents of X while, (3) ensures that, after enough number of iterations, each weak parent has the chance to be included into the candidate parent set.

In every iteration, the candidate parent set contains at most one transformed variable for a gene, because the time delayed network has no multiedges existing between two genes. This property reduces the learning complexity.

As described above, the selection of the candidate parents is done partially on a random basis, leading to an unstable structure. This might result in bias for selecting parents in the next iteration, and thus give a biased network as output. In addition, this problem might make the learning process fail to converge. We propose a new criterion instead of using KL-divergence, which reduces the degree of the random sampling and stabilizes the score so that the score improves smoothly.

The new criterion $\tau(X; Y)_t$ for variables X and Y, can be computed as follows:

$$\tau(X ; Y)_1 = MI (X ; Y) \tag{5}$$

$$\tau(X ; Y)_t = \alpha \times \tau(X ; Y)_{t-1} + (1 - \alpha) \times M_{Disc} (X ; Y \mid M_{t-1}) \tag{6}$$

where t indicates the t-th iteration for $t > 1$ and M_{t-1} represents the network learned from the $(t-1)$-th iteration, α is a parameter to adjust the accumulation rate where $0 \le \alpha \le 1$. Note that $\tau(X; Y)_t = MI(X; Y)$ if $\alpha = 1$ and $\tau(X; Y)_t = M_{Disc}(X; Y|M_{t-1})$ if $\alpha = 0$. Generally, we set $\alpha = 0.5$ which indicates that the substructures appearing repeatedly in previous iterations have the similar weights to the substructures in the current iteration. The formulation of τ $(X; Y)_t$ includes $\tau(X; Y)_{t-1}$, and thus recursively includes $(\tau(X; Y)_{t-2}, ..., \tau(X; Y)_1)$, each of which has different proportion. That is, τ_t is based on all learned networks, from M_1 to M_{t-1}, and each network contributes a part to the final τ_t. The bias and the nondeterministic nature of random sampling in one network is complemented by other good networks, which avoids bias in the final network. It can be observed that correct structures appear repeatedly and thus they have greater chances of remaining in the current network. This reduces the effect of rapid change of KL divergence, resulting in improved convergence. Note that KL-divergence is based only on the previous single network. Any bias in the previous network might affect the current network and even the subsequent networks. It is easy to see τ_t is decomposable, as both MI and M_{Disc} are decomposable.

Another significant problem in learning is that it is time consuming to make inference on $P_{Mt-1}(X, Y)$ in M_{t-1} for calculating $\tau(X; Y)_t$. Ong, Glasner, & Page (2002) estimated that it would take 9 months to do inference on a network with about 200 genes by the junction tree algorithm directly. Sampling is proposed to tackle the problem. One can check Friedman et al. (2000) for the details.

Structure Learning

Transformed network can be learned by any classical learning algorithm. We propose an algorithm, learning by modification (LBM), which is motivated by the K2 algorithm (Cooper & Herskovits, 1992). Due to decomposability of Bayesian score, we can find the best parents for each variable independently. For every variable V_i, and its candidate parent set, K2 includes new variables as its parents one by one as long as the inclusion of the new variable can improve the score of the network maximally as compared to other candidates.

Figure 3. An example: Given a variable X and its candidate parent set CPS = {A, B, C, D, E}, in which B, C are the parents of X. Suppose following subsets of CPS give the scores to X in descending order: {B, C} > {A, B} > {A, C} > {A, B, C} > {A, C, D} > {A, C, D, E} > {A} > {B} and all other subsets give the scores smaller than B. K2 selected {A} and {A, B} in order but missed {B, C} because K2 fails to capture the combined effect of the two parents; learning by elimination selects {A, C, D, E}, {A, C, D} and {A, C} in order; while learning by modification selects {A}, {A, B}, {A, B, C} and {B, C} in order.

K2	learning by elimination	learning by modification
{A}	{A, C, D, E}	{A}
↓	↓	↓
{A, B}	{A, C, D}	{A, B}
	↓	↓
	{A, C}	{A, B, C}
		↓
		{B, C}

One problem of K2 is that it does not consider the combined effect of the parents to a particular variable in the early iterations. Sometimes, this problem leads to a low score network. In addition, there is no way to remove selected false parents from the parent set. We illustrate the effect using an example in Figure 3.

An alternative way, learning by elimination, involves initially setting the parent set as the candidate parent set and then iteratively deleting a variable from the parent set which maximizes the score. The process stops when further removal of any variable from the parent set would not increase the score. The algorithm considers the combined effect starting from the beginning and removes the variables that are not parents one by one. Still, the false parents in the parent set can introduce noise which reduces the combined effect. If there are some false parent variables, there is a similar problem as K2: the true parent might be removed at the beginning with no chance to return. See the second column of Figure 3 for an example.

In Figure 4, we propose a method called learning by modification (LBM) to overcome these problems. LBM is a heuristic algorithm for finding a parent set (PS) of V_i by maximizing $Score(V_i|PS)$. It is iterative in nature. In every iteration, it includes exactly one new variable into PS and then deletes zero or more variables. The two merits of LBM are as follows.

First, LBM ensures PS contains as few false parents as possible. As few parents mean the combined effect of the true parents will not be diluted, true parents V_j of V_i have a better chance of getting a higher $Score(V_i|PS È \{V_j\})$ and hence, they get a better chance to be included into PS. In other words, it avoids the problems of backward selection where the parent set contains too many false parents.

Second, unlike K2, Step (a) of every iteration of LBM always includes a variable V_j into PS irrespective of whether $Score(V_i|PS È \{V_j\})$ is greater than $Score(V_i|PS)$ or not. This idea avoids the problem of K2, where the noises of the false parents may prevent the true parent of V_i from being included into PS.

Figure 4. Outline of the learning by modification algorithm

- Let CPS be the candidate parent set of V_i and PS = {} is the parentset.
- Compute the Bayesian score S = Score(V_i|PS)
- Repeat the following procedure until PS does not change:
- Set S = Score(V_i|PS È {V_j}) and PS = PS È {V_j} where X È CPS maximizes Score(V_i|PS È {V_j}).
- Repeat following procedure until PS does not change: Select a variable V_j È PS which maximizes Score(V_i|PS −{V_j}). If Score(V_i|PS −{V_j}) > S, then set S = Score(V_i|PS − {V_j}) and PS = PS − {V_j}.

The goodness of LBM was also demonstrated by our experiments on simulated data. We found that the parents selected by LBM are better than both K2 and backward selection methods. Figure 3 illustrates the algorithm using a simple example.

Because we assume there is no loop in the same time slice, we do not detect loops formed solely by edges with time delay 0. In practice, the algorithm is fast and accurate.

Semi-Fixed Bayesian Network

When referring to gene regulation, most works simply model that a gene is directly regulated by other genes. However, the regulation of genes in fact occurs at various levels, including transcription, translation, splicing, posttranslational protein degradation, and other processes (Kolpakov, Ananko, Kolesov, & Kolchanov, 1998). To give a correct description of the gene network, we cannot just consider the gene expression level (that is, the level of mRNA transcription).

Based on the biological knowledge, it is known that protein plays a key role in gene network (Wyrick & Young, 2002). In fact, protein-DNA interaction and protein-protein interaction are the main activities in the regulatory system (Kolpakov et al., 1998). Therefore, when predicting microarray gene expression data, proteins should be included. Although their expression levels are still diffcult to measure in the large scale, it is good if we can treat them as hidden variables. The following are the advantages of modeling proteins as hidden variables:

- The model will become more meaningful, more interpretable, and closer to real-life system (Barbara, Jameson, & Witting, 1999; Elidan et al., 2000; Friedman, 1997, 1998).
- In the model, the proteins are decision-relevant. The network without considering hidden variables may omit some dependencies (Barbara et al., 1999; Elidan et al., 2000).

Introducing hidden variables introduces advantages and increases the complexity of the network learning. Moreover, microarray gene expression datasets often have missing values.

Considering the above challenging issues, Bayesian network forms a natural choice with the advantage of supporting several principled methods for learning the causal relationships with incomplete data, both hidden variables and missing values (Friedman, 1998). Successful application of Bayesian network can be found in domain of learning with hidden variables for several applications (Barbara et al., 1999; Elidan et al., 2000; Friedman, 1997, 1998). The most widely used method for structure learning is expectation maximization (EM) algorithm (Friedman, 1998). In E step, the algorithm calculates the score of each possible structure using the structure and parameters learned from previous iteration. Selection of the structure and parameters, which maximizes the score, is done in M step. The procedure is repeated until convergence criteria are met. In our problem, such a kind of learning is diffcult because the algorithm needs to learn the relationship among the hidden variables and the observed variables. In addition, it is diffcult to predetermine the correct number of hidden variables. To learn the optimum number of hidden variables is computationally complex. Besides, in the presence of hidden variables, the network is no longer decomposable, and this makes the learning diffcult (Friedman, 1998).

A system which models the gene network as a directed graph with hidden variables is proposed to tackle the problem (Liu, Sung, & Mittal, 2004a). In the model, the number of hidden variables is predefined using the biological knowledge and, in addition, the relationships between hidden variables and observed variables are partially fixed. A modified EM algorithm (Liu et al., 2004a) is also proposed, which employs the advantages of the semifixed structure to decompose the network, thus learning such networks effciently. Also, an approximation method to perform inference on the joint probability of two genes is presented in order to speed up the learning procedure.

Model Gene Network as a Semifixed Network with Hidden Variables

In the gene regulation system, the regulation process can be divided into two main steps. The first step is gene expression, which is represented by $g_i \rightarrow r_i \rightarrow p_i$ where g_i is a gene, r_i and p_i are the corresponding mRNA and protein, respectively. $g_i \rightarrow r_i$ is the transcription and $r_i \rightarrow p_i$ is the translation process. The transcription effciency that is represented by mRNA level can be measured by microarray. The second step is the gene regulation, which is represented by $p_i \rightarrow g_i$. In this step, the generated protein p_i, possibly in collaboration with some other proteins, regulates the target gene g_i. These two steps are the most important steps in the gene regulatory system. All other steps such as protein degradation just adjust the expression and the regulation strengths. Let $Pa_j = \{g_1,..., g_k\}$ denote a parent set of gene g_j such that each $g_i \in Pa_j$ regulates gene g_j. We note that all proteins $\{p_1,..., p_k\}$ in Pa_j act in a combinative manner to regulate g_j. In other words, the proteins may combine together to form a complex, and then bind to the binding site of the target gene and regulate it, or bind to their own binding sites, and then collaboratively regulate the target gene, or a mixture of the above two ways. An example network is shown in Figure 5(a). Considering a single node representing the proteins' combined influence as the direct regulator to regulate the target gene, the model can be further simplified, as shown in Figure 5(b).

Figure 5. Simplified gene regulation system. (a) Gene expression system can be simplified as the interaction of genes and proteins. (b) The system can be further simplified because the combined proteins are the direct regulator to the target genes.

v_1	v_2	v_3
	1	1
1	0	1
1	1	1
0	1	1

(a)

v_1	v_2	v_3
(0.4, 0.6)	1	1
1	0	1
1	1	1
0	1	1

(b)

Based on the above discussion, for each gene g_j, we propose a hidden variable h_j, which represents the combination of a set of regulatory proteins expressed from Pa_j. Thereupon, Pa_j regulate h_j, then h_j regulates g_j. Based on the simplified regulation system, each gene is regulated by at most one hidden variable and the hidden variables are regulated by one or more than one genes. Such a model means the interaction exists only between gene ↔ protein or among proteins, and there is no edge from gene to gene or hidden variable to hidden variable. This model is termed as a semifixed network and is formally defined as follows:

- A semifixed network $N = < V, E >$ where vertices $V = O \cup H$, $O = \{g_1,..., g_n\}$ is a set of observed variables representing the expression levels of genes, and $H = \{h_1,..., h_n\}$ is a set of hidden variables representing the expression levels of combined proteins) and E is the edge set.

- For each $e_k \cup E$, $ek = (g_i, h_j)$ or (h_j, g_i). Thus, N is a bipartite graph on two partitions O and H.

- For each $g_i \cup O$, there is exactly one incoming edge (h_j, g_i) while there can be many outgoing edges.

- For each $h_i \cup H$, it has exactly one outgoing edge (hi, gi) while there can be many incoming edges $\{(g_{i1}, h_i), (g_{i2}, h_i),..., (g_{ik}, h_i)\}$ where $Pa(h_i) - Pa_i = \{g_{i1}, g_{i2},..., g_{ik}\}$.

Compared to learning general networks with several hidden variables, learning the semifixed network is easier because the number of hidden variables is fixed and the relationships between hidden variables and observed variables are partially known.

Semi-Fixed Structure EM Learning Algorithm

When there is no hidden variable in the network and no missing values in the gene expression data, the probability of the variables given a network structure can be expressed as the production of the probabilities of independent subnetworks:

$$P(X_1...X_n : N_o, D) = \prod_i P(X_i | Pa(X_i)) \qquad (7)$$

where X_1 to X_n are observed variables and No denotes the network without hidden variables. D is a complete dataset.

The decomposability property reduces the learning diffculty in the following manner. With score functions such as minimum description length (MDL) and Bayesian scoring metric, learning the structure of a network can be decomposed to learn each independent subnetwork seperately (Friedman, 1998; Friedman et al., 1999), whereas, in the presence of incomplete data, the decomposability property is not valid and this makes the learning diffcult (Friedman, 1998). However, if all parameters of all hidden variables are assigned, hidden variables are observed and thus, in a sense, the incomplete dataset becomes "complete."

A useful property of semifixed network is that when all parameters of hidden variables have been assigned (as the number of hidden variables and partial relationships of hidden variables and observed variables are known ensuring that all hidden variables can be assigned parameters), the network can be decomposed into independent subnetworks. Each subnetwork comprises of a gene g_j, a hidden variable h_j and a parent set of h_j $(Pa(h_j))$(as shown in Figure 5(b)). The probability is decomposed as:

$$P(g_1...g_n, h_1...h_n : N_{o,h}, D) = \prod_i P(g_i|h_i)P(h_i|Pa(h_i)) \tag{8}$$

where $g_1, g_2,..., g_n$ are observed variables (genes), $h_1, h_2,..., h_n$ are hidden variables and $N_{o,h}$ denotes the network with hidden variables. D is an incomplete dataset. Based on different decomposition methods, the decomposition of scores is also different. In our work, Bayesian score is used. For the detail of Bayesian score, please refer to Friedman et al. (2000). When the network No has no hidden variable, the score is decomposed as follows:

$$Score(N) = \sum_i Score(g_i|Pa(g_i)) \tag{9}$$

For a semifixed network $N_{o,h}$, hidden variables are included. We can show that its Score can be decomposed because the hidden variables are attached to the corresponding genes, as follows:

$$Score(N_{o,h}) = \Sigma(Score(h_i|Pa(h_i)) + Score(g_i|h_i)) \tag{10}$$

Proof

Given all hidden variables, $N_{o,h}$ is decomposable. By Formula 9, Score($N_{o,h}$)=ΣScore(v_i|Pa(v_i)) where vi is a gene or a protein, in $N_{o,h}$: $\{v_1, v_2,..., v_{2n}\}$ = $\{g_1, g_2,..., g_n, h_1, h_2,..., h_n\}$. Therefore, it is easy to see ΣScore(v_i|Pa(v_i)) = Σ(Score(h_i|Pa(h_i)) + Score(g_i|Pa(g_i))) where Pa(g_i) = h_i in $N_{o,h}$. Thus, Formula 10 is proven.

With the aim of computing a network $N_{o,h}$ which maximizes Score($N_{o,h}$) using the property in

Equation 10, we propose a EM algorithm known as semifixed structure EM(SSEM) algorithm to learn such network. The principle of the EM algorithm is as follows: In each iteration, given an initial network structure N_{i-1} and a parameter set θ_{i-1}^{oh} (which includes both the parameters of observed variables θ_{i-1} and hidden variables θ_{i-1}), the step 1 is to calculate the missing values and hidden variables to build a complete dataset are calculated. The second step is to find a better structure Ni and a better parameter set θ_i based on the new complete dataset. A detailed description of the algorithm is shown at the end of this chapter.

For step 1, the missing values and hidden variables can be filled up as follows: Given N and θ, for a missing value of a variable v_i, supposing $Pa(v_i)$ is the parent set of v_i in N and $D = \{d_1,..., d_k\}$ is the discrete values of v_i, we fill up the missing value of vi by a vector $S = (s_1,..., s_k)$ where $s_j = P(v_i = d_j|Pa(v_i))$. This is illustrated in the following example:

Example

The variable v_1 has parents v_2 and v_3. As shown in Table 1 (a), there is a missing value in an instance: $\{v_1, v_2, v_3\} = \{(), 1, 1\}$ where () indicates a missing value. Suppose $P r(v_1 = 0|v_2 = 1, v_3 = 1) = 0.4$ and $P r(v_1 = 1|v_2 = 1, v_3 = 1) = 0.6$, we fill up the instance by $\{v_1, v_2, v_3\} = \{(0.4, 0.6), 1, 1\}$. It means, the filled value adds 0.4 count to the case $v_1 = 0$ and 0.6 count to the case $v_1 = 1$. As shown in Table (b), there are 1.4 cases for which $v_1 = 0$ and 2.6 cases for which $v_1 = 1$. In other words, $P r(v_1 = 0) = 1.4/4 = 0.35$ and $P r(v_1 = 1) = 2.6/4 = 0.65$.

The values of hidden variables are treated as missing values too and are computed in a similar fashion. Given the filled dataset, N_{i-1} and θ_{i-1}, step 2 can learn Ni and θi using general structure learning methods. The general method to learn the structure from a complete dataset is to decompose the network into independent subnetworks, then, to learn the structure of each subnetwork independently. Because we fix partial structure, we can decompose it as the independent subnetworks, each of which has a target gene, a hidden variable and a parent set of the hidden variable (similar to Figure 5 (b)). The main objective is to find the optimal parents for each hidden variable. Learning parents from a large number of candidates is a diffcult task. As a gene network is a sparse network (Someren et al., 2000), a popular technique is to first measure the dependencies of candidates to the target variable and to choose the best k genes as candidate parents. Then, the search for the parents from the candidate parent set can be performed. Friedman et al. (1999) proposed to calculate the dependency by KL-divergence(as Equation 11):

Table 1. Example of filling in missing values

V1	V2	V3
	1	1
1	0	1
1	1	1
0	1	1

(a)

V1	V2	V3
(0.4, 0.6)	1	1
1	0	1
1	1	1
0	1	1

(b)

$$MI(X,Y|M) = \sum_{x,y} \overline{P}(x,y) \log \frac{\overline{P}(x,y)}{P_M(x,y)} \tag{11}$$

where MI(X, Y|M) is the mutual information of variables X and Y with respect to the network M, P(X, Y) is the observed joint probability of X, and Y and P_M(X, Y) is the estimated joint probability of X and Y given M.

Although we can compute $P_M(g_i, h_i)$ given the filled dataset, we cannot compute $P(g_i, h_i)$ to measure the dependency of g_j and h_i, as h_i is hidden. We propose an alternate way to measure the dependency: in each subnetwork, the target gene is the only descendant of the hidden variable. The probabilities of the hidden variable is passed to the target gene. Therefore, $MI(g_j, h_i|M)$ can be reflected by $MI(g_j, g_i|M)$. Thus, the MI can be calculated as following:

$$MI(g_j, g_i|M) = \sum_{g_j, g_i} \overline{P}(g_j, g_i) \log \frac{\overline{P}(g_j, g_i)}{P_M(g_j, g_i)} \tag{12}$$

where $P(g_i, g_i)$ is the observed probability distribution of genes g_j and g_i while $P_M(g_i, g_i)$ is the estimated probability distribution of gene g_j and g_i in network M. Performing inference on joint probabilities in a big dataset is quite time intensive. Thus, we approximate the joint probability of g_i and g_j as follows:

- If $g_j \in Pa(g_i)$, then $g_j \rightarrow h_i \rightarrow g_i$. $P_M(g_j, g_i) = P_M(g_i|g_j)PM(g_j) \approx P_M(g_i|h_i)P_M(h_i|g_j)P_M(g_j)$. Note that in this case, $P_M(g_j, g_i) = P_M(g_i, g_j)$.
- Otherwise, g_i and g_j are conditionally independent and $P_M(g_j, g_i)$ can be approximated as $P_M(g_j)P_M(g_i)$.

By the above approximation, only the joint probabilities of the gene pairs with the parent-child relationships need to be calculated.

The detail of the iterative algorithm is as follows:

- In iteration i, give N_{i-1}, θ_{i-1} and the original incomplete dataset D_0.
- In E step, the missing values and the values of hidden variables of D_0 are filled up based on the inference of N_{i-1} and θ_{i-1}. Then, we obtain a complete dataset D_{i-1}. The structure N_i is learned based on D_{i-1} by maximizing Score(N_i : θ_{i-1}, D_{i-1}). Because of the decomposability, we learn the parents for each gene g_i independently:

    1. Fnd k genes with best MI score with respect to g_i to build the candidate parent set CPS.
    2. Fnd the parent set PS $\in$ CPS which maximum Score(SS_i : θ_{i-1}, D_{i-1}), where SS_i

is a substructure PS $\rightarrow$ h$_i$ $\rightarrow$ g$_i$.

   o   Repeat the procedure until convergence.

- In M step, θi is learned based on Ni which maximize Score(N$_i$: θ_i, D$_{i-1}$).
- Repeat the procedure until convergence or until the predefined number of iteration is reached.

In the above procedure, the network structure and parameters are refined iteratively. To get the initial network structure N$_0$ and parameters θ_0 :

- Learn the D$_0$ as a complete dataset. Pa$_i$ for each g$_i$ and the dependent probabilities are gotten.
- For each gene g$_i$, add a hidden variable h$_i$. Set the Pa(hi) = Pa$_i$ and P(h$_i$|Pa(h$_i$)) = P(g$_i$|Pa$_i$).
- A complete dataset D$_0$ by filling D$_0$ based on the network structure and dependent probabilities is obtained.
- N$_0$ and θ_0 can be learned from D$_0$.

Conclusion

Learning gene networks is an important and diffcult task. With the use of microarray data, it has gained even more attention and has become one of the central tasks in the post genome era.

Several facts hinder the research on learning gene networks from microarray gene expression data: the NP-hard property, the data (dimension) problem, the stochastic nature, and so forth. Although many methods have been proposed to tackle these problems, few of them could give reasonable results on large-scale data. To learn the complex cellular network, some strategies are possibly useful:

- Integrating with more biological information. Gene network is a simplified presentative of complex cellular network, which includes genome, proteome, and metableome. It is natural that if we have more types of data source, we would get better learning performance. Recent papers (Imoto, Higuchi, Goto, Tashiro, Kuhara, & Miyano, 2004; Irit, Tanay, Raijman, & Shamir, 2005; Tamada, Kim, Bannai, Imoto, Tashiro, Kuhara et al., 2003) have reported that combining different types of biological data sources is useful in determining the structure of a gene network. The frequently used data sources are protein interaction, transcription factor, cell cycle information, and so forth. Given more related information, the learning models could be more realistic and the results they produce would become more biologically relevant.

- Combining multidatasets. One of the main problems in learning gene networks is the insuffciency of microarray data. Accurate results cannot be deduced from thousands of genes tested in tens of measurements. If we could combine several datasets with or without the same time intervals, we would have a greater chance of obtaining correct pictures of networks. Several issues need to be considered to achieve effcient dataset combinations: 1) The datasets may be obtained under different scenarios. The expression and regulation patterns of the datasets may be different. There will be some overlap and some intersupplement, which need to be handled carefully. 2) The datasets may have different time intervals. For example, in Spellman's dataset (Spellman et al., 1998), the time intervals of the subsets vary from 7 minutes to 30 minutes. The strategies to combine different microarray dataset are important for the purpose.

- Use of gene over-expression and disruption data. Such types of data provide the chance to observe the effect of specific genes directly. The goodness of these data has been reported in some recent papers (Akutsu, Kuhara, Maruyama, & Miyano, 1998; Pe'er et al., 2001; Rice, Tu, & Stolovitzky, 2005; Rung, Schlitt, Brazma, Freivalds, & Vilo, 2002).

References

Akutsu, T., Kuhara, S., Maruyama, O., & Miyano, S. (1998). Identification of gene regulatory networks by strategic gene disruptions and gene overexpressions. In *Proceedings of the Ninth Annual ACM-SIAM Symposium on Discrete Algorithms* (pp. 695-702).

Akutsu, T., Miyano, S., & Kuhara, S. (1999). Identification of genetic getworks from a small number of gene expression patterns under the Boolean Network model. In *Proceedings of the Pacific Symposium on Biocomputing (psb)* (pp. 17-28).

Arkin, A., Shen, P., & Ross, J. (1997). A test case of correlation metric construction of a reaction pathway from measurements. *Science, 277,* 1275-1279.

Barbara, G., Jameson, A., & Witting, F. (1999). Learning Bayesian networks with hidden variables for user modeling. In *Proceedings of the International Joint Conferences on Artificial Intelligence Workshop: Learning About Users* (pp. 29-34).

Brazhnik, P., Fuente, A., & Mendes, P. (2002). Gene networks: How to put the function in genomics. *TRENDS in Biotechnology, 1*(20), 467-472.

Chen, T., Filkov, V., & Skiena, S. (1999). Identifying gene regulatory networks from exprimental data. In *Proceedings of the International Conference on Research in Computational Molecular Biology (recomb)* (pp. 94-103).

Chen, T., He, H., & Church, G. (1999). Modeling gene expression with differential equations. In *Proceedings of the Pacific Symposium on Biocomputing (psb)* (vol. 4) (pp. 29-40).

Cooper, G., & Herskovits, E. (1992). A Bayesian method for the induction of probabilistic networks from data. *Machine Learning, 9,* 309-347.

D'haeseleer, P. (2000). *Reconstructing gene networks from large scale gene expression data.* Unpublished doctoral dissertation, University of New Mexico.

D'haeseleer, P., Liang, S., & Somogyi, R. (2000). Genetic network inference: From co-expression clustering to reverse engineering. *Bioinformatics, 16(*2), 707-726.

Dutilh, B. (1999). *Analysis of data from microarray experiments, the state of the art in gene network reconstruction.* Unpublished doctoral dissertation, Department of Theoretical biology and Bioinformatics, Utrecht University.

Elidan, G., Lotner, N., Friedman, N., & Koller, D. (2000). Discovering hidden variables: A structure-based approach. *Neural information processing systems (nips)* (p. 479-485).

Friedman, N. (1997). Learning belief networks in the presence of missing values and hidden variables. In *Proceedings of the 14th International Conference on Machine Learning* (pp. 125-133).

Friedman, N. (1998). The Bayesian structure EM algorithm. *Uncertainty in artificial intelligence* (p. 129-138).

Friedman, N. (2004). Inferring cellular networks using probabilistic graphical models. *Science, 303*(6), 799-805.

Friedman, N., Linial, M., Nachman, I., & Peer, D. (2000). Using Bayesian networks to analyze expression data. In *Proceedings of the International Conference on Research in Computational Molecular Biology (recomb)* (pp. 127-135).

Friedman, N., Murphy, K., & Russell, S. (1998). Learning the structure of dynamic probabilistic networks. *Uncertainty in artificial intelligence* (pp. 139-147).

Friedman, N., Nachman, I., & Peer, K. (1999). Learning Bayesian network structure from massive datasets: The "Sparse Candidate" algorithm. *Uncertainty in artificial intelligence* (pp.206-215).

Goldsbrough, P. (2001). Biotechnology in agriculture (2nd ed.). Lecture Notes. Department of Horticulture & Landscape Architechture, Purdue University, West Lafayette, IN, USA.

Gransson, L., & Koski, T. (2002). Using a dynamic Bayesian network to learn genetic interactions (Tech. Rep.). Graduate School of Biomedical Research, Linkoping University.

Hartemink, A., Gifford, D., Jaakkola, T., & Young, R. (2001). Using graphical models and genomic expression data to statistically validate models of genetic regulatory networks. In *Proceedings of the Pacific Symposium on Biocomputing (PSB)* (vol. 6) (pp. 422-433).

Hasty, J., McMillen, D., Isaacs, F., & Collins, J. (2001). Computational studies of gene regulatory networks: In Numero molecular biology. *Nature Reviews Genetics, 2*(4), 268-279.

Imoto, S., Goto, T., & Miyano, S. (2002). Estimation of genetic networks and functional structures between genes by using Bayesian networks and nonparametric regression. In *Proceedings of the Pacific Symposium on Biocomputing (psb)* (vol. 7) (pp. 175-186).

Imoto, S., Higuchi, T., Goto, T., Tashiro, K., Kuhara, S., & Miyano, S. (2004). Combining microarrays and biological knowledge for estimating gene networks via Bayesian network. *Journal of Bioinformatics and Computational Biology,* (1), 77-98.

Irit, G., Tanay, A., Raijman, D., & Shamir, R. (2005). The factor graph network model for biological systems. In *Proceedings of the International Conference on Research in Computational Molecular Biology (recomb)* (pp. 31-47).

Kim, S., Imoto, S., & Miyano, S. (2004). Dynamic Bayesian network and nonparametric regression for nonlinear modeling of gene networks from time series gene expression data. *Biosystems, 75,* 57-65.

Kolpakov, F., Ananko, E., Kolesov, G., & Kolchanov, N. (1998). Genenet: A gene network database and its automated visualization. *Bioinformatics, 14,* 529-537.

Lee, A., Sung, S., Kim, Y., & Kim, S. (2003). Inhibition of lipopolysaccharide-inducible nitric oxide synthase TNF-α and COX-2 expression by sauchinone effects on I-κBα phosphorylation, C/EBP and AP-1 activation. *British Journal of Pharmacology, 139,* 11-20.

Liang, S., Fuhrman, S., & Somogyi, R. (1998). REVEAL, a general reverse engineering algorithm for inference of genetic network architectures. In *Proceedings of the Pacific Symposium on Biocomputing (psb)* (vol. 3) (pp. 18-29).

Liu, T., Sung, W., & Mittal, A. (2004a). Gene network modeling through semi-fixed Bayesian network. In *Proceedings of the European Conference on Artificial Intelligence (ecai)* (pp. 373-377).

Liu, T., Sung, W., & Mittal, A. (2004b). Learning multi-time delay gene network using Bayesian network framework. In *Proceedings of the 16th IEEE International Conference on Tools with Artificial Intelligence* (pp. 640-645).

Murphy, K., & Mian, S. (1999). Modelling gene expression data using dynamic Bayesian network (Tech. Rep.). Computer Science Division, University of California, Berkeley, CA.

Ong, I.M., Glasner, J.D., & Page, D. (2002). Modelling regulatory pathways in E. coli from time series expression profiles. *Bioinformatics, 18,* 241-248.

Pe'er, D., Regev, A., Elidan, G., & Friedman, N. (2001). Inferring subnetwork from perturbed expression profiles. *Bioinformatics, 17(*Suppl. 1), s215-s224.

Rice, J., Tu, U., & Stolovitzky, G. (2005). Reconstructing biological networks using conditional correlation analysis. *Bioinfomatics, 21*(6), 765-773.

Rung, J., Schlitt, T., Brazma, A., Freivalds, K., & Vilo, J. (2002). Building and analysing genome wide gene disruption networks. *Bioinformatics, 18*(Suppl.2), S202-S210.

Segal, E., Shapira, M., Regev, A., Pe'er, D., Botstein, D., & Koller, D. (2003). Module metworks: Identifying regulatory modules and their condition-specific regulators from gene expression data. *Nature Genetics, 34*(2), 166-176.

Someren, E., Wessels, L., & Reinders, M. (2000). Linear modeling of genetic networks from experimental data. In *Proceedings of the International Conference on Intelligent Systems for Molecular Biology (ismb)* (pp. 355-366).

Spellman, P., Sherlock, G., & Futcher, B. (1998). Comprehensive identification of cell cycle regulated genes of the yeast saccharomyces cerevisiae by microarray hybridization. *Molecular Biology of the Cell, 9,* 3273-3297.

Tamada, Y., Kim, S., Bannai, H., Imoto, S., Tashiro, K., Kuhara, S., et al. (2003). Estimating gene networks from gene expression data by combining Bayesian network model with promoter element detection. *Bioinformatics, 19*(Supl. 2), ii227-ii236.

Wahde, M., & Hertz, J. (2000). Course-grained reverse engineering of genetic regulatory networks. *Biosystems, 55,* 129-136.

Wyrick, J., & Young, R. (2002). Deciphering gene expression regulatory network. *Current Opinion in Genetics and Development, 12,* 130-136.

Endnote

[1] Because the time interval between consecutive time slices is short, only few loops can be formed within the same time slice.

About the Authors

Ankush Mittal is presently serving as an associate professor at the Indian Institute of Technology, Roorkee. He earned a bachelor's degree in computer science and engineering and a master's degree in computer science and engineering from the Indian Institute of Technology (Delhi)(1996 and 1998, respectively). Dr. Mittal earned his PhD from the National University of Singapore, Electrical and Computer Engineering Department. Previously, he was a faculty member in the Department of Computer Science, National University of Singapore (2001). His research interests include image processing, bioinformatics, and e-learning. He has published more than 100 papers in top journals and conferences.

Ashraf A. Kassim is with the Electrical & Computer Engineering Department of the National University of Singapore (NUS) and vice-dean of the NUS School of Engineering. He obtained his Bachelor of Engineering with first class honors and Master of Engineering in electrical engineering from NUS, before receiving his PhD from Carnegie Mellon University (1993). Prior to joining NUS, Dr. Kassim was involved in machine vision research at Texas Instruments. His main research interests are in the areas of computer vision, image and video processing. He has over 100 international journal and conference publications. He has been a program and organizing committee member of a number of international conferences. Dr. Kassim is an editor of *Machine Vision and Applications Journal*.

***

Arnaldo J. Abrantes was an associate professor with the Electronics, Telecommunications and Computer Engineering Department of Instituto Superior de Engenharia de Lisboa (ISEL). Dr. Abrantes received a PhD from the Technical University of Lisbon, Portugal (1998). His research interests include computer vision, multimedia information retrieval, and machine learning. Dr. Abrantes develops his activities at ISEL, within the group of Multimedia and Machine Learning.

Mansoor Alam is a professor of electrical engineering & computer science at the University of Toledo, Ohio (USA). Dr. Alam earned a bachelor's degree in engineering from Aligarh Muslim University, and an ME in electrical engineering from the Indian Institute of Science, Bangalore (1969 and 1971, respectively). Dr. Alam earned a PhD in electrical engineering from the Indian Institute of Science, Bangalore (1974). He has served as the undergraduate director of the computer science & engineering program, and as graduate director, EECS Department at UT. He has held previous faculty positions at the University of Windsor, (Ontario, Canada), and at the University of Petroleum and Minerals, (Dhahran, Saudi Arabia). His research interests include fault-tolerant systems and reliability, MPLS networks, scheduling algorithms in multi-service routing switches, performance analysis of high-speed networks, and Internet QoS control.

Gary Bradski is a consulting professor in the Stanford University, Department of Computer Science AI Lab. He is also vice president of engineering at Rexee Inc. He is currently interested in the application of multi-grid techniques and statistical models to computer vision. He was integral to the development of the following vision libraries: the Open Source Computer Vision Library (OpenCV), the Statistical Machine Learning Library (MLL comes with OpenCV), and the Probabilistic Network Library (PNL). These vision libraries helped develop a notable part of the commercial Intel performance primitives library (IPP) and are all available for commercial or research purposes at http://sourceforge.net.) Dr. Bradski also organized and worked on the vision system for Stanley, the robot that won the DARPA Grand Challenge autonomous race across the desert.

Arunkumar Chinnasamy is an analytics consultant for leading banks in the Asia Pacific and is currently developing scoring models for risk and marketing. Chinnasamy received his Bachelor of Engineering degree in information technology from India and master's degree from the National University of Singapore under the supervision of Dr. Ken Sung and Dr. Ankush Mittal. After graduation, he did research in National University of Singapore and A*STAR, and has published international papers in data mining applications in life sciences.

Rajesh Chowdhary is currently pursuing his PhD in computer science from the National University of Singapore. Chowdhary received his BTech from the Indian Institute of Technology, Bombay, and MSc from Imperial College, London. His research interests include Bayesian networks, biomedical informatics, machine learning, gene regulation, and genome data mining.

Ben Daniel (PhD candidate, University of Saskatchewan), has a broad interdisciplinary research interest, mainly in applied artificial intelligence in education (AIED). Currently his active research foci are on the application of Bayesian belief network in ill-defined areas and imprecise data sets and analysis of complex social systems, social software, content analysis, virtual learning communities, distributed communities of practice, learning objects, and knowledge management. Daniel's a member of the Laboratory for Advanced Research in Intelligent Educational Systems (ARIES) in the Department of Computer Science and the Virtual Learning Community (VLC) Research Laboratory at the Educational and Communications Technology Unit at the University of Saskatchewan, Saskatoon, Saskatchewan, Canada.

Qian Diao grew up in the Luoyang, Henan province in the middle of China. She attended Nanjing University of Aeronautics and Astronautics, where she earned her BE and ME in automation (1994 and 1997, respectively). Dr. Diao earned her PhD in pattern recognition and intelligent systems at Shanghai Jiao Tong University (2000). After graduating, she came to the Intel China Research Center as a researcher (July, 2000). She has since joined the Intel Santa Clara site as a research scientist (April 2006). Her main research interests include text mining, pattern recognition, and the algorithms of machine learning and computational statistics, especially in graphical models, support vector machine, and semi-supervised learning.

Christos Faloutsos is a professor at Carnegie Mellon University (USA). He has received the Presidential Young Investigator Award by the National Science Foundation (1989), seven "best paper" awards, and several teaching awards. He has served as a member of the executive committee of SIGKDD, and has published over 140 refereed articles, one monograph, and holds five patents. His research interests include data mining for streams and networks, fractals, indexing for multimedia and bio-informatics data bases, and performance.

Sumeet Gupta is currently a PhD student at the Department of Information Systems (School of Computing) in the National University of Singapore. He graduated with MBA from NUS Business School, Singapore. His research interests are in e-commerce with a specific focus on IT post-adoption, Internet shopping, and virtual communities. His research work has been accepted in *Decision Support Systems*, and *Information Resource Management Journal*. Gupta has presented his research work at ICIS, AMCIS, ECIS, and PACIS.

Wei Hu earned his BE and ME at Harbin Engineering University, Department of Computer and Information Science (1992 and 1995, respectively). Dr. Hu earned his PhD at the Chinese Academy of Sciences, Institute of Computing Technology. (1998). He worked as a research associate at Hong Kong University in the Department of EEE (1998 to 1999). He joined Intel China Research Center as a researcher (March 2000). His main research interests include algorithms and applications of machine learning and computational statistics, such as graphical models and semi/unsupervised learning. Currently Dr. Hu is focusing on the subject of personal multimedia mining, especially video mining, to extract and fusion of the audio/visual/text information.

Kaizhu Huang is a researcher at the Fujitsu Research and Development Center Co. Ltd., Information Technology Laboratory. He earned a bachelor's degree in automation from Xi'an Jiaotong University, and an ME in pattern recognition and intelligent systems from the Chinese Academy of Sciences Institute of Automation (1997 and 2000, respectively). Dr. Huang earned a PhD in computer science and engineering from the Chinese University of Hong Kong (2004). His current research interests include machine learning, pattern recognition, image processing, and information retrieval.

Seiya Imoto is an assistant professor at the University of Tokyo, Institute of Medical Science, Human Genome Center, laboratory of DNA information analysis. He earned his BS and MS both in mathematics from Kyushu University (1996 and 1998, respectively). Dr. Imoto earned his PhD in mathematics from Kyushu University (2001). His current research interests include statistical analysis of high dimensional data by Bayesian approach, DNA micro-array gene expression data analysis, gene regulatory network analysis, and computational drug target gene discovery.

Pedro M. Jorge is an assistant professor at the Polytechnic Institute of Lisbon, and member of the Institute for Systems and Robotics. He received the MSc degree from the Technical University of Lisbon, Portugal (1995). His research interests include machine learning, computer vision, and statistical signal processing. Jorge develops his activities at Instituto Superior de Engenharia de Lisboa, within the group of Multimedia and Machine Learning.

Michael Kane is a PhD student in the Statistics Department at Yale University. He received a BS in computer engineering and MS in electrical engineering at Rochester Institute of Technology. Previously, he worked as a research scientist in Eastman Kodak's Commercial and Government Systems Division (later, the International Telephone and Telegraph's Space Systems Division). His research interests include statistical/machine learning, Bayesian statistics, wavelet analysis, and data analysis.

Hee-Wong Kim is an assistant professor at the National University of Singapore, Information Systems Department. He has previously worked as a senior consultant at EDS. He currently serves on the editorial board of *Journal of Database Management*. His research work has been accepted or published in *Journal of the Association for Information Systems*, *Communications of the ACM*, *International Journal of Human-Computer Studies*, *Journal of the American Society for Information Science and Technology*, *IEEE Software*, *Data Base*, *Information and Management*, and *Decision Support Systems*. He has presented his research work at ICIS, HICSS, ECIS, PACIS, AMCIS, IRMA, and DSI.

Irwin King earned a BSc degree in engineering and applied science from California Institute of Technology, Pasadena and an MSc in computer science from the University of Southern California, Los Angeles, (1984 and 1988, respectively). Dr. King earned a PhD in computer science from the University of Southern California, Los Angeles (1993). He joined the Chinese University of Hong Kong (1993). He is a member of ACM, IEEE Computer Society, International Neural Network Society (INNS), and Asian Pacific Neural Network

Assembly (APNNA). Currently, he is serving the Neural Network Technical Committee (NNTC) under the IEEE Computational Intelligence Society. He is also the Vice-President of the Asia Pacific Neural Network Assembly (APNNA). He is a member of the Editorial Board of the *Neural Information Processing—Letters and Reviews Journal* (NIP-LR). His research interests include content-based retrieval methods for multimedia databases, distributed multimedia information retrieval in peer-to-peer systems, and statistical learning theory. He has published over 100 papers in these areas.

Helge Langseth works as an associate professor at the Norwegian University of Science and Technology (NTNU) Department of Computer and Information Sciences (2006). Dr. Langseth earned his PhD in mathematical statistics from the Norwegian University of Science and Technology (NTNU) (2001). His thesis was entitled *Bayesian Networks with Applications in Reliability Analysis*. He has been working with reliability applications at SINTEF Safety and Reliability for more than 10 years. His main research interest is to use Bayesian network models in decision support systems.

João M. Lemos is currently full professor of systems, decision, and control at the Department of Electrical Engineering and Computers of IST, Technical University of Lisbon, Portugal. He is also the leader of the research group on Control of Dynamic Systems at INESC-ID. He earned his PhD from IST (1989). After extensive periods of work at the University of Florence, Dr. Lemos has been devoted to problems on computer-based systems and control, including adaptive control and multiple model based algorithms for control and estimation. He published over 25 research papers in peer reviewed scientific journals and 100 communications on international symposia.

Tie-Fei Liu is a post-doctoral fellow in the Department of Biological Science at the National University of Singapore. Dr. Liu earned a Bachelor of Medicine degree from the Third Military Medical University of China and a PhD from the Department of Computer Science of the National University of Singapore. Currently, his research interests are computational biology and bioinformatics.

David Lo earned his bachelor's and master's degrees in engineering science from the University of Western Ontario, Department of Electrical Engineering (London, Ontario) (1991 and 1994, respectively). He worked for a medical equipment company as a senior system developer for 5 years before he returned to school. In November 2004, he joined STMicroelectronics as an R&D consultant for the System-on-Chip Platform Automation group. Dr. Lo earned a PhD in electrical engineering from Carleton University, Ottawa, (Canada) (2005).

Jianye Lu is a PhD candidate at Yale University Computer Science Department. Before attending Yale, he earned his bachelor's and master's degrees in computer science from Tsinghua University, China, (2000 and 2002, respectively). Lu then worked as contractor at the Intel China Research Center (2003). His current research interest is computer graphics, including material weathering, architecture reconstruction, and sketch-based modeling. His previous projects include visual tracking and motion planning for mobile robots.

Jiebo Luo is a senior principal scientist with Kodak Research Laboratories. He serves on the editorial boards of several journals (T-PAMI, T-MM, PR, JEI) and participated in the organizing or program committees of numerous conferences and workshops. He is an adjunct professor at the Rochester Institute of Technology and has advised PhD and MS students at various universities. Dr. Luo is a Kodak distinguished inventor and a senior member of the IEEE. His research interests include image processing, pattern recognition, computer vision, medical imaging, and multimedia communication. He has authored over 100 technical papers and holds over 40 U.S. patents.

Michael R. Lyu is a professor in the Computer Science and Engineering Department of the Chinese University of Hong Kong. He earned a BS in electrical engineering from National Taiwan University, a MS in computer engineering from the University of California, Santa Barbara, and a PhD in computer science from University of California, Los Angeles. He has worked at the Jet Propulsion Laboratory, Bellcore, and Bell Labs and taught at the University of Iowa. Dr. Lyu's research interests include software reliability engineering, software fault tolerance, distributed systems, image and video processing, multimedia technologies, and mobile networks. He has published over 220 papers in these areas. Dr. Lyu is frequently invited as a keynote or tutorial speaker to conferences and workshops in the United States, Europe, and Asia. He has been an associate editor of *IEEE Transactions on Reliability*, *IEEE Transactions on Knowledge and Data Engineering*, and the *Journal of Information Science and Engineering*. Dr. Lyu is an IEEE Fellow.

Dimitris Margaritis is an assistant professor at Iowa State University, Department of Computer Science (USA). He earned an MS from the State University of New York at Stony Brook, and a PhD in computer science from Carnegie Mellon University. He is interested in artificial intelligence and machine learning, with emphasis on learning the structure of graphical models from centralized and distributed data and their uses in modeling very large databases and bioinformatics applications.

Jorge S. Marques is an associate professor with the Electrical Engineering and Computers Department of Instituto Superior Técnico, Lisbon, and member of the Institute for Systems and Robotics. He earned a PhD and the Aggregation title from the Technical University of Lisbon, Portugal (1990 and 2002, respectively). His research interests are in statistical image processing, shape analysis, and pattern recognition. Dr. Marques was president of the Portuguese Association for Pattern from 2001 to 2003.

Gordon I. McCalla is a professor at the University of Saskatchewan, Department of Computer Science (Saskatoon, Canada). His research interests are in applied artificial intelligence, focused particularly on user modeling and artificial intelligence in education (AIED). Working with colleagues and students in the ARIES Laboratory at the University of Saskatchewan, Dr. McCalla has explored many issues, including granularity in learning and reasoning, educational diagnosis, learner modeling, tutorial dialogue, instructional planning, peer help, and learning object repositories. A current focus is a data-centric approach to e-learning called the "ecological approach." Dr. McCalla is a former president of the International AIED Society.

Satoru Miyano is a professor at the University of Tokyo, Institute of Medical Science, Human Genome Center. He earned his PhD in mathematics from Kyushu University (1984). Currently his research group is developing computational methods for inferring gene networks from micro-array gene expression data and other biological data, for example, protein-protein interactions and promoter sequences. The group also developed a software tool called Genomic Object Net for modeling and simulation of various biological systems. This software is now commercialized as Cell Illustrator. Dr. Miyano's research group is also intensively working on developing the gene networks of the human endothelial cell by knocking down hundreds of genes. With these technical achievements, his research direction is now heading toward the creation of systems pharmacology.

Vipin Narang is currently pursuing his PhD in computer science at National University of Singapore. He received his bachelor's degree and MS (Research), both in electrical engineering, from the Indian Institute of Technology, New Delhi (2000 and 2002, respectively). His research interests include Bayesian networks, stochastic models, machine learning, Bayesian statistics, gene regulation, and developmental genetics.

C. Notarnicola received the physics degree (summa cum laude) from the University of Bari, Italy (1995), with a thesis on the inversion of a scattering model with neural networks, and the PhD from the University of Bari, Italy (2002). Her dissertation title was "*Multisensor Data Fusion for Soil Physical Parameters Extraction.*" From 2002 to 2004, she was with the Physics Department, University of Bari, working in the framework of the Nowcasting Project. Her research interests include soil models, data fusion, and inversion problems with Bayesian and neural networks techniques. In 2004, she worked with Politecnico di Bari in the framework of an Italian Government PON project for the application of data fusion techniques to degraded areas characterization. Now, she is with Carlo Gavazzi Space SpA in Milan, Italy, working on land cover/use analysis and classification techniques with high-resolution remotely sensed data.

Sudhanshu Patwardhan is presently working at Advanced Technologies Cambridge (Cambridge, England) as a program manager for British American Tobacco's Genomics Programme. He is one of the earlier clinician scientists who moved into applying Bioinformatics research techniques to the drug discovery and development process in the pharmaceutical industry. Following his medical training in India (University of Pune), he pursued a Diploma in Bioinformatics (Bioinformatics Center, University of Pune) and an MBA in Managing Bioscience Companies (Keck Graduate Institute, California). His work on integrating "omics" data at Eli Lilly's Systems Biology division in Singapore received critical acclaim in academic and industry circles.

Luigi Portinale is a full professor of computer science in the Computer Science Department of the University of Eastern Piedmont "A. Avogadro" at Alessandria (Italy). He earned a Laurea degree in computer science (summa cum laude) and a PhD in computer science from the University of Torino (1988 and 1994, respectively). His main interests are in the field of artificial intelligence, with particular attention to case-based reasoning and the use of Bayesian belief networks for reliability applications. He has published several papers on the above topics in international journals, international conference proceedings and books. He has been program chair of the European Workshop on Case-Based Reasoning on 2000, as well as member of several program committees of international conferences. He's a member of the Italian Association for AI (AI*IA) and of the American Association for AI.

Andreas Savakis is professor and department head of computer engineering at the Rochester Institute of Technology, Rochester, NY. Dr. Savakis earned a BS and MS from Old Dominion University and a PhD from North Carolina State University, all in electrical engineering. Before joining RIT, he conducted postdoctoral research with the University of Rochester and was with the Eastman Kodak Company Research Laboratories. His research interests include image processing and computer vision algorithms and their real-time implementation. Dr. Savakis is a senior member of the IEEE and was awarded the IEEE Third Millennium Medal.

Sachin Shetty is a PhD candidate in the modeling and simulation program. He holds a Bachelor of Science in computer engineering from Mumbai University, and a Master of Computer Science from the University of Toledo. His research interests are learning distributed Bayesian networks in peer-to-peer networks, multi-agent systems to simulate the behavior of terrorist networks, and self-organization of agents in peer-to-peer networks.

Min Song, director of Wireless Communications and Networking Laboratory, is currently an assistant professor in the Department of Electrical and Computer Engineering at Old Dominion University (USA). He earned a PhD in computer science from the University of Toledo (2001). His main research interests include communication networks modeling, simulation, and analysis, data mining of terrorist communications, architecture of packet switches and routers, network information security, and wireless sensor networks. During the past five years, he has published more than 44 articles in referred journals, international conferences, and books. He is a member of IEEE and IEEE Communication Society.

Wing-Kin Sung is an assistant professor in the Department of Computer Science, School of Computing, NUS. He is also a senior group leader in Genome Institute of Singapore. Dr. Sung earned both his BSc and PhD in the Department of Computer Science from the University of Hong Kong (1993 and 1998, respectively). His research interest is computational biology. Prior to joining NUS, Dr. Sung worked as a post-doctoral fellow at Yale University, participating in the development of algorithms for DNA mapping and for evolutionary tree reconstructing. In addition, he also worked as a senior technology officer in the E-Business Technology Institute (ETI).

Sebastian Thrun is an associate professor at Stanford University and director of the Stanford AI Lab (SAIL). Thrun is interested in AI, robotics, and machine learning.

Zenglin Xu is a PhD candidate in the Department of Computer Science and Engineering of the Chinese University of Hong Kong. He earned a BS in computer science and technology from Xian Polytechnic University, China, and a MS in computer software and theory from Xian Jiaotong University, China (2002 and 2005, respectively). His research interests include machine learning, pattern recognition, evolutionary algorithms, and information retrieval.

Juan-Diego Zapata-Rivera is an associate research scientist in the Research & Development Division at Educational Testing Service in Princeton, NJ. He earned a bachelor's degree in computer science from EAFIT University in Colombia (1995). Dr. Zapata-Rivera earned a PhD in computer science (with a focus on artificial intelligence in education) from the University of Saskatchewan, Canada (2003). His current research interests include the design, development, and evaluation of innovative assessment-based learning environments, Bayesian student modeling and the use of inspectable student models as communication tools and as mechanisms to gather and share assessment information with students, teachers, and parents.

Yimin Zhang is a researcher at Intel China Research Center. He joined Intel in March 2000. He earned a BA from Fudan University (1993), MS from Shanghai Maritime University (1996) and a PhD from Shanghai Jiao Tong University (1999), all in computer science. In his PhD years, his research was focused on Chinese semantics and Chinese information processing. Before he joined Intel, he worked in Huawei Tech. Ltd. (China) as a software engineer for one year and was responsible for developing telecommunication software. At Intel, he has been involved in several projects related to natural language processing, especially focusing on Chinese-named entity extraction. He also took part in a project for analysis of advanced workload, such as language modeling, and so forth. Recently, he began to lead a team at ICRC to develop DBN technologies to support an extensive area of future applications like noise-robust speech recognition, biometrics, and so forth.

Zhangbing Zhou earned a BE in mechanical engineering from China University of Geosciences, and an ME (2000) in control theory and engineering from the Chinese Academy of Sciences, Institute of Automation (1995 and 2000, respectively). He is currently a member of technical staff in Mobility R&D Center, Bell-Labs China Lucent technologies. His research interests include machine learning, Semantic Web technologies, and databases.

Foreword Author

K. R. Rao earned a PhD in electrical engineering from The University of New Mexico, Albuquerque (1966). Since 1966, he has been with the University of Texas at Arlington (USA) where he is currently a professor of electrical engineering. He, along with two other researchers, introduced the Discrete Cosine Transform in 1975 which has since become very popular in digital signal processing. He is the co-author of the books *Orthogonal Transforms for Digital Signal Processing* (Springer-Verlag, 1975) (also recorded for the blind in Braille by the Royal National Institute for the blind), *Fast Transforms: Analyses and Applications* (Academic Press, 1982), and *Discrete Cosine Transform-Algorithms, Advantages, Applications* (Academic Press, 1990). He has edited a benchmark volume, *Discrete Transforms and Their Applications* (Van Nostrand Reinhold, 1985) and has co-edited a benchmark volume *Teleconferencing* (Van Nostrand Reinhold, 1985). He is the co-author of the books, *Techniques and Standards for Image/Video/Audio Coding* (Prentice Hall, 1996), *Packet Video Communications over ATM Networks* (Prentice Hall, 2000) and *Multimedia Communication Systems* (Prentice Hall, 2002). He has also co-edited *The Transform and Data Compression Handbook* (CRC Press, 2001), *Digital Video Image Quality and Perceptual Coding* (with H.R. Wu) (Taylor and Francis, 2006) and *Introduction to Multimedia Communications: Applications, Middleware, Networking* (with Z.S. Bojkovic and D.A. Milovanovic) (Wiley, 2006). He has also published a book, *Discrete Cosine and Sine Transforms*, with V. Britanak and P. YIP (Elsevier, 2007). Some of his books have been translated into Japanese, Chinese, Korean, and Russian and also published as Asian (paperback) editions. He has been an external examiner for graduate students from universities in Australia, Canada, Hong Kong, India, Singapore, Thailand, and Taiwan. Rao was a visiting professor in several universities (Australia, Japan, Korea, Singapore, and Thailand). He has conducted workshops/tutorials on video/audio coding/standards worldwide. He has supervised several students at the master's (59) and doctoral (29) levels. He has published extensively in refereed journals and has been a consultant to industry, research institutes, law firms and academia. He is a fellow of the IEEE.

Index